KING JOHN

The head of the effigy of King John in Worcester Cathedral, probably made about twenty years after his death.

KING JOHN

W. L. WARREN

UNIVERSITY OF CALIFORNIA PRESS

Berkeley   Los Angeles   London

UNIVERSITY OF CALIFORNIA PRESS
Berkeley and Los Angeles, California

ISBN 0-520-03643-3

Library of Congress Catalog Card Number: 77-20332

2 3 4 5 6 7 8 9

Printed in the United States of America

PATRI MATRIQUE

Contents

Illustrations

ILLUSTRATIONS

MAPS

x

Preface

The reign of King John has a perennial fascination both for the
general public and for professional historians; but while the former
has been left, by and large, with the Victorian assessment of the
man, the latter have been induced by half a century of research
to depart from it. It is a lamentable feature of the age in which we
live that a gulf has developed between the expert and the general
public, and while there may be some excuse for it in the more
abstruse branches of the natural sciences, there is none whatever
in the field of history. It is a gulf that I have attempted in this book
to bridge – reassessing the reign of King John in the light of the
most recent research, and presenting it in a way that is, I hope,
both readable and sound.

My debts to the work of many scholars are inevitably multi-
tudinous. I have endeavoured to catalogue them fully in the notes,
but I cannot omit to acknowledge here my particular indebtedness to the writings of Lady Stenton, Sir Maurice Powicke, Professor C. R. Cheney, Professor S. Painter, Professor F. Barlow,
Dr A. L. Poole, Mr H. G. Richardson, and Mr J. E. A. Jolliffe.
Any merit that the book possesses I would most happily credit to
them; but I should add that without my wife's forbearance and
encouragement it would have taken much longer to write, and
without her cogent criticism it would have been sadly defective.

I would also like to add here my thanks to Professor Harry
Rothwell, of the University of Southampton, for his kindness in
allowing me to use the translation of Magna Carta he has made
for his volume of *English Historical Documents* (*1189–1327*).

W. L. W.

The Queen's University,
Belfast 1960

The Genesis of a Sinister Reputation

'I am become as it were a monster unto many.' *Psalm lxi.* 6

1. THE DESCENDANTS OF MELUSINE

For over fifty years, from 1154 to 1216, England was ruled by a man from Anjou in France and two of his sons. They were King Henry II, King Richard I, and King John. Henry's claim to the English throne was derived from his mother Matilda. She was the only child of King Henry I to survive him, and after the death of her first husband, Emperor Henry V of Germany, she had been married to Count Geoffrey of Anjou.

These Angevin rulers of England had marked characteristics of personality. They were passionate and dynamic, with clever minds and strong wills. They had a hot temper which sometimes prejudiced their calculated schemes. They seemed, even to contemporaries, a little larger than life. Their minds and bodies appeared to work faster than those of normal men. When they conceived anything it was usually on a grand scale; their will matched their conception, and their vast resources were bent to its realisation. Henry II was 'a human chariot' drawing everything after him.[1] He never seemed to take a moment's rest: in church even he scribbled or drew pictures; while hearing matters of business he would be mending his hunting gear; in relaxation he would hunt from dawn until sunset, pushing through woods and mountain passes, and even then weary his court after supper by remaining on his feet. To be in his household was to know the fury of Hell, said his courtiers.[2] Richard I, differing from his father in build and colouring and in his zest for war, was like him in a ruthless energy that brooked no opposition: the builders of his castle at Les Andelys were startled one day by a shower of blood, but the king forced them on, 'and even if an angel had descended from heaven to urge its abandonment he would have been sworn at.'[1] John defied every man, seeming to challenge his whole world single-handed. For six years he brushed aside the denunciations of the great Pope Innocent III, gathering the Church in England into his fierce hands and squeezing out of it all opposition and nearly all life. 'He feared not God, nor respected men.'[2]

The violent temper of the Angevins, their vicious reaction to being thwarted, was almost pathological in its intensity. A misplaced word of praise for the king's enemy, William the Lion of Scotland, threw Henry II into a fit of rage one morning in which he fell screaming out of bed, tore up his coverlet, and threshed around the floor cramming his mouth with the stuffing of his mattress. Frequently he would chew the rushes of the floor in his fury.[3] Richard, believing that he had got the worst of a bargain on one occasion, flew into a blind rage, like a wounded boar, it is said, and no one dared come near him.[4] The chronicler Richard of Devizes remembered John as a young prince breaking out in frustrated fury at Chancellor Longchamp: 'His whole person became so changed as to be hardly recognisable. Rage contorted his brow, his burning eyes glittered, bluish spots discoloured the pink of his cheeks, and I know not what would have become of the chancellor if in that moment of frenzy he had fallen like an apple into his hands as they sawed the air.'[5]

'From the Devil they came', growled St Bernard, 'and to the Devil they will return.'[6] There were many who agreed with him. Popular gossip told of their descent from a devilish ancestress – it was a convenient explanation of their demonic energy, their ferocious ruthlessness. In the days of long ago, when all fairy stories are credible, a count of Anjou, men said, returned from a distant journey with a strange woman whom he married. She was evidently a lady and very beautiful, but there was much that was odd about her: she had no relatives or friends, she seldom went to church, and when she did always made some excuse to leave before the Consecration. In time her husband became so puzzled by this behaviour that he instructed four of his knights to stay close by her when next she entered the church, and prevent her slipping out. Just as the Consecration was beginning she made as if to leave, but the knights trod on the hem of her robe to detain her. As the priest raised the Host above his head she uttered a scream, wrenched apart the fastening of her cloak to escape from it, and still shrieking flew out of the window. She was Melusine, daughter of Satan, and no evil spirit, as is well known, can look upon the Body of Christ. In her flight she dragged two of her children with her; but two remained and from them were descended the Angevin kings of England. Henry II's sons, with characteristically profane humour, were prone to joke about the story, and to people who protested against their fighting among themselves they replied: 'Do not deprive us of our heritage; we cannot help acting like devils.'[1]

2. THE CHRONICLERS AND THE ANGEVINS

It is hardly surprising that these kings cast strong shadows, and provoked violent reactions, nor that men argued about their achievements and defects. Anyone studying their lives in contemporary writings has to be prepared for enemies vilifying them and friends trying to redress the balance with exaggerated praise.

Until the development, comparatively recently, of detailed studies of administrative records, assessments of medieval kings have been based largely upon the information supplied by contemporary chroniclers, and the opinions and judgements of near contemporary ones. Exclusive reliance on chronicle material, however, inevitably subjects the historian to the limitations of the chroniclers themselves. He may transcend the prejudices of his sources but he cannot improve their quality. One generation will produce chroniclers of perspicacity, wide interests, and sound methods, while the next is served by gossip-columnists, or hack compilers of bare-bones annals. It is, as it happens, possible to know some of the 12th century kings of England better than any of the 14th century because the chronicles, biographies, and memoirs of the earlier period are of wider range and higher quality.

Surviving administrative records illuminate the past in a different way from the chronicles. It is difficult material to use, but can be made to yield insights into the problems and methods of medieval kings which contemporary commentators often failed to appreciate. It supplements the chronicles, and may sometimes remedy their deficiencies. But chronicles never cease to be important. History written from administrative records alone would be as defective, for opposite reasons, as that written exclusively

3

from literary sources. This is because what actually happened is only one element in history: men's opinions, and their reactions to what they, often mistakenly, believed had happened are at least of equal importance. The historian who has studied the royal records is often in a better position to know the facts than the contemporary chroniclers, but the information they record is the sort of information upon which men made up their minds at the time, and so framed their attitudes and actions. It is from beliefs not facts that action often springs. The deeds of the legendary King Arthur were as much a part of men's thinking in the 12th century as the deeds (often ill-understood) of the real King Henry II; but the historian would not appreciate this if he had studied only the archives. Moreover, men are slow to change impressions once formed in the light of new facts, and are prone to respond to contemporary problems with out-of-date notions in their minds. The historian must take account of such things if he is to understand the past, and not merely to establish a sequence of events; and he can learn more than facts alone from chroniclers who are representatives of the age in which they lived.

From this point of view annals written in a remote corner of the realm are not without value: they show, at least, what men of those parts heard, and, reading between the lines, the historian can recover their assumptions and prejudices. But though the historian may welcome any source of information, he will, of course, write with less confidence where the chronicles are poor. He may use the skill of a detective and the imagination of a dramatist in reconstructing the past from scattered scraps of information, and produce a synthesis that is at once coherent and convincing; but his conclusions will inevitably be less sure than when he is guided by the knowledgeable writings of intelligent and discriminating contemporaries.

Such considerations are particularly relevant to the reigns of Henry II and his sons. The persisting images are of Henry as a strong and beneficent ruler, of Richard as a glamorous hero, and of John as a villainous failure; but these sharp contrasts reflect the attitudes of the more influential of the chroniclers rather than real differences of personality. The dominant impression of Henry is closest to reality, that of John furthest removed. All three, as a matter of fact, were heartily disliked by many people in their own day – for they were hard and domineering men – but a considered judgement was passed on Henry by chroniclers of perspicacity and sound historical sense, Richard's reputation was glorified by an enthusiastic hero-worshipper, while John's was blighted by scurrilous gossip-mongers.

The reigns of Henry II and Richard I coincided with the finest period of historical writing in the middle ages. The material for Henry II in particular is so copious and from such varied sources, including some of the highest quality, that he can be seen in the round as a living, flesh-and-blood figure. He can be viewed from the point of view of someone who hated him, from that of someone who respected him, and from that of someone who loved him. The personality of the man comes out in trivial but illuminating details: Walter Map tells of him tipping his sailors after a very stormy Channel crossing, and portrays him hailed as a great king by the common people who would seize him and bear him aloft when he went among them.[1] Adam of Eynsham recalls how he begged a Bible from the monks of Winchester to give to his friend Bishop Hugh of Lincoln, who had happened to remark on the supreme value of Holy Scripture and of how difficult it was to get hold of copies. (Hugh was embarrassed by the gift and returned it to the monks.[2]) Gerald of Wales recalls that Henry worried about his waistline, and, more seriously, that he was interested in history and advised the monks of Glastonbury where to look for the tomb of King Arthur.[3]

In considering Henry's deeds, contemporaries were inclined to dwell on his faults, and not without reason. He was a slippery negotiator and earned the nickname 'Proteus' that John of Salisbury, for one, bestowed on him in private correspondence.[4] He had sufficient compunction to try to avoid actually breaking his word, but he readily bent it to the limits of its flexibility. His violence and duplicity were generally deplored. Men expected him to come to a miserable end, and were not disappointed. Gerald of Wales wrote a lively account of his reign on the theme of the wheel of Fortune: his dizzy rise, with God's help, to vast power and European glory, followed by his tumble, when he forfeited that help by his sinfulness and opposition to the just claims of the clergy, until at the end his empire was crumbling about his ears. The sting came in the title of the book, for Gerald called it a manual *For the Instruction of Princes*.[5] One day a man less sophisticated in his hostility to Henry gratuitously hurled a

stone at him from the walls of Bedford castle.[1] But this spirit did
not last, and William of Newburgh, one of the most judicious of
medieval chroniclers, records what Henry's reputation was in
Richard's day: 'the experience of present evils has revived the
memory of his good deeds, and the man who in his own lifetime
was hated by nearly all men is now declared to have been an
excellent and beneficent prince.'[2] The winnowing of time has
isolated a just judgement. Henry deserved to be remembered for
the peace and prosperity he brought to wide dominions, for curbing the self-interest of the over-mighty, and for the benefits of rapid
justice and good administration.

Richard I comes alive in the pages of *The Journey of the Crusaders*.
Its anonymous author tells of him conducting the siege of Acre
so eagerly that even when ill he insisted on being carried before the
walls on a litter so that he could discharge his crossbow at the
infidel. Again it is the incidental anecdotes that are most reveal-
ing: riding with his knights one day he suddenly wheeled his
horse aside to attack a wild boar with his lance, and then when
the wounded beast sprang at him he courageously stood his ground
and despatched it with his sword.[3] Roger of Howden shows him in
a less favourable light, fighting a mock duel with bulrushes against
the noblest knight of the French king's entourage, losing his temper when his helmet was knocked over his face, and being pet-
tishly rude to his chivalrous adversary.[4]

Like his father, Richard was very generally disliked in his own
day. He was an ungracious boor who added sodomy, it was believed, to the normal carnal indulgences of a prince. He was ob-
sessed by fighting and preferred war itself to tournaments. Gerald
of Wales held that 'he cared for no success that was not reached by
a path cut by his own sword and stained with the blood of his
adversaries.'[5] He was lionhearted but soulless. He was by no
means unintelligent, and, as with his father and brother, such
abilities as he possessed were out of the ordinary; but of the three
he was the most limited. Warcraft was his speciality and everything else was sacrificed to indulging it. If a castle were takable,
Richard would spot its weakness, and in an age when the siege
was the principal military operation he had plenty of opportunity
to win renown. Men respected his skill and his strategic sense,
but there was little for which to love him. He might seem heroic
at a distance – on crusade, or in captivity in Germany – but those

who lived under his rule received the news of his death with relief.[1] Death dealt kindly with him, however, and his reputation, so precarious while he lived, was retrieved by the starry-eyed panegyrist of *The Journey of the Crusaders*. There he is extolled, with the accompaniment of every rhetorical device, as a leader comparable to a hero of classical epic or a *chanson de geste*. Hence, though he went to an unmourned grave, he was hardly cold in it before the gallant crusader began to displace the harsh, cold warrior as the persisting image.

No such good fortune attended John. The era of great historical writing came to an end shortly after he ascended the throne. William of Newburgh stopped writing in 1198, a few months before John became king; Roger of Howden died in 1201, and Ralph Diceto in 1202. Gerald of Wales lived on at least until 1216, but spent his time writing his memoirs of earlier days. While Henry and Richard stand out clearly in the writings of contemporaries, John seems to recede into the distance. The biography of William Marshal, earl of Pembroke, assumes a unique importance because it sometimes, but all too rarely, takes us into John's presence. Among the contemporary chroniclers (and only two wrote anything more than the barest annals) was no one who knew him personally, no one who lived in his court and knew his ways. Roger of Howden had written a great chronicle of the reigns of Henry II and Richard I from the intimate knowledge of his own service in the royal household. (He realised the importance for history of documentary evidence, and transcribed many texts into his work.) Ralph Diceto, dean of St Paul's, knew everyone of importance, and could write of them in familiar terms. Gerald of Wales too was intimate with all the great men of his day – at Paris and Rome, as well as in England. The creator of the image of Richard 'Cœur de Lion' was with his hero at the siege of Acre, and wrote, as he himself says, while the event was still warm in his memory; but no such eye-witness rode with John on his exciting dash through France to rescue his mother from the enemies who had trapped her at Mirebeau in 1202. The chroniclers of his reign do not even record what John looked like as king (very likely they did not know), and were it not for the effigy in Worcester cathedral (made perhaps some fifteen years after his death) it would be impossible to get a picture of him in the mind's eye.

On the other hand, the royal archives survive in greater abundance for John's reign than for any of his predecessors, though they are far from complete. It is possible to read there the orders that he sent out to individuals, what he had for his Christmas dinner in 1211, a meticulous description of the jewels he possessed, and even his tailor's bills. It is known, for example, that one night he lost five shillings playing games of chance with Brian Delisle, that he had a valet named Petit, a laundress named Florence, and a bathman named William. The historian can establish that on such and such a day he was at Windsor, or Ludgershall, or York, and that he issued these or those orders, but for most of the time he follows John himself at a distance, unable, quite, to catch up with him.[1]

Of the strictly contemporary chroniclers the best are Gervase of Canterbury and Ralph of Coggeshall. Gervase was a monk of the cathedral monastery at Canterbury; the inmates were the only people he knew well, and matters touching the interests of his house were his primary concern in writing his chronicles. The cathedral monastery, and its cell at Dover, however, were particularly well placed to catch news from travellers, and Gervase has much valuable information about events abroad. He was modest about his own work: he recognised that there was a grander kind of history than the mere recording of information, but professed himself no more than a compiler of facts.[2] He was indeed over-modest for he appraised the information that came to him with discriminating judgement. Unfortunately he was reticent in passing opinions about the Angevin kings and hinted at his dislike of them instead of expressing it openly. Nonetheless, his death in 1210, six years before that of King John, is a serious loss to the historian.

Ralph, abbot of the Cistercian abbey at Coggeshall in Essex, lived on until the last year of John's reign. His *Chronicon Anglicanum*, however, is less than its title implies. It is, indeed, hardly a chronicle at all for there is only a pretence at a continuous narrative; rather it is a notebook in which Ralph recorded (often by insertion in what he had already written) interesting information that came to his ears. What he understood by interesting information chiefly concerned the Cistercian order and the neighbourhood of his house. The weather and the crops, phenomena in the heavens, and strange happenings in East Anglia, have as big a place as King John. On certain great events of the day, how ever, he questioned knowledgeable visitors to the abbey, and hence his work contains information and opinions that are available nowhere else.[1]

The only other contemporary chronicles are the scrappy annals of anonymous monks at Dunstable, Worcester, and Tewkesbury, at Margam in Glamorgan, and Waverley in Surrey. They were men of honest intention and sober purpose, not given to dressing their account of events in showy ornament; but their experience was narrow and their knowledge fragmentary. Moreover, all the chroniclers were members of religious orders and their feelings about John were inevitably distorted by one obnoxious feature of the reign which they were unable to escape. He refused to receive an archbishop appointed by the pope, brought an interdict upon the country in consequence, and retaliated by seizing the clergy's revenue. For six years, from 1208 to 1214, they were caught in a war between Church and State, and found themselves lying well within the range of the royal artillery. For the chroniclers, personally involved and not too widely informed, the facts they recorded were as prejudice itself. It was only with the greatest difficulty that they could ever bring themselves to speak well of John: all his acts were seen through the distorting glass of a particular tyranny. Their inevitable hostility to him remains, however, generalised and diffuse, lacking edge and clarity of focus. For them, in their monastic retreats, he was an oppressive force, but an impersonal and unsubstantial figure.

The dearth of contemporary witness forces the historian to draw upon two writers who set down what they knew of John's reign more than a decade after his death: Roger of Wendover, and an anonymous canon of the Austin priory at Barnwell near Cambridge.

Some time in the late 1220s this anonymous canon became concerned at the lack of recent history in the priory's library. It had a copy of an abridgement of Roger of Howden's great chronicle, but this stopped with the year 1201, and he determined to continue it himself, supplying for the years in between what he and his colleagues could remember. Often this was very little: a mention of the capture of Constantinople by western knights, the date of a Church council or the death of a bishop. It is very meagre before the year 1212, though after that they could remember more and it becomes a valuable source of the last four years of John's reign and the early years of his son, Henry III.

The chronicle is rather weak on chronology, but compensates for this by including brief comments on what is recorded. These are particularly valuable, for this anonymous annalist was precisely the sort of political commentator one could wish for. He was penetrating and impartial, had a judicious perception of the interplay of cause and effect, and an admirable sense of perspective.[1] He was, of course, a member of the clergy, and he knew how much the clergy had suffered during the Interdict; but he takes a detached view of it: it was not all John's fault, 'our sins brought it upon us'. The country, he believes, had been unhappy under John's rule, but he does not make John out to have been a particularly evil man: Englishmen deserted him and few mourned his death, but this was because he extracted so much money from them, and showed generosity to aliens whom alone he trusted. 'He was a great prince certainly but hardly a happy one, and, like Marius, he experienced ups and down of fortune.' 'Ireland, Scotland, and Wales all bowed to his nod – a situation which, as is well known, none of his predecessors had achieved – and he would have thought himself as happy and successful as he could have wished, had he not been despoiled of his continental possessions and suffered the Church's curse.'[2]

There is much mature judgement in this, and John would have been fortunate if the abiding impression of his reign had been left in the hands of the Barnwell annalist. Obviously the Barnwell annalist did not guide posterity: neither here nor in the earlier chronicles is that King John whom the 19th century historian J. R. Green portrays in his enormously influential *Short History of the English People*:

'In his inner soul John was the worst outcome of the Angevins. . . . His punishments were refinements of cruelty, the starvation of children, the crushing of old men under copes of lead. His court was a brothel where no woman was safe from the royal lust, and where his cynicism loved to publish the news of his victim's shame. He was as craven in his superstitions as he was daring in his impiety. He scoffed at priests and turned his back on the mass, even amidst the solemnities of his coronation, but he never stirred on a journey without hanging relics round his neck. . . .'[3]

The man primarily responsible for this was Roger of Wendover.

3. 'THE TERRIBLE VERDICT'

Roger of Wendover was a monk of St Albans who wrote a great chronicle that began with the creation of the world. Some ten years after John's death he set down an account of the reign. What is immediately striking about this is that he seems to know more about John's reign than men who were writing shortly after the events they described. He knows what John said to his nephew Arthur before he made away with him. He can give illustrations of the way the king terrorized the clergy: crushing an archdeacon under a cope of lead, threatening to slit the noses of papal servants and to pluck out their eyes. There is a story of a Jew of Bristol who had a tooth knocked out daily until he revealed where he had hidden his treasure. He gives John's blasphemous oath ('By God's teeth'), and tells how he made free with the wives and daughters of his barons. He explains that John lost Normandy to the king of France because at the critical stage of the campaign he was uxorious and idle: 'Let be, let be, whatever he now takes I shall one day recover.'[1] Historians have often used these stories freely: here at last is the meat after a diet of thin gruel. Now we can know what John was really like, for here are anecdotes that clearly characterise him.

What the historians who use these anecdotes about John seldom make clear, however, is that Wendover's chronicle is full of anecdotes of a highly dubious nature. There is one about a washerwoman who tried to earn an extra penny by plying her trade on the Sabbath, and was sucked dry by a small black pig as punishment. There is one about a loaf of bread baked on the Sabbath that ran with blood when a knife was put to it. There is one (it is eighteen pages long) about a peasant named Thurkhill from the village of Twinstead in Essex who, in 1206, was led through the realms of Purgatory by St Julian.[2] As Wendover tells it the story has many realistic touches, from the man's name and the place where he lived to precise details about the torture chambers of the underworld: in one, for example, stand cauldrons of inky water so bitter that if a piece of wood is thrown in the bark instantly peels off it. It is a grim and lively story; but is it true? Wendover certainly seems to think it as authentic as his stories about John; and it is difficult to see on what grounds historians should reject the former while accepting the latter.[3]

If Wendover's anecdotes about John are examined more closely, some of them begin to dissolve at a touch. Take the one that illustrates the personal peril which, he alleges, beset the clergy in 1208 during the Interdict: 'About that time the servants of a certain sheriff on the confines of Wales came to the royal court bringing in their custody a robber with his hands tied behind his back, who had robbed and murdered a priest on the highway; and when they asked the king how he wished such cases to be dealt with, he replied at once, "He has slain an enemy of mine, loose him and let him go".'[1] Doubt is cast on this story by the royal records which show that at this very time the king ordered that anyone injuring a member of the clergy by word or deed should be hanged from the nearest oak tree.[2] As soon as doubt sharpens criticism it can be seen that Wendover's account bears the hall-marks of worthless gossip. The details are lamentably vague ("... the servants of a certain sheriff on the confines of Wales ...") until the king's reply is reached, and then his actual words can be given. It is the quoted words that constitute the damning part of the story, but in such a context they can hardly be admitted as evidence.

The fact that Wendover can give others of his stories in more circumstantial detail does not help to authenticate them. Think of the story of the peasant Thurkhill. Consider, too, the tale of the fiendish treatment of an archdeacon: in 1209, Wendover writes, a royal servant, Geoffrey the archdeacon of Norwich, was talking over the excommunication of John by the pope with some of his colleagues at the Exchequer. He held that it was not safe for men in holy orders to serve the king any longer. A report of his tender conscience reached the ears of John who, in a fury, sent Sir William Talbot to arrest him. He was imprisoned in chains, clad in a cope of lead, and deprived of food, so that weakened and crushed he died an agonising death.[3] There is undoubtedly something wrong with this story for Geoffrey the archdeacon of Norwich, so far from dying of a surfeit of lead in 1209, became bishop of Ely in 1225. If Wendover had any concern with facts he would surely have discovered this much. As it happens, the genesis of the story can be tracked down in earlier writers. In 1212, it seems (not 1209 as Wendover thought), a man named Geoffrey, who came from Norwich, was apprehended for being involved in a baronial conspiracy and died after long confinement in prison. He was not a very important person and is mentioned only incidentally in the other chronicles. In none of them is there any hint of the alleged horrific torture.[1] Wendover has brought the incident vividly into the light of day, and one might at first glance assume that he had access to better information than the earlier writers; but since he has the wrong year, the wrong cause, and the wrong man, the odds are heavily against him being right about the leaden cope.

To be fair to Wendover, he was not setting up to be a careful historian, and it is unfortunate that his stories have been seized upon because they seem to supply a great want in more reputable chronicles. His purpose in writing was didactic, as he admits in his preface:

> 'First we will address a word to certain stupid cavillers who ask what is the point of recording men's lives and deaths, and the various chances that befall them; or of committing to writing the various prodigies of heaven, the earth, and the elements? Now we would have such persons know that the lives of good men in past times are set forth for the imitation of succeeding times; and that the examples of evil men, when such occur, are not to be followed but shunned. Moreover, the prodigies and portentous occurrences of past days, whether in the way of pestilence or other chastisements of God's wrath, are not without admonition to the faithful.'[2]

Naturally, therefore, he was more interested in the effectiveness of his sermons than the authenticity of the stories with which he illustrated them. He was making an edifying pot-pourri, and he modestly called his book 'Flowers of History'. It is a pity that his showiest blooms turn out to be artificial.

The stories that Wendover told about John have gone echoing down the long corridors of History, and have reverberated in the popular consciousness of the past. To some extent this is due to their intrinsic memorableness; but they would never have sounded so loud had it not been for Matthew Paris.

Wendover, as it happens, was no stylist. He is more para-phrased than quoted, for his prose is flat and pedestrian, and dulls even the brightest tale. (It has trapped some unwary historians into thinking him 'objective'!) Matthew Paris succeeded Wen-dover as historiographer at St Albans in 1235, and he took up his predecessor's humdrum work and refurbished it. Paris was no punctilious historian either, and wrote with strong partisan prejudices. He hated foreigners, lawyers, theologians, civil servants, papal 'interference', and any form of taxation. He was violently nationalist and pro-baronial, and did not hesitate to write tendentiously. But he was a superlative literary artist. He worked wonders with Wendover's text, polishing it here, propping it up with an epigram there, putting speeches into silent mouths. 'By God's feet, now at last am I king and lord of England,' he makes John say on hearing of the death of his chief official. He seems to have been rather pleased with this invention, for on writing an abridged version of his chronicle he transferred it to the death of another and greater royal official where, on second thoughts, it seemed more appropriate![1]

The portrait of John that emerges from Paris is, in consequence, even further removed from reality than that in Wendover, but it is eminently more readable. One of the new passages that Paris introduced is particularly arresting. He would have us believe that in 1213, when John was hard pressed by enemies both at home and abroad, he sought to gain a protector by offering to make England tributary to the Moslem ruler of North Africa, and to abandon Christianity, 'which he considered false', and to embrace Islam. Paris, as a born raconteur, fills out his story of the experience of John's envoys with much picturesque detail, so that even so essentially improbable a tale takes on some semblance of authenticity. When the envoys had penetrated innumerable and terrifying guards to reach the emir's presence, he says, they found him reading a copy of the epistles of St Paul in Greek. He confessed that he was profoundly impressed by Paul, but could not stomach his desertion of the faith of his fathers. Indeed, the emir felt so strongly about apostasy that the mission was hopeless from the start. Nonetheless he was interested to hear what the envoys had to say. Speaking to their brief, they dwelt glowingly on England's prosperity and happy condition under an illustrious monarch. They overdid it: instead of seeing England as a desirable acquisition, the emir only became incredulous that John should propose submitting it to the rule of another.

'The ambassadors were retiring discomfited', writes Paris, 'when the emir became aware of the third member of the party,

Robert the clergyman, who was small and swarthy with a mis-shapen hand (for two fingers stuck together) and a face like a Jew. He called for him to be brought back for he had noticed that while the others had done the talking Robert had remained silent and detached, and it occurred to him that so ill-favoured a person would not be sent on so delicate a mission unless he was thought to be particularly shrewd and intelligent. More-over, he realised from the man's tonsure that he was a member of the clergy. So keeping him back and dismissing the others, the emir had a long private talk with him, which Robert after-wards related to his friends. The emir wanted to know if King John were a man of sound morals, if he were virile and bore lusty sons, adding that if Robert did not reply truthfully he would never believe a Christian again, certainly not a tonsured one. So Robert, promising on his word as a Christian to tell the truth, was obliged to admit that John was a tyrant not a king, a destroyer instead of a governor, crushing his own people and favouring aliens, a lion to his subjects but a lamb to foreigners and rebels. He had lost the duchy of Normandy and many other territories through sloth, and was actually keen to lose his kingdom of England or to ruin it. He was an insatiable extorter of money; he invaded and destroyed his subjects' property; and he had bred no worthy children but only such as took after their father. He detested his wife and she him. She was an incestuous and depraved woman, so notori-ously guilty of adultery that the king had given orders that her lovers were to be seized and throttled on her bed. He himsel was envious of many of his barons and kinsfolk, and seduced their more attractive daughters and sisters. As for Christianity he was unstable and unfaithful. When the emir heard this he no longer merely despised John: he loathed him.'[1]

Here, for the first time, emergent in full colour, is the traditional impression of King John. What posterity made of it rather de-pended on its own historical predilections. Tudor historians tended to dismiss the atrocities: they fastened instead on John's defiance of the pope and thought of him as an heroic precursor of Henry VIII badly let down by treachery. There is no mention of Magna Carta in Shakespeare's *King John*. Nineteenth century historians, however, preoccupied with personal morality, reverted to the

Paris portrait. 'His history stamps him as a worse man than many who have done more harm', said the great Bishop Stubbs, 'chiefly on account of his own personal share in the producing of his own deep and desperate humiliation.'[1] 'Foul as it is,' wrote J. R. Green, 'Hell itself is defiled by the fouler presence of King John.' He is quoting from Matthew Paris – Paris at his most irresponsibly epigrammatic. 'The terrible verdict of the king's contemporaries,' commented Green solemnly, 'has passed into the sober judgement of history.'[2]

Paris can hardly be called a contemporary: he was not even born when John came to the throne. His 'terrible verdict' was based on a crude legend, bits of malicious gossip gathered together with undiscriminating zeal by Roger of Wendover. But whence came that legend, burgeoning while John was barely cold in his grave? The Barnwell annalist, it should be noted, knew nothing of it, or if he did his scrupulosity dismissed it. We may suspect that the fact that Wendover was writing at St Albans has something to do with the legend's appearance in his chronicle. Standing on the great north road and not far from London, St Albans felt the pulsing blood of English political life. Its antiquity and vast estates brought it dignity and fame. Its abbot was a great man of the realm, taking his place among the most eminent of the baronage. His abbey was patronised and visited frequently by members of the ruling class. It was not by chance that Wendover and Paris are spokesmen for the baronial interest in the political troubles of their own day. Nor would it be surprising if they reflected a baronial attitude about the immediate past. The most likely source for Wendover's stories about John is the abbey's guests, who, with little prompting, would recall the brave days when they had brought down the tyrant, who could clearly remember their father saying . . . who had it direct from a man in the court that. . . .

Wendover's tales are powerful evidence of the hatred men bore their late king. In their garbled inaccuracy and palpable implausibility they do not take us very close to the real King John, but they do make us ask this: why were men prepared to tell such tales about him? Why did he leave so noisome a reputation behind him?

Gaining a Kingdom

'O remember not the sins and offences of my youth.'
Psalm xxv. 6

I. MOTHER AND FATHER

John was born at Oxford on Christmas Eve 1166. He was the eighth of the children Eleanor of Aquitaine is known to have borne to Henry II, and remained the youngest of the seven who survived the hazards of medieval childhood. Three of them were girls: at the time of John's birth Matilda was ten, Eleanor and Joan were still infants. None of the boys was a nursery companion for John: Henry, the heir apparent, was eleven, Richard nine, and Geoffrey eight – old enough, that is, to be learning to sit a horse, for, men said, if it were not begun before the age of seven it would never be learned at all.

John's mother was forty-five at the time of his birth, but still, despite frequent pregnancies, possessed of full vigour. Indeed, boundless energy was as characteristic of her as of her husband, though he was eleven years younger. Twenty-five years later Richard of Devizes could write of her as 'even now unwearied by any task and provoking wonder at her stamina.' Richard thought her 'an incomparable woman: beautiful yet gracious, strong-willed yet kind, unassuming yet sagacious (which is a rare combination in a woman)'. Nonetheless, he could not resist insinuations about her scandalous youth: 'Many knew what I wish none of us knew. This very queen was at Jerusalem in the time of her first husband – let no one say more about it, though I know it well. Hush!'[1]

She was, in truth, a fit mate for a demoniac Angevin. Henry, however, was her second husband. As a black-eyed beauty of fifteen, and duchess of Aquitaine in her own right, she had been married to the heir to the French throne, who became King Louis VII in 1137. Intelligent and witty, beautiful and queenly, she was the natural focus of the new fashion of courtly love: gallants trailed her with flatteries, troubadors composed love-songs in her honour. Her sister, Petronilla, was carried away by the heady atmosphere and eloped with a married man – the king's brother at that. Eleanor was more discreet and probably perfectly virtuous, but gossip said that she had more than flirted with Geoffrey of Anjou, a handsome hero of the jousting field, and told even worse stories of her adventures in the Holy Land when she accompanied her husband on crusade.

At the time of their marriage Louis had been a gallant young knight, eager to learn the courtly ways of the more sophisticated south; but after a few years he threw over dalliance for religious devotion. It came about as a consequence of Petronilla's elopement. Her paramour, Louis' brother, was married to a sister of the Count of Champagne. Eleanor persuaded her husband to support the guilty pair against Champagne's protests, and it came to war. In the course of it, at the siege of Vitry, the king's mercenaries got out of hand and fired the cathedral. Over a thousand women and children who were sheltering there perished in the flames. Louis was deeply shocked. The crusade was part of his self-imposed penance, and he became increasingly devout and abstemious. He cut his hair short so that he looked like a monk, and passed many hours in prayer. It made him a high-principled and respected king, but it was no sort of life for the vivacious and amorous Eleanor. She joined the crusade in the hope of excitement and made a nuisance of herself to the army. She discharged her high spirits by dressing herself and her ladies in armour and cavorting like an Amazon, and requited her husband's lack of attention by basking too freely in the admiration of her uncle, Raymond, prince of Antioch. It was even said that Saladin became enthralled by what he heard of her, that they exchanged love letters and planned to elope, and that Louis had to drag her back from taking ship at Tyre. This, however, can be no more than an engaging piece of fancy, for at the time Saladin was twelve years old.[1]

Within two years of returning from the Holy Land, King Louis was minded to take another wife. It was not merely that he and Eleanor found it difficult to get on together: more serious was the fact that in eleven years of married life she had borne him only two children and both of them daughters. The fortunes of the Capetian dynasty rested on having a son to succeed. Louis was very worried: he despaired of Eleanor giving him an heir and determined to try elsewhere. Having a son was much more important even than retaining control of Aquitaine in his wife's name. He was too much of a gentleman to charge her with adultery as many thought he might have done, but instead had the marriage declared void on the grounds of consanguinity, which in the 12th century were very wide.

At Easter 1152, then, Eleanor ceased to be queen of France; but as duchess of Aquitaine she was still mistress of half of France south of the Loire. In her large inheritance she was a ruler virtually independent of the Crown: she had to do homage for it to the king, but he could not interfere in her administration, and the homage of the several counts of the duchy was rendered to her and not to him. So exalted, indeed, was the dignity of the dukes of Aquitaine that the ceremony of installation, when they were invested with the ducal coronet, was a sacred rite closely modelled on a royal coronation. The snag lay in exercising this dignified authority and in controlling the duchy. The dukes usually retained the county of Poitou in their own hands, but the other counts were very insubordinate. They were loyal to their duke in that they would turn out to fight for him against anyone else, but they expected to be left alone in their counties, and were apt to show their resentment of interference by armed defiance. The counts too, however, often had difficulty in controlling their fiefs (as feudal holdings were termed) and in exacting obedience from their vassals. Even in Poitou, where the dukes exercised comital authority, they had to reckon with the intractable independence of local lords, sheltering behind the walls of powerful castles. Only on their family estates, which included the city of Poitiers, where no lord stood between them and the minor knights and citizens, could the dukes enforce regular obedience.

Aquitaine was notorious for the factious independence of its vassals, but though notorious it was not unique. Indeed, it was characteristic of much of France in the 12th century that the real power of the greater lords was not commensurate with their feudal dignity. A count was often better placed to exact real obedience from more subordinates than was a duke who received the homage of several counts. Oaths did not, by themselves, create power, though everyone still adhered to the old oath-takings out of deference for ancient custom, and in the belief that only thus was society held together at all. The king himself could not enforce his commands or collect a tax outside the *Île de France* (the area around Paris) which he ruled directly. A mere count could often defy him successfully, unless the king could bring up enough of his other vassals as allies to suppress the rebel. Often enough the great tenants of the Crown would stick together to maintain their independence: the count of Flanders, for instance, could usually depend upon the support of the duke of Normandy. Through the chain of oath-takings the ruler of Paris, who bore the title of king, was lord of everyone; but he properly called himself King of Frenchmen (*Rex Francorum*) rather than King of France (*Rex Franciae*). When a man took an oath of homage to a lord (and he would have to if he wished to hold his fief by proper title) he was bound to follow him in war; but he did not feel obliged to obey all his lord's commands, unless his lord could raise enough troops to enforce his will.[1]

Nonetheless, as duchess of Aquitaine Eleanor was a very desirable match. Even if she had been ugly there would have been plenty of suitors seeking the ducal dignity and hoping to make its authority mean something. She, for her part, needed a protector, and, if possible, someone with enough real power of his own to make her authority effective. She found one in Henry of Anjou.

Henry, fifteen years old, had recently succeeded his father Geoffrey. The counts of Anjou were powerful men: they rendered homage directly to the king without the intervention of any duke, and they were at least as strong in their county as the king was in the *Île de France*. They had reduced their vassals to obedience after long years of determined warfare, and maintained an imperious independence that kept out not only the king's emissaries, but the pope's emissaries too. Moreover, they had taken over the county of Maine and the lordship of Touraine. For the latter they had to do homage to the counts of Blois, which was an annoying indignity, but nothing more. Maine they claimed to hold directly from the king, though the dukes of Normandy demanded homage for it. This was liable to be a source of friction, but Count Geoffrey had removed it by taking over the duchy of Normandy himself. He did so in right of his wife Matilda whom he had married in 1128. She was the widow of Emperor Henry V of Germany, and a

20

dowager empress was a good catch for a mere count; but more than that, she was the daughter of Henry I, king of England and duke of Normandy, and, since he had lost his son when the White Ship foundered off Barfleur in 1120, his heiress. When the old king died, however, his daughter's throne had been usurped by her cousin, Stephen of Blois. Matilda had managed to get a foothold in western England, and for as long as the young Henry, her son, could remember, civil war had been raging there between the partisans of the rivals. Count Geoffrey did not trouble himself with his wife's claims in England, but in 1141-4 he conquered Normandy and ruled it in his wife's name as regent for their son.

It was Count Geoffrey's intention that at his death Henry should be content with the duchy of Normandy and the kingdom of England, if he could secure it, and that the ancestral fiefs of the Angevin house should pass to his second son, who bore his father's name. When Count Geoffrey died in 1152, however, Henry cheated his brother and took over Anjou, Maine, and Touraine, leaving him only the castles of Chinon, Loudun, and Mirebeau. So when Henry married Eleanor at Whitsuntide in the same year they joined together fiefs that stretched unbroken from Cherbourg to Bayonne; and in addition Henry took up the shadowy claim of the dukes of Normandy to be overlords of Brittany, and his wife's shadowy claim to be overlord of Toulouse and the Auvergne. Two years later this great dominion was extended northwards across the Channel as far as the Cheviots. Since he was fourteen Henry had been making expeditions to England in support of his mother's cause. He had not been able to unseat King Stephen, but in 1153 he concluded a favourable truce whereby Stephen was to reign undisturbed for the rest of his life, but recognised Henry as his heir. A year later Stephen died, and on 17th December 1154 Henry and Eleanor were crowned in Westminster Abbey.[1]

Henry's principal problem throughout his reign was how to control and administer the wide dominions he had acquired. The traditional solution to such a problem was the delegation of powers and responsibilities to the greater landholders; but it was a solution begotten of necessity in the turbulent days of the 9th to the 11th centuries, and it was fraught with the danger that through absorbing regal powers the great barons would leave the ruler with little more than a position of honour, and set up states within the state. This, indeed, was the situation in France, and

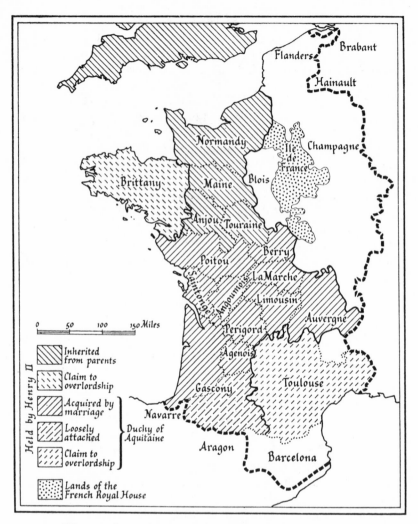

Held by Henry II

- Inherited from parents
- Claim to overlordship
- Acquired by marriage
- Loosely attached
- Claim to overlordship

Duchy of Aquitaine

- Lands of the French Royal House

0   50   100   150 Miles

Flanders   Brabant

Hainault

Normandy

Champagne

Île de France

Brittany

Maine   Blois

Anjou   Touraine

Berry

Poitou

Saintonge

Angoumois

La Marche

Limousin

Auvergne

Périgord

Agenois

Toulouse

Gascony

Navarre

Aragon

Barcelona

1. The continental possessions of Henry II about the time of John's birth.

Henry, as duke of Normandy and count of Anjou, paid his king no more than a nominal deference; could he himself maintain a more real authority over all the men who acknowledged him as lord? In the peripheries of his domains, on the Welsh and Scottish borders, in Ireland, Brittany, and southern Aquitaine, Henry had to allow his barons to run on a free rein; but in the rest, in England, Normandy, Anjou, Maine, Touraine, and (to a lesser extent) in Poitou, the Limousin, and the Auvergne, he ruled more directly through officials removable at will, personally selected from among the lesser land-holding classes or even the low-born. Centralised administrations were operated in each of the provinces by a justiciar (in England) or seneschals (on the continent), under the regular supervision of the king; and administrative writs conveyed instructions to sheriffs, viscomtes, prévôts, or lesser officials in the localities. Itinerating commissions, and the travelling court of Henry himself, kept everything under review, ensured that the ruler's will was obeyed, and dispensed justice.[1]

In ruling this way Henry II was adapting and developing methods practised by his Norman predecessors, but he made them operate successfully over a greatly extended area only by his own tireless energy in general supervision and attention to points of detail. Life for his courtiers was hard and uncertain, and those with long memories recalled nostalgically the well-ordered court routine of Henry I. His grandson could not abide regular hours. He would sit up half the night wrestling with a knotty legal problem, and even when he did go to bed could be woken to receive urgent news. He hated to be idle himself and dashed about his realms making sure that his officials were not idle either.[2]

Peter of Blois, who was for a time the king's secretary, vividly reconstructed life at Henry's court in a letter to some of his friends. 'If the king has promised to remain in a place for a day – and particularly if he has announced his intention publicly by the mouth of a herald – he is sure to upset all the arrangements by departing early in the morning. As a result you see men dashing around as if they were mad, beating their packhorses, running their carts into one another – in short giving a lively imitation of Hell. If, on the other hand, the king orders an early start, he is certain to change his mind, and you can take it for granted that he will sleep until midday. Then you will see the packhorses loaded and waiting, the carts prepared, the courtiers dozing, traders fretting, and everyone grumbling. People go to ask the maids and the doorkeepers what the king's plans are, for they are the only people likely to know the secrets of the court. Many a time when the king was sleeping a message would be passed from his chamber about the city or town he planned to go to, and though there was nothing certain about it, it would rouse us all up. After hanging about aimlessly for so long we would be comforted by the prospect of good lodgings. This would produce such a clatter of horse and foot that ?'' Hell seemed let loose. But when our couriers had gone ahead almost the whole day's ride, the king would turn aside to some other place where he had, it might be, just a single house with accommodation for himself and no one else. I hardly dare say it, but I believe that in truth he took a delight in seeing what a fix he put us in. After wandering some three or four miles in an unknown wood, and often in the dark, we thought ourselves lucky if we stumbled upon some filthy little hovel. There was often a sharp and bitter argument about a mere hut, and swords were drawn for possession of lodging that pigs would have shunned.'[1]

Though it led a scrambling sort of existence the life of the court was enriched by the many foreigners who came to visit the most eminent prince of Christendom. There were embassies from Norway and Sweden, Germany, Italy and Sicily, Navarre and Castile, and the Holy Land. The king's roving agents, Richard of Ilchester and John of Oxford, came in to report on their travels, which took them from one end of Europe to the other. Henry the Lion, duke of Saxony, who had married the eldest daughter of Henry and Eleanor, spent some time in exile at the court of his father-in-law. There was, too, much learned discourse for Henry liked to employ scholars in his service, and loved to join in an argument. 'With the king of England there is school every day,' wrote his secretary, 'constant conversation of the best scholars and discussion of questions.' Henry was well educated for a layman: he spoke Latin and French, and could understand most of the other west European languages. When business was over, and it was too dark to hunt with his hawks or hounds, he would retire to his chamber with a book.[2]

But though the court was cultured it was serious and hardworking; we hear little of the gentler side of medieval life – it was no place for talk of chivalry and the composition of *aubades*, such as Eleanor had been used to at Poitiers and Paris. The king did not encourage tournaments: he left that to his empty-headed but splendidly gay eldest son, who set up a separate establishment as soon as he was old enough to do so. One who shared the young Henry's enthusiasms wrote that it was he 'who made chivalry live again, for she was dead, or nearly so. He was the door by which she entered. He was her standard bearer. In those days the great did nothing for young men. He set an example and kept men of worth by his side. And when men of high degree saw how he brought together all men of worth they were amazed at his wisdom and followed his lead.'[1] But not King Henry II: he preferred to be surrounded by men trained in the schools or in the administrative service. King Philip of France (who succeeded Louis VII) one day pointed the contrast between the English and French courts. It had been proposed to settle a quarrel by a combat of four-a-side. Philip mockingly suggested that his champions, four barons distinguished on the jousting field, should meet four men of comparable standing in King Henry's entourage, William FitzRalph, William de la Mare, Richard de Villequier, and Richard d'Argence. The first of these was too old to fight, the second ill, the third gouty, and the fourth a victim of quartan fever.[2]

2. THE DEVIL'S BROOD

There was little home life in the peripatetic court for the children of Henry and Eleanor. During the last stages of her frequent pregnancies the queen would stay for a little while at some convenient castle or hunting lodge, wherever the court happened to be in England or on the continent, and as soon as possible the baby would be put in the hands of a nurse and brought up by tutors and guardians. John normally spent Christmas at least with his father, but it is possible that he saw little of his mother, for soon after his birth his parents became estranged, and Eleanor retired to Poitou, there to plot mischief for Henry with her older sons. Writers who liked their history spiced with mythology recalled the 'prophecies' of Merlin and spoke of Eleanor as 'the eagle of the broken covenant who shall spread her wings over two kingdoms,' and of her sons as the 'lion cubs who shall awake and roar loud.'[3]

The disparity of age between Henry and Eleanor was perhaps

primarily responsible for their growing animosity: at forty-five she had passed the prime of her beauty, while he, eleven years her junior, was still in the full vigour of his lustful passions. That he kept several concubines was notorious. There was even a widespread belief in England that he had seduced Alice, daughter of King Louis by his second marriage, while she was in his care as the betrothed bride of his son Richard. One chronicler holds that he had a child by her who did not survive; and Gerald of Wales alleges that he planned to divorce Eleanor so that he could marry her.[1] After 1174 he lived openly with a high born mistress, Rosamund Clifford (known in popular ballads as 'Fair Rosamund'), and when she died had a splendid tomb made for her before the high altar in the nunnery of Godstow near Oxford. Some of the legends that gathered round Eleanor's name told how she had poisoned her rival, or had her bled to death while she was taking a bath.[2]

When little more than a year old John was entrusted to the abbey of Fontevrault in Anjou, perhaps in the vain hope that he would become a novice. Later he spent some time in the private household of his brother Henry, who was eleven years older, where he may have learned the rudiments of the sports of hunting and war, as befitted a gentleman. His academic education (for his father was a great believer in literacy) seems to have been entrusted to Ranulph Glanville, the king's most senior official in England.[3] Beyond such bare facts as these little is known of John's youth: the chroniclers were hardly aware of his existence, for fourth sons, even of a king, are among the more insignificant of God's creatures, and it was against the odds that he would succeed to the throne. There is, however, one incident of his childhood days, probably apocryphal, recorded in *The Story of Fulk Fitz-Warin* (which, written in Anglo-French in the early 13th century, recounted the adventures, part fact, part fantasy, of a sort of baronial Robin Hood). Fulk, it seems, was a playmate of John's at the king's court, but frequently quarrelled with him:

'It happened one day that John and Fulk were alone in a chamber playing chess. John took the chess board and struck Fulk a great blow with it. Fulk, feeling hurt, kicked John hard in the stomach, so that he banged his head against the wall, became dizzy and fainted. Fulk was frightened, and was glad that there was no one in the room but themselves. He rubbed John's ears and brought him round. John went wailing to his father the king. "Hold your tongue," said his father, "you are always squabbling. If Fulk has done what you say, you probably deserved it." He called his tutor and ordered him to be well beaten for complaining."[1]

But though the chroniclers have little to say of John in his younger days, he began to have an influence on the course of history from the age of six, for the problem of his future supplied the occasion for a civil war in King Henry's dominions.

The possession of four healthy sons was a comfort to any ruler who took thought for the succession; but it posed the problem of providing for those who were not to assume the crown. Henry hoped that his sons would help him rule his wide dominions and relieve the strain of keeping a firm hand on the ill-assorted parts, with their different languages and customs. He tried, therefore, to settle the future division as early as he could, so that the boys could be brought up with their prospects in mind.[2] His eldest son, Henry, would of course take his own inheritance: Anjou, Maine and Touraine, Normandy and England. It was common practice of the day on the continent to associate the heir in rule with the reigning king; so when Henry was only seven (in 1162) the barons were made to do homage to him, and it was proposed to have him formally crowned. Regalia were actually prepared, but unfortunately the king was at loggerheads with his archbishop of Canterbury, Thomas Becket, and the ceremony was put off from year to year until 1170.[3] From then on there were two kings in England, and contemporaries called them the Old King and the Young King to distinguish them. Already in 1158, at the tender age of three, he had been betrothed to Margaret, the eldest daughter of King Louis by his second marriage. She was still in her cradle, but was handed over to the care of her future father-in-law, in accordance with the custom of the day. Her dowry, it was agreed, should be the Vexin, a strip of territory on the Norman border which the two kings disputed. Until the children were old enough to marry the Vexin was entrusted to the Knights Templar. This seemed an amicable settlement of an old dispute, but Henry, with characteristic double-dealing, had the children married only two years later.

Aquitaine was administered by Henry in his wife's name, but it remained her property for which she did homage to the French king. Her inheritance, it was proposed, should go to their second surviving son, Richard, and in 1172 when he was fourteen he was solemnly installed at the church of St Hilary in Poitiers.

For Geoffrey a bolder move was planned. Henry claimed to be overlord of Brittany, a shadowy claim which the Normans had asserted before him. The Bretons were not ready to acknowledge any subjection; but their duke, Conan IV, who ruled precariously, was very much under the influence of the king of England, for he had inherited the earldom of Richmond in Yorkshire and looked to Henry for help against his turbulent vassals. His only child, a daughter, Constance, was secured as a bride for young Geoffrey. In three years of campaigning Henry knocked the fight out of the Bretons and in 1169 forced them to do homage to Geoffrey as heir to the duchy. When Conan died two years later the succession took effect. Geoffrey was then eight years old.[1]

But what was to be done with John? It was a question which bothered Henry: 'Lackland' he called him, and the name stuck.[2] In 1171, however, a splendid opportunity opened. In north Italy there lived the count of Maurienne whose fiefs stretched from the upper Rhône valley and the shores of Lake Geneva to the river Aosta and Turin, and embraced all the western passes through the Alps. His hold on these strategically important territories was shaky, he had no son, and he was very short of money; but he had a marketable asset in two daughters. Envoys passed back and forth and Count Humbert closed a bargain by agreeing to part with his eldest daughter, Alice, and to make John his heir, for 5000 marks.* At Candlemas 1172 King Henry and the count met at Montferrand to complete the transaction and journeyed back

---

* A mark, a common term of account, was two-thirds of a pound sterling (i.e., 13s. 4d.). No attempt is made in this book to express the sums given in contemporary records in terms of modern money. The value of money can be assessed only in relation to current prices, and no easy correlation can be made between medieval and modern price scales. A parish priest of John's day was doing very well if he had an annual income of £10; but a large illuminated Bible could cost all of that. John could buy 4000 plates and 500 cups from Staffordshire in 1205 for as little as £2 13s. 7½d. On the other hand, the same amount of money spent on steel would have bought far less in John's day than it would in the 20th century—only about a fifth as much. See E. V. Morgan. *The Study of Prices and Value of Money* (Historical Association Pamphlet, 1952),

to Limoges together. Unfortunately the count took it into his head to ask an awkward question: he himself, he said, was providing a handsome endowment for his daughter, what was Henry doing for his son? Henry seems to have given no prior thought to this, but there came into his head on the spur of the moment the traditional holding of a cadet of the Angevin house: the castles of Chinon, Loudun, and Mirebeau. There and then he assigned them to John. The Young King, however, was indignant at this: the castles were part of his own inheritance and he refused to let John have them. It was not so much that they would be a serious loss as the principle of the thing. For two years now he had been a crowned king, but his father had allowed him to perform only ceremonial functions. Here was a typical example of the way his father prejudiced his interests without even consulting him. He was old enough to be ruling for himself, and he demanded to be entrusted with England or with Normandy, or with Anjou, where he and his wife might set up their own court. Henry seems to have treated this merely as a display of childish ill-temper, but he woke up a few mornings later to find that his heir had slipped away to his father-in-law. He woke up too to the fact that his neglected wife and her ex-husband had been planting troublesome notions of independence in his son's mind; and when his envoys reached Paris to bring the young Henry back they were greeted by Louis with the words: 'Your master is king no longer – here stands the king of the English!'[1] As soon as she heard the news Queen Eleanor, who was then staying at Poitiers, sent Richard and Geoffrey to join their elder brother. She herself, heavily disguised, attempted to follow them, but was caught by her husband's men and taken to imprisonment at Winchester.[2]

The sparks of a family quarrel set off a powder keg of general discontent. Smarting under the vigorous suppression of their freedom of action, a majority of the barons throughout the Angevin dominions threw off their allegiance to the Old King in factitious fidelity to the Young King. Louis had a special seal made for his protégé, and with it he recklessly granted pensions and fiefs to any French baron who would follow him.[3] Henry kept his head and deployed his mercenaries in a series of successful campaigns. The rebels came to heel, and his boys to beg their father's pardon; but it took him the best part of two years to do it, and by then Alice of Maurienne was dead and John's prospects with her.

As part of the price of settlement, however, the Old King obliged his heir to agree to an endowment for John. A castle and a lordship in each part of the Young King's future inheritance were made over to him. A few weeks later the earldom of Cornwall fell vacant, and that too was reserved for John.[1] In 1176 another bride was found for him: he was betrothed to his second cousin Isabelle, daughter of the earl of Gloucester, and made heir to the earldom. By this time he had ceased to be 'Lackland', but a title and a stake in every portion of his eldest brother's inheritance was a poor substitute for the virtually independent principality that had been planned for him in Maurienne, and which Richard and Geoffrey would achieve.

The Young King, after the abortive rebellion of 1172–3, was still not allowed any real responsibility by his father, but Richard and Geoffrey were. By adding the Angevin inheritance to the possessions of his Norman predecessors King Henry II was taking on as much as any medieval king could hope to control effectively. Only his fierce energy enabled him to hold down Aquitaine and subdue the Bretons as well. When he tried to bring Wales under his control in 1165 even he had to admit that he was over-extending himself. It was a relief, therefore, to let Richard and Geoffrey take some share of the burden. Richard in particular soon established an awesome reputation as a tamer of Aquitainian tigers. At the first growls of independence he would turn up with a troop of professional soldiery, ruffianly thugs hired from the over-populated Low Countries. They were despised by all true knights, condemned by the Church, and regarded with horror by the country people upon whom they would descend like a swarm of locusts. In time of peace Richard kept their rapacity in check with iron discipline, but at the first sign of rebellion he would unleash them. It was no use his enemies taking refuge in castles, for Richard would detect a weakness in even the most allegedly impregnable of them and exploit it with precocious skill.[2] His success provoked the jealousy of his brothers Henry and Geoffrey so much that in 1183 they joined forces to aid his hard-pressed vassals: no Angevin wasted time on fraternal affection. Richard, however, soon showed that he was more than a match for them too, and was only prevented from winning a crushing victory by the sudden death of the Young King from dysentery.

It was a sad blow to his father, and, indeed, to his father's subjects. The Young Henry was the only member of the family who was popular in his own day. It is true that he was also the only one who gave no evidence of political sagacity, military skill, or even ordinary intelligence, but such, after all, are not looked for in a fairytale prince, and the young Henry had all the trappings of a hero of romance or *aubade*. He was tall, handsome, gay, and splendidly improvident. He had the sort of charm that makes even gross irresponsibility seem nothing more than the mischievousness of a lively boy. Unable to pay his mercenaries he would let them loose to rifle abbeys and holy shrines, but even this did not mar his reputation with the chroniclers. Songs, poems, and histories were written to honour his name, and he died lamented by all, perhaps because men saw in his liberality and affability their only hope of escape from the determined ruthlessness of his father and brothers.[1]

The Old King naturally expected that Richard would step into the shoes of his dead brother and release Aquitaine for John, but Richard did not take kindly to the idea. He liked to go his own way, and having made something of the dukedom he had no wish to exchange it for the shadow of authority that the Young King had had in England, Normandy, and Anjou. When his father broached the subject he asked for a day or two to think it over, but mounted his horse and rode off for Poitou. In a typical outburst of wrath Henry told John that he should go and seize the duchy for himself.[2] It was said only to be regretted, but at sixteen John was of an age to be fending for himself, and he joined his brother Geoffrey for another round of fratricidal strife.

Gerald of Wales, in his gossipy way, draws a comparison between the two younger brothers. They were rather alike, he thought: 'one was corn in the ear, the other corn in the blade.' Unlike their older brothers who were both tall, and their father who was of medium height, they were rather short, though 'reasonably well-built for their size.' John, in fact, never grew to more than 5ft 5ins.[3] Geoffrey, now in his middle twenties, was perfectly capable of conforming to the martial standards of the ruling class; but unlike many of those prominent in the art of war, and its substitutes the hunt and the tournament, he had brains and a facile tongue, and rated cunning at least the equal of combat – indeed he was Ulysses and Achilles both. 'He was not easily deceived, and one would have called him most sagacious were it not for his readiness to deceive others.' The trouble with Geoffrey was that his honey-tongued eloquence was merely a top dressing on a scoundrelly hypocrisy. Roger of Howden can hardly mention his name without an epithet of abuse, and thought him the real trouble-maker among the brothers.[1] John, at this time, appeared to Gerald as still the spoilt baby of the family. He was impatient of correction and gave no thought to the morrow. He preferred fopperies and luxury to the stiffening experience of knightly exercises, and was as wax to receive the stamp of vice. His immaturity was pronounced and he could not be restrained from childish levity. Gerald did not altogether despair of him for he thought that he would outgrow his childish follies; but it is not a pleasant sketch. The one good thing that could be said of him was that he was generally obedient to both his parents.[2]

Although Henry himself was responsible for this fresh outburst of fighting among his sons, he had no wish that it should continue, and intervened to separate them. It was clear, though, that some opportunity had to be found for his youngest born to make a man of himself. John thought that his chance had come in 1185 when the patriarch of Jerusalem arrived in England with an exciting proposition. The ruler of the Holy Land, King Baldwin IV, was wasting away with leprosy, and the patriarch was looking for a successor. Since the royal house of Jerusalem was a junior branch of the house of Anjou, and since Henry was the pre-eminent prince of Christendom with three healthy sons, it was natural that he should expect to find one in England. Indeed, he had actually brought the royal standard and the keys of the Holy Sepulchre with him. He addressed the assembled court at Reading and made such a moving appeal that everyone was reduced to tears.[3] King Henry, however, was not a man to be swayed for long by emotion; he had his own sources of information and doubtless knew that the Holy Land was rift with political rivalries and uncertainties. The king of Jerusalem was little more than commander-in-chief of the feudal army there: beyond that his authority was negligible. When the patriarch came for his answer to another council meeting at Clerkenwell on 18th March 1185 he found that a little show had been staged for him. Henry solemnly requested his barons to advise him as they thought best for his soul's safety, and promised to abide by whatever they should decide. They deliberated and gave as their unanimous opinion that he should not abandon the work to which he was pledged by his coronation oath: the realm needed him. The patriarch's hopes were finally dashed when Henry further refused to let any of his sons go, though John begged on his bended knees for permission.[1]

Despite the trouble they had caused him, Henry still valued the help his sons could give in controlling the turbulent extremities of his empire. Richard had brought much needed discipline to Aquitaine, and Geoffrey had begun to bring order out of chaos in Brittany. There remained Ireland, nominally under his allegiance, but dangerously disordered. He had marked it out as John's task before the patriarch of Jerusalem arrived, and though John himself might be entranced by brighter prospects, his father was not to be deflected from his purpose.

3. LORD OF IRELAND—A LOST OPPORTUNITY

The name of Ireland was well enough known to the middle ages if only for the zeal of the Celtic missionaries who had tramped Europe in the 7th century when the Franks were still more than half pagan. But as a country it was poor, it was backward, and with square-rigged ships and the prevailing winds it was not easy to get at. The Romans had not been seriously tempted, the Anglo-Saxons had not bothered; only the Norsemen, late starters in the *Völkerwanderung*, had shown any interest, but then they were eccentrically adventurous and pushed on even to Iceland and Labrador.[2] Nevertheless, prestige was reckoned by the acre in the middle ages, and Ireland was so much fresh territory to be conquered – when one had nothing better to do. King William Rufus had stood on the shores of Pembroke and thought about it. King Henry II seriously contemplated it in 1155 when he was young and inexperienced, but his worldly-wise mother, the Empress Matilda, had persuaded him that he had enough to do on the continent.

Henry's interest, however, coincided with that of an Englishman, Nicholas Breakspear, who sat in the chair of St Peter at Rome (the only Englishman ever to do so) as Pope Adrian IV. He was very distressed by what he heard of the state of the Irish Church. Not only were the days of the saints long gone by, the church there had fallen well behind a Europe which had experienced a century of ecclesiastical reform. It was still even organised on a tribal basis with power in the hands of hereditary abbots. A strong hand was needed and Adrian looked hopefully to the king of England. He sent him a papal commission (known from its opening words as the Bull *Laudabiliter*) authorising the conquest of Ireland, and an emerald ring by which he might invest a ruler of it. For years the bull and the ring lay in the treasury at Winchester unused; but in 1171 Henry, having neglected the conquest of Ireland himself, had been obliged to take note of its impending conquest by others.[1]

In 1166 Dermont McMurrough, king of Leinster, whose brigandage and adultery had brought against him a more than usually formidable combination of enemies, landed in England in search of assistance. Henry had too much on his hands at the time to give personal attention to Ireland, but he was happy to welcome Dermont as a vassal and gave him permission to advertise for free-lances. Dermont aroused the interest of some of the barons of the Welsh March who were battle-hardened from continual skirmishing against their neighbours and ready for fresh employment for their swords. They soon achieved a striking success. The Irish were not used to fighting men in armour, they were staggered by the showers of arrows from the Welsh archers whom the adventurers brought over, and terror-stricken by the rearing, pounding hoofs of the war-horses. When the Irish learned to take cover in woods, or disperse themselves in bogs they were more difficult to defeat, but the adventurers did well at the first encounter. They married Irish heiresses and set about establishing principalities for themselves.

This was not what King Henry had anticipated. He could not tolerate any of his barons setting up independent bases and sources of power. He tried handicapping them by cutting off reinforcements; he tried bullying them by distraining upon their English lands; but they had the bit between their teeth and would not be stopped. The only solution was to take control of Ireland himself. He landed with an imposing force in 1171, obliged the Anglo-Norman *conquistadores* to acknowledge his overlordship, reserved the ports of Dublin, Wexford, and Waterford, with their hinterland, for himself, and offered the Irish chieftains his protection if they would become his vassals. They were glad to do so. In six months Henry established his authority, but it was an authority that had to be continually exercised if it were to remain effective. He could not do it personally. The Irish chieftains soon reverted to their tribal feuds, and the Anglo-Norman adventurers identified themselves with local interests and profited from the state of anarchy. John de Courcy, for one, gained an epic success in the north of the country and looked like becoming lord of the whole of Ulster.

Henry had first thought of assigning Ireland to John in 1177, but at that time he was too young to be thrust on to a pioneering frontier, and the Crown's interests had to be left in the ineffective hands of a viceroy in Dublin.[1] But in 1185 John was nineteen, and it was high time that he took his share of the burden of bringing peace and order to every part of the Angevin dominions. His father therefore knighted him, fitted him up with an army of 300 knights, and loaned him a detachment of Chancery clerks. He sailed from Milford Haven on 24 April.[2]

Adrian IV's bull had anticipated the formation of a kingdom of Ireland; but there was a snag in making John king immediately – the current pope, Lucius III, refused his sanction. So John went with the title of Lord of Ireland (*Dominus Hiberniae – dominus* being the title accorded a king before he was actually crowned). It was not until after Lucius' death in November of the same year that Henry was able to secure papal approval, and with it a crown of peacock feathers and gold; but by that time John's expedition had ended in fiasco.[3]

Ireland was virtually *terra incognita* to English chroniclers. They knew something of the adventures of the early conquistadors – it was a popular story – but they found it hard to understand what was going on there. So far as John's expedition of 1185 was concerned they merely recorded his departure and humiliated return (if indeed they mentioned it at all). It is very frustrating for John's biographer that as soon as he appears on the stage of history a curtain falls. It is not, however, an entirely impenetrable curtain, for Gerald of Wales was on the expedition. King Henry had asked him to go for he knew more about Ireland than anyone else in the royal entourage. He had relatives among the Anglo-Norman settlers and he had made a journey of exploration; indeed, he wrote the first guide book to Ireland for tourists, and a very interesting one too – for the sort of tourists who like their topography mixed with fable and folklore.[4] Gerald's writings on contemporary events are very copious, but he is not a chronicler in the normal sense at all. He often starts a narrative but it soon gets lost in personal opinion, gossip, classical parallels, and rambling reflections. Nothing can be learned from him of John's movements in Ireland, but we do get a good idea of what went wrong.

John's expedition gave, it seems, a very clear illustration of his want of serious purpose. He took a lot of young hangers-on with him, and they all burst into laughter when the bearded Irish chieftains came in to renew the homage they had first done to his father: shaggy beards had gone out in great-grandfather's day. The ridicule of striplings had an effect which even the most pessimistic observer of the Irish scene would not have predicted: the chieftains sank their perennial differences and united against the foreigner. They even managed to inflict a defeat on some of John's mercenaries. The Anglo-Norman settlers stood aloof. Inevitably they disliked having their independence inhibited by the presence of their overlord, and should have been warmed by sympathetic generosity, but they found themselves passed over in the making of new grants in favour of the young courtiers John had brought with him. The barrels of silver pennies supplied by King Henry were emptied in riotous living. The unpaid mercenaries resorted first to plunder and then to desertion. In September John crawled back home to his father, laying the blame for his failure on the intrigues of the erstwhile viceroy, Hugh Lacy.[1]

Gerald of Wales was tempted to say, 'that is what comes of spurning the patriarch of Jerusalem,' but moral didacticism was only one side of his personality: he had an aristocratic eye for the art of war and he acutely criticised the military methods that had been used. Knights equipped in the French fashion were no use in rough wooded country. The cavalry charge, which relied for success on close ranks of men and horses, had no place here: lightly armed horsemen who could pursue the enemy into the hills were needed. Then again, the customary heavy armour of knights, and the high, curved saddles that lancework required, made it difficult for men to mount and dismount quickly, which was often necessary in a scrambling, skirmishing kind of warfare. Large numbers of Welsh bowmen should always be employed to keep back the Irish slingers who could move around with great rapidity and agility. Finally, if the country were to be held securely, it could be done not simply by building large numbers of castles, but by building them according to a strategic plan, advancing them steadily in leapfrogging movements.[2]

This was sound advice, but new methods are not learned over-
night, and victory might well have eluded John anyway. It was
certainly not to be the last time that an apparently well equipped
expedition came to grief in Ireland. King Henry was obliged to
turn again to the conquistadors for his administrators, for they at
least knew what they were about: John de Courcy was made
viceroy. Certainly John could not have put up a worse show. Whatever excuses could be made, men could point out that at an age
when Richard had cowed and crushed the proud barons of southern France, John had shown himself nothing more than a feckless
waster.

While John had been throwing away his opportunities and his
father's money in Ireland, his brother Geoffrey was fatally wounded
in a tournament.[1] He left behind him a daughter, Eleanor, and
a posthumous son, Arthur, so there was no possibility of intruding
John into Brittany, but it did give him a better chance of succeeding to the throne. Richard was still unmarried: the Princess Alice
to whom he had been betrothed in 1169 was still being trailed
around in King Henry's household, but the old king seemed dis-
inclined to release her, and Richard himself showed no desire for
matrimony. The king and he were on bad terms. Richard's refusal to part with Aquitaine had been met by Henry's refusal to
recognise him formally as heir. There was always the possibility
that Henry would divide his dominions and let John have the
crown of England.

To exacerbate the situation there was a new king ruling in
France, and Philip II had one overriding ambition: to break up
the Angevin empire. He first tried simple assault, but this got him
nowhere for it only made the quarrelsome Angevins unite against
him, and he had to make a hurried peace. So then he tried the
more subtle tactic of setting them against each other. Philip had
none of the courtesy and gentlemanly uprightness of his father;
intrigue and deceit came naturally to him, and old age and suspicion made easy victims. He fostered rumours that Henry had
seduced Alice and would never let Richard have her, and that he
intended to disinherit him. Richard was keen to go off on crusade
and try his skill on castles more worthy of it than those of his
vassals. The third great effort of Western Europe to clear the
Holy Land of infidels was being prepared; but anxious as he was
to join the French and German knights, Richard feared that his

father would trick him behind his back, and have the barons do homage to John while he was away. Philip, eagerly taking up his cause, demanded that Henry have Richard formally recognised as his heir, and that John join the crusade.[1] When he refused they made war on him.

Together they were too much for the old king who was worn out and ill. He was hounded from castle to castle. When he was driven even from Le Mans, his birthplace, he wearily sued for peace. The summer of 1189 had been a hot one, and when Henry came to humble himself before Philip at Gisors, thunder rumbled and lightning struck between them. He promised everything that was demanded of him: to give up Alice, to have his barons do fealty to Richard, to pay Philip an indemnity of 20,000 marks. He asked only one thing: to be given a list of those who had deserted him. When the list was brought he was horrified to find that the first name was that of John. Many no doubt thought that the old king's days were numbered, and that their future lay with Richard. John, cynically weighing the situation, had joined them. Broken-hearted and cursing, Henry was brought to Chinon, and there, on 6 July 1189, he died.[2]

4. COUNT OF MORTAIN

Richard was crowned king on 3 September 1189 in Westminster Abbey. A bat flittered round the throne in broad daylight as the ceremony was being performed and the superstitious shivered.[3] Richard, however, was not a man to be deterred by portents. He was anxious to be off on the exciting adventure of a crusade. Already before he was crowned he had ordered a muster of ships. Everything was sacrificed to raising money for it, even good government. His father's officials, who had been loyal to the last, were made to pay heavily to gain the new king's goodwill. Sheriffs were discharged from office, and new ones were installed who would pay to be admitted. Everything was for sale – privileges, lordships, earldoms, sheriffdoms, castles, towns, and suchlike, writes one contemporary.[4] 'He relieved all those whose money was a burden to them,' says another.[5]

The new king attempted to solve the problem of keeping England quiet during his absence by a number of balancing acts. The large sums demanded of office holders helped in this respect: private ambitions were gratified, but people who had paid heavily for their privileges would be anxious to preserve the *status quo*. The principal office in the administration, the justiciarship (which in the absence of the king amounted to a viceroyalty) was divided between a bishop and a baron: Hugh de Puiset, the aristocratic bishop of Durham, and William Mandeville, the aged earl of Essex. Into the office of chancellor (which controlled the Great Seal) he put a man who had served him well in the administration of Aquitaine, William Longchamp. Longchamp was furthermore made bishop of Ely, and legatine power was sought for him from the pope.

Richard also tried a balancing act with possible rivals for the throne. Geoffrey Plantagenet, one of Henry II's illegitimate sons, a man of some personality and ability, who had stood by his father to the end, was put quite out of the running by being obliged to take priest's orders. He had been in minor clerical orders for some time. Richard urged him into regular celibacy by giving him the archbishopric of York. Henry's other bastards did not, apparently, present much danger. There remained of course, John, and his nephew Arthur – Geoffrey of Brittany's son. The late 12th century had not made up its mind about rules of inheritance and both had a good claim. Arthur, however, was only four years old, and as a complete stranger it would be unlikely that he would be an effective rallying point for any who thought to profit from a change of ruler. So Richard's choice, as his heir, fell for the time being upon him. John was so liberally compensated that, it was hoped, it would not be worth his while jeopardising a magnificent appanage by reckless rebellion. Between Richard's accession and his departure his brother was loaded with titles, fiefs, and revenues. As soon as he became king Richard carried out his father's expressed but unfulfilled intentions: John was made count of Mortain in Normandy, and married to the heiress who had already been marked out for him, Isabelle of Gloucester. The archbishop of Canterbury protested at the marriage of second cousins without papal licence, but it went through nonetheless.[1] Gloucester was a valuable honor (as the greater fiefs were termed) and, as earl, John received the third penny of the profits of justice in the shire. He was allowed, of course, to retain the fiefs that he had previously been holding, and it was understood that he could regard Ireland as virtually his own. To these Richard added several more castles and fiefs, including the important honor of Lancaster. Most remarkable of all was the grant of six counties, Nottingham and Derby, Dorset, Somerset, Devon and Cornwall. What the grant of the counties meant was that the revenues from them that were normally paid into the royal exchequer went instead to John. To ensure, however, that the royal government retained some control of the territories granted to John, the king reserved to himself the more important castles within them. Furthermore he exacted an oath from John to stay out of the country for three years, by which time, no doubt, he expected to have returned from his crusade.[1]

On the face of it these arrangements were adroit, but they were easily upset. The first thing that happened was that the earl of Essex died. Richard, impatient to be gone, put Longchamp into the justiciarship with Bishop Hugh, and added secular make-weight by putting in two well-tried servants of the Crown, Hugh Bardulf and William Brewer. Longchamp, as chancellor and papal legate in addition, was well on the way to upsetting the balance of power. Moreover, the queen-mother, Eleanor, pleaded with Richard to release John from his oath to stay out of England, and he imprudently did so.[2]

The trouble with balancing acts is that they only work if every-one in the act does his share of preserving the balance. Neither Longchamp nor John was prepared to. Longchamp was am-bitious; John was thinking of the succession. People were worried by the king's departure, for many feared that he would never return alive. Before the French and English contingents started, news was received that Emperor Frederick Barbarosa had been drowned in a river in Cilicia while on his way to the Holy Land with the German knights by the overland route. There was a feeling too that since the king was responsible for peace and order within his dominions there would be no security when he left. 'As the earth grows dark when the sun departs, so the face of the kingdom was changed by the absence of the king,' writes Richard of Devizes. 'All the barons were disturbed, castles were strength-ened, towns fortified, ditches dug.'[3] It was every man for himself and none more actively than John. If Richard did die suddenly to be the man in possession would be a stronger title than mere designation as heir. John paraded the country with an armed re-tinue and did not check his followers when they spoke of him as the next king.[4]

There was no one who could restrain him. The men who had

plenty of experience in running the country while the king was across the Channel, and knew how to handle over-mighty subjects, were with Richard on crusade. They included Ranulph Glanville who had been Henry II's justiciar and John's tutor.[1] His mother had gone too. Longchamp, indeed, was anxious to keep John down: he was very loyal to Richard and accepted Arthur as his master's heir; but when he tried to do anything he found that his own overweening ambition had alienated everyone. Richard was no judge of men and had blundered badly in leaving Longchamp to guard his interests. Longchamp was a Norman by birth with little or no acquaintance with the people of England, whom, indeed, he affected to despise. He was eager to push his family's fortunes: his brother Henry was made sheriff of Herefordshire, his brother Osbert was given the sheriffdom of Yorkshire, and later those of Norfolk and Suffolk also. He used his authority to secure rich heiresses and wardships for them, and increased his own power by shutting Bishop Hugh out of the Exchequer when he conducted official business. The barons despised him as a jumped-up jack-in-office; the bishops resented his authority over them as papal legate; and even the clerks of the administration could not abide him. Chroniclers heaped abuse on him and said that his grandfather was a runaway serf. When this accusation is found in medieval chronicles it is usually untrue, but it is a sure sign of extreme unpopularity.[2] Much of the abuse was probably unfair: he seems to have had some administrative gifts, and much of his unpopularity was very likely due to the zeal with which he raised money for the unfillable coffers of King Richard. His virtues, however, are beside the point: his vices, real or supposed, made him a perfect scapegoat. 'The laity found him more than king, the clergy more than pope, and both an intolerable tyrant,' says Newburgh.[3]

John went to work on him with a will. He himself had set up a court modelled on that of a king. He had his own justiciar, his own chancellor, a seal-bearer, a seneschal. Some such structure was perhaps necessary for the running of his wide estates, but it gave the appearance of a rival administration. His castles at Lancaster and Marlborough were the resort of anyone who felt aggrieved by Longchamp. Hugh of Nunant, bishop of Coventry, who conceived a violent hatred for Longchamp, became his intimate adviser. There was little good that could be said of Nunant

himself: the story is told that when he confessed his lifelong catalogue of sins on his deathbed, no confessor could be found who
would absolve him.[1] But for the moment all animosities were sunk
in hatred of Longchamp. John was able to put himself forward as
the champion of baronial interests against the chancellor's interference. Gerard of Camville, fearing an inquiry into his work as
sheriff of Lincolnshire, resisted a demand to surrender his shire
and the castle of Lincoln, saying that he would do so only to John.
The chancellor laid siege to Lincoln, John seized the castles of
Tickhill and Nottingham. It looked like a struggle for supremacy
between the two of them.

Unfortunately for John, Walter of Coutances, archbishop of
Rouen, arrived in England at this moment. Hearing of the disordered state of England while he was in Sicily, King Richard
had sent Coutances home with wide powers to do whatever he
thought fit. The archbishop was a man of noble birth and administrative experience, sagacious and tactful. If Richard had had
any sense he would have appointed him justiciar in the first place.
Whilst many people were hostile to Longchamp, few wanted open
war, and the archbishop of Rouen was welcomed as a mediator.
Longchamp was prepared to climb down for his commission as
papal legate had lapsed with the death of the pope, and he was
realising the extent of the opposition to himself. Unfortunately,
however, he was no sooner softening his words than his agents
got him into trouble again. John's half-brother Geoffrey arrived
in England in September 1191 to take up his archbishopric of
York. He, like John, had been told by Richard to stay out, so the
chancellor's men had reason to oppose his landing. They acted,
however, with shocking violence. Disembarking at Dover,
Geoffrey took refuge in the priory of St Martin, but he was dragged from the altar there and imprisoned in Dover Castle. Longchamp protested that this was not done by his order, but for the
unscrupulous militants around John it was a good excuse to take
up arms against him again. They marched on Windsor where he
had set up his headquarters, and he fled for safety to the Tower of
London.[2]

The archbishop of Rouen proposed in a council at London in
October that Longchamp be deposed from the office of justiciar.
This was agreed to by the assembled barons and bishops, and
Longchamp, after giving up his brothers as hostages, retreated

from the country. The archbishop then produced his trump card – a mandate from Richard giving him power to take over as justiciar if necessary. This was a blow to John. He had had his moment of popularity when he led the opposition to an unpopular minister, and he had hoped to take over as regent; but no one could object to Walter of Coutances running the country as Richard's representative.[1] John's bright prospects of succeeding to the throne as a figure of popular acclaim were waning fast. It no longer even seemed inevitable that Richard would die childless, for news arrived that he had married while in Cyprus. The queen-mother had bullied him into taking Berengar of Navarre, whom she had brought from Spain for the purpose.

John was reduced to wild schemings. He followed Richard's own example of a few years before and intrigued with King Philip of France. Philip had given up the crusade at the end of 1191 because he wanted to get home to take possession of part of Flanders, whose count had died at the siege of Acre. At the same time he was hopeful of doing some mischief to Richard who had stayed behind to push on to Jerusalem. He held out a tempting offer to John: let him take the cast-off Alice as his wife and the dominions that Richard held of the French Crown should be his. John was actually about to take ship from Southampton when his mother arrived home. She would stand for no nonsense of this kind, and threatened that if he went the Crown would seize his estates.[2] He stayed, but he did not stop intriguing. He even negotiated with Longchamp for his return – with no very serious purpose perhaps, but he liked to show how powerful he was. The chancellor had taken heart from the fact that the new pope regarded him as still the official legate in England. In March 1192 he landed at Dover, took refuge with his sister, who was wife of the castellan there, and demanded a proper trial on the charges for which he had been deprived of the justiciarship. Worried and anxious, the royal officials begged John to help them get rid of the chancellor. When they had begged him enough to satisfy his pride, he came to a council meeting at London and lorded it over the assembly. If we can believe Richard of Devizes he was quite brazen: 'The chancellor will not fear for anything, or beg favours from anyone, if he has me for friend. He offers me £100 within a week if I steer clear of the quarrel between you and him. You see it is money I want. I think I have said enough for wise men to understand,' and so he stalked out. The distracted officials had to raid the treasury to bribe him to sanction their proceedings against Longchamp; and more than that, everyone at the council meeting took an oath of fealty to him as Richard's heir.[1]

John went around confidently saying that Richard would never come home. It began to look as if he might be right. The summer of 1192 came and went, parties of English crusaders began arriving home, but there was no news of the king. Christmas was spent in ignorance of what had become of him. Then startling news arrived: he was a prisoner in Germany. Returning from the Holy Land by a route made tortuous by storms, shipwreck, and the presence of many enemies on the Mediterranean coast, Richard had fallen into the hands of a man most personally hostile of all – Duke Leopold of Austria, whom he had insulted at the siege of Acre. The duke handed him over, at a substantial transfer fee, to Emperor Henry VI, to whom it seemed like the answer to a prayer. The emperor was faced in Germany by the opposition of the duke of Saxony, who was married to Richard's sister. In Italy he was striving against the king of Sicily, with whom Richard had formed an alliance on the way to the Holy Land. What could be better than to have Richard himself in his hands? He could use him as a bargaining counter, and the ransom money would pay for the conquest of Sicily.

King Philip was delighted at the news. He was a friend of the Hohenstauffen ruling house in Germany, and he had exciting hopes of buying Richard from the emperor and releasing him only at the price of the break-up of the Angevin dominions. Henry would not part with Richard so readily – he was far too valuable to himself – but he encouraged the French king's hopes, for it enabled him to push up the ransom price and put pressure on England for prompt payment. Philip was not the man to let any chance slip; even if he could not get hold of Richard, he could make the most of his captivity. The government in England had been thrown into near panic by the king's misadventure, so Philip gathered mercenaries and Danish help for an invasion of Richard's lands, and in hope of disrupting the opposition played on John's ambition for the promotion of civil war. The selfishness of Philip's intentions should have been obvious for he had set the Angevins against each other before; but John was ready to take a gambler's chance. He hurried to Paris in January and did homage to Philip in expectation of his brother being deprived of his continental possessions by French troops, and undertook to set aside his own wife and marry Philip's sister. Returning to England he sent privately to the Scots and the Welsh inviting them to join him in rebellion. For the government, burdened with the problem of raising money for the king's ransom, it was a critical situation. Richard alone remained undisturbed: 'My brother John,' he said, 'is not a man to win land for himself by force if there is anyone to put up a mere show of resistance.'[1] It was a crippling disparagement and John long felt the effects of it. As it turned out, the force that he was able to muster was not very imposing: the bishop of Coventry, who had counselled him throughout the Longchamp affair, brought his men out, and the restless Welsh helped him; but the barons remained loyal and the king of Scots stood aloof. The government, stiffened by the queen-mother who knew how to cope with her sons, fortified the royal castles, laid prompt siege to John's, and mustered a home-guard against the threatened invasion. So frustrated were John's efforts that he agreed to a truce and the payment of the share of Richard's ransom from his own lands. It was a truce only though, not a settlement. When Philip heard early in the autumn that the emperor and Richard had agreed to terms, he sent his ally an urgent message: 'Look to yourself for the devil is loosed,' and John fled to the French court.[2]

Philip's message was not strictly accurate: until the emperor received a portion at least of the 150,000 marks demanded for the ransom Richard would be held in captivity. The plotters thought that they still had a chance. They plied Henry with offers: would he surrender Richard to them for the same money? Would he keep him in captivity a year longer? 'Behold how they love him,' says Roger of Howden.[3] Henry, however, merely showed the offers to Richard. He had no wish to see the Angevin dominions undone. The agreement with the king of England strengthened his position within the empire and his financial credit. Moreover, he had grand ambitions to make the imperial title mean an overlordship of Christendom. By the terms of the agreement Richard did homage to Henry and made England a fief of the empire, and as ruler of half of France he would make a useful ally against its king. Richard could turn on a courtly dignity and charm and his relations with the emperor had grown cordial: he was allowed to hold court, to receive the many people who came to visit him, and to transact business with the government in England. When the first instalment of the ransom arrived in February 1194 he was released and given an escort of German knights. As soon as he landed the castles still holding out for John surrendered miserably. The castellan of St Michael's Mount, indeed, is said to have died of fright when he heard Richard was back. At Nottingham in March the king held a council and asked for judgement on the rebels. John, it was decreed, should appear for trial within forty days or forfeit his lands and all claim to the kingdom.[1]

John did not come to stand trial; he lay low in Normandy. Richard found him there in May. The king had gone over as soon as he could to drive Philip away from his sieges of Norman castles. On his way he stopped at Lisieux to spend the night with a former servant of his who was archdeacon there. The story goes that he noticed that his host was ill at ease. 'What is the matter?' said Richard. 'Oh, I know, you have seen my brother John, do not deny it. Tell him to come to me without fear. He is my brother and should not be afraid. I will not hold his folly against him.' The archdeacon fetched John from his hiding place: 'Come out, you are in luck. The king is gentle and merciful, kinder to you than you would have been to him.' Trembling, John came out and threw himself at his brother's feet. Richard raised him up with a kiss, saying, 'Think no more of it, John; you are only a child who has had evil counsellors,' and took him to sup off a freshly caught salmon.[2]

Richard's patronising forgiveness was the culminating humiliation for John. The 'child', as Richard called him, was 27 years old, but could show a record only of failure and dishonour. Throughout his life so far he had been overshadowed by brothers who had made a name for themselves in the world (as their father had done) at the age of fifteen. In his efforts to emulate them he had shown only caricatures of their qualities: where the young Henry had been gay, he was frivolous, where Geoffrey had been cunning he was sly, where Richard was bold he was merely bombastic. The expedition to Ireland had been a fiasco; his assumption of authority in England during Richard's absence had been a hollow mockery. He stood in 1194 as a traitor and a fool. Such a reputation long clung to him, and in some quarters was perhaps never entirely displaced; but, in fact, the real John had not yet emerged.

It was as if, hitherto, he had been afflicted with the pressing need to rival his brothers' prowess; but from now on he began to escape from it, and emerged as much more like his father than any of them. As king he was to show a grasp of political realities that had eluded the young Henry, more fierce determination than ever Geoffrey could boast of, as sure a strategic sense as Richard displayed and a knowledge of government to which the heroic crusader never even aspired. Only the Old King himself is comparable to the later John in his powers of organisation and the ability, invaluable in a ruler, to bend his energy to points of administrative detail.

No one could have suspected all this in 1194, but it is possible that during the five years that followed, Richard himself, and his immediate entourage, began to acquire a respect for the reformed John that then emerged, for he spent them serving his brother faithfully on the field of battle and in the council chamber.

Richard's forgiveness of his brother's treachery did not extend to reversing the verdict of the council at Nottingham: John was left landless (apart from the titular lordship of Ireland) and was set to earn the recovery of his property. He aquitted himself well: he conducted a lightning siege of Evreux that secured the castle within a day, and defended Normandy while Richard marched south to deal with trouble along the Loire. As a result, reports Roger of Howden, Richard, in 1195, 'laid aside his ill-will' and restored to him the county of Mortain and the honour of Gloucester, with an annual allowance of £2000.[1]

In the following year John countered Philip's seizure of Nonancourt by seizing Gamanches, and then led a party of Richard's mercenaries on a raid into French territory as far as Beauvais, capturing its martial bishop and razing his castle of Milli.[2] When war was renewed in 1198 John was again to the fore, containing Philip's attack on the Norman border town and waylaying and capturing a party of eighteen French knights and many men-at-arms.[3] In a desperate attempt to set the Angevin brothers against each other once more, Philip, early in 1199 after concluding a truce with Richard, sent to tell him that John had deserted to the French side, and offering to show him a letter to prove it. Richard believed him, according to Roger of Howden, and ordered the seizure of his brother's property; but John kept his head and successfully protested his innocence.[4]

It was as well for John that he spent the years from 1194 quietly building up credit with the men who mattered at court: in 1199 Richard was still only 41, but his death came sooner than anyone could have expected. In the winter of 1198–9 a ploughman near Limoges turned up a Gallo-Roman hoard and rumour inflated its value. Richard claimed that the lord of the place was cheating him of his due treasure-trove, and went in the spring to lay siege to the castle of Chalus. In a poor state of repair and ill-defended, it presented only a minor problem to Richard's talents. He was indeed too contemptuous of it, and without bothering to don his armour he went reconnoitring round it with his mercenary captain, Mercardier. He was struck in the shoulder by a bolt from a crossbow, the wound festered, and ten days later, on 6 April 1199, gangrene killed him. He died bequeathing his jewels to his nephew Otto of Saxony, and his inheritance to his brother John.[1]

5. RICHARD'S HEIR

At the time of Richard's death John was, ironically enough, staying with his rival, his nephew Arthur of Brittany, son of his elder brother Geoffrey. As soon as the news reached him he rode off with only a few companions for Chinon where the Angevin treasury was kept.[2] It was a prudent move for anyone who wished to control the springs of government. His great-grandfather, Henry I, had spurred his horse for the treasury at Winchester as soon as he heard that his brother, William Rufus, had been killed in the New Forest. The fact that John had been designated heir by Richard on his deathbed was influential but not decisive. The officials tried to carry out their master's last wishes, but the barons were not bound by them. Kinship with the royal house was essential for succession, but precedence in blood was not yet clearly established. Feudal custom in the matter was hardening, but there was no uniformity between one part of the Angevin empire and another: the customs of England, Normandy, and Anjou were at variance.* A law book attributed to Ranulph Glanville, Henry II's justiciar, is doubtful whether a younger brother or the son of a dead older brother has a better claim to a feudal inheritance: it gives arguments on both sides and rather

---

* Aquitaine did not constitute part of the problem in 1199 for Eleanor was still its duchess; Richard had merely been associated with her in the rule of it as duke.

favours the nephew.[1] On the other hand, to a contemporary legist of Normandy 'the younger son is the nearer heir to the inheritance of his father than the child of the elder brother who died before the father.'[2] In the circumstances of a contested succession, acceptance by a sufficient number of influential men to secure investiture was what really mattered.

The biography of William Marshal gives a glimpse of the debate going on. The news of Richard's death was brought to William on 10 April at Vaudreuil just as he was going to bed. He dressed hurriedly and went to call on Archbishop Hubert Walter of Canterbury, who was staying nearby. 'My lord,' he said, 'we must lose no time in choosing someone to be king.' 'I think,' said the archbishop, 'that Arthur should rightfully be king.' 'To my mind that would be bad,' said Marshal; 'Arthur is counselled by traitors; he is haughty and proud; and if we put him over us, he will only do us harm for he does not love the people of this land. He shall not come here by my advice. Consider rather Count John: he seems to me the nearest heir to the land which belonged to his father and brother.' 'Marshal,' said the archbishop, 'is this really your desire?' 'Yea, my lord, for it is just. Undoubtedly a son has a better claim to his father's land than a grandson; it is right that he should have it.' 'So be it then,' said the archbishop, 'but mark my words, Marshal, you will never regret anything in your life as much as this.'[3] William Marshal was a paragon of feudal propriety and something of an elder statesman to the house of Anjou, and his opinion carried great weight.

From Chinon John rode for the abbey of Fontevrault, where Richard's corpse had been taken for burial at the feet of his father. From there he went on to Beaufort-en-Vallée to call on Richard's widow, in the company of Bishop Hugh of Lincoln who had officiated at the funeral; but there they found themselves among enemies. Constance of Brittany had not been idle: while John was securing the treasury, she had entrusted her twelve-year-old son to the care of King Philip and raised forces to seize Richard's lands for him. An army of Bretons had taken control of Angers, and there on Easter Day (18 April) a gathering of barons from Anjou, Maine, and Touraine had accepted Arthur as rightful successor: their customs, they said, required it.[4] John hurried to Le Mans, but the citizens received him coldly and the garrison would not admit him. The Breton army and a force under King

Philip were converging on the town, and it was only by slipping away before daybreak on Easter Tuesday that John managed to avoid capture.[1] He found that he was safe in Normandy, for the Normans had no wish to put themselves under the rule of a Breton; and at Rouen on 25 April John was acclaimed duke and invested with a coronet of golden roses.

Meanwhile William Marshal and the archbishop of Canterbury had gone to England to plead his cause. The realm was disordered and uncertain, as it always was when kingless, but there was little sentiment for Arthur of Brittany. The justiciar, Geoffrey FitzPeter, was for John. He and the two envoys from the continent summoned the barons to Northampton and prevailed upon them to take an oath of fealty.[2] There was not much enthusiasm, but the alternative seemed worse. John took a Norman army down to Le Mans to punish it for not supporting him: its walls and castle were flattened, its leading citizens made prisoner; but he was anxious to get across to England as soon as possible for the all important ceremony of coronation. His mother had brought up Richard's mercenaries under Mercardier from Chalus, and leaving the situation in Anjou and Maine to them, he hurried back to the Normandy coast. On 25 May he landed at Shoreham with a few friends, and two days later, on the feast of the Ascension, at Westminster Abbey, he was crowned.[3] The youngest son had gained the throne.

3

Losing a Duchy

'I became a reproof among all mine enemies, but especially
among my neighbours: and they of mine acquaintance were
afraid of me; and they that did see me without conveyed themselves from me.'   *Psalm xxxi.* 13

1. THE FIGHT FOR AN INHERITANCE

The situation on the continent was so precarious that John could
not afford to remain long in England. Within three weeks of leaving Normandy he was disembarking again at Dieppe with reinforcements of English troops. Normandy had accepted him without question as Richard's successor; Aquitaine was being held for
him by his mother; but these two great duchies of the Angevin
empire were sundered by the counties which had declared for
Arthur.[1] John had a few adherents in Maine, Anjou, and Touraine who were holding out in scattered strongholds; the private
mercenary army of Richard's boon companion, Mercardier, was
happily stalking the country to plunder 'traitors'; but the towns
were dominated by the Bretons and their allies. This was serious
because the principal roads of medieval France intersected at
Angers and Tours, and John had to hold them if he were to control
both northern and southern France. The stretch of river and road
linking the two towns was the strategic hub of the Angevin empire,
and his enemies had realised it: as soon as Richard's death was
known the Bretons moved up the Loire to Angers, and the French
down it from Blois to Tours.

John was not able to hurry south immediately because Philip
distracted him by driving a wedge into Norman territory where
the Seine and its tributaries ran across the border. The English
troops were thrown into a counter-attack and managed to hold
Philip back but not to force him back. A lull followed while both

II. The struggle for an inheritance, April to September 1199.

sides drew breath, and short truces were arranged. John needed time to muster local forces for the defence of Normandy. Philip too was glad of a respite, for Richard's death had caught him ill-prepared; but he was not interested in anything more than a short truce. The two kings met at the frontier to parley in the middle of August, and Philip was challenged to say why he had gone to war against a man who had done him no injury. The excuse he gave was that John had taken possession of Normandy without seeking his overlord's permission and doing homage.[1] Richard's failure to make clear provision for the succession had indeed obliged John to act precipitately, but he insisted that he was ready to do homage and give his lord reasonable satisfaction. Philip, however, pitched the price of peace impossibly high. He demanded Anjou, Maine, and Touraine for Arthur, and a critical slice of the Norman March for himself.[2]

John had no hesitation in rejecting these terms outright. He had been gathering strength and was by now in a better position than Philip probably realised. Fortunately for John, Richard had been making preparations for a new offensive against the French at the time of his death. Moreover, his brother's alliances with the princes of the lower Rhine held firm. These were of vital importance. Philip was able to harry Normandy much better than his predecessors had done because he had acquired, as the dowry of his first wife, a strip of western Flanders which gave him convenient bases along the Norman border. Richard had countered this by bribing the princes of the Low Countries into alliances, and so threatening Philip in the rear. If Normandy was to be safe John had to do the same. Early in August Count Baldwin of Flanders had visited John at Rouen and done homage, and a week later the count of Boulogne came to renew his alliance at the ducal palace on the Isle of Andelys in the Seine.[3]

Feeling safer in the north, John believed that he could ignore the French bridgehead across the Seine and its tributaries and give his attention to Anjou. When, in September, Philip struck at the castle of Conches, John took no notice and marched south. The initiative was clearly in his hands for as soon as he moved Philip broke away from Normandy and headed south too. At John's approach the commander of the Breton forces wavered. William des Roches, the most powerful baron in Anjou, was acting as the right arm of Constance and Arthur, but his own future was in the forefront of his mind. His authority as constable in Anjou, Maine, and Touraine was recognised by the French king, but he doubted if this would mean anything if John were on the warpath, and he was ready to bargain. Philip foolishly gave him an excuse for changing sides: bursting into Maine to forestall John he seized and razed the castle of Ballon. It was being held for John by an old follower of his father, but William claimed that it was part of his jurisdiction and objected to it being destroyed. Philip dismissed the objection brusquely saying that consideration for Arthur would not deter him from dealing as he pleased with what he captured. With this as a face-saver, William opened negotiations with John and offered to arrange a settlement with the Bretons. His offer was accepted, and John promised in return to respect William's position and advice. At Le Mans on 22 September Constance and Arthur were brought in and made their peace.[1]

Forsaken by the very people for whom he had hastily gone to war, Philip was not anxious to continue it. The papal legate who had arranged the truce with Richard at the beginning of the year was still in France and ready to mediate. Through his good offices the two kings agreed to suspend hostilities over Christmas and to meet personally afterwards. When they did meet, at the frontier on 15 January 1200, they were obviously both predisposed to peace. They stood talking for a long time and were seen to embrace warmly.[2] The consequence was a treaty formally concluded at Le Goulet on 22 May.

2. THE TREATY OF LE GOULET

The basis of the peace was perfectly simple: John was accepted as the rightful heir of Richard to all the fiefs that his father and brother had held on the continent, with a few minor modifications of the border. John, in turn, acknowledged that he held them from the king of France as his overlord. These were the principal features of the treaty that men would take away with them, and many might think that John's firm stand had been completely successful. But anyone who could remember Henry II in his heyday would realise from the specific provisions of the treaty that John's position vis-à-vis his overlord was in fact inferior to that of his father.

The border was rearranged to allow Philip custody of some of the townships and small fiefs that had been in dispute between him and Richard, and these were to be demilitarised. Other fiefs which the French king coveted, and which were liable to be a cause of friction, were assigned as a dowry to John's niece, Blanche of Castile, who, it had been agreed, should marry Philip's heir, Louis. They were only young children at the time, but as contemporary custom allowed, Philip was to take possession of the child bride and her dowry. There was no very serious loss to John involved in these arrangements – the prospect of a firm peace would more than offset them, and anyway his territorial power was not thereby materially weakened.

The portions of the treaty that had more serious import were those that governed John's feudal position. In return for the formal bestowal upon him of his fiefs he agreed to pay 20,000 marks as 'relief' to his overlord.[1] The relief was a succession duty, a customary payment which any feudal lord could demand of a vassal entering upon his inheritance. Whether the lord would receive it, or could deprive the vassal of the fief for failure to pay, depended on the reality of his own authority. The significance of the relief demanded of John lies partly in the enormous sum asked, but even more in the demand itself and the agreement to pay. No one had ventured to ask it of Henry or Richard; they had simply taken possession and no one dared say them nay. The performance of the traditional act of homage was as far as they had gone in acknowledgement of the French king's titular supremacy.[2]

Moreover, in the course of the treaty Philip ventured to prescribe certain of John's feudal relations with his own vassals. Arthur, as heir to Brittany, was acknowledged to be John's vassal, but John agreed not to diminish Arthur's prerogatives in any way without a judgement of his court. His predecessors had been more peremptory in their dealings with barons in disfavour. Furthermore, he was required to receive back into homage the rebellious lords of Angoulême and Limoges and to allow them to remain in full possession of their rights. Finally, he disavowed the close dependence upon himself of the count of Flanders and the count of Boulogne. These men were tenants-in-chief of the French Crown, but had formed alliances with the Angevins and been granted fiefs in Normandy and England. Being thus the vassals of both the king of England and of France they had often been persuaded by financial bribes to resolve their conflicting feudal loyalties in favour of the former.[1] John, however, acknowledged that 'they are or ought to be rather the vassals of the French king than of us,' and promised that in future he would not countenance their disobedience to their rightful lord.

Here then, in the Treaty of Le Goulet, are signs of a new relationship between the Angevin and the Capetian, or rather, to speak more accurately, some practical expression of a feudal dependence that had hitherto been largely theoretical. When Henry II performed homage he had been merely nodding to a historical survival – the antique fiction that the man who was crowned king at Rheims was the ruler of France. In reality, in 1154, the real ruler of more than half of France was Henry himself, and most of the rest was controlled by lesser but still virtually independent princes. The effective power of the king was exercised in a region around Paris which was somewhat smaller than the duchy of Normandy alone. Henry II's sons had, in their struggles with their father, turned to the French king as an ally and invested his feudal prerogatives with a more than usual significance, and in so doing they had dented the armour of their father's independence. Richard had played this game effectively while he was count of Poitou, but when he succeeded his father he had adopted Henry's position without serious qualification. It is in the peace terms of 1200 that the first distinct glimmers of a new reality investing the old fiction are apparent. The emergence of the monarchy as the dominating force in French political life was something that contemporaries firmly grasped only after Philip had deprived John of most of his continental possessions; but there in the Treaty of Le Goulet were embedded the prognostications of it.

3. 'JOHN SOFTSWORD'

Gervase of Canterbury, well placed in that busy town to catch the gossip of pilgrims and cross-Channel travellers, reports that in 1200 many carping critics and ill-wishers called John 'Softsword' for making peace with King Philip.[2] Gervase himself thought the slur inapt. Since he was writing after experience of John's persecution of the Church, he could add, with much bitterness, that any apparent softness was later changed to a flintiness that none of his predecessors could equal. But apart from that, Gervase felt that John was being prudent in preferring peace to war. He was right.

A peace policy at the beginning of the new reign was closer to necessity even than to prudence. Richard's preparations for war in 1198, and John's mustering of forces in 1199 were impressive. Gleaming new castles stood as bastions on the frontiers; mercenary troops stood to arms by the thousand. But behind them lay an economy at full stretch and a Normandy suddenly weary of war. The harsher truths of the military situation escaped contemporary chroniclers, though some, like Gervase, had an inkling of them. Therein, however, lies the explanation of John's readiness for peace in 1200, and, more important, a clue to the collapse of Normandy when war was renewed.

The military strength of the Angevin domains was geared to static defence. Henry II had no aggressive designs on his neighbours because even his vast energy was consumed in the task of holding and administering what he had already. It was only with great reluctance, and because his hand had been forced, that he crossed the Irish Sea. Even then, to conquer Ireland properly and to subjugate it to his officials was beyond him. It had to remain a lawless province for private adventurers on the edge of his domains. Hence Henry limited his objective, sensibly, to giving his subjects peace.

Castles were relied upon for the defence of the long frontier with France. The medieval castle had many uses, and defence was often only a secondary one. Primarily, castles were centres of authority. They served as headquarters for administrative officers, as guard-houses for hostages, gaols for prisoners, barracks for mercenary troops, as repositories for money, jewels, archives, and stores of every sort.[1] But on the Norman frontier in the 12th century, the castle was developed, more than anywhere else in Europe, with an eye to its function as a unit in an integrated system of defence. As such it had many advantages. For one thing it made for an economical use of manpower. On a long frontier lacking natural protection, a comparatively small number of men holding a chain of forts could hold up a large invading army until sufficient defending forces could be mustered. Forts could be by-passed of course, but a prudent invader would not risk leaving many untaken castles in his rear. The castle-guard might cut off his communications and reinforcements; and a defending force, stepping safely from castle to castle in his rear might prevent his withdrawal. It was necessary to have a relief column ready to help beleaguered forts, for few castles were expected to withstand a prolonged siege. It was common practice of the day for a castellan to treat with his besiegers and agree to surrender unless his lord came up with help within a specified time. There was no dishonour in this: it spared the invaders' resources but preserved the delaying function of the castle.

A strategy which relied upon the castle had, however, to accept two great disadvantages: high cost, and the limitations of static defence. The capital cost and the repair bills were considerable, even for the relatively simple type of castle consisting of a great tower and an outer wall. In addition, the development of siege-craft in the later 12th century made much reconstruction of old castles necessary. The cost of the more sophisticated castle, designed to withstand a prolonged siege by the latest techniques learned in the Holy Land, was almost prohibitive. Richard's castle at Les Andelys (Château Gaillard) cost more than twice the regular annual revenue of Normandy, and took three years to build (though even that struck contemporaries as a remarkably short time).[1]

Unfortunately, castles, even when sown as thickly as in the Norman marches, offered little protection against stabbing, plundering raids. Indeed, the cost of maintaining a castle could be greatly increased by laying waste the *châtellenie*, the neighbouring bundle of lands, rents, and services, upon which the guard supported themselves.[2] Moreover, static defence obliged the Angevins to meet the enemy on their own ground. Their towns went up in flames and their vassals were ruined if they went to war. Even a counter-attack could cause serious damage to the people it sought to defend. In one raid in 1198 Philip burned Evreux and seven neighbouring towns, but it was the defenders themselves who fired Neubourg.[3] By attacking here and there without stopping to mount serious siege operations, King Philip could keep the defences of Normandy at full stretch, reduce the revenue available to his opponents by wasting the land, and put up the bill for maintaining the castles by the damage he caused to the fortifications and the *châtellenies*. Castles, then, were a deterrent to full-scale invasion, but a poor protection against a ruthless raider.

The best answer to Philip's tactics lay in a standing army ready to counter-attack at any moment. This was Richard's solution: in addition to building new castles and reconstructing the old ones, he sought to remodel his feudal army. Nearly every baron, as a condition of holding his fief, was obliged to serve his overlord, when summoned, with a stipulated number of knights – men expensively mounted and equipped for the cavalry charge. Such a force was still the age's answer to full-scale invasion, but it was a ponderous weapon and not easily adapted for defence against raiders. It was often ill-trained, and it was difficult to keep it in the field for longer than six weeks. Richard therefore sought to raise a smaller but long-service troop of cavalry; but since he was unwilling to bear the cost of recruiting it from free-lances, he sought help from his English vassals. Those of them who were not personally involved in the defence of Normandy were asked to provide 300 knights to serve for a year. This was a small fraction (about a twentieth) of the number of knights for which they were liable at home, but since it cost three shillings a day to keep a knight in the field, the burden was not a light one. Richard's request met considerable opposition, and he only got his way by applying harsh pressure.[1] It is clear, in fact, that there was a deep unwillingness to serve abroad among English knights and little feeling of personal concern with the fate of the king's continental dominions. It came out strongly against John in later years.

Richard's need of a long-service army was increased by a development in the practice of war for which he himself was largely responsible. When earlier generations had sought to settle their disputes by war they had fought according to ancient customs, much as they would in a duel or a tournament.[2] They challenged mustered troops, manœuvred for position, and then either mount-ed a siege, gave battle, or agreed to terms. They fought in the spring and summer. A 'cold' war might be kept going throughout the year, but actual fighting was suspended for the harvest, and a series of truces would then normally carry them through to Christmas. When the festivities were over a conference would be held (St Hilary's Day – 13 January – was a popular date), and if no agreement was then reached they would fit out again for the campaigning season. War, in any age, is a destructive and peril-ous business; but fought by this ritual it was kept, at least, within sensible bounds. Richard, however, made the campaigning season an anachronism of an amateurish past. Several of his vassals, when he was count of Poitou, had defied him in the autumn, fully expecting to have the winter months to rally their kinsmen and friends, but had been shocked to find him hammering at their gates as soon as he could get there. There was no 'close season' for Richard: he fought all the year round. It was ungentlemanly but effective. He did the same as king – on a larger field of operations. To a contemporary Englishman, William of Newburgh, the all-seasons war was madness, sheer madness. As if the pestilence and famine that struck England in 1196 were not enough, he wrote, 'the minds of the brawling princes were harder even than this scourge, fierce as it was, for in their passion for war they ran winter, summer, and autumn together.'[1] Newburgh was a Yorkshire-man who had little enthusiasm for the struggle in France. There were many northern barons who shared his repugnance, and the way they expressed themselves was by resisting the king's requests for aid.

Richard's day-in, day-out, preoccupation with war forced him to rely very much on mercenary troops. The term 'mercenary' covered a wide range of professional soldiers, from the socially respectable to utter pariahs. High up were the skilled craftsmen and engineers who built and worked the siege engines. In the middle were the crossbowmen who manned the castles, and the Welsh archers who excelled in ambushes, as skirmishers, and as scouts. Right at the bottom were the disorderly *routiers*, the ruffians recruited into companies of foot and hawked for sale by enterprising captains. The over-populated Low Countries were a common recruiting ground and the *routiers* were often known as 'Flemings' or 'Brabantines', but the outcasts and criminals of every nation were to be found among them. They plundered without much regard to friend or foe, and were feared and hated as much by the people of the rulers who hired them as by their opponents in war.[2] Mercenaries were by no means a new element in medieval warfare. Even the Norman kings, in the heyday of the feudal army of mounted vassals, had hired them as a means of converting English silver into forces for the defence of their continental possessions.[3] But by the end of the 12th century both the Angevin and the Capetian rulers were relying on mercenaries as the main-stay of the military arm. They were very useful: there was no argument about where or when they were liable for service; they had greater tactical flexibility; they would happily spend

long months guarding castles – all they asked was to be paid.
With them as a standing army there was no respite for rebels or
enemies. Unfortunately there was no respite for the taxpayer
either.

Kings gain distinction, wrote Henry II's treasurer, by the
virtues of their kingship, but their power rests on money: 'Their
power rises and falls as their available wealth flows or ebbs; those
who lack it are a prey to their enemies, and those who have it
prey upon them.'[1] The wealth of the Angevin dominions was the
wonder of Europe. The Germans who escorted Richard back to
England on his release from captivity were astounded at the
prosperity of London, and wished they had demanded an even
higher ransom.[2] The prosperity of his dominions, however, is no
safe guide to the state of a king's finances. The Angevins were rich,
but their commitments were too great. The machinery of government had to be kept going from the Cheviots to the Pyrenees,
from the bogs of Meath to the mountains of the Auvergne.
Long stretches of exposed frontier had to be defended with expensive castles. By parsimony, caution, and careful husbandry,
Henry II had left his treasury well stocked with barrels of silver
pennies, but they had been recklessly dissipated by Richard's
eagerness for war. The king's dominions were prosperous, it is
true, and none more so than England; but their wealth was not
available simply for the taking. Silver had to be wheedled by fair
means or foul out of subjects' purses; and the Angevins increasingly found that the traditional sources of revenue brought in far
too little for their needs. Furthermore, any taxation provokes
resentment, and none more so than when it is for a purpose ill-
understood and little approved, of novel device and heavy in-
cidence.

The strain on his subjects' willingness or even capacity to pay
for Richard's ambitions had been severe ever since he became
king. The Crusade had been prefaced by extraordinary efforts
to raise money. Some lords had gone so far as to mortgage their
estates to the Jews in order to fit themselves out for the expedition;
and some, unequal to the task of redeeming their pledges, had
preferred to remain in the Holy Land. The financial burden of the
Crusade had been quickly followed by civil disturbances during
Richard's absence, and then by the unprecedented sacrifices
demanded of everyone for his ransom.[3] With his release there

began a heavy expenditure on war with Philip or preparations for it. Every year for five years the bills mounted for the building or remodelling of castles, the laying in of equipment, the purchase of Rhenish alliances, and the hire of mercenaries.[1] Richard kept himself in ready cash by borrowing recklessly from international finance houses, and left it to the ministers of his several dominions to meet the debts he contracted. The screws had to be put on to every source of revenue. The Jewish money-lenders of the realm were protected like a herd of prize cattle, valued for the milk that could be extracted from them in protection money. Pressure was redoubled to extract fines from the luckless suitors in the royal courts.[2] In 1198 the ministers in charge of the government in England, casting around for extra means of taxation, revived the principle of the ancient Danegeld and set about assessing everyone's real property as a basis for it. Many of the clergy tried to escape liability and were threatened with outlawry to bring them into line.[3]

It is not surprising that the complaints and lamentations mounted steadily in volume. Of course, loudness of complaint is no sure guide to inability to pay; but the inability of Richard's government, for all its remarkable exertions, to keep pace with his expenditure is shown by the shifts to which it resorted. A note of desperation is sounded by the Exchequer's hectoring of debtors.[4] A sign that responsible government was on the verge of collapse was the change of the Great Seal in May 1198 and the proclamation that charters sealed with the old one were no longer valid, so that people had to pay for renewal.[5] It is possible that Richard's daring, and indeed foolhardy, attempts to snatch a victory by capturing Philip in the autumn of 1198 were inspired by the knowledge that the war could not be prolonged. 'There is not a penny left in Chinon', he gaily sang; but even he had to realise some time that power ebbs when the money ceases to flow.[6] The salvation, momentarily, was that Philip was in difficulties too.

Normandy was in a sorry state by Richard's death. The deficiencies of defence by castles had never been clearly exposed in the days of Henry II, so that Philip's onslaught in 1193 had given a rude shock to complacency. The key fortress of Gisors surrendered at a knock. The border barons, exposed and vulnerable beyond their expectations, readily subordinated their oaths of allegiance to their material interests. Hugh of Gournai, for one, changed sides like a shuttlecock. Those Norman clergy whose jurisdictions straddled the political frontier were alarmed at the drop in their revenues. Walter of Coutances, archbishop of Rouen and high in Richard's counsels, was so shocked by what he saw on returning to his see from Germany that within a fortnight he had negotiated a local truce. Richard repudiated it.[1] Even when there was no fighting, Normandy was crippled by expenditure on defence. It is doubtful if more than thirty of the duchy's forty-five castles could be maintained from the normal revenues, and extraordinary taxes could not be taken indefinitely. In plain fact, Normandy was bankrupted by the tasks Richard imposed upon it, and only credit operations and the flow of English silver averted collapse. The large-scale use of mercenaries reduced the battle areas to a shambles. There was a brutality abroad that no one could remember in previous wars: Philip put out the eyes of prisoners and Richard soon imitated him. Areas far removed from the front became disordered. Bishop Hugh of Lincoln, journeying south in 1199 to seek Richard in Aquitaine, was warned at Angers that 'nothing now is safe, neither the city to dwell in nor the highway for travel.'[2] To crown all, pestilence and famine ravaged the countryside for several seasons in succession. Apocalyptic preachers gained a ready audience: Anti-Christ, swift rumour ran, had been born in Egypt, and the world was in its death-throes.[3]

Hence the situation that faced John at his troubled accession was one of serious overstrain in material resources and morale, and a deep uncertainty that the struggle could be carried on at all. Richard himself had agreed to a truce in November 1198, and after Christmas extended it for five years.[4] It lapsed with the king's death, but its renewal was imperative, and, if possible, its conversion into a stable peace. John handled his hard-pressed resources well in 1199: he gained recognition throughout his brother's dominions by threatening with his forces without actually putting them to peril and loss. He was showing the wisdom of his father in not pushing his luck further. The peace of Le Goulet cost him 20,000 marks and required another heavy tax in England, but even this was cheaper than war. The contrast with Richard's gusty bravado and reckless resort to expensive adventures no doubt justified to small minds the epithet 'Softsword', but if John had tried a firm sword it would have shattered in his hand.

4. THE ANGOULÊME MARRIAGE

Now that his authority was recognised by his overlord, John set about the equally important task of making sure that it was recognised by his vassals also, and spent the summer of 1200 in a tour of his continental dominions. It was more than an opportunity for the barons to pay their respects, for he took an army with him and made it a demonstration of power. In June he visited Maine, Anjou, and Touraine, and took hostages from those he did not trust.[1] In July he crossed over to his mother's lands and made a grand circuit that brought him back to Poitiers at the end of August. (*See Map III.*)

The duchy of Aquitaine had stood apart from the troubles of John's succession because technically it belonged to his mother alone. She was its hereditary duchess and Richard had merely been associated with her in ruling it. In July 1199 she prudently confirmed her position by renewing homage to Philip at Tours, but in the following September she formally made over her inheritance to John as her rightful heir, commanding her vassals to do him homage and receive him peaceably.[2] The legal title was clear, but the command that John be received peaceably was little more than a pious hope. Richard had met his death, as he had spent the greater part of his life, fighting rebels in Aquitaine. It was an unquiet and factious province threatening always to erupt in disorder and rebellion. Indeed, of all the barons of the Angevin dominions those of Aquitaine (with the possible exception of those in Ireland) were the most presumptuous in their exercise of local lordship. This was not so much because they had been granted extensive privileges by the duke as because they had no tradition of loyalty and wore their feudal obligations very lightly. Only armed force could keep them in order. These were troubled waters in which King Philip longed to fish. Indeed, he had already cast bread upon them when in the Treaty of Le Goulet he required John to receive the homage of Count Aymer of Angoulême and his nephew, the viscount of Limoges, and restore all their property to them.[3] Richard had imperfectly suppressed their rebellious independence; could John contain them better? In taking any army with him on tour in the summer of 1200 he was showing that he meant to rule in the only way the barons of those parts respected.

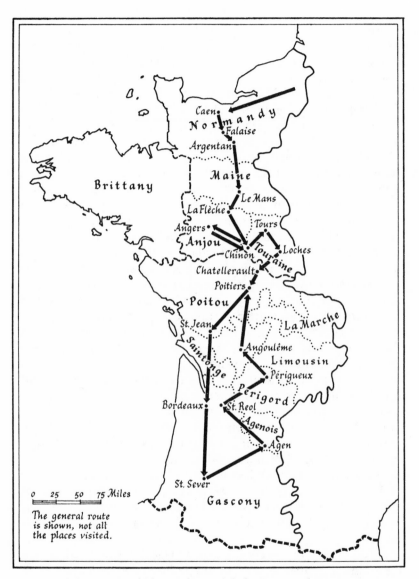

III. John's tour of his continental fiefs, June to August 1200.

About this time, on the look-out for any chance of strengthening his position, John had it in mind to put himself on the marriage market. It is true that a slight difficulty existed in that he already had a wife, but, conveniently for him, John had contracted a marriage that it would be easy to have declared void. Isabelle of Gloucester, to whom John had been betrothed by his father in 1176, and married in 1189, was his cousin. In the technical language of the matrimonial law they were related in the third degree of consanguinity, and could not be validly married unless the pope himself relaxed the strict rule.[1] Archbishop Baldwin was appalled when he heard in 1189 that John had actually married Isabelle, forbade them to cohabit, cited John to appear before his court, and laid an interdict on his estates when he failed to do so. John was able to circumvent the archbishop by appealing to a papal legate who was visiting England at the time, and the interdict was lifted. Presumably he was able to assure the legate that a dispensation was being sought, but none was ever received. Archbishop Baldwin died shortly afterwards and no one else sought to press the matter of the flaw in the marriage bond. John gained Isabelle's dowry and the earldom of Gloucester, and the two remained in the convenient position of being married in due form but with dubious validity.

For ten years Isabelle played no part in John's public life, and it is doubtful if she played much of a part in his private life either; certainly she bore him no children. She was not even crowned with him in May 1199. He had considered breaking the frail tie earlier, and in 1191 had toyed with the idea of marrying King Philip's sister Alice, whom Richard had unchivalrously cast off.[2] Soon after he became king John set about freeing himself. The question of the validity of his marriage was put first to three Norman bishops and then to three in Aquitaine. The reason for the two trials is uncertain, but the final result is not: John was pronounced a single man.[3]

He thought at first to contract a marriage that would strengthen his southern frontier in the foothills of the Pyrenees. Richard had formed an alliance with the Spanish kingdom of Navarre, by marrying King Sancho's daughter, and it had served him very well. John hoped to preserve the alliance, but unfortunately Navarre was threatened by the hostility of the neighbouring kings of Castile and Aragon, whom, it could be expected, Philip would recruit as allies. The answer was to reach behind Philip's men and threaten them in the rear – in the manner of the Rhenish alliances. Portugal offered a good opening for it had been friendly with England ever since 1147, when a party of English crusaders helped to liberate Lisbon from the Moors; and furthermore its king had a marriageable daughter. Portuguese ambassadors were at John's court early in 1200, and a return embassy was commissioned by him in July, just after the start of the southern progress.[1] Within a few weeks, however, John cast aside this plan for another. On 24 August, as the royal tour of Aquitaine was nearing its close, he married the daughter of Count Aymer of Angoulême.[2] It was a fateful marriage: the loss of the continental dominions stemmed from it, or so at least most contemporaries firmly believed; yet very cogent arguments could be advanced in its favour.[3]

The Angoumois, which the family of Angoulême held in close grip, lay at the heart of Aquitaine. A network of Roman roads crossed it, and its towns dominated the passage from Poitiers to Bordeaux, and from the central mountains of France to the sea. Its strategic significance was therefore considerable. Its importance, however, was matched by the pride of its count. Not content to pursue a *de facto* independence by ignoring the dukes of Aquitaine, he had asserted a *de jure* independence and performed homage direct to the king of France.[4] Richard had been seriously troubled, and though he had beaten Count Aymer in the field, he had not cowed him in spirit and was still fighting him at his death. Aymer had appealed for help to King Philip and hence figured in the peace treaty of Le Goulet. A marriage between John and the heiress of Angoulême therefore made very good political sense. It healed a running sore, gave John the reversion of the county, and at the same time salved the count's touchy pride. Unfortunately, in taking Isabelle, John was butting his head into a political and personal situation of great delicacy: in accepting him she was obliged to break her engagement to a neighbouring baron, Hugh le Brun, lord of Lusignan.

The Lusignans were the most important barons of Lower Poitou, and moreover were an illustrious crusading family. Hugh had recently distinguished himself on the Third Crusade, and his uncle Geoffrey had gained a heroic reputation second only to that of Coeur de Lion himself. At this very moment another uncle, Aumary, was reigning as king in Jerusalem. It is not surprising that they should have so excelled in war because they had spent many years sharpening their skill and blunting their lances in rebellion against the Angevin rulers of Aquitaine. In 1168 they had slain Patrick earl of Salisbury whom Henry II had appointed to govern the duchy; and in 1188 Geoffrey de Lusignan had murdered a personal friend of Richard, then count of Poitou.[1] But a turning point in their history had come when they joined the Third Crusade. Richard could forget even personal affronts in his admiration of prowess on the battlefield, and in the Holy Land he and the Lusignans had struck up a firm friendship. Hugh had even gone to visit him in Germany while he was a prisoner of the emperor; and after his release Richard had turned the friendship to good account by pitting the Lusignans against their troublesome neighbours of Angoulême. It was easy to do this because the two families were rival for the rich, sprawling county of La Marche to the east.[2] Richard, in fact, retained La Marche in his own hands, dangling it before the Lusignans, no doubt, as a prize to be won, and in the meantime giving them other nibbles of his largesse. Hugh's younger brother, Ralph, was given a rich heiress who brought him the county of Eu in Normandy, which shows that Richard was prepared to pay highly for their services even though he withheld La Marche.[3]

Hugh must have realised, of course, that his hopes rested largely on bonds of friendship that were unlikely to survive Richard's death in 1199. In the troubled days of John's succession, Queen Eleanor was prepared to bid high for the support of Poitevin barons and Hugh might have struck a profitable bargain; but with his eyes on La Marche he took the extreme measure of kidnapping her, it is said, and released her only on condition that she surrendered the county to him. When, therefore, John became his mother's partner in the lordship of Aquitaine in September 1199 he had to recognise a *fait accompli*, and in the following January he received Hugh's homage for the county.[4]

Subsequently (though the actual date is uncertain), Hugh contracted to marry the daughter and heiress of his former rival Count Aymer. The negotiations that preceded this *volte-face* are unknown. Perhaps Hugh wished to consolidate his position by calming the inevitable hostility of Count Aymer to his success in gaining La Marche; or Aymer himself may have suggested it as the only way of salvaging his pride now that the county had slipped beyond his grasp. The only thing that can be said for certain is that John appeared upon the scene and disrupted the whole project.

It must have been distressing for John that these old rivals should patch up a quarrel that had conveniently preoccupied them for several years; but more than that, the prospect of Hugh le Brun eventually uniting in his hands the lordship of Lusignan and the counties of La Marche and Angoulême was deeply disturbing. The whole balance of power in Aquitaine would be threatened. Indeed, Hugh, ruling territories as large as the whole duchy of Normandy, would have been in a position to dictate the price of his allegiance. If he chose independence and put himself under the protection of the king of France Aquitaine would be cut in half and John's chances of holding it negligible. For John to take Isabelle himself was the most, perhaps the only effective way of averting the danger. If John put the matter to his counsellors, such considerations must have outweighed any fear of Hugh le Brun's indignation at losing his fiancée. William Marshal, for one, would have been pleased to see the Lusignans curbed, for he bore them a personal grudge which he made no effort to conceal. They had murdered his uncle, Earl Patrick, while he was unarmed. He himself had been captured by them in ambush and vividly remembered lying one night as their prisoner while they amused themselves by seeing who could throw a great stone farthest.[1]

On the other hand, it is possible that John did not stop to consider questions of policy. Rumour had it that Isabelle entranced him. It is the way of gossip, of course, to prefer spicy conjecture to the complexities of politics, and no one really knew what had gone on at Angoulême in the summer of 1200; but certainly John's precipitancy gives some colour to the notion. A betrothal would have served his political purposes for the time being, and would have been a sort of *ballon d'essai*, testing reactions before he committed himself to such a drastic reversal of policy. It would also have been more decorous for Isabelle was little more than twelve.[2] But no, John married her. Passion and policy, it seems, ran in close harness.

5. THE REVOLT OF THE LUSIGNANS

At the beginning of October 1200 John crossed to England with his child bride, and on the 8th they were crowned together in Westminster Abbey.[3] He then took her down to Wiltshire (which was a favourite country retreat of the Angevins) and left her at Marlborough while he set off on another royal tour. John's journeys in 1200–1 look like the first part of a grand design to explore the whole of his inheritance. Within two years of his accession, and despite serious political preoccupations, he managed to see much of it, from the Marches of Spain to those of Scotland. No previous king had gained a knowledge so personal and systematic. John wished to see for himself. It was characteristic of him.[1]

In the autumn of 1200 he toured the English midlands. From Wiltshire he went to Gloucester and explored the Welsh March up to Bridgnorth. Thence he turned into Staffordshire and followed the Trent to Nottingham. From there he went to Lincoln to keep an appointment with the king of Scotland who had been summoned to do homage for his English fiefs. An old superstition said that calamity would befall a king who entered the city of Lincoln, but John paid no attention to his courtiers' warnings, and went in to see the new cathedral being built, and to offer a golden chalice at the altar.[2] Death did indeed strike on this occasion, not at the king but at the aged Bishop Hugh. It was a sad moment for Hugh was famous for his saintly life, his great work as a pastor, his sharp tongue, and his pet swan. He had been one of the great characters of the 12th century episcopate. Henry II had loved him though he often felt the lash of Hugh's criticism. Indeed, it was Henry who had forced him into the bishopric, despite Hugh's protests that his appointment had been uncanonical. John shared his father's affection and visited Hugh in his last illness. He remained at Lincoln for the funeral, and put his own shoulder to the coffin as it was borne to its last resting place.[3]

After the funeral John turned south through Stamford and Northampton, to rejoin his wife for Christmas festivities at the royal hunting lodges south of the Thames. But on the first day of the new year he was off again, picking up the track of his autumn tour at Lincoln, and heading this time for the north-east coast. The prospect of winter snows could not keep him from following the coast as far north as Bamborough in Northumberland, and then traversing the Scottish March to Carlisle. From Cumberland he turned back into Yorkshire and made his way down the eastern slopes of the Pennines to Nottingham again. By then it was the middle of March and he went down to Canterbury for a ceremonial crown-wearing on Easter Day.

Meanwhile trouble was being spawned in Poitou. It was only to be expected that the ancient turbulence of the Lusignans would revive when John sought to fence off their ambitions. For several months they had remained surprisingly quiet, perhaps in the hope that John would generously compensate them for their loss, perhaps because his recent parade of strength had awed their usual allies. But John made no move to placate them. Indeed his treatment of the Lusignans brought to light a serious weakness in his character as a ruler. Unlike Henry and Richard, he could never quite bring himself to be generous in victory. Success invariably bred in him an overbearing confidence, and he could not resist the temptation to kick a man when he was down. It was one of the really objectionable features of his character which no one could miss. It brought its own retribution of course, for it not only perpetuated enmities but soured the loyalty of possible friends.

As Easter 1201 approached, old Queen Eleanor was becoming very worried by whispers of gathering trouble. She was weak and bedridden now, but still alert and influential. She had gone to Spain to fetch her grandchild, Blanche of Castile, for the marriage that had been arranged with the French king's son; but it had fatigued her intolerably, and feeling that her days of service were over she had retired to the abbey of Fontevrault in Anjou.[1] Fontevrault was by way of being the spiritual home of the Angevins. Henry and Richard were buried there, and Eleanor no doubt expected to join them soon. She deserved a quiet retirement, but she was not to enjoy one. Disturbed by the rumours from Poitou, she roused herself from a serious illness and sent for the viscount of Thouars.

Amery of Thouars was not a strong character: interest and fear frequently jostled him from one political adherence to another; but his estates made him the most powerful baron of Poitou and gave him virtual control of the approaches into the county from the north. Lesser men would follow his lead. In the troubled days just after Richard's death he had joined Eleanor in attacks on Arthur's supporters in Anjou. John had need of his help then and had put the castle of Chinon in his hands and made him seneschal of Anjou and Touraine; but at the moment of triumph, at Le Mans in September 1199, had taken these offices away again.[2] It was not John's way to give anything to powerful men if he could possibly avoid it: he distrusted them too much. Eleanor realised that, in the event of war in Poitou, Amery's continued loyalty to John was very doubtful in consequence, and she set herself to remedy her son's mistake. By a triumph of feminine diplomacy she persuaded Amery to write to John with assurances of loyalty, warning him of impending trouble, and beseeching him to come over and give a clear lead to those who were inclined to support him. Such was Eleanor's anxiety that she herself wrote to John at the same time, explaining what she had done, and had her personal attendant, Guy Diva, write too, in the hope that he would realise that these were not merely the worries of an old woman.[1]

John, however, remained fairly sanguine, and did not bother to satisfy his mother's entreaties by going over himself until the beginning of June. Meanwhile he gave the Lusignans a few kicks by instructing his officials to take over Hugh's county of La Marche and to harry Ralph in his county of Eu and 'do him all the harm they could'.[2] Distress of this kind was a normal way of coercing vassals, but legally it should only have followed a judgement of the ruler's court. Strong rulers, however, were apt to make light of legal propriety where rebellion was concerned, for they would not have remained strong for long if they had been more puncti-lious. John's predecessors had got away with such high-handed-ness in England because, short of civil war, there was no means of calling them to account, and on the continent because their over-lord the king of France did not dare. But John's feudal position was not so strong as theirs had been: the Treaty of Le Goulet showed that. Pushing his overlordship was Philip's way of develop-ing the strength of the monarchy, and John really had to go very carefully with his continental vassals if he wished to avoid trouble with the king. He seems, however, to have preferred a showdown, and the Lusignans were not slow to provide the occasion. They appealed to the king of France against John, accusing him of unjustly attacking and despoiling them.[3]

Shortly after Easter John ordered his English vassals to come to him at Portsmouth at Whitsuntide ready for a campaign. The feudal army was hardly the best weapon for the situation, and John did not, in fact, intend to take it. When the knights assembled he relieved them of the money they had brought with them for expenses and sent them home again.[4] This was certainly one way of raising money to hire mercenaries that avoided the resistance and delays that had accompanied Richard's requests; but it was a shifty method to which men could hardly be expected to take kindly.

King Philip was embarrassed by the appeal of the Lusignans for it came at an awkward time. He had enough on his hands with a struggle with the Church over his bigamous marriage to Agnes of Meran. He had been glad of the Treaty of Le Goulet and hesitated to prejudice it. John's mustering of forces in 1199 and his progress through Aquitaine had been very impressive, and Philip could not yet know how strained were the resources of the Angevin in money and loyalty. It was impossible to ignore the appeal, but he handled it gingerly. When John crossed the Channel, Philip called on the Lusignans to stop the sieges by which they were harassing the government of Poitou, and went to meet John personally at the Norman border to talk the matter over with him. John was invited to pay a state visit to Paris at the end of June, and was entertained sumptuously at the royal palace, which Philip vacated for the occasion.[1] In an atmosphere of mutual goodwill a compromise was easily reached on the Lusignan affair: Philip said he would not press the matter of the appeal if John would do his feudal duty and give his vassals the opportunity to bring their grievances before his court. It was a sensible solution and the rivals parted amicably.

The summer of 1201 was a good time for John. Constance of Brittany, who had given him so much trouble, died in August, fully reconciled to him, and John saw to the execution of her will.[2] Feeling generous, he settled a handsome dowry on Richard's widow Berengaria, and opened negotiations for an alliance with her father, King Sancho of Navarre.[3] Everything seemed to be going well for him. The friendship of Thouars and Angoulême secured his position in Aquitaine; he had only to cross the Channel with his mercenaries and the king of France met him with fair words. His mother's anxieties had clearly been groundless. Unfortunately it was just such feelings of security that encouraged John to acts of high-handed folly. He would keep to his arrangement with Philip and give the Lusignans a trial in his court, but he would make sure that they were humiliated in the process.

Instead of opening his court to the Lusignans so that they could present a case for redress before their fellow barons, John took the initiative. He charged them with treason against his brother and himself, and invited them to prove their innocence, if they could, by fighting a judicial duel with royal champions. There was nothing legally improper in this procedure, but to force it on the Lusignans was a stupid provocation. The choices before them were to abase themselves, to fight the duel and very likely lose, or to appeal again to Philip. They appealed, of course. They scorned to fight the professional duellists whom John had been recruiting, and insisted that they were answerable to no one but their peers. To their supreme overlord, the king of France, they protested that the duke of Aquitaine was denying them justice.[1]

Philip was obliged to intervene. He remonstrated with John and extracted from him a promise that a fair trial would be held. But John was slippery: he prevaricated, he delayed fixing a date for the trial, and when he did fix it, declined to give the defendants a safe conduct to the place of meeting.[2] He thus sought to gain the excuse that a fair trial had been offered and refused, but Philip could not allow himself to be flouted in this way. It was his feudal duty to see that the Lusignans received justice: his prestige and authority were at stake. He insisted that John give him three castles as security for fulfilling his promise; but John could still invent elaborate excuses and sent the archbishop of Canterbury to make them to Philip in December.[3] By Easter 1202 Philip's patience and diplomacy were exhausted: he ordered John to appear before the court of French barons meeting at Paris to answer for his default of justice. John replied that by ancient agreement the duke of Normandy was obliged to attend the French court only when it met on the frontier between their territories. Philip, however, was as wily as John: the summons, he said, was addressed not to the duke of Normandy, but to John as duke of Aquitaine, count of Poitou, and count of Anjou. John was being driven into a corner. He promised to obey the summons on 28 April and to surrender two border castles as security for submitting to the court's decision. But he had one manœuvre left: he neither surrendered the castles nor appeared at Paris on the appointed day.[4] Henry II had treated a similar summons with scorn and also with impunity, but the authority of the French Crown was vastly greater in 1202 than it had been in 1152.[5]

Philip had the assembled barons proceed to judgement on John for his failure to obey the citation. As a contumacious vassal he was declared to have forfeited his fiefs of Aquitaine, Poitou, and Anjou. The moment had come for Philip to break the Angevin hold on France. He formally declared the feudal ties linking him with John to be severed and threw his forces against the Norman border. He knighted Arthur of Brittany and erected him as John's successor in all his fiefs save Normandy. At Gournai in July 1202 Arthur did homage for them. Normandy itself Philip was determined to retain for the French Crown.[1] The judgement of the French court in April had not, it seems likely, formally deprived John of the duchy of Normandy: after all, he had been summoned specifically in virtue of his other titles. The propriety of Philip's taking Normandy was therefore in question, and Norman prelates in captured territory hesitated to do him homage and wrote to the pope for advice. Normandy, however, was the lintel of Angevin power on the continent and Philip was not to be baulked of making certain of it for himself. Whatever deficiencies there were in the judgement of 1202 were filled in by supplementary judgements expropriating John in the following year.* Philip did not need a judgement of his court as an excuse for attacking John, but he did to justify to the rest of the barons the expropriation of one of their number. The destruction of his rival was to be as complete and legal as Philip could possibly make it.

John naturally endeavoured to persuade his subjects that Philip's assault on Normandy was an unwarranted and greedy aggression. In a letter of 7 July to Cistercian abbots whom he had asked for a loan, he said, 'You are sufficiently aware of what is common knowledge: how the king of France contrary to the peace which was made between us, and which was confirmed by oaths and charters, unjustly attacks us and strives by all means in his power to deprive us of our inheritance.'[2] In reality of course the war and the consequent loss of the continental possessions were John's own fault. The chroniclers thought so, but tended, with superficial judgement, to think that the marriage with Isabelle of Angoulême was the cause of it all.[3] According to one chronicler, John himself told Isabelle in 1205 that she had cost him his continental lands.[4] But the marriage was a distant and indirect cause.

* This description of the two trials of John is guesswork from scraps of evidence, for the chronicle accounts are meagre, conflicting, and confused, and there has in consequence been much argument among historians as to what actually happened. For a summary of the arguments see Appendix.

Hugh le Brun's grievance over Isabelle was swallowed up in the greater one of John's investment of his lands and castles. This in turn was swallowed up in Philip's determination to maintain his feudal prerogatives and the jurisdiction of his court. The French king's hostility to the house of Anjou admittedly made the continuance of peace for very long improbable, but the war which began in 1202 John brought upon himself by bullying important vassals and trifling with his overlord.

6. MIREBEAU AND ITS AFTERMATH

King Philip was more ready for war in May 1202 than he had been a year earlier. For one thing he was more secure at home. He had defied the papacy in his bigamous marriage to Agnes of Meran in 1196, and in January 1200 an interdict had been imposed on his lands. It was a troublesome situation from which he had only escaped by the death of Agnes in July 1201. Furthermore, John's position had seriously deteriorated in the meantime: he could no longer call upon the Rhineland princes to take Philip in the rear because they had departed on crusade. They never actually arrived in the Holy Land for the crusade was deflected against the Christians of Byzantium and sacked Constantinople. It was an unfortunate business altogether, but Philip profited from it: instead of helping John, Baldwin of Flanders became emperor of Byzantium and ended his days as a prisoner of the Bulgarians. It was little comfort for John that in July 1201 his nephew Otto had been recognised as Holy Roman Emperor by the pope, for it was only with the greatest difficulty that Otto was holding out against a formidable rival, Philip of Swabia.

In 1202 Philip of France was 37 years old, and John only two years his junior; but age was the only thing in which they were closely comparable. Men still thought of John as a feckless young man, the baby of the family, irresponsible and troublesome to his elders.[1] It had yet to be seen whether wearing a crown would stiffen his back. No one, on the other hand, could think of Philip as a young man. He did not even look it for his hair had already gone. From the age of fifteen the fate of France had lain in his hands, and responsibility had matured him early. He was not by nature a man of courage or a commanding personality: he trembled much from fear of assassination and he would mount only the most docile of horses. But experience had taught him self-discipline and an understanding of men. While John had been fooling with his friends in Ireland, Philip had been pitting his wits against the crafty Henry II. While the summit of John's achievement had been to bring down Chancellor Longchamp, Philip was manœuvring against Saladin in the Holy Land. While John, in 1202, was still learning the job of ruling, Philip was bending perfected abilities to the prime ambition of his life: the destruction of Angevin power. It was no mere neighbouring prince of comparable age and experience with whom John trifled in 1201–2, but a man who felt himself to be the heir of Charlemagne, and who had schooled himself to discharge the responsibility that this implied. What he lacked in boldness he made up for in determination.[1]

Philip brought no new tactic to his campaign in 1202. A bold sally down the valley of the Loire was for more venturesome spirits than his, and he left it to Arthur and the Poitevins. Normandy was his objective and the siege of its frontier fortresses his method. So for John the situation at the outbreak of war was similar to that at his accession: Philip biting piece by piece in the east, and rebels plundering in the south. His reaction was likewise similar. He was not ready for immediate operations and stayed at first behind the protective screen of Norman castles; but as soon as his recruiting officers had brought him in enough mercenaries to give him a mobile army, he turned south to the vulnerable and strategically vital heartland of his empire.[2]

He was not a moment too soon. Near Le Mans a courier met him with an urgent note from his mother. She had left Fontevrault and was heading for Poitiers, but Arthur and the rebels were close on her heels bent on capturing her. John at once revealed his Angevin blood. The ability of Henry II and Richard I to pop up as through a trap-door, with the suddenness of a demon king, had never ceased to astound their contemporaries, and it was not lacking in John. A detachment of his army was rushed through a forced march of eighty miles and more, and caught up with his mother at Mirebeau within forty-eight hours. It was then the night of 31 July. The rebels had seized the town and broken into the castle; Eleanor was trapped in the keep. As John had swept to the rescue he had picked up William des Roches, the seneschal of Anjou. William knew Mirebeau and was prepared to direct the attack on the understanding that John would be guided

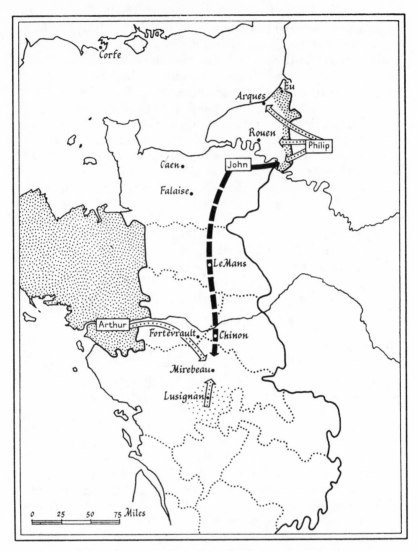

IV. War of 1202–4, first phase Spring to Autumn 1202.

by him as to what to do with Arthur, if he were captured. The rebels had gone confidently to their rest that night. They had barricaded all the gates save one: William des Roches led the storming of it as dawn broke. Geoffrey de Lusignan was still breakfasting on a dish of pigeons when John's men swept round him. The besiegers, who had now suddenly become the besieged, hastily scrambled for the safety of the castle, but were too hotly pursued to organise a stand there. In no time at all Eleanor was able to issue from the keep and rejoin her son. No one of importance among the rebels escaped.[1]

John was naturally exultant. He wrote to tell the English barons of his victory.

> 'Know,' he said, 'that by the grace of God we are safe and well and God's mercy had worked wonderfully with us, for on Tuesday before the feast of St Peter ad Vincula, when we were on the road to Chinon, we heard that the lady our mother was closely besieged at Mirebeau, and we hurried there as fast as we could, arriving on the feast of St Peter ad Vincula. And there we captured our nephew Arthur, whom William de Briouze delivered to us, and Geoffrey de Lusignan, Hugh le Brun, Andrew de Chauvigni, the viscount of Châteleraut, Raymond Thouars, Savary de Mauléon, Hugh Baugé, and all our other Poitevin enemies who were there, being upwards of two hundred knights, and none escaped. Therefore God be praised for our happy success.'[2]

It was indeed a first-rate achievement, well-nigh miraculous thought some. Everyone was impressed, including the French chroniclers. Not until Crécy were English arms to gain so resounding a success. The troops in the Norman marches were heartened by the news, and William Marshal sent a message across the lines to taunt Ralph de Lusignan with the fate of his brothers.[3] Philip was badly shaken. He had been concentrating on the siege of Arques, but he called it off and hurried south to see if he could retrieve anything from the disaster. He was too late: John was carting his prisoners, heavily manacled, back to Normandy. He took his time over the journey – parading them, perhaps, as a warning to others. Burning and plunder along the border were all that Philip could do to relieve his chagrin.

Arthur and Geoffrey de Lusignan were incarcerated at Falaise.

79

The keep of the castle at Caen was cleared of other prisoners and Hugh le Brun locked up there, securely fettered. Most of the less important prisoners were shipped over to England and put in Corfe castle or other strongholds. The strictest measures were taken to prevent the captives escaping, and visitors could speak with them, if at all, only under the most stringent precautions.[1] John's capture of all the important rebels at a stroke meant, of course, that rebellion was left leaderless. Their vassals were now directly subject to his commands, and their castles fell into his hands. The serious threat from within his dominions had been cut off short.[2]

By the autumn of 1202, then, John faced Philip with most of the trump cards in his hand, but he still managed with incredible foolishness to lose every trick. Over-confidence born of success, and his inveterate distrust of powerful subjects, were primarily responsible. He immediately threw away an ace in William des Roches. William's switch to support of John had been instrumental in securing his inheritance in 1199, at the price of giving him control of Anjou and Touraine and the first voice in John's council. He was ambitious, it is true, but while his ambitions coincided with John's interests his support was invaluable. It was he who had directed the attack on Mirebeau – on the understanding that should Arthur be captured, he would have chief say in what should be done with him.[3] With William as an ally John could have tackled Philip in Normandy confident that the strategically vital counties along the Loire were in safe hands. But in the flush of triumph, John thought that he could cut William down to size. Arthur was removed from his reach, and his advice was blatantly ignored. In consequence he deserted, and took with him Amery of Thouars, who was his neighbour in northern Poitou. John retaliated by splitting William's administration between two of his own henchmen, but they had to fight William and his supporters for control of it. John's communications with Aquitaine were thereby disrupted and his resources fatally divided.

To retrieve this unfortunate and quite unnecessary situation John tried to come to terms with the Lusignans. He sought to conciliate them by releasing them early in 1203; but he was two years too late. They made him an oath to remain loyal and gave him castles and hostages in pledge for it, but they soon broke their word. William Marshal, for one, was horrified that John should in this way put a head back on the trunk of Poitevin dis-affection. What Mirebeau had silenced John himself revived.[1] He could not make a similar mistake with the prisoners at Corfe, for many of them were soon dead. Their fate was held against him, though it was hardly his fault. The twenty-five prisoners there, it seems, planned a break-out and gained possession of the keep. They were surrounded and their food supplies cut off to reduce them to submission. Twenty-two of them starved to death rather than give in.[2]

Much more harmful to John's reputation was the death of Arthur of Brittany.[3] The true story was known to very few, but ugly rumours circulated. Fifty years later Matthew Paris was not at all sure what had happened, and could only hope that it was not true that John had murdered him.[4] Arthur simply disappeared, and rumours that he was dead began to circulate before in fact he was. John was hard put to it to know what to do with Arthur while he had him. It would have saved him much trouble and a shadow on his conscience if he had delivered him up to William des Roches. But Arthur had become a serious rival to John after his disinheritance by the French court, and he distrusted William too much.

A story came to the ears of Ralph of Coggeshall that John was advised to have Arthur blinded and castrated, so as to elimin-ate him as a rival. But this seemed barbarous and stupid to Hubert de Burgh, who had charge of Arthur at Falaise, and he stopped the two men who were sent from doing it. It occurred to Hubert, however, that the Bretons might calm down if they believed they had lost their leader, so he took it upon himself to announce that Arthur was dead. Unfortunately he had miscalculated the mood of the Bretons, for, believing that their duke had been murdered, they swore vengeance on John. Realising his mistake, Hubert now gave out that Arthur was still alive, but no one believed him.[5] Whether or not this story of Coggeshall's is true, it was certainly a tradition among the Bretons that a solemn assembly in 1203 had denounced John for the murder of their duke.[6]

Arthur was more than the hereditary prince of the Bretons – he was a great symbol, a symbol of a mythically glorious past and a hopeful future. His name itself was significant. He was the child of Constance of Brittany and Geoffrey, son of Henry II, born a few days after his father's death. The Angevin family had wanted the baby to be called 'Henry' after his grandfather, but Constance refused, knowing the unpopularity of the Angevin connection among the fiercely independent Bretons. It was an age when many European peoples were groping in the murky past for something with which to bolster an incipient nationalist sentiment, and the Bretons had taken the legendary King Arthur as their own. So the baby was named Arthur. As a means of endearing a half-Angevin to the Bretons it worked. King Richard sought to make himself guardian of his nephew when the boy was ten years old, but the Bretons had hidden him away, preferring, says William of Newburgh, to bring him up themselves 'under the mighty omen of his name'. For long they had dreamed of a fabulous Arthur, 'now with high hopes they nurture a real one, according to the views of certain prophets expressed in their grand and famous legends of Arthur.'[1] It was all a lot of foolish nationalist mythology, thought the Barnwell annalist, and God punishes such sinful pride; but it was no use telling the Bretons so.[2]

Shakespeare, of course, knew the story of Hubert de Burgh resisting the blinding of Arthur, and made it the dramatic hinge of his play about John's reign. But his source, Holinshed, did not reveal the probable end of Arthur. One of the few people who were in a position to know what happened was William de Briouze, lord of Brecon – the man who had actually captured Arthur at Mirebeau. He had been a strong partisan of John at his accession and was his constant companion throughout the Normandy campaigns. Some time after 1207, however, he fell from favour, probably because he had become too powerful for John's peace of mind. John demanded hostages from him as surety for his loyalty, but his quick-tongued wife, Matilda, refused to hand over her sons to the man who, she said, had murdered his nephew.[3] After that John gave her no peace until she too was dead in his prison.

The Briouzes were patrons of the Cistercian abbey of Margam in Glamorgan, and a series of annals written there seem to reflect much information supplied by William. It is therefore particularly interesting that they contain a detailed account of Arthur's end:

'After King John had captured Arthur and kept him alive in prison for some time, at length, in the castle of Rouen, after dinner on the Thursday before Easter,* when he was drunk and possessed by the devil (*ebrius et daemonio plenus*), he slew him with his own hand, and tying a heavy stone to the body cast it into the Seine. It was discovered by a fisherman in his net, and being dragged to the bank and recognised, was taken for secret burial, in fear of the tyrant, to the priory of Bec called Notre Dame des Prés.'[1]

It is not difficult to believe that John could have killed Arthur in a typical fit of Angevin drunken rage, and he was certainly at Rouen at the alleged time; so it is not improbable that the Margam annals give the only authentic account.

In 1210 William de Briouze, after trying in vain to recover John's goodwill, fled for refuge to the French court. It was probably only then that Philip learned what had really happened to Arthur. He had suspected for some time, though, that Arthur was dead: as early as 1204, says Ralph of Coggeshall, he heard that Arthur had been drowned.[2] It is possible that he had his court condemn John for the murder: the annalist of Margam thought so, and Philip's son Louis asserted as much in 1216; but no one is sure when, or if he really did. If John were formally condemned, it is surprising that Philip did not exploit the propaganda value of it more widely. What he did do, as soon as he believed that Arthur was no longer alive, was to taunt John with his disappearance: to all overtures for peace he replied, 'first produce Arthur'.[3]

At Mirebeau Arthur's sister, Eleanor, had also fallen into John's hands, and with her brother's death she became his closest hereditary rival. In striking contrast she lived on to die of old age in 1241. She remained a prisoner, but John treated her generously. She was given an allowance from the Exchequer, and he sent her gifts of clothes, fur-lined capes, shoes, and fine linen from which to make chemises and sheets – 'not however of the king's finest cloth,' ran the precise instructions to his agents, 'but if they have none suited for this except the king's finest cloth, to purchase it as good as they can with the king's money.' Since he also sent her ornamented saddles and reins, her imprisonment cannot have been very close. Indeed, she spent some time with the queen, and with the daughters of the king of Scotland who were hostages for a treaty.[4] The murder of one rival in a drunken rage, thoughtful

* 3 April 1203.

kindnesses to another who was orphaned and captive in a strange land – such are the inconsistencies of John's character.

Few men in England either knew or cared what had happened to Arthur. If they did hear tell that he had been killed, they were likely to believe that he deserved it – after all he had been captured in rebellion against his liege lord and while attacking his grandmother. This was Pope Innocent III's reaction when the French king attempted in 1216 to make a political issue of Arthur's fate: he was a traitor to his lord who deserved the most shameful death without formal trial.[1] In France, though, the attitude was different: the Bretons could not forgive John the murder of their champion, and Philip used it as a stick with which to beat him. The triumph at Mirebeau had completely miscarried. After it John should have been riding crests of the waves; instead he foundered in the troughs. He had only himself to blame.

7. 'DESERTED BY HIS OWN MEN'

In the autumn of 1202 John was faced with war on two fronts: the Bretons were breathing fire in the west and had seized Angers; Philip was assaulting his castles in the east. In addition, the defection of William des Roches and the viscount of Thouars had infested both banks of the Loire with rebels right across his territories. In November John went south to see for himself what the situation there was like, and evidently found it very serious for he soon returned to Normandy to prepare for a full-scale campaign. Trusting to the chains of castles on his eastern flank to hold up Philip, he started collecting stores and mustering men at Argentan, a convenient focus of roads in central Normandy. From this time on, however, events began to overtake his plans before he could develop them.[2] (*See Map V.*)

In January 1203 news reached him that Queen Isabelle was being hard pressed by rebels at Chinon in Touraine. He set out to rescue her with a posse of mercenaries; but he had no sooner passed through Alençon on his way south than he heard that its count had gone over to Philip. John had dined with him only a couple of days before, and the sudden fear of being surrounded on all sides by enemies robbed him of all resolution. Instead of emulating his dash to Mirebeau he cowered in Le Mans. A detachment of mercenaries under Peter de Préaux went on to Chinon

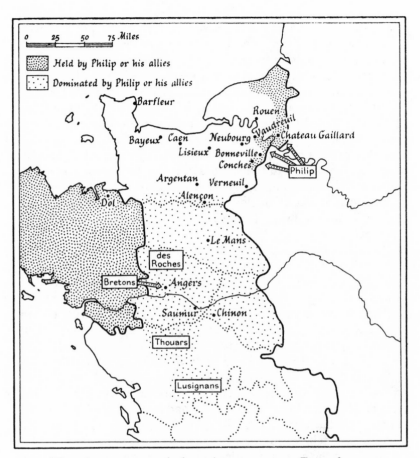

0   25   50   75 Miles

Barfleur

Rouen
Vaudreuil
Bayeux Caen Neubourg Chateau Gaillard
Lisieux Bonneville
Conches
Philip
Argentan Verneuil
Dol Alençon

Le Mans

des Roches

Bretons Angers

Saumur Chinon

Thouars

Lusignans

v. War of 1202-4, second phase Autumn 1202 to December 1203
(showing places mentioned in the text)

and rescued Queen Isabelle, and then the whole party moved cautiously back to Argentan by a devious route.[1]

From then on John seems to have had his tail between his legs. He seemed unable to do anything except to make the blunder of killing Arthur in April. Philip got in touch with the rebels in the central provinces and organised a defence against the expedition John was thought to be preparing at Argentan, but he need not have bothered for it never materialised. When campaigning weather came again in the spring it was Philip and not John who made an expedition to the Loire. He took a boat in perfect safety down the river to Saumur, right in the middle of the Angevin empire, and encouraged the Poitevin rebels by joining them in attacks on castles in Aquitaine. The heart of John's inheritance had been torn out.

John was now trapped in Normandy, and as soon as Philip returned to renew his pressure there, its defences began to crack. Conches was taken. Vaudreuil suddenly surrendered. This last was a staggering blow for it was a vital link in the defensive chain. It had recently been provisioned and its men paid; it bristled with armaments, and John was sending in more supplies by boat when its commanders opened the gates to Philip. Its surrender was everywhere the talk of the day, and derisive songs were sung about its 'glorious defence'. John evidently feared a general lowering of morale in consequence, which he hastened to avert by issuing letters patent saying that the castle had been surrendered by his order and that no blame attached to its defenders. It is unlikely that anyone felt reassured.[2]

All along the eastern frontier Philip was through the outer ring and pressing hard against the inner defences. John seemed helpless, uncertain where to buttress the sagging walls, or where to counter-attack. He flitted here and there from Rouen, more in desperation than with set purpose. The initiative lay wholly in Philip's hands, and at the end of August he brought his siege-train up to Château Gaillard. This was the great challenge. Clinging to precipitous cliffs on a bend of the Seine, Château Gaillard was the bar to Rouen. More than that, it was the symbol of Angevin rule in Normandy. Richard had lavished loving care on this, his 'Saucy Castle'. He had built it to be untakeable.[3] Angevin wealth had been poured into it to mock the ambitions of the king of France. Philip drew back his fist to punch the mocking face.

John now had a focus for his efforts. He had no fear of the castle being taken by storm, and little fear of treachery surrendering it, for it was in the hands of an Englishman, Roger Lacy, who had no stake in Normandy. The only problem was provisions, for even the strongest castle can be taken by hunger. John therefore planned to run supplies in through Philip's blockade, while mustering troops to break up the siege. His plan for beating the blockade had all the boldness and dash that had given Richard his great reputation, and which made King Philip seem by comparison an unimaginative slogger. It was to be a night operation. Victuals and armaments for the beleaguered fortress were to go up the river in seventy supply boats that Richard had built, accompanied by a naval detachment and a commando force of Flemish *routiers*. At the same time William Marshal was to lead a sizeable army of knights and footsoldiers up the left bank of the Seine. Just before dawn the land force would fall upon the French encampment, while the naval forces would smash the pontoon which Philip had thrown across the river and rush the supplies into the castle. The whole plan miscarried. It was not to be the last time that John would find his agents unable to carry out his imaginative schemes. The rowers in the boats found the current too much for them; they fell behind schedule, and the land force went into the attack before the naval party had reached the bend of the river. In consequence the French were able to muster all their forces against each attack in turn. The land army was routed; the water-borne troops tried to smash through on their own but were driven back with heavy loss. The river ran thickly with blood.[1]

John did not renew the attempt. Instead he swung all his available forces right across Normandy and threw them against the Bretons. Perhaps he hoped, by crushing Philip's allies, to draw him off from Château Gaillard, as the victory at Mirebeau had drawn him from the siege of Arques. At any rate it was a move of desperation that achieved little. Dol was sacked. Its cathedral was set on fire and the mercenaries plundered happily. It was the last serious military enterprise that John was to mount from Norman soil.

Looking back, the chroniclers could see 1203 only as a year of shame. No tale, as yet, of heroic defence stood out to brighten the dark picture of collapse. Many men were bewildered at John's apparent helplessness. By Roger of Wendover's day, gossip mongers had provided an explanation: he spent his nights in riotous living, it was said, and lay abed all morning with his young wife. He was so infatuated with Isabelle, said the whispering tongues, that she must have bewitched him. 'When messengers came to him saying, "The king of France has made war on your territory, he has taken such and such castles and dragged off the castellans tied to horses' tails, and he disposes of your property without anyone stopping him," the king replied, "Let be, let be, whatever he now takes I will one day recover", and no one could get any other answer out of him.'[1] The French historian, Charles Petit-Dutaillis, has suggested that John suffered from cyclothymia, a mental derangement which shows itself in periods of violent activity alternating with periods of utter lethargy.[2] But this is merely to put a medical term on tainted testimony. The administrative records show that John was busy all the time, though nothing he did helped to save the defences of Normandy from collapse.

The real reason for his helplessness is treachery – of the kind that had brought his relief column for Chinon to a wavering halt in January 1203. The biographer of William Marshal says that treachery ran through Normandy like an epidemic at the end of 1202, and both Gervase of Canterbury and the Barnwell annalist were convinced that treachery among the Normans was such that resistance to French invasion was impossible.[3] John, in fact, was deserted by the duchy's natural defenders, its barons: local resistance to Philip played no effective part in the campaign, and the only castles to hold out resolutely were ones commanded by English castellans. Treachery, however, did not merely rob John of the support of his vassals: it robbed him personally of resolution. Ralph of Coggeshall had no doubt of it: the king, he says, 'could bring no help to the besieged because he went all the time in fear of his subjects' treason'.[4] Whether by nature or as a result of these nerve-racking experiences in Normandy, John frequently showed himself highly sensitive to fears of treason in later years. Treachery, then, worked a double mischief: it sabotaged the machinery of resistance, and it unnerved the king. In the last analysis Normandy was lost behind the castles in the hearts of the Normans themselves before Philip launched his attack.

The roots of the Normans' reluctance to be defended go back beyond John's reign. Loyalty to the Angevin house had sagged

badly in Richard's day. Resistance to Philip had been perfunc-
tory in 1194 until Richard brought in English troops and relieved
Verneuil;[1] and Philip might easily have seized the duchy while
Richard was a prisoner in Germany, if the French barons had not
been reluctant to attack the lands of an absent crusader.[2]
In fact, the Normans were already becoming weary of Angevin
rule before Henry II died. It is not surprising that English chroniclers failed to recognise it, but it was sensed by Gerald of Wales,
who was a familiar figure in both the Angevin and Capetian courts
and preferred the latter. One day he talked it over with Ranulph
Glanville, who was then running the administration of both England and Normandy. 'Why is it,' asked Gerald, 'that whereas,
when the Normans first acquired the duchy they defended it so
successfully that, as history books tell us, they forced the French
kings to flee for safety, but now, when the dukes have become
rulers of England and of great continental fiefs, they seem much
less powerful and able to defend themselves?' Ranulph did not
dispute Gerald's facts, but thought the reason was that just before
the Normans came the Franks had suffered so much in war that
their manpower was exhausted, and was only now picking up
again. Ranulph, clearly, had not much idea of the passage of time
since the 9th century, but he was right in feeling that the balance
of effective power was swinging in favour of the French kings.
The resources of the Angevins might seem greater but they were
deployed too far. The compact resources of the Capetians, on the
other hand, could be concentrated much more easily against one
objective. Gerald, however, was not altogether satisfied with this
answer. He could offer a reason of his own, and one suspects that
in posing his question he was really trying to draw Ranulph on to
listen to it. It was his view that in taking over England the Norman dukes had learned to rule as monarchs, and their new
authoritarianism had broken the Normans' spirit. 'How can they
raise necks trodden down by the harshness of notorious tyrants,'
he asks, 'to resist the arms and fierce courage of free Frenchmen?'
He assures us that Ranulph agreed with him. When he came to
record this conversation, Gerald had thought of another reason.
Success in war, he says, accompanies a pursuit of the arts of
peace. The careers of Alexander and Caesar illustrated it, and the
same thing was happening in France. An allowance must be made
for Gerald's cultured prejudices, but there was something in what

he said. By the end of the 12th century Paris had outstripped her rivals, Chartres, Laon, Rheims, or Orleans, as the intellectual centre of France; and the court of King Philip set the tone in social and literary fashions which fifty years before would have flowed from the courts of Aquitaine or Toulouse. The Young Henry and Richard had for a time captured the imagination and pens of panegyrists, but Philip was their successor not John. The French monarchy, conscious of being the heir of Charlemagne, was once more drawing the minds of all Frenchmen into its orbit.[1]

Angevin rule in Normandy was, indeed, already a guttering candle when John came to the throne. It went out when Philip blew hard upon it. Only bold leadership had hitherto shielded its dimming flame. When Richard was in captivity the loyalty of the Normans had faltered because they were then as sheep that have no shepherd, said William of Newburgh. The biographer of William Marshal put the same thing another way: 'The Normans', he says, 'were not asleep in the days of the Young King. Then they were grain but now they are chaff, for since the death of King Richard they have no leadership.'[2]

What helped Richard, of course, was the conviction of the Normans that he would be successful: he always was. Whether they warmed to him or not, they acknowledged him as master. Prudence revived their loyalty when he was near. John, unfortunately, had no such reputation. On the contrary, he came to the throne tainted with the failures of misspent youth. Few could think him more than half the man his brother had been. 'A feckless young man who takes things easy', was how Robert of Auxerre described him. 'A very foolish youth', said Newburgh.[3] Richard himself did John incalculable harm when he mocked from his prison, 'My brother is not a man to win land for himself if there is anyone to put up a mere show of resistance.' 'Lackland', 'Softsword', the tags echoed round Europe. Everyone underestimated him. He might have looked soft on top but there were cruel teeth underneath – as subsequent events only too clearly showed, said Gervase of Canterbury sourly.[4] There was a trickle of truth, though, in the common impression: John could be tough, he could be ruthless, he could plan a bold manœuvre, but he never displayed the courage that rouses and inspires. Moreover he was liable to panic.

To fill the gap left by shrinking loyalty, John took measures that made it shrink even more. He worked on the assumption that his barons would be treacherous and relied more and more on his mercenary captains. When in October 1201 he received the fealty of Juhel of Mayenne, the greatest baron in Maine, he sought to insure himself by taking charters from Juhel's knights and townsmen by which they promised that if their lord were unfaithful to John they would fight against him and do all the harm they could.[1] How striking is the contrast with the letter he wrote to the *routiers* who followed Martin Algais when their leader was captured: 'Since the commencement of our war no misfortune has happened which we have taken more to heart than what has befallen our beloved and faithful Martin Algais, for, as God is our witness, we are greatly irritated and incensed thereat. . . . And know that the service of Martin Algais we esteem more highly than the service of any other person.'[2] As John put his trust increasingly in his mercenaries, so he put their captains in positions of administrative authority. Gerard d'Athée, for instance, was made seneschal of Touraine, Brandin seneschal of La Marche, and Lupescar (*The Wolf*) put in charge of a Norman bailiwick.[3] Nothing could more quickly widen the gulf between ruler and ruled than such employment of these hardened and unscrupulous professional soldiers. Perhaps they did not take up office in person – their skill was needed elsewhere – but the profits of office went into their pockets, and profits were all they were interested in. 'Do you know', says the biographer of William Marshal, 'why King John was unable to keep the love of his people? It was because Lupescar maltreated them, and pillaged them as though he were in enemy territory.'[4] This was no mere idle gossip. It is easy to understand how the Normans felt when the abbess of Caen can be seen offering the king 40 marks for protection against Lupescar and for having him restore what had been taken from herself and from the tenants of the abbey's estates.[5]

Giving mercenaries the run of the land was symptomatic of a breakdown of the normal administration of Normandy in 1203. It had been one of the best ordered regions in the whole of Europe, but the tribulations of war, the long insupportable burden of defence expenditure, and the tensions of unwilling loyalty, were reducing it to chaos. It was only English treasure that kept the war going at all. Coin was shipped across the Channel to pay the castle-guards in January. In February the wages of John's servants were in arrears and urgent letters were sent for more. The total sum shipped from England that year was twice the normal revenue of the duchy. Yet even this was insufficient, and in the last months John was borrowing from anyone who had money to lend.[1]

Conditions forced a reversion to a more primitive kind of rule. Lands were distributed to supporters in return for the service of knights in imitation of an earlier feudalism, which a money economy was everywhere else replacing. John became detached even from the barons who still held to him, and surrounded himself with 'bachelors', young, unknighted warriors who were bound to him in personal service.[2] By the autumn of 1203 the duke of Normandy was like a stranger in an alien land, moving about with an armed escort. In October he went all the way round by Lisieux and Herbertot to get from Verneuil to Rouen, instead of going through Neubourg: 'It was not the straight way, but the other seemed dangerous to him, for he would have come upon his enemies.'[3]

John's counsellors themselves began to despair. 'Sire,' said William Marshal, 'you have too few friends, and if you challenge your enemies to fight you will be crippled.' John pretended to be undaunted. 'Whoever be afraid,' he said, 'let him flee; I shall not go for a year.'[4] But he was like a rabbit trapped in a patch of corn which the mower is steadily reducing. It could not be long before the rabbit scuttled to escape, and the critical moment came in December. The biographer of William Marshal remembered it vividly:

'The king stayed but a short time in Rouen and gave out that he intended to go to England to seek counsel and help from his barons, saying that he would return immediately. But since he took the queen with him many feared that he would stay in England until too late. Preparations were quickly made for the king had already sent his baggage on privately. On the first night he slept at Bonneville, not in the town but in the castle, for he feared treason, indeed he had been warned that most of his barons had sworn to hand him over to the king of France, and though he pretended to be unaware of their intention he kept well away from them. He told Marshal and those in whom he trusted to be ready before daybreak; and so he slipped away

Château Gaillard at Les Andelys on the Seine, built by Richard I to guard the approaches to Rouen. The king of France captured it in March 1204 after a siege of nearly seven months.

without taking leave while he was supposed to be asleep, and by the time his departure was discovered he was seven leagues on. He made for Bayeux by way of Caen, riding more than twenty leagues that day – leagues of the Bessin too, which are longer than French leagues. Thence he went on towards Barfleur where many of his followers bade him farewell: it was perfectly clear that they could not expect him back soon.'[1]

Whether or not their suspicions were justified at the time, events seemed to confirm them, for John sailed from Barfleur on 5 December and never came back at all.

8. NORMANDY LOST

Christmas spent in the safety of Canterbury seems to have put new heart into John. Certainly he had no mind to abandon the struggle and when he came to Oxford to talk with his barons at Epiphany the situation might not have seemed as bad as it had done when he was down among the threatened castles of the Seine valley and creeping treason was rasping at his nerves. He immediately set about making preparations for his return. A great display of strength was what was needed to create in the Normans the loyalty of self-interest. It would take time to gather everything together, but he thought he had it. Philip, admittedly, had torn the network of defensive castles in the eastern march of Normandy, but the net still held him. While Château Gaillard still defied him he had neither siege engines nor time to spare for the well-fortified city of Rouen. It was unfortunate that the attempt to provision Château Gaillard had failed, but it could hold out for some time yet. It was well manned by determined men, and its able commander, Roger Lacy, was conserving victuals by sending all non-combatants out of the castle. Even should it fall and Philip move on to Rouen, he would find the city hard to take. Within its strong walls and triple fosse had been garnered every cartload of supplies that John's officials could collect. It defenders had been reinforced by those loyalists who had slipped away from the territories captured by Philip, and they were commanded by the brave and trustworthy Peter de Préaux. Moreover, its citizens were among the staunchest upholders of the Angevin connection for it had brought them great wealth and privileges. Civic liberties had been freely granted to them, and they enjoyed unrivalled trading rights throughout the Angevin dominions. Only the certainty of John's complete defeat would persuade them to take a chance on Philip's generosity.

Confident that Philip had more than enough to occupy him for many months in eastern Normandy, John concentrated his attention in the west. Among his last acts before departure had been the fortification of the river Touques, which divided the duchy in half through Lisieux. Some contemporary observers criticised this, believing that he should have pressed all his available resources into the eastern castles that were still untaken.[1] But John was prepared to let them go if he could defend the eastern half of Normandy, and there was strategic justification in his thinking. Let Philip expend himself on the well nigh impregnable fortresses of Château Gaillard and Rouen. Central Normandy around Caen, and the Cherbourg peninsula, were as yet untouched by war. They were protected by the southern fortresses from Pontorson to Verneuil, and by his defensive line on the Touques. With this region as a base, he could mount the overwhelming counterattack on which he now fixed his hopes. All else had failed, but the great crushing hammer blow could still be mounted from the vast resources of England, if only he had time to tap them.

He put his problems to a council of barons at Oxford in January. There were several who were ready to join an expedition to Normandy to save the lands they held there, but what the king wanted above all was money with which to recruit mercenaries. His urgent need of help could not be denied, and the king was hinting openly that if he had received proper support earlier he would not be in such difficulties now. Those of the barons who held their land in return for military service (and most of them did) agreed to aid him with two and a half marks for every knight for which they were liable.[*][2] This was a welcome grant, higher than any that had been made in previous years. The exchequer records show the royal officials adding to it with all the urgency they could muster: heavy levies (known as 'tallages') were taken from the towns, the goods of merchants lying at the ports were

---

[*] Such a payment, in lieu of actual service by the knights, was known as 'scutage', that is to say, 'shield-money'. It was paid in a lump sum by the baron in respect of all the service he owed, and then recovered from his knights. The baron's personal service could not be commuted in this way: if he did not wish to serve he had to make a private bargain with the king.

taxed at a fifteenth of their value, concessions and privileges were readily offered to anyone prepared to pay for them. The dominant note everywhere was the scraping together of money. As supplies came to hand they were passed across the Channel.[1] John grew more sanguine: his terrors abated and he prepared to return. On 6 March he even went so far as to make arrangements for wild animals to be trapped in the New Forest and sent over with horses, dogs and falcons, so that he would be sure of his hunting when he arrived.[2]

Ironically, it was on the very day that John gave instructions about his hunting gear that the fate of the duchy was sealed: Château Gaillard fell. It was not starved into submission or cravenly surrendered, it was taken by storm. This was the crowning moment of Philip's long career of siege operations: he had beaten not only John but Richard too, the only man who had seemed his peer in castle-building and siege craft. Little blame can attach to the defenders of the garrison. Perhaps, looking back, they could recall small tactical errors on their part, but they had heroically contested every inch of the ground and caused more casualties among the attackers than they had suffered themselves. If there was a weakness in the defence it can be ascribed to a curious lapse by its designer who had allowed a tongue of rock to remain as a bridge across the deep ditch which surrounded the great central keep. Even when Philip had breached the outer walls he should still have been faced by the unapproachable stone cliffs of this massive citadel. As it was his sappers were able to shelter under this fixed bridge and chip away at the foundations of the keep. Unable to get at them in any other way, the defenders burrowed from the inside and scared the Frenchmen off. But mine and counter-mine seriously weakened the fabric of the wall, and realising this Philip brought up a huge trebuchet and hurled great stones at it until the wall collapsed. After six months of siege the defenders were now face to face with their attackers, but still they fought on fiercely until every one of the hundred and fifty-six who remained alive had been disarmed and made prisoner.[3]

The news was received with consternation in England: Philip was now free to attack Rouen much earlier than had been expected. Unless the city could hold out longer than Château Gaillard, which seemed unlikely, the whole weight of the French army could be thrown against western Normandy before the new army, on which all hopes had been pinned, could be ready. John hurriedly went into conference with his advisers and greater barons at London. Emergency measures were taken. Stores were rushed into Rouen. Messengers were sent on fruitless missions to the king's nephew in Germany and those of the Rhineland barons who had not gone on crusade.[1] It was decided to parley with Philip to see if something could be salvaged from the imminent wreck. Fortunately a papal legate, intent on making peace between the warring kings, was in England at the time of the council. In the second week of April a powerful delegation, consisting of the archbishop of Canterbury, the bishops of Norwich and Ely, William Marshal, and the earl of Leicester, went over with the legate to speak with Philip. The pope had been anxious, ever since war had been renewed two years before, to get the kings to stop quarrelling and go off to the Holy Land. John had spent a lot of money on embassies to Rome to express his readiness for peace and to plead that Philip wronged him. But to all papal entreaties and warnings of his soul's peril, Philip had remained resolute, though he was careful not to seem obdurate. He received the delegation: he was prepared, he said, to make peace – but only on his own terms. Let John hand over Arthur or (since nothing had been heard of Arthur for a twelvemonth) his sister Eleanor, and surrender his claim to all his continental lands. Obviously, even the hazardous chances of war were preferable to these terms; discussion was pointless, the English envoys and the papal legate went their several ways.[2]

Sad to relate, it was on 1 April 1204 that John's mother died, with the news of the fall of the 'Saucy Castle' to take with her to the grave.[3] Of all her sons Richard had been her favourite: the 'great one' she called him. She had been great herself in her own way. In the tapestry of her life were woven all the threads of the Angevin story. Her second marriage to the young Henry of Anjou had laid the foundations of a great continental dominion. Her influence had swayed its fortunes at critical times. Now, on her deathbed, it was being shattered by the son of the man who had divorced her.

Shattering Philip's next moves certainly were. He sized up the situation to a nicety. Rouen was the great prize. One of the richest and most splendid cities of all France, it had for a generation been the pulsing heart of the Angevin empire.[4] Much of Philip's life had been spent hammering at the line upon line of castles that kept it from his grasp. Now, after two years of concentrated effort, he had battered his way through. The prize lay before him, a few leagues down the Seine. To everyone's surprise, and to his own credit as a military commander, he turned away. His forethought penetrated John's schemes. He must have seen that if the defenders of Rouen held him up long enough for John to convert the wealth of England into a brand new army, he stood to lose all that he had so far gained. On the other hand, if the rest of Normandy were in his hands it would be pointless for Rouen to hold out alone. So he took a chance and turned away. Instead of taking his army and his great siege train down the Seine, he put his knights on horseback again and led them swiftly into the wooded hills of southern Normandy where many of the rivers of the province had their source. (*See Map VI.*) Up the river Risle he went to the shadow of Mont d'Amain. Here he turned the defensive line of the Touques by crossing the river at its shallow headwaters, and plunged into the valley of the Orne. It was what a later age of military commentators would describe as a brilliant left-hook. Argentan gave him no trouble; Lupescar and his mercenaries withstood him for a week at Falaise, and then threw in their hand and joined his forces. The place where William the Conqueror had been born was thus delivered into the French king's hands. His next objective was the ancient capital of the duchy, Caen, where the Conqueror was buried. It surrendered without a fight. All around barons and townsmen hastened to do Philip homage. There in the month of May 1204 was demonstrated the basic reason why Normandy could not be defended: the Normans, their loyalty dried up, deserted as soon as it was safe to do so.

Meanwhile, at the beginning of May, the Bretons had ruptured the defences in the south-west corner of the duchy. Burning to avenge the death of their prince they by-passed Pontorson, broke the gate of Mont St Michel, seized Avranches, and stormed up through the Bessin to join Philip at Caen. Thence the French king despatched detachments to receive the surrender of the Cherbourg peninsula and to take the remaining fortresses on the southern frontier. He himself led the bulk of his army eastwards through Lisieux to Rouen where the last scenes of the drama were to be enacted.

Normandy was virtually lost and John knew it. At the end of

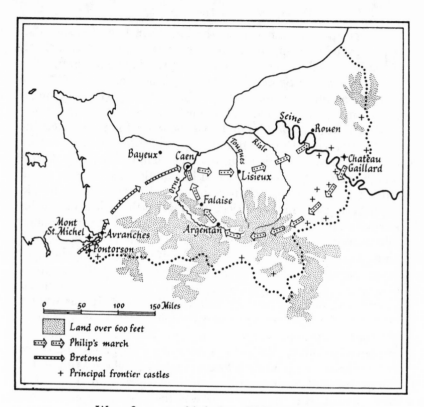

VI. War of 1202-4, third phase Philip's capture of
central Normandy in the summer of 1204

May a faithful clerk, Peter de Leon, arrived at Shoreham with the administrative archives from Caen and the king sent him carts to convey them to London.[1] In Rouen the determination of the citizens to resist the French king was wilting fast. This was very understandable. Their civic and trading privileges were what weighed with them most, and while the Angevin rulers could guarantee these none could be found more loyal than they. But now such guarantee was gone. Philip, moreover, played his economic cards as carefully as he had played his strategic ones. He freely confirmed the civic liberties of the towns that he had taken, and by lending a ready ear to requests for more, threatened Rouen with a crop of rivals. The military commandant, Peter de Préaux, realised that only the direct intervention of John could avert collapse. To save the city from needless destruction he arranged an armistice with Philip on 1 June and agreed that if his lord brought him no help within thirty days he would surrender. Urgent messages were sent to John, but he had given up hope: no help could be looked for from him, he is said to have replied, but everyone should do what seemed to him best.[2] There was no point in prolonging the issue: Rouen admitted Philip on 24 June, before the thirty days were up. The duchy of Normandy, save only for the Channel Islands, was lost to the English Crown.

It is difficult to see how John could have averted disaster. Not even the ablest commander can hold a disaffected province indefinitely against a determined invader. With all the available resources at full stretch, he was never able to bring a strong force to bear against the French army save only for the abortive night attack to relieve Château Gaillard at Les Andelys. Philip had the luck, and the hearts of the Normans. Richard himself could not have beaten that combination. If Richard had lived for another five years, though, there would have been one notable difference in the course of the campaign. The king himself would have been on the heights above Les Andelys as dawn broke, to give the signal for the combined attack on the French camp; however ready the Normans were to surrender, Philip would not have been able to march up the valley of the Orne to Caen without fear of a sudden assault by Richard and his household cavalry; and even when all else had gone, Richard would have been urging the citizens of Rouen to arms, and parrying the first assault with blows from his great sword. John stayed in England biting his nails.

4

King of England

'Man walketh in a vain shadow, and disquieteth himself in vain: he heapeth up riches and cannot tell who shall gather them.' *Psalm xxxix.* 7

I. DIVIDED COUNSEL

The year which followed the surrender of Rouen is for the historian of John's reign one of tantalising obscurity. More than ever he laments the death of Howden in 1201. The dramatic events of 1202–4 in Normandy could not, of course, fail to leave a mark on even the most meagre and annalistic of chroniclers, and with the aid of scissors and paste the historian can piece together the sequence of events with fair confidence, though he is left groping ineffectually after the fate of Arthur and the alleged trials of John at the French court. But when Normandy had fallen the chroniclers found little to say, and were it not for the administrative records one would be driven to suppose that John did practically nothing between the abortive negotiations of April 1204 and an expedition planned for June 1205. Roger Wendover, indeed, plying his prejudiced pen some twenty-five years later, said just this. John, he would have us believe, received the news of the collapse of his power in France with sanguine unconcern: 'he was enjoying every kind of pleasure with his queen, in whose company he believed that he possessed all that he wanted; moreover he put his trust in the vast quantity of money he had collected, as if by that he could bring back the lands he had lost.'[1]

Wendover clearly had not read the *Close Rolls*, the *Curia Regis Rolls* or the records of the Exchequer. There he would have found, had he the wit to interpret them, striking testimony to John's indefatigable attention to the business of government.[2] It is probable that there had never been a king who devoted himself so keenly to the job of ruling. Certainly no one had seen anything like it since Henry II died in 1189, and his multifarious cares had kept him out of England for long periods, and the administration in the hands of officials. John was on the move all the time, dragging his household round and round the midlands, down to Devon in the summer of 1204, up to Yorkshire in the spring of 1205. And wherever he went he would sit with his justices hearing pleas. It was a privilege to have one's case tried by the king himself, and men would offer as much as £100 for a royal audience; but John was quite content to take as little as half a mark and to judge the most ordinary of cases, as well as those where his personal intervention was essential to the litigant. His travels brought him for only short periods to Westminster, but when there he could be found sitting in at an Exchequer session, hearing the accounts of the sheriffs presented for audit and intervening to make a change in a sheriff's liabilities. In November 1204 he initiated a far-reaching reform of the currency that put coins of good design and full weight into the hands of the people and new confidence into trade.[1] John's government was alive and enterprising, and it owed much of its vigour to the zealous activity of the king himself.

But what of Philip's victories? How did John meet the challenge of the loss of Normandy, and the problem that followed upon it of French troops invading Poitou? Why was no positive move made until the spring of 1205? Here the administrative records are of little help and the chronicles silent or obscure. There are only a few trailing whispers of what was going on between John and his barons, and of these we must make what we can. They hint at a truculent baronage, a nervously suspicious king, and divided counsel.

From a military point of view the situation admitted of only one response – an expedition to Poitou. While Queen Eleanor lived she stood as the rightful lord of Aquitaine and the French court's disinheritance of John could not be pressed against the southern lands of his house. Hence her death in April 1204 was of great political importance: it removed the legal obstacle to Philip's further progress, and as soon as Normandy was effectively in his hands he despatched a strong force of mercenaries to link up with William des Roches in Anjou and to invade Poitou. John's representative there, the seneschal Robert of Thornham, was able and trustworthy, but had long been struggling with the rebellion of the Lusignans and their friends, and try as he would he could not resist this new rush of foes. He himself was made prisoner. Thouars made a brief resistance, but its viscount soon came to terms with Philip and the whole county was overrun save for the fortress of Niort and the seaport of La Rochelle.[1] But here Philip's triumphal advance came to a halt. Angoulême was held by John in right of his wife (for Count Aymer had died in 1202) and could not be attacked with feudal propriety; and south of Angoulême the rest of the barons of Aquitaine were rallying to the Angevin cause. It cannot be supposed that it was love of John or respect for the Angevin connection that roused them, rather it was their lively fear that their independence would be more in jeopardy from a triumphant king of France than a ruler in distant England. Whatever the cause, here was the first stiffening of resistance, here Philip's onslaught expended itself, and here was the opportunity to mount a counter-attack. If an attempt were to be made to recover Normandy direct, all supplies would have to be carried in a great fleet of ships and the shore itself seized before equipment could be landed; but in the south there was now a defendable base. Not Normandy but La Rochelle and Bordeaux should have been on the lips of the military high command at John's court. John himself immediately realised the change in the situation. Twenty-eight thousand marks raised from the scutage and by the busy royal officials were handed over to the brother of the archbishop of Bordeaux to raise, it is said, a force of 30,000 troops in Gascony to be ready for the king's coming.[2]

Military considerations, however, were not the only ones to be reckoned with: there were political considerations too, and on these all enterprise foundered. An expedition on the scale necessary for victory required the support, or at the very least the co-operation, of the barons of England; but Aquitaine was nothing to them. It was virtually a private concern of the king, a problem assumed by Henry II when he married Eleanor. If the king insisted on them following him to Poitou they would probably have to follow him as their liege-lord or pay a fine to escape service; but they had no interest in it, and he could not oblige them to bring the knights they owed him as king of England. Normandy, now, was different. There were, as like as not, already some murmurs of discontent at the waste of effort and money on foreign enterprises of any kind, but many barons had estates in Normandy and a lively concern about their fate. Normandy and England were not easily disentangled from each other. They were the most closely linked, indeed the only closely linked provinces of the Angevin empire. It is true that the Norman families established in England by the Conqueror and his successors had in the course of time shown a tendency to split into Norman and English branches; but this tendency had been deliberately resisted by Henry II who used his influence over succession to insist that baronies were indivisible and the English Channel a mere fact of geography.[1] In consequence the capture of Normandy by the French king hit many of John's vassals very hard. It posed political and legal problems that were absent from the loss of Anjou and Maine. The Anglo-Norman baronage was in 1204 forcibly split into two: those whose Norman interests were paramount did homage to Philip; those who could not afford to jeopardise their English holdings had followed John back to England. Only three of the latter, the earls of Chester, Pembroke, and Leicester, had extensive holdings in Normandy, but it must have been the lesser men who had only a few manors to lose, but to whom a few manors meant much, who suffered the most worry and harboured the most bitterness. One or two were clever enough to take forethought for the political consequences: Ellis of Wimberville and Alan Martell had similar holdings on both sides of the Channel, and while they were at the siege of Arques together they agreed to an exchange, so that Ellis took the English and Alan the Norman lands.[2] But most men held on to their lands until too late and were faced with a difficult choice, and ultimately a serious loss.

At first, and indeed for many years, the losses did not seem irrevocable. It is true that both kings behaved nominally as if they were: in October 1204 John confiscated the English lands of those who had remained in Normandy, and Philip set a term within which those who had followed John should come and make their peace with him or suffer confiscation. But John clearly thought the confiscations temporary and was prepared to allow men to buy their lands back, save, perhaps, in cases of overt treachery. Here was an opportunity for making money and he took it, but, bent as he was on recovering Normandy, he had no interest in making the division permanent. Similarly Philip was prepared to allow the English barons a certain amount of latitude: he did not want to oblige them to support John's attempt at the forcible recovery of Normandy if he could help it.[1] The situation therefore remained for the barons both worrying and expensive.

It is not hard to guess the sort of arguments that went on in baronial halls and the king's council in the autumn of 1204, and which ultimately crippled all effective action. For John Normandy was only one of his losses, and his first concern was with the safety of Aquitaine. The extinction of his base in western Normandy shifted his strategic thinking to southern campaigns for the recovery of his inheritance. The barons, at least those who had Norman estates, and they numbered among them the greatest and most influential, would have none of this. If they had made any arrangements at all for the safety of their Norman fiefs they were only of a very temporary kind: they had left younger sons there, or had bought Philip's forbearance for a few months. Robert earl of Leicester, and William Marshal earl of Pembroke had, for example, taken advantage of their official negotiations with Philip in April 1204 (after the fall of Château Gaillard) to make private arrangements about their estates: they had given him 500 marks each that he would not touch their Norman lands for a year and a day, and they had promised to do him homage at the end of that time if their estates were still in his hands. When they had reported what they had done to John, he seems to have thought it quite a sensible arrangement: at the time he was still confident of being able to mount the counter-attack from western Normandy that would bring him victory, so their promise of homage counted for nothing.[2] But now, with all Normandy held by Philip, such temporary arrangements obliged those who had made them to look for speedy remedy. They could not wait upon the outcome of a southern campaign. So far as they were concerned, only two sources of action were open to consideration: an expedition to Normandy as soon as practicable, or a formal peace between the two kings in which the vexed questions of private ownership of land and the complications of feudal relations would be settled. The important earls of Leicester and Pembroke might be supposed from their terms with Philip to have anticipated a campaign; but in fact William Marshal, at least, regarded the arrangement as a *pis aller* at a critical moment – what he really hoped for was a peace which would enable him to serve two masters. It was he who had sensed most acutely the frailty of the Angevin hold on Norman hearts, and had firmly told John that there was no hope for him there. He was famous through two kingdoms for his military prowess, his chivalry, his unwavering adherence to the minutiae of feudal proprieties, and his attitude must have swayed most forcibly the minds of his colleagues.[1]

William Marshal's rank, power, and long history of loyalty to the Angevin house gave him a high place among the counsellors of the king, but there were other counsellors as close or closer, who would take a different view. They would remind John, if he needed reminding, that any formal peace could not fail to prejudice his just claims. Thus did action wait upon wrangle. The months slipped away and a grim winter closed tightly upon the country-side. The rivers froze after Christmas and the Thames could be crossed on foot. The ground was so hard that no ploughshare could bite into it until March. The winter sowings were almost ruined by the ferocity of the cold; vegetables and herbage were shrivelled up. When spring finally came and an expedition could be thought of, corn was selling at famine prices. Oats fetched ten times the normal price, and men were paying half a mark for a few pence worth of peas or beans.[2] A sorry land was England in 1204–5.

2. SUSPICION AND DISCONTENT

There are indications, slight but palpable, that there was an estrangement between the king and the barons in 1204–5 that went deeper than disagreement over tactics against Philip of France. We cannot get close enough to descry its lineaments, but a want of confidence, suspicion and discontent rumble through these months like distant thunder. John was never really at ease with his barons; with few was he on friendly terms, with almost none was he intimate. It was not that he was a misanthrope or devoid of humanity: he kept a large and lively household that he liked to see well-fed, well-dressed, and gay; but his friends were servants, paid mercenaries, landless knights and young bannerets, or poor men whom he took up, cultivated, and trusted with his business.

There were, of course, always barons about the court, there as duty called, or on private business, or because the king was in the vicinity and they deemed it politic to pay their respects; but there were very few who were hailed as friends or could be said to have the king's ear. John had kept on, as head of the administration, King Richard's justiciar, Geoffrey FitzPeter, and he was earl of Essex. But he was earl of Essex by luck not birth. His background was exclusively that of a royal official, who as a young man close to the fount of royal patronage had picked up a minor heiress, Beatrice de Say. By a stroke of fate the line of the Mandeville earls of Essex became extinct in 1190, Beatrice had a claim and her husband pushed it successfully. John belted him as earl on the day of his coronation. Such a man, landed only in right of his wife, can hardly be accounted a member of the aristocracy.[1]

William Marshal had also started his career as a landless servant, though of a very different kind. He was the second son of the second marriage of John FitzGilbert, marshal of the court to Henry I. His memories went back to the day when, as a young hostage in the civil war, he had played conkers with King Stephen. As a younger son he had started life with no land and no money, but with good connections and a fortune in his invincible lance. He might have become a professional soldier, but he had more than a trace of gentility in his blood, and a love of chivalry and honour that drew him into the company of the wellborn, and he preferred to remain an amateur, picking up a rather precarious living from the generosity of rich patrons or from the sale of horses and prisoners that he captured in tournaments. Tournaments those days were violent affairs, differing only from real battles in being fought for no other purpose than enjoyment of fighting and within the code of the chivalric cult. Fatalities were not infrequent, and the victors could hold the vanquished to ransom and take their armour and valuable chargers. Such was the sport of the 12th century aristocracy, when not engaged in real war, or that other simulacrum of war, the pursuit and slaughter of wild animals. So young William Marshal made his way in the world, playing for this or that gentleman's team against challengers, until Fortune smiled on him. Queen Eleanor patronised him, and Henry II made him tutor in chivalry to his eldest son and paid for his services with the heiress of Richard FitzGilbert, earl of Pembroke. In right of his wife he was lord of Striguil in the Wye valley, of the palatine county of Pembroke in west Wales, and of Leinster in Ireland. He increased this princely holding by buying half the lands of the earls of Giffard for 2,000 marks in 1191.

On the same say that Geoffrey FitzPeter was made earl of Essex, John belted William as earl of Pembroke. He deserved the honour for he had rendered long service to the Angevin house with his lance, his sagacious counsel, and his tact as a negotiator. Although a comparative newcomer to the ranks of the great landowners he was respected by the barons as the bosom friend of kings and princes, as a man of proved courage and valour, as the finest exponent of aristocratic pursuits, and the very soul of chivalric honour. He was duly respectful to John, whom indeed he had helped to the throne, and was ready to lend his help and advice in any of the king's difficulties. John was mindful of the character and experience of William, kept him often by his side in Normandy, and suffered him to speak frankly; but affection and intimacy were wanting between them. For William, the great days of golden memory had been the days when he was tutor and friend to the Young Henry: John had his respectful and loyal service but not his devotion. John, for his part, could not altogether suppress a prickling resentment of William Marshal's great prestige and influence; they could not see eye to eye on the policy to be pursued in 1204, and relations in after days might have been strained to open breach, had not William been ever mindful of his feudal duty to his liege-lord.[1]

A baron much favoured by John in the early years of the reign was William de Briouze, lord of Bramber in Sussex, Radnor, Brecon, and Abergavenny in Wales, and Barnstaple and Totnes in Devon. He at least came of an ancient baronial house, though until recently only a minor one. The family originated at Briouze in Normandy and had been given the castle and rape of Bramber by William the Conqueror. By the time he succeeded his father in 1180 he had already established a reputation as a determined and ruthless fighter in the turbulent Welsh March, terrible alike to his neighbours and to the Welsh. King Richard knew how to use such a man, rough, fearless, and ready for anything that brought him profit. William was with him when he met his death at Chalus. John knew how to use him too, and he was usually by the king's side in 1202–3 or acting as his personal agent. He was probably one of the few men who knew what had happened to Arthur, and his friendship with the monks of Margam abbey in Glamorgan has secured for us the only reliable knowledge of the murder. His power increased rapidly under John: he was made the most powerful baron in south Wales, he was given Limerick in Ireland, rich marriages were arranged for his numerous children, one of his sons was given a bishopric. Many years later people in Wales were saying that William extorted the rich peninsula of Gower from John by threatening to leave him in the stress of war in 1203. Perhaps this was idle gossip; but Briouze was certainly pushingly ambitious, and his friendship with the king, if such it can be called, was one rather of mutual usefulness than of affection. John gave him lands, but withheld the coveted title of earl, and from 1206 was looking for ways of keeping his power in check. Ultimately John was able to break William de Briouze, though he helped to break himself in the process. In 1204, however, they were allies, but this probably brought the king no closer to the rest of the baronage, for many hated Briouze as a ruthless rival and resented his access to royal patronage.[1]

Perhaps the only one of the greater barons with whom John was on terms of back-slapping intimacy was his half-brother, William Longsword, earl of Salisbury, a bastard son of Henry II. He was intelligent and useful to John. He was often entrusted with diplomatic missions, put in command of military operations, and has the distinction of gaining the first great English naval victory off Damme in 1213. John liked to send him a tun or two of wine, play cards with him, and lend him a few marks when gambling left him out of pocket.[2]

While those whom he could readily trust were few, those whom he could readily distrust were many. With the desertion of the Norman barons so recent and so catastrophic, John's confidence in his English vassals could not be high. If Philip invaded England how many of them too would hasten to desert? Most of the English earls had been in Normandy for the campaign and doubtless not a few had been privy to conspiracy or treasonable talk. How many had crossed the Channel after him only because their English estates tethered them unwillingly to his side? In 1203 when John felt himself wronged by Philip's aggression and stabbed in the back by treachery he had laid his woes before the pope. Innocent III had tried to help him by instructing the archbishop of Rouen to command all rebels to return to their allegiance. It is significant that similar papal letters were sent at the same time to the archbishop of Canterbury.[3]

John had for some time suspected the most powerful of his

barons, Ranulph earl of Chester, of treasonable designs. Ranulph was a big man in Normandy as well as England, and held fiefs there for which he owed as many as fifty knights in military service. He had married the widowed Constance of Brittany, so the young Arthur was his stepson. It is unlikely, though, that Ranulph felt any affection for the boy: his marriage to Constance had been a political one, and she thought so little of it that she subsequently went off and married Guy of Thouars without bothering to obtain a divorce. Nonetheless, John accused him in April 1203 of plotting with the disaffected Bretons. April 1203 was, of course, a bad time for John: all his plans were going awry and he had murdered Arthur in a drunken rage. Ranulph was made a butt for the king's bad temper. He behaved with dignity and tact, and the trusted Roger Lacy, constable of Chester and commandant of Château Gaillard, went surety for him. John's suspicion simmered down, but it was ever ready to boil up again. In December 1204 he suddenly denounced Ranulph for an alleged alliance with the rebellious Welsh chieftain Gwenwynwyn, and sent in his sheriffs to seize the earl's estates.[1] Again it was but a puff of unwarranted fear that soon blew over, but it is symptomatic of the tension that plagued John and kept his barons ill at ease and anxious.

The king's apprehension was not all a matter of wild fancy and vague suspicion: the barons did not attempt to disguise their discontent. Like their Norman *confrères* they had been held down by the heavy hand of Angevin government. Since the abortive rebellion of 1173 they had lost many of the castles that had been in their families for generations, and which were commonly coveted as a mark of baronial status – the only proper residences for men of great military dignity, part of the panoply of feudal lordship. They had, moreover, been systematically excluded from all positions of power and influence in the administration of the realm. Their privileges as feudal lords were subject to investigation by low-born royal servants, ever on the look-out for a flaw in a title or an excuse to interfere. It was well known to be dangerous to leave a young son or a widow to the mercies of kings who were always short of money. Their grievances had not crystallised out into formal demands yet, but they grumbled and were uncooperative, querulous and restive. It had been necessary, in order to rally support for John's claim to the throne, to promise that every man would recover his rights.[2] They had evidently not received what they felt were their rights for the cry went on throughout the reign. According to Roger of Howden the earls made trouble in 1201 when John summoned them to join him at Portsmouth for the crossing to Normandy. They went instead to hold a protest meeting at Leicester and issued a joint statement saying that they would not cross 'unless he restored to each of them their rights'. John wielded the big stick and took hostages. They came to heel, but changed only their public attitude, not their minds.[1]

The sense of grievance was not overlaid by the desperations of war. In the early months of 1205 the country was threatened with invasion by the allies of the French king, and John was urgently looking for reassurances of loyalty. At a council at Oxford in March of that year, the barons took an oath 'that they would render him due obedience', but they demanded a *quid pro quo* and compelled John to promise 'that he would by their counsel maintain the rights of the kingdom inviolate, to the utmost of his power.'[2]

Such vague and inchoate expressions of grievance do not attract much attention from the constitutional historian, who prefers the clear statements of Magna Carta. But it should be remembered that the expression of grievance went back to the first moments of the reign, and therefore took its origin before John ascended the throne. Doubtless he incurs responsibility for failing to find a remedy, and certainly for aggravating the cause, but in England as in Normandy John was assuredly called upon to meet the cost of his predecessors' rule.

It was only natural that John's suspicion and apprehension should find a focus in the threat of invasion. Philip was expected, in his moment of triumph, to attempt it for he had threatened it as far back as 1193. Mindful of the possibility of baronial desertion, John took steps to forestall it in January 1205. An avowal of fidelity was required from every adult male of the population, and the whole country was put in a state of emergency. All able-bodied freemen were traditionally expected to turn out for the defence of the homeland. In 1181 Henry II had issued an edict laying down the equipment each freeman was to have according to his wealth, and making provision for its inspection.[3] John well remembered these local levies for they had been called out to suppress his rebellion as Count of Mortain. He was not satisfied with their organisation in 1205 and insisted on every male over twelve years of age 'from the greatest to the least' entering into a sworn association 'for the general defence of the realm and the preservation of the peace.' A 'constable' was to be appointed in every hundred,* city and group of neighbouring townships, who would muster the local forces under the orders of a chief constable appointed in every shire. The fear of subversion as well as assault from outside runs clearly through the ordinance, and it must have been clearly apparent to anyone who took the oath 'against foreigners and against any other disturbers of the peace.' Anyone who failed to take the oath, without reasonable excuse, was to be taken to be a manifest enemy of the king and the kingdom.[1] There can be no clearer witness than this to the fears that beset King John in the bitter winter of 1204–5.

In February the threat of invasion assumed more definite shape: King Philip, adept at getting others to do his work, enlisted the help of Renaud count of Boulogne, and Henry duke of Brabant. These men were brothers-in-law squabbling over the inheritances of their wives, who were daughters of the last count of Boulogne. Philip patched up their quarrel and set them hunting greater game – the putative inheritance of their wives in England. They were well-born ladies these, granddaughters of King Stephen of England and his wife, Matilda of Boulogne, robbed, they thought, by Henry II of their rightful English estates. Let their husbands go with drawn swords to maintain their claim, promised Philip, and he would follow with his army in a month. Such at any rate was the rumour that ran round the worried realm of King John. The royal officers along the south and east coasts were alerted and instructed to allow no ships to leave port or to sail the waters of their jurisdictions without written permission from the king.[2] John stood at bay, but not yet daunted: he would strike back.

3. THE EXPEDITION THAT STAYED AT HOME

Meeting his barons in formal conference at the end of March, John pushed them into agreeing to a policy of aggressive defence. Orders were issued to the sheriffs on 3 April to see that a tenth of the knight service of every shire attended the king fully equipped at London on 1 May 'ready to go in his service wherever he should bid them, and to remain in his service in defence of the realm as

---

* The hundred was an administrative subdivision of the shire.

might be necessary.'[1] Like his brother in 1197, John did not want the old-fashioned feudal army to turn out on service for forty days; he wanted a smaller force for a longer period, and so required every nine knights in the country to equip a tenth.

This muster of a cavalry force was soon swallowed up in grandiose plans for which more than a month was necessary, indeed the muster may have been postponed as John's plans matured. The chroniclers seem to think that what he had in mind was an expedition to Poitou, but those who tell of it did not realise that two separate expeditions were being prepared. The headquarters of one of these was established at Dartmouth, the obvious point of departure for Poitou. John's bastard son Geoffrey (who emerges at this moment from complete obscurity) was given command of a force of mercenaries who were to embark there. Much greater preparations, however, were made in the Solent to ship the king and his barons from Portsmouth, and this could have been the point of departure for an expedition to Normandy. It seems likely, then, that John planned a pincer movement, engaging Philip on two fronts. A concentrated attack from Poitou would, from the tactical point of view, have been preferable, but such a plan as this offered a reasonable solution to the dispute over policy which had held up action hitherto.[2]

Throughout April and May England was bustling with activity. The king's busy officials had never been busier, marshalling the resources of the country for a gigantic effort. A barrage of royal writs issued from the chancery covering everything from the building of great ships to the collection of nails for horseshoes. Around the coast workmen were impressed to build galleys or to convert commandeered merchantmen. Along all the roads to Southampton and Dartmouth carts trundled laden with bacons, venison, hurdles, quarrels for crossbows, wool for sails, and barrels of money for everything. From royal castles all over the country, save the vulnerable frontier areas, the king's hired crossbowmen set out for a preliminary muster of land forces at Northampton. Here the king reviewed them in the third week in May and conferred again with his barons. Nothing hitherto had been seen like these preparations: they eclipsed even those for Richard's crusade in 1190. Gervase of Canterbury has it that nearly 1,500 ships were got ready at Portsmouth. It is well known that as soon as chroniclers get into three figures they are prone to wild exaggeration, but certainly the effort was prodigious and the results enormously impressive. Something like a quarter of the year's revenue was spent on military and naval preparations alone.[1]

The Solent must have been a grand sight in the first week of June when the king brought the court down to Porchester castle, and the great armada was made ready for sea. The seamen and men-at-arms, it seems, were filled with enthusiasm for the expedition, but there was little prospect of them being well led for under the fluttering banners of the barons there was disquiet and misgiving.

It was a wretched culmination to John's vigorous preparations. He could not even count on the assistance of Earl William Marshal for their relations had been strained for several weeks. The long months of indecision and the weeks of preparation had eaten up the respite that the earl had bought from the king of France. Some time before Easter he talked John into letting him go to parley with Philip. John naturally wanted to do what he could for so important a vassal, and seems to have authorised him to take an oath to the French king if this would save his Norman estates from confiscation.[2] The biographer of Marshal says that John commissioned the earl to see if he could bring Philip to discuss peace terms, but he is very likely trying to give official dignity to a venture at personal diplomacy by his patron. A formal peace would have suited William better than anything. The king's principal adviser, Archbishop Hubert Walter, suspected as much and was at some pains to let it be known in France that the mission had no authority to negotiate a treaty. If the biographer's assertions are worth anything they point to that divided counsel which robbed John of proper support at this crucial time.[3]

Earl William certainly succeeded in saving his Norman estates. He did so by performing to King Philip 'liege-homage on this side of the sea.' It is a curious formula for which no precedent can be found in feudal law, and its precise meaning is not clear. John did not like the sound of it. He upbraided William and accused him of taking an oath 'against me and to my disadvantage'. William denied it, saying that he had acted in accordance with John's permission that he might take an oath to save his estates. There was room for doubt though, and the king was justified in replying that he would put the matter to the judgement of his barons. A nice feudal issue is involved. It was quite normal to hold separate fiefs of different lords and to do each of them homage in respect of these fiefs, but one could only owe personal service to one lord. If the two lords went to war against each other, one rendered to each the knights' service that was owed from the separate fiefs (and in recognition of which one had done homage), but personally followed to war that lord to which one owed allegiance (and to whom one had taken an oath of fealty). The formula invented by Philip and William implied something more however: it implied that William had divided his allegiance: that in England he was John's man, but on French soil he was Philip's man. It is hard to accuse so upright and feudally correct a man as William Marshal of duplicity, but this comes very near it. The best that can be said for him is that he had no wish to hide anything and that he had perhaps misunderstood the verbal permission that John had given him.

John, however, had good cause to feel uncertain of William's loyalty, and apprehensive of what he would do when the expedition reached France. Brooding over it one day early in June as he sat on the sea shore watching the armada assemble, the king returned to the charge he had made earlier. William again insisted that he had not exceeded the terms of the king's permission. John then put the matter to the crucial test: 'Come with me', he said, 'and fight for the recovery of my inheritance against the king of France to whom you have performed homage.' At this the earl balked: he could not do it, he said. This to John was manifest treason, and he called to the barons standing near for judgement. Before anyone could answer William turned to them and said, 'Let this be a warning to you: what the king is planning to do to me he will do to every one of you when he gets the upper hand.' The king angrily called for judgement, but the barons looked askance at each other and backed away. 'By God's teeth', swore John, 'it is plain to see that none of my barons are with me in this: it looks ugly, I must take counsel with my bachelors.' He led his entourage of young men aside and they agreed with him that Marshal could have no valid excuse for not going with his lord on the expedition. But as one of the more experienced of them pointed out, if William protested the justice of his case, the lie could be given him only by challenging him to a judicial duel, and who among them was good enough to beat Marshal? There was a murmur of concurrence at this and no one was rash enough to offer himself as the king's champion, so John gave up in disgust and went off to his dinner.[1]

Only Marshal's biographer tells us of this incident so we cannot altogether rely on its accuracy in detail; but of one thing we can be certain – the impression it creates of John at odds with his barons on the eve of the great expedition is only too close to the truth. Whether or not, like Marshal, they could offer an excuse, the fact of the matter is simple: they did not want to go.

If he were aware of their reluctance, John chose to ignore it and went on with his preparations until all he waited for was a favourable wind. At this point the only two men who had the courage to speak frankly, Archbishop Walter and William Marshal, came to him and sought to dissuade him from embarking. They used every possible rational argument: it was rash, they said, for him to put himself in enemy territory where he had no safe place of refuge; the French king could muster far more troops than he could take oversea; it was no use putting himself in the hands of the Poitevins whose fickleness and treachery were proverbial; if he went England would be undefended and it was well known that the count of Boulogne was ready to invade; he was taking a gambler's chance and risked losing all that he still had while trying to recover what he had lost; and what was to happen if he met his death – he had no heir to take up the reins of government. When nothing they could say succeeded in moving him to change his mind, they fell to the ground and grasped his knees, 'swearing that, for certain, if he would not listen to their entreaties, they would forcibly detain him lest the whole kingdom be thrown into confusion by his going.'[2] What they feared, and what the king assumed, was that if he attempted to put to sea he would be faced by something like a sit-down strike. Weeping and wailing with frustration and shame, still arguing and protesting, John was practically dragged off to Winchester where his counsellors thought, perhaps, to calm him down. It was to no avail. Next day he was back at Portsmouth where the sailors and common soldiers were loud in their indignation at the barons' conduct. He boarded the royal galley with a few companions and cruised up and down the Channel, but after three days, finally convinced of the impossibility of going, he put into Studland in Dorset and called the expedition off.[3]

The vast labours of the spring of 1205 gave birth to nothing more than the despatch of the subsidiary expedition to Poitou from Dartmouth, and of a supplementary one under the earl of Salisbury to reinforce the garrison of La Rochelle. They were too late to relieve two of the isolated strongholds that had heroically flown John's flag for long months in conquered territory. When Chinon was no longer defensible at Easter, its garrison came out fighting until all had been forcibly disarmed. Loches was overwhelmed at midsummer. Hubert de Burgh had held the former, Gerard d'Athée the latter. John helped to pay their ransoms and brought them to England.[1] Such were men in whom he could repose trust and friendship; such were men whom the barons hated; but can one wonder at the king's partiality?

4. THE DEFENCE OF AQUITAINE

John did not see in the abandonment of the expedition the abandonment of Aquitaine itself. His mind was very much on holding it, as the flurry of writs sent to his officials there clearly witness. He saw to it that the defences of the Channel Islands were strengthened for they now formed an important link in his chain of communications with the south of France. Loyal knights and burgesses from Poitou visiting England were lodged at the king's expense. Money was spent during the winter months on having eight large transport ships made for the king's use. In January 1206 a mission was sent out with a cargo of treasure to discuss the king's interests with his supporters. It was not a high-powered diplomatic mission: it was composed exclusively of workaday royal officials.[2] Since the barons had let him down so badly it is not surprising that he should have made what he could of his own resources and trusted only to servants. The remarkable thing, however, is that when the king himself set sail for Poitou in the early summer of 1206 very many barons went with him. No contemporary chronicler explains this change of front; indeed the secular events of the year are treated fleetingly if at all in English chronicles. It is possible that John had brought pressure to bear on his barons individually. He was constantly on tour throughout the winter, rarely staying more than a day or so at any one place. In February 1206 he went north to Yorkshire, and returned south via Cumberland, Lancashire, and Cheshire, and there may be a connection between this tour and the high proportion of barons

The obverse of an impression of the Great Seal
used in John's reign.

from northern England who personally accompanied the king to Poitou.[1]

Active preparations were set in train at the end of April. The necessary muster of ships began: vessels were commandeered in the southern ports, fitted out with landing gear and required to be at Dartmouth on the eve of Whitsun.[2] The king's officials in the Channel Islands were ordered to send out recruiting officers into the shipping lanes 'who know how to talk wisely and warmly to the steersmen and the sailors and to move and induce them to come quickly into our service, and to assure them of our peace and goodwill and safe conduct.'[3]

Something more modest, but at least more effective, than the armada of 1205 seems to have been what John had in mind; but the several hundred vessels that put out from port at the beginning of June must have been an impressive sight. On 7 June the fleet put into the great harbour of La Rochelle. It was then virtually a frontier town that had been defending itself against the king's enemies for many months; but the king's arrival was the signal for a great demonstration of support by the baronage of Aquitaine, and his vassals flocked to his banner. John, however, kept his head: this was not the time for a full-scale campaign against Philip, for it was necessary first to consolidate what he had. His mother's inheritance was in danger of being lost to him both in the north and the south. All Poitou had gone over to Philip save for the city of Niort which Savary de Mauléon bravely held. While in the south the castle of Montauban was known to be the headquarters of men who thought they could profit by defying John.

His answer to this situation was to lead his army in a series of raids. (*See Map VII.*) First he marched from La Rochelle to encourage the defenders of Niort, and went on half-way to Poitiers before turning south, as if to let the Poitevins know that he had returned. Then in July he shifted his headquarters south to the Garonne and laid siege to Montauban. His enemies there doubtless felt themselves secure, for most men thought the place impregnable and told each other that Charlemagne himself had been unable to take the place after seven years of effort. It took John fifteen days. His siege engines battered it into a shambles and his English troops then showed their prowess by a successful assault on the walls. The captives were illustrious and the spoil prodigious.[4]

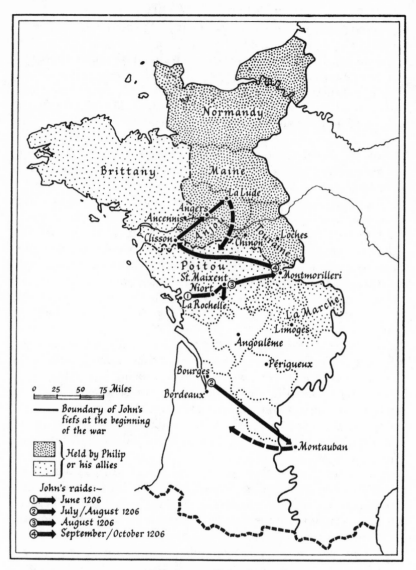

VII. John's expedition in 1206

In August he returned to Niort and led a raid across Poitou to the border with Berry. At this point the viscount of Thouars, that weathercock of fortune, whom Philip had made seneschal of Poitou, returned to his old allegiance, a sure sign of the success of John's manœuvres. This brought northern Poitou into his hands and gave him confidence to try a raid into Anjou. He struck across the border where Poitou, Brittany, and Anjou meet, and came up to the Loire at Port Alaschert. There, so the chronicler of the abbey of St Aubin at Angers relates, 'he made the sign of the Cross over the water with his hand, and trusting to the help of God forded the stream with all his host, which is a marvellous thing to tell, and such as was never heard of in our time.'[1] On 8 September and for a week following he held court at Angers, the home of his ancestors. He went on as far north as La Lude on the border of Maine, but then turned back for Poitou. He had made his gesture to his traitorous vassals, but he did not wish to challenge the full might of the French king.

Philip, however, was alarmed: he gathered his army and marched to the Poitevin border, but made no attempt to recover the territories that had been lost to him beyond it. He was still digesting Normandy and wanted time to complete his meal: he would rather stabilise the situation in the south than involve himself with the fickle Poitevins. John's success had been impressive, but he was not keen to press his good fortune too far. So both kings were ready for a truce and concluded one on 26 October to last for two years. The situation was frozen as it then existed: each king was to retain the allegiances he then held for the two-year period, and any dispute between them was to be settled by a truce supervision committee of four barons jointly appointed. Trade and communications were to proceed without let or hindrance.[2]

John had good reason to be satisfied with the success of his venture: Poitou was largely in his hands once more and his mother's inheritance made secure. He had, moreover, gained valuable experience of mounting a seaborne operation, and had seen at first hand what the situation in Aquitaine required. His readiness to conclude a long truce suggests that he realised that great as his effort had been a greater one was needed if the lost provinces were to be recovered.

On the whole it was probably as well for John that he pursued limited objectives and was content with a small measure of success in 1206. The problems of politics and logistics involved in Poitevin operations were formidable. England was the source of adequate resources if he could persuade the barons to release them for his use, but the battlefield was at the far end of a long sea journey. The navigation of Ushant was a perilous voyage at the best of times, but there was now added to it the dangers of a hostile coast. The mere ferrying of supplies would involve armed convoys; the shipment of a large army would be a naval operation of the first magnitude. Command of the Channel and of the approaches to La Rochelle or Bordeaux were essential before an expedition could even be contemplated, and there was always the danger of a French counter-attack on England while the king was on the western seas. The king's small administrative service had laboured manfully to organise the musters of 1205 and 1206, but it was overtaxed: several officials were responsible for half a dozen different jobs at once. Operations on the scale necessary for success would have to be planned carefully. It would all cost an unprecedented amount of money. England was rich and prospering, but the traditional sources of crown revenue were inadequate to the king's needs. The inner history of the reign, writ large in the records, but barely perceived by the chroniclers, is the attempt of John to gear the country to military enterprises novel both in magnitude and character.

5. THE BIRTH OF THE ROYAL NAVY

Mastery of the seaways to Poitou was the most obvious of the new tasks forced upon the English government, for the country had at this time no naval tradition. By the time of William the Conqueror the Normans had little interest in sea-faring: though still wanderers and land-hunters all over Europe, they had forsaken the ship for the horse. If, in the late 12th century, an expert on naval affairs or a skilled navigator were wanted he was fetched from the Mediterranean.

The existence of the Channel, of course, obliged rulers of England and Normandy to some limited concern with the sea. Kings kept ships at their disposal. Henry II had at least one royal galley, long, low, and slim, and called an *esnecca* (which betrays the origin of its lines in the Scandinavian ships of Viking days).* This was

* The Norse ships were called *derki*, dragons, or *snekkjur*, sea-serpents.

always ready to put to sea for swift passages by the king across the Channel. In addition there were always vessels on hand for conveying the king's messengers and officials, his hunting gear, household effects, and administrative paraphernalia.[1] These in no sense constituted a fleet but were the maritime equivalent of the administration's carts and pack-horses. In addition the Crown could call on the services of vessels belonging to the Cinque Ports. William the Conqueror had required from the seaports of Hastings, Dover, Hythe, Romney, and Sandwich a maritime service equivalent to the knight service due from military vassals. Hence the leading men of the Cinque Ports were more like barons than burgesses, and Henry II on occasion so addressed them. They were traditionally required to provide fifty-seven ships for a service of fifteen days in the year, an adequate time for the simple needs of the Norman kings, but insufficient for the more extensive operation of their Angevin successors. When kings required a fleet, as Henry II did to go to Ireland in 1171, or Richard to go on crusade, they hired or commandeered merchant ships.[2]

To Richard perhaps goes the credit for first perceiving the value of maritime operations in support of land forces. No one who had been to the Holy Land could fail to learn it. Richard is said to have built in 1196 seventy *cursoria*, vessels that were seaworthy but primarily designed for river work, to assist in the defence of the Seine valley. It was these which John had used in 1203 in his abortive attempt to relieve Château Gaillard.[3] At the same time Richard felt the need for a permanent depot on the English coast whence supplies might be conveniently ferried to the continent. The site he selected was a good natural harbour on a barren bit of an island in the Solent, which shared the double high tides of the neighbouring port of Southampton, was easy of access from the royal manors in Hampshire and Wiltshire, and was under the wing of the royal castle at Porchester. The men whom he encouraged to take up plots of land on the new site laid the foundations of what was to become the naval dockyard and thriving town of Portsmouth.[4]

Richard, however, had nothing that can be called a naval policy. It was the loss of the northern coast of France and the transformation of England into an island fortress that made a clear policy imperative. John's government responded promptly and efficiently to the challenge. Even before Normandy had been lost, John had shown a grasp of the value of economic sanctions and naval operations. In 1201 he put an embargo on exports of wheat to Flanders to persuade the Flemings to return to their old allegiance, and fined merchants who contravened his orders.[1] Trade with France was not prohibited, perhaps for fear of economic repercussions, but it was subjected to a levy of a fifteenth of the value of the cargo, and wool could only be exported by special licence. Every port was instructed to appoint six or more of its wisest and wealthiest inhabitants, together with one man in holy orders, and a man of knightly status to assess and levy the tax.[2] In July 1202 John sent from Rouen to the barons of the Cinque Ports to bid them prevent Philip bringing up supplies by sea to his siege of Arques:

'We are given to understand', he wrote, 'that the king of France is fitting out ships to bring victuals by sea to his army at Arques. And we therefore command and enjoin you by the bounden fealty to us, that as you love us and we trust in you, and as you have sworn to do us good service, you so guard the sea that no provisions may reach him there by sea; and we will closely guard the land so that none or very little shall reach him that way; and so act and conduct yourselves in this matter that we may be bounden to you and your heirs for ever. And if you see two of our galleys on the sea, speak with those who are in command of them, for they will be ready to do what you shall point out to them as seeming expedient for our honour. Witness ourself at Rouen, 21st day of July.'[3]

All this suggests a close control of shipping from English ports, a grasp of the value of sea-power, and the presence of royal warships cruising off the coast. What we do not see before the loss of Normandy is the presence of any considerable war fleet for offensive operations: the king was still dependent on the ship service of the Cinque Ports. This was not, of course, to be despised and John was careful to ratify the Cinque Ports' privileges by solemn charter in 1205, but it was in some ways as antiquated as the feudal army was on land. What John needed was the maritime equivalent of his mercenary troops, and he soon set about getting it. By 1204 he had forty-five galleys on call round the coast from King's Lynn to Gloucester, and a flotilla of five in Ireland, under four commanders.[4] From 1205 onwards the records tell of ships being built and fitted out specially for the king's use. The sum of £368 was spent on building galleys at London that year, and Alan Bolifrey, on the king's order, supervised the construction of eight large transports.[1] It is impossible to know how many ships were built for him altogether, but what is certain is that once a royal navy was started it expanded rapidly. In three years from 1209 to 1212 twenty new galleys and thirty-four other vessels were launched for the king. A new mole was constructed at Portsmouth to contain them, and sheds were erected on it to store the tackle during the winter months.[2]

The galleys (*galeae*) were the principal warships, equipped with sail but fitted also with oars for speed and independence of the wind. Oars were ordered by the thousand at a time, and cloth for sails by the thousand ells. The rowers with their oars took up much of the space in the holds of the galleys, so we meet with other vessels in the king's service for passengers and cargo. There were what the accounts call simply 'ships' (*naves*), the ordinary square-sailed merchantmen, and 'busses' (*buzae*), slow and heavy but capacious transports. Both of these could be fitted with wooden 'castles' at bow and stern (the forecastle and poop of later days) and platforms in the rigging for the discharge of missiles in naval engagements.

Of course the king did not expect to provide all the ships for a major expedition. He still had to rely on commandeered merchantmen. The Patent Rolls show him at work for the expedition of 1206:

'The king to the constable of Southampton, and William Fortin, and William de Langetot, greeting.

We command you as you love us, our honour, and the peace of our kingdom, and regard your own safety and welfare, to hasten immediately on receipt of these letters without let or delay to the ports of Southampton, Kilhaven, Christchurch, and Yarmouth, and the other ports in your bailiwicks, and detain for service all vessels fit for passage that are able to carry eight or more horses. Man them with able seamen at our cost and send them to Portsmouth, so that without hindrance they be there on the eve of Pentecost, or if possible earlier. And be careful that each ship be provided with ladders and hurdles. And remember to enrol the names of the owners of the ships and the number of seamen in each ship, also the number of horses which each ship can conveniently carry. And if any ship be laden with merchandise or anything else, cause it immediately to be unloaded and taken into our service, at our livery, as aforesaid.

And in the same hour that these letters reach you dispatch, night and day, to each individual port, trusty messengers to the fleets to transact in your stead whatever business you shall be unable to direct in person. And let this matter be executed with such diligence that we may not be losers by your default. And intimate to the inhabitants of every port that if they fail to act in this matter according to your orders, they alone shall be held answerable. And write to us at London on the Sunday next after the Ascension of Our Lord concerning the steps you have taken in this business, retaining these letters as your warrant.

Witness Geoffrey earl of Essex at Lambeth, 29 April.'

Here is the government of King John acting with typical energy, directness, and despatch.[1] 'Hasten immediately', work 'night and day'. This is the authentic tone of Angevin government, the trademark of King John.

The swift emergence of England as a maritime power in these years demanded, and received, administrative rethinking. Orders to sheriffs and bailiffs were all very well, but operations of the new scale required a continuous guiding hand. The problem was to superintend the expanding royal navy, see to its upkeep, fitting out, and manning, and to integrate it, when an expedition was contemplated, with the Cinque Ports' fleet and the impressed merchantmen. The names of William of Wrotham and Reginald of Cornhill recur frequently in connection with naval matters from the earliest days of the reign. From 1198 William of Wrotham had been head of an organisation for taxing the produce of the tin mines in Devon and Cornwall, and since part of his duties was the shipment of tin abroad he early gained experience of maritime affairs. Reginald of Cornhill, sheriff of Kent, came of a merchant family and was a close relative of the Henry of Cornhill who had been the organising genius of Richard's crusading fleet. In 1204 they, and the obscure William of Furnell, were put in charge of the levy of a fifteenth on cargoes for France, and appear as 'chief keepers of the ports' issuing licences for the export of wool. Wrotham and Cornhill, together with William Marsh and John la Warr, were responsible for the flotillas of galleys dispersed around the coasts in 1204. Soon William of Wrotham emerges as the chief expert with overriding authority in all maritime matters. He commissioned ships for the king's service and paid for them directly out of the issues of the tin mines, recruited and paid the sailors who manned them, kept a close watch on shipping through his officers in all the ports, and issued licences for the shipment of many commodities. The cargoes seized from enemy ships were sold by him and the profits passed through his accounts. When the sheriff of Southampton had to build the new mole at Portsmouth, William of Wrotham went down to tell him how to do it. He exercised, furthermore, a jurisdiction in maritime disputes.[1] By 1208, in fact, he is controlling an organisation that is similar in all essentials to that which by the 14th century is being called the admiralty.

It was, however, purely an administrative appointment that William of Wrotham held: he did not take the ships to sea. The post of Admiral of the Fleet, if one may antedate the use of the term, fell to John's half-brother, William Longsword, earl of Salisbury. Novel uses were found for the fleet: in 1210 during an expedition to Ireland, John sent a detachment of six galleys under Geoffrey Lucy 'to search out pirates'. But if we can pick a date when Britannia began to rule the waves, it is very likely 1212. The fleet was then fully in command of the Channel and its approaches, and could spare twenty galleys to harry the Welsh coast. Throughout the summer of that year French merchantmen fell to English warships as prizes; Wrotham disposed of thirteen; three, laden with cloth, were taken in the port of Barfleur itself.[2] In May of the following year the navy was for the first time called upon to save England from invasion. It fell upon the French fleet at Damme and so crippled it that King Philip had to abandon his plans. 'Never since the days of King Arthur', says the biographer of William Marshal, 'did so much booty come into England.'[3] It is surprising that a nation so proud of its naval history has not honoured King John more.

6. JOHN'S METHODS IN ADMINISTRATION

The development of an administration for coping with the necessity of a navy reveals at once the adaptability and inventiveness of

John's government – seizing upon existing offices and developing them to new purposes. This is not the only interesting thing about his government. He who studies the development of royal administration will find himself going back with some assurance to the beginning of John's reign, but further back he will grope uncertainly. This may seem at first glance the result of an accident – the survival of systematic collections of Chancery documents dating from that time. There is more to it, though, than the mere chance that fire, damp, and hungry rats have made away with earlier collections. It seems in fact much more likely that the beginning of John's reign is the moment when the systematic keeping of archives by the Chancery starts. As far back as the early 14th century men interested in the royal archives found themselves in much the same position as a modern historian: clerks in the royal service compiling lists and abstracts of the, by then, almost unmanageable mass of archive material, began to find themselves at a loss when they took their researches beyond 1199. They came across undated charters and had to list them as 'believed to be of the reign of Henry II.' By contrast they found from the first years of John's reign neat copies of dated charters on rolls of parchment. Henry II's charters were undated because they were merely a written record, very often made some time after the actual event, of arrangements made orally. This is readily seen from the words with which they open: 'Know that I *have* given and by this charter confirmed . . .' It is only in the next generation that men come to think of a grant as actually conveyed by the document that recorded it and liked to have the date clearly recorded. What we see in John's reign is the clear emergence of a conscious bureaucracy, punctilious about its method and records. John himself had something to do with this development, so we must look at it more closely. This is not merely a matter of administrative history, for the personality of John is writ large on the records that survive, and we can get closer to him there than through the pages of any chronicle.[1]

The government of England at the beginning of the 13th century was at once remarkably sophisticated and curiously primitive, having developed institutions and methods that put it ahead of contemporary secular governments in western Europe, yet still wedded to conceptions that take us back to the earliest monarchy of England. The king governed as well as ruled and had a multitude of agents to help him. His will was made effective in the furthest reaches of the realm by local officials ranging from the man who was appointed to collect a customs duty in a certain port, to the man who was responsible for the royal interests in a whole county or group of counties. There were sheriffs, constables, coroners, bailiffs, stewards, reeves, and foresters. These were directed and controlled by officials who formed a central 'civil service', operating as the administrative section of the king's Household, as distinct, that is, from the purely domestic side of the Household. The mouthpiece of the king was his Chancery, the secretariat which expressed his will so far as it was desired to do this in writing. Its head was the chancellor, who kept the Great Seal. The royal revenue was handled by the Treasury and the Exchequer, the one dealing with the actual cash that came in, storing it and dispensing it as instructed, and the other dealing with the audit side. There was a corps of judges, learned and experienced in what was often referred to as 'the law and custom of England', and many temporarily appointed judges who helped man the teams that went on circuit round the county courts.

Several of the organs of this administration had reached that high stage of development at which rational reflection upon their methods becomes both desirable and possible. About 1190 a legal treatise was written called *De Legibus et Conseutudinibus Angliae*. Ranulph Glanville, justiciar from 1180 to 1189, is credited with producing it. It is possible, though, that it comes from the pen of one of his pupils and successors as justiciar, Hubert Walter or Geoffrey FitzPeter, both of whom were high in King John's service. It maps with admirable clarity the jungle of customary procedure in the judicial courts, and is an invaluable handbook to the 'writs of course' which Henry II and his advisers had developed to initiate swift actions in commonly recurring types of cases. It is evidence at once of the maturity of the legal system and the intellectual qualities of its chief practitioners.[1]

The Exchequer too had its handbook, the *Dialogus de Scaccario*, written by Richard FitzNigel, bishop of London and treasurer of the Exchequer from about 1160 to 1198. It describes in its first section the organisation and numerous personnel of the office, their duties and perquisites, and explains how the accounts of the sheriffs were audited and recorded at the Easter and Michaelmas sessions, how the coin was assayed, and receipts given in the form of tallies. In the second section it describes the sources and methods of collecting royal revenue and the processes of collecting debts. The Exchequer had to perform far more than the mere mechanical operations of revenue collecting and accounting: its chief officers had to determine judicially what was due to the king and treated the office as a court of law.

The English Exchequer had long been the wonder and envy of Europe. The record of a Michaelmas audit, a Pipe Roll as it is called, survives from as early as 1130. Its business had since then increased much in complexity and its methods had developed accordingly, but it was already in John's time very conscious of a weight of tradition, and Richard FitzNigel is not far behind his 17th century successors in his regard for the 'ancient course'. About the middle of Henry II's reign its personnel had become so numerous and its twice yearly sessions so lengthy that it was decided to give it a more or less permanent abode, and it was established in the royal palace at Westminster that King William Rufus had built. It was in a turret there overlooking the Thames that Richard FitzNigel sat on the day that the idea of writing his treatise came to him. The Exchequer officials rented houses close at hand from the abbot of Westminster, and so helped to give the area its first beginnings as the administrative centre of the country.[1] It was only some time after the Exchequer had taken up residence at Westminster that it came to be thought of as a place at all; hitherto it had been a session – the king's financial officers in session to receive in audience the Crown's debtors. We are in danger of a serious anachronism if we think of it as a 'department of state' much before the reign of John.

No treatise was written on Chancery procedure, but it also had developed to a high level of efficiency, excelled only by the grander purposes of the Papal Chancery. While the latter was perfecting the formulae of its papal bulls, impressive by their size and grandiloquence, the English Chancery was working in the other direction, cutting out all superfluities of expression and concentrating on evolving documents that expressed the king's will explicitly with the minimum of wasted effort and parchment. Even so, the Chancery's admirable brevity could hardly keep pace with the expansion of the royal business it had to conduct, particularly with the development of the writs of course initiating actions in the royal courts: the skins of sheep being bred in increasing numbers in England in the 12th century were put to good use for parchment, and Poland did a lucrative trade in wax for seals. Strictly speaking the Chancery was part of the chapel of the royal Household. That it should have been this in origin is not as strange as it might seem for men trained in the service of the Church were, until the 12th century, the only people who normally practised the skills of reading and writing. In Anglo-Saxon days the king would call upon one of his chaplains to pen a document when one had to be written. By the time of the Norman Conquest the English kings had developed a regular secretariat, but still in the days of John's great-grandfather the Chancery did its work in a corner of the hall where the king was staying, closed off by a screen. Indeed it was from the screen (*cancella*) that the chancellor derived his name. It is an indication, though, of how important the office had become by John's time, that on the day of his coronation he appointed as chancellor the most exalted clerk in the kingdom, Hubert Walter, archbishop of Canterbury. 'We have', remarked a caustic bystander who remembered Thomas Becket, 'seen a chancellor become archbishop, but this is the first time that we have seen or heard of an archbishop becoming chancellor.'[1]

What the records of John's time seem to reflect, if we glance at them cursorily, is the existence of more or less independent departments of state, handling the chief business of government, executive, financial, and judicial. The departments are indeed there in form, and it is convenient to talk of them as such, but the outward appearance is deceptive, and departmentalism was flatly contradictory to the practice of the day. It might seem obvious to any modern bureaucrat that the increasing complexity and wide ramifications of the royal business demanded specialised departments, but any tendency of practical problems of administration to draw men to think this way in the time of John was inhibited by the dominating administrative conception of the day. This was that all aspects of government were in the king's hands personally. Government may have increased in range and complexity but it had not changed its nature: fundamentally John should govern as his Anglo-Saxon predecessors had done, by going about the country and seeing to it himself. He needed help, of course, because of the burden of the work; but his helpers were not so much specialised officials as aides-de-camp in his G.H.Q.

Government was still basically unitary in conception: even when the Exchequer had in practice 'gone out of court' (as men put it) and taken up residence at Westminster, it is still thought of as being part of the king's Household (the *Curia Regis*) – it was not an independent department but still part of the itinerating court which had happened to be left behind at Westminster because it was too cumbersome and inconvenient to take along.

Day by day, when in England, John traversed his realm seeing what had to be done, consulting with his advisers, and instructing his Chancery staff to set the necessary machinery in motion. Nor was he concerning himself solely with a general oversight of the administration, with high matters of state, and general questions of policy: the most ordinary business of government was equally a part of his concern. As he journeyed he would receive payment of debts, hear pleas of robbery or rape and the most mundane of civil actions, and dictate letters personally about ordinary administrative matters. His helpers might handle a lot of routine business, but the king was equally ready to do it himself. There was no question of a formal division of labour: what the king handled himself and what he left to his assistants was largely a matter of time and opportunity.

Similarly, just as the king was ready to handle all aspects and all grades of business, so his officials, at least in the higher echelons, were expected to have a general competence. Their personal abilities might cut them out for special responsibilities, but they did not become narrow specialists. Take William of Wrotham as an example: he acquired special responsibility for naval administration with the title of Keeper of the King's Ports and Galleys, but he remained warden of the stanneries, helped to supervise the currency reform of 1205, ran the mints at London and Canterbury, was keeper of the revenues of the vacant bishopric of Bath, and was a circuit judge in 1206. In addition he was archdeacon of Taunton and a canon of Wells. No doubt much of the actual work of the offices he held was performed by a deputy, but he was the man responsible and had to know what he was about.

As with men so with 'departments'. The Exchequer at Westminster was no mere financial agency. It was a detached portion of the Household that remained representative of the whole Household. It had its own secretarial staff that could act as a detachment of Chancery. One could get a perfectly valid charter drawn up and sealed there, for the Exchequer held a duplicate of the Great Seal. One could get a hearing before royal justices there too. Some of the normal Exchequer business was judicial in nature and its chief officers were known indifferently as 'barons' or 'justices', but they were perfectly competent to handle non-financial judicial business. Indeed the king expressly said in 1201 that cases settled before the justices at Westminster had equal validity with those held 'before the king himself or his chief justice'.[1] Sitting in a non-financial capacity the justices at Westminster would sometimes be referred to as the justices of the Bench (*de banco*) to distinguish them from the justices with the king (*coram rege*). In the course of time the former will become the Court of Common Pleas and the latter the King's Bench division, but one has to be careful not to antedate any separation of function. Of course the justices at Westminster might find that a case before them presented problems that only the king himself could decide, and refer it to the itinerating court; but this does not affect the general principle that the Westminster Bench was not a subordinate court dealing with only a limited class of pleas. The justices accompanying the king also had to hold up cases until they could take his advice or until he came to sit with them personally.

The volume of business handled by the Household detachment at Westminster tended to expand or contract according to whether the king was in England or not. When he went abroad the Exchequer would absorb all the other elements of the Household that he did not take with him, and become the sole central administrative authority, under the direction of the justiciar, who was the king's *alter ego* for administrative matters. When the king was in England, on the other hand, it was open to him to limit the Westminster detachment's competence. John had a penchant for witnessing the judicial duels in which, in the manner of the day, conflicting statements by parties in a case were put to the test, and he sometimes required that all such cases be put before him. He might, as he did in 1209, shut down the Westminster Bench altogether and concentrate pleas in the itinerating Household. But in general the offices at Westminster were the Household in little, the administrative equivalent of a chapel-of-ease.[2]

To some extent the preservation of this system in the face of inevitable pressures towards departmentalism reflects a shortage of personnel of the requisite ability. Lacking sufficient men the king had to extract every ounce out of those he had, and narrow specialisms were at a discount. If the men seconded to the Exchequer at Westminster because of their financial acumen had the ability to cope with other kinds of business, then let them. It also reflects, though, King John's determination to rule as his father and great-grandfather had done, personally and directly, despite the crushing burden of business that royal government now entailed. Even if he had to dole out portions of the work to personal assistants, he would keep his hand in at everything, joining his justices on the bench, sitting in with his financial experts at sessions of the Exchequer. Departmentalism was resisted not so much because John set his face against it, as because he inhibited its development by personally ignoring it, and by using his hired help in a way that ignored it too. It was indeed a *tour de force* of personal monarchy. It required unbounded energy and universal competence. John had it; but once his dynamic personality was removed from the scene departmentalism proceeded rapidly.

John's personal concern with even the minutiae of administration was all the more remarkable in that it was largely unnecessary. The English administration had learned to run itself. It had been obliged to. The union of England with extensive continental dominions had kept the king at a distance for long periods. Henry II was out of England for two-thirds of his reign; Richard had visited it for only five months in nine and a half years. There were always many matters for which the king's *fiat* was essential: the disposal of lands and castles, the appointment of bishops and abbots, the resolution of knotty problems of law which custom did not seem to cover. Messengers hurried to and fro. But for all the routine matters, and for many that were not routine but which the king had given authority to his delegates to determine, the administrative machine operated under the justiciar, who used the Exchequer seal for solemn documents and his own for administrative writs.

It could break down: politics and personal animosities had interfered with some of its operations sadly in the days of Longchamp, but it had been quickly restored to order by William of Coutances and Hubert Walter without the personal intervention of the king. It was efficient and impartial. William of Newburgh had been moved to remark on the collection of the ransom money for Richard that 'No one was able to say, such and so great am I, pray have me excused.'[1] Its respectability should not perhaps be overestimated: a certain amount of petty corruption and venality were inseparable from the operations of government until very modern times. The abbey of Abingdon slipped £5 a year into the pocket of the sheriff of Berkshire 'that he would deal leniently with the abbot's men.'[2] Many little tyrannies came to light only when their perpetrator was safely removed by death from the possibility of seeking vengeance. But the royal ministers were aware of the problem and tried hard to combat it. Powerful commissions of enquiry were sent out now and again, usually at intervals of four years, to investigate the operations of local officials. The Crown could hit hard when it detected or suspected malpractice: twenty sheriffs were pitched out of office in 1170.[3] The Crown, in short, had developed an administrative machine that could run itself without much maintenance or excessive grinding of gears. Gervase of Canterbury felt bound to say that England was very well governed while John was fighting on the continent in 1202.[4]

It was open to the king, therefore, to continue to leave the business of government entirely in the hands of his justiciar and chancellor; but this was not John's way. Coming to England briefly for coronation in May 1199 and staying for little more than a fortnight he appointed a new chancellor and shook up the Chancery organisation. Returning at the end of February 1200, staying for two months, and taking stock of his new kingdom for the first time, he had 119 judicial pleas put before him; and even when he crossed the Channel again he sent instructions to his justices or had them hold pleas until he returned.[5] He was as fascinated with the daily business of governing as his brother Richard was with war. The royal records give the lie direct to Wendover's readiness to believe that John was idle and insouciant. Ralph of Coggeshall knew better: John, he says, 'ruled indefatigably'.[6]

John's impact on the administration was rather like that of an energetic young director appointed to the board of an old established and rather conservative business. Indeed the comparison is a very close one. Yet John was not so brash as to suppose that he knew all there was to know about the business, nor to imagine that youthful energy was a good substitute for wise old heads.

His first move, indeed, was to bring back into the royal service as chancellor the finest administrative brain that even the brilliant 12th century had seen, that of Hubert Walter. No one living had a firmer grasp of the intricacies of royal government, yet even in old age his mind was adaptable and fecund with suggestions for coping with new problems. He was still chancellor on the day of his death in 1205. Matthew Paris would have it that when John heard that his great servant was no more, he turned to the by-standers and said, 'By God's feet, now for the first time am I king and lord of England.' This was pure invention by Matthew Paris; but in putting it in his chronicle as a clever remark in line with what he mistakenly imagined John's character to be, he was forgetting that Hubert Walter was chancellor because John asked him to be, and that he remained chancellor because John wanted him. Perhaps the most remarkable thing about this anec-dote is that it has been accepted as perfectly true by many his-torians. It only goes to show how powerfully traditional concep-tions can inhibit critical faculties.[1] Hubert Walter was certainly a man whose word carried irresistible authority. The royal justices will defer to his judgement; his advice will persuade John to call off an expedition.[2] It is possible that John bridled sometimes against Hubert's caution and restraint – he would not have been a true Angevin if he had not – but as with his father, his judgement was even stronger than his temper, and Hubert stayed in office, the indispensable adviser of his still young master.

The first results of the energetic new broom sweeping vigor-ously under the guidance of an experienced old hand were seen on the day of the coronation. The king, acting on the suggestion, he said, of Hubert Walter, issued a 'constitution' regulating the fees payable at the Chancery for the issue of documents under the Great Seal. Charges had been exorbitant under his predecessor, he said, and he wished to restore the scale of Henry II's day. For instance, the cost of having a charter of confirmation prepared was reduced from £9 5s. to 18s. 4d., while an ordinary letter of pro-tection was to cost no more than 2s. No doubt this was a gesture of reform calculated to appeal to the aristocracy, the greater churchmen, and the merchant classes, who commonly sought such documents; but it reveals John's immediate concern with the way his bureaucracy operated. Moreover, the low charges prepared the way for insisting that no charter should be accepted as evidence in the royal courts unless it had been confirmed by the new king, without incurring the opprobrium of doing so only as a means of levying a heavy tax on title deeds.[1] This insistence helped to curb forgeries, and enabled the administration to build up collections of copies of charters granted by John's predecessors, but unrecorded in the royal archives. The earliest surviving Charter Roll is in consequence, from the first year of John's reign, tangible evidence of the new precision and respect for the value of archives as an aid to efficient administration.

Actually copies of all sorts of documents as well as charters were put on what are called the *Rotuli Chartarum* for the earliest years of the reign. But once the principle of regular enrolment of outgoing documents had been established, a clear mind got to work differentiating the classes of documents, and so within a short time we have separate rolls for Letters Patent and Letters Close.[2] The corollary of archive keeping was an archive keeper, and we first hear of one in John's reign – William Cucuel. John knew him well and hailed him personally in a postscript to an ordinary official letter: 'Salute vos Willelme Kukku Wel.'[3]

7. PERSONAL GOVERNMENT

John's determination to rule personally and directly kept him busy through many of his waking hours as he traversed the country on ceaseless journeyings. A few days here, a few days there, round and round he went. Travelling about from manor to manor was the ancient habit of all lords. Medieval society was far from static: certainly the peasantry was static, but the upper classes were continually on the move. The mother of this restlessness was necessity: in the days when rents were tendered in kind it was often simpler to go to eat them where they were produced than to transport the food itself. In point of fact the royal food rents had long been commuted to money payments. Richard FitzNigel could just remember peasants from royal estates bringing victuals into the Household before Henry I sent commissioners round to value them in terms of coin.[4] But old ways of life persist, and the king still journeyed the rounds of his manors and castles. There were solid advantages of personal supervision of the royal estates and forests in this. Renovations and additions to royal castles commonly follow closely upon a royal visit. A farm here would be restocked, one there put out for rent. Moreover, it brought the king into contact with his barons and enabled him to size up the situation in the country at first hand.

King John had nowhere that could be called a home in any recognisable modern sense. Nowadays a sovereign will have four or five royal residences visited more or less regularly at certain seasons of the year. Even the most frequently visited of John's residences must be numbered at a score or more, and they saw him for only a few days at a time. He had London quarters at the Tower, and a palace at Westminster. A pre-eminence must be assigned to the castles at Windsor, Winchester, Nottingham, Ludgershall, and Marlborough for special apartments were kept ready for the king there; but any of the sixty-odd other castles which were more or less permanently in royal hands could expect to have to put him up for a night or two, and royal lodgings there were kept, if not in a state of perpetual readiness, at least in a state of repair. Then again there were unfortified royal residences, hunting lodges mostly, at Bere Regis and Gillingham in Dorset, Freemantle in Hampshire, Clarendon in Wiltshire, Feckhenham in Worcestershire, Brill in Buckinghamshire, Geddington in Northamptonshire, Clipston and Kingshaugh in Nottinghamshire.[1]

Customary as it is, in historical novels especially, to see a medieval king in the great hall of a castle in the evening, or entertaining guests at a hunting lodge, it is just as appropriate to think of him picnicking by the roadside, rather formally no doubt, as he went his incessant way. The king's Household, for much of its time, was a cavalcade of horsemen, pack-animals, carts, and wagons. The king's chapel is no quiet place of worship for it goes in the leather pouches of a packhorse. The king's featherbed, with its linen sheets, rugs, and fur coverings, the rich hangings of his bedchamber, his portable urinal, and his bathtub go with him. His wardrobe (*garderoba*), consisting of strong chests holding his robes and personal valuables, ready cash, and important documents, travelled in one or more 'long-carts'. His kitchen equipment went in two one-horsed *carettes*.

A host of officials ministered to the domestic needs of the travelling household. Besides the dignified servants like the Seneschal, the Chamberlain, the Marshal who organised the bodyguard, and the Butler who brought in victuals, there were intermediate men of standing like the Master Dispenser of the Bread, the Master Dispenser of the Larder, the Clerk of household expenses, and a horde of lesser servants who had their place in the almonry, the hall, the butlery, the pantry, the kitchens. There was the Usher of the Chamber who made the king's bed, Florence who washed his clothes, Ralph who tailored them, and William the bathman who dried them when they were wet. There were something in the order of a hundred and fifty persons of dignity to be given presents at Christmas time, and a numberless retinue who were glad to pick up scraps.[1]

It is unlikely that the king and his intimate companions remained with the baggage train while it was on the move. Heavy carts could not make much more than two and a half miles per hour, and bad road surfaces could reduce them to a crawl. A river swollen by heavy rains could hold them up for several days.[2] The great lack in medieval communications was sufficient bridges. The roads were perfectly adequate, however, for well-mounted horsemen. An express messenger would expect to cover 35–40 miles in a day. John frequently shifted his court 20–30 miles in a day and sometimes more.[3] One suspects that the heavy baggage was sent by a direct route along the projected itinerary while John and a few horsemen went off to stay with a sheriff, a baron, or an abbot, and rejoined the main party later. While the wagons went to Nottingham he would ride off to his lodges at Clipston or Geddington. The Household might be set up at Marlborough or Winchester while the king went hunting at Freemantle or inspected his ships at Porchester. The Household was, in fact, the steadily moving focus of a still more widely roving king. It was Carlisle on 25 June 1212 while John himself was being entertained at the justiciar's manor house at Ditton. We know that he was there because he raided the justiciar's flower garden and sent his mistress a chaplet of roses by the hand of Philip Marc's groom.[4]

It was not easy to keep the itinerating Household supplied with ready cash from the Treasury in the Tower of London. John would send down to the Exchequer officials at Westminster, and Robert of Winton or Peter of Ely would come riding back with it, escorted by a small troop of cavalry. Silver pennies were the only currency in use: the 'pounds', 'shillings', and 'marks' that one meets with in the records were accounting terms only. The pennies were packed in barrels or £100 sacks. Sometimes there was a delay because the Exchequer itself was waiting for cash to come in and had not enough on hand to send to the king. What seemed ridiculous was that money owed to the king was going up from say Dorset to London, while the king was waiting at Dorchester for an Exchequer draft, having no money to pay his expenses. The Household, flexible in its methods, and being not greatly en- amoured of centralisation, eventually thought of a way round this difficulty. The simple solution was to collect money direct into the Chamber which handled the king's privy purse, as the court moved about, and to give the debtor a chit for presentation at the Exchequer.

The idea of local collection was supplemented by that of local depositories. It had in the past been found useful to have forward dumps of cash in time of war. The shipments of English coin going out to the king in Normandy in 1202 by-passed the Norman Ex- chequer at Caen and went straight into safe-deposit in Rouen. Similarly in England, while the continental expeditions of 1205 and 1206 were being prepared, money was collected into Exeter and Porchester. Bristol became an important provincial treasury in March 1204 when the 'Treasure of Ireland' was brought over from Dublin and lodged there. For convenience when the king was heading north, large sums were deposited with the castellan of Nottingham. In 1207 such provincial treasuries were put on a regular footing. Bristol, Devizes, Marlborough, Corfe, Exeter, Nottingham, Salisbury, and Rochester received sizeable drafts from the central Treasury, and added to it any surplus that the Chamber collected locally, to hold until the king had need of it.[1]

Inevitably this peripatetic life was a hard one. The itinerary had to be planned many days ahead, if only to allow the Butler chance to have wine brought up from the cellars at Bristol and Southampton, and the Baker to have flour laid in at a castle on the way against the king's coming. With so many mouths to feed, little delay on account of bad weather could be allowed. Henry II had been frugal in his habits, and seems not to have cared much for ease and comfort. John was not given to extravagance, but he liked to live more liberally than his father had done. The rigours of living in temporary quarters out of chests and boxes were mitigated to some extent by sumptuous clothing and good food. New robes at the king's gift were one of the perquisites of service in the Household, and John did not stint the money for he liked to see his men well dressed. He was more generous even than he need have been, and sent gifts of new tunics and dresses to the wives of his crossbowmen.[1] He liked his own comfort and had a dressing gown. This was a novelty, apparently, for his accountant knew no name for it and had to resort to a circumlocution: 'For the surcoat of the lord king for getting up in the night, 20 shillings.'[2] His wife had no reason to complain of her dress allowance: in 1204–5 for instance, Reginald of Cornhill, who with his London connections was useful as a purchasing agent, supplied her with 110 yards of linen, an ermine fur, eight towels, a small brass bowl, nine and a half yards of scarlet cloth, a hood of lawn, another of rich ermine, fur gowns, and robes. John did not forget his first wife, the countess of Gloucester, either, and often sent her presents of cloth and wine.[3]

The purchase of sugar, almonds, cinnamon, nutmeg, ginger, and other spices, gives evidence of rich eating. Indeed sugar appears for the first time on the accounts of any king of England in 1206. A great feast was always prepared for Christmas and Easter. For Christmas at Tewkesbury in 1204 four thousand plates and five hundred cups were purchased from the pottery works already thriving, apparently, in Staffordshire. Four hundred yards of linen 'for making napkins' were also bought. Christmas 1211 was spent at Windsor, and the constable of the castle rendered account of the payments he made for it: for 60 pounds of pepper, 18 pounds of cumin, ½ pound of galingale, 3 pounds of cinnamon, 1 pound of cloves, ½ pound of nutmeg, 2 pounds of ginger, £3 5s. 4d. For 3 blankets, 2 large knives, 24 towels, 103 yards of canvas for sacks and cloaks, 1500 cups, 1200 pitchers, 10,000 herrings, 1800 whiting, 4000 dishes, 900 haddocks, 3000 lampreys, and for cartage and work on apartments and tables, £32 12s. 11d.[4]

We do not know much about King John's recreations; but we do know that he was a connoisseur of jewels, and that he liked to read, to gamble, and to hunt. He built up a very fine collection of jewels. Some were purchased by his agents abroad; but the king also added to his collection by accepting jewels as part payment for debts owed to him. His friend, Abbot Sampson of Bury St Edmunds, bequeathed to him, on his death in 1212, his palfreys and his jewels. He well knew the king's tastes for in 1203 John had bought a sapphire and a ruby as a gift for St Edmund's shrine, but liked them so much himself that the abbot suggested that he keep them for his own lifetime. In 1205 Pope Innocent III sent him four rings, set with an emerald, a sapphire, a garnet, and a topaz, with a letter explaining their emblematic meaning. Part of the king's collection, minutely inventoried, was deposited for safe keeping (together with gold flagons, goblets, dishes, combs, clasps, crosses, candelabra, and phylacteries) at monasteries up and down the country. But John always liked to have some of his jewels with him and special chests were made for them.[1] On one occasion he lost the jewels that he wore around his neck. A man named Bartholomew found them and brought them to the king, who was so pleased that he gave him an annuity of 20s. from the rents of Berkhamsted where he was born.[2]

John had a small library that he carried round with him. He borrowed books from the abbot of Reading and lent him a copy of Pliny in return. In the spring of 1205, when the king was at Windsor, he asked Reginald of Cornhill to send him two tuns of wine and 'a history of England in French'.[3] When not reading he often liked to spend a leisure moment playing games of chance for small stakes with his half-brother William Longsword, or with his henchmen, Henry Neville and Brian Delisle.[4]

Like most medieval kings, John was addicted to the hunt. 'He haunted woods and streams and greatly delighted in the pleasure of them.'[5] In most parts of England, and especially in Surrey, Hampshire, and Wiltshire, the Severn valley, and around Rutland and Huntingdon, game were specially protected for the king over wide stretches of land. There was a great practical use behind the sport: the Household depended for its supply of fresh meat very largely on royal venison and game birds. But at the same time, hunting was clearly one of John's passionate interests. His huntsmen and falconers followed him everywhere, even overseas on campaign. He would pay a high price for good hawks: two marks to a man who brought him two goshawks from Ireland, sixty shillings to the falconers of the king of Scotland who brought him three falcons. He kept on good terms with King Sverrir Birkibein of Norway, sending him a shipload of corn occasionally, so as to ensure a good supply of the favoured Norwegian birds. A Danish merchant, Nicholas Dacus, was allowed to bring his ship into English ports and trade free of all customs duties, on condition that he supplied a hawk every time he came. John hunted sometimes on holy days and eased his conscience by liberal alms to the poor: a hundred paupers were fed at Newcastle in 1209, 'because the king went into the woods on the feast of St Mary Magdalen'; four hundred and fifty paupers were feasted at Eiswell in 1212, 'because the king went to take cranes, and he took nine, for each of which he feasted fifty paupers.'[1]

As the court journeys it takes on local colour from the sheriffs, castellans, and bailiffs who come in to see the king, stay to give him counsel, and in passing to put their names as witnesses to the documents he issues that day, and so leave us a memento of their presence. So too, barons, bishops, abbots, come in to court as it passes near them, or they will come, perhaps, from afar, seeking some grant, privilege, or concession. The king will consult them about local affairs: he will, if he chooses, take their advice about current matters of business. There was usually some business on hand concerning the disposal of baronies that had fallen vacant, or whose heir was a minor, and the allocation of castles. Many barons were apt to think that such things were the prime business of government.[2]

As the cavalcade drew into a temporary resting place there would usually be waiting for it a number of suitors with cases to plead before the royal justices, or perhaps before the king himself. Some were there because they wanted a judgement at the highest level, others because a plea begun before the royal justices in the county courts or at Westminster had been adjourned to the itinerating court. There were always some cases which were, as Henry II once put it, 'of such great moment that they could not be settled without the lord king, and others which for their doubtfulness must be put before the lord king or those acting for him.'[3] The inconvenience to litigants and witnesses of chasing an itinerating court was a grievance of long standing, and one which John and his officials recognised and tried to mitigate by adjourning a case until the king should come to the neighbourhood of the parties. John carefully planned his itineraries weeks ahead, and a litigant seeking on his own account to put a plea before the king could find out where he would be on any particular day by enquiry at the Exchequer chambers at Westminster, or, if the Exchequer were closed for vacation, at the Treasury in the Tower of London.[4]

The late 12th and 13th centuries were one of the great formative periods of English common law. There was as yet, in John's day, no principle of case-law, no strict adherence to precedents; but the royal justices were gathering and passing on to their apprentices a great store of judicial experience and wisdom from the many cases that came before them. Henry II had encouraged anyone with a grievance to have recourse to the royal courts by providing plenty of opportunity, by designing swift actions initiated by writs drawn up in common form, and by offering, at a fee, the use of a 'jury of recognition'. These juries were panels of men of standing in the neighbourhood, put on oath to answer from their local knowledge certain questions put to them by a royal justice. A commonly recurring type of case, for instance, was that of a man who complained that another was depriving him of his inheritance from his father. The plaintiff would sue out of Chancery, at a small fee, the writ called *Mort d'ancestor* which instructed the local sheriff to empanel a jury and have it view the property in question. When the case came up before the king's justices when they visited the county court, the jury would be asked the two crucial questions: was this property in the hands of the plaintiff's ancestor on the day he died, and is the plantiff his closest heir?[1] Only the Crown's authority could put a man on oath to answer in this way, so the use of a jury was a privilege to be sought only in the royal courts. The response to this and like methods of proferring royal justice was overwhelming. The king could hardly get enough justices to cope with the increasing demand.

The volume of business naturally threw up many cases which did not fall within the terms of recognised procedures, presented novel features, involved arbitrary royal action in the past, or which brought up the relations between great magnates that the visiting justices did not feel competent to determine themselves. It was the king's duty to see that every freeman in the realm had justice done to him, and therefore to resolve complications or uncertainties in the administration of the law. He might leave much of it to his advisers and the judicial experts whom he kept in his Household, or he might, if very conscious of his duty and interested enough to undertake hard work, tackle a good deal of it himself. John tackled it himself with unflagging zeal. Even the most pressing political problems, crises, and crushing misfortunes could not throw him so far off balance that he neglected personal concern with his subjects' need of justice. Even in March 1216, when the country was rift by civil war, and French invaders stood on English soil, he was commissioning four justices to hear a case at Northampton about the right to present to an ecclesiastical benefice 'according to the law and custom of England.'[1]

Nor did he concern himself solely with weighty matters or uncertainties of the law: as he journeyed he would have the justices who were with him take on ordinary cases that were waiting at the county court for the circuit judges to come their rounds. In this way he relieved the burden resulting from the vast increase in litigation, and kept in touch with the ordinary processes of his courts and the small needs of small men. He was sitting himself with his justices when the case came up of a boy who had thrown a stone and accidentally killed another. The king was 'moved to pity' says the record, and closed the case by granting a pardon. He was 'moved to pity' too when a defendant, Hawise of Winston, protested before him that her husband had conspired with the plaintiff to abuse the procedures of the court to cheat her of land she had inherited. Even when unable to sit with his justices he seems to have kept an eye on what passed during the day: Geoffrey FitzPeter and William Cantilupe allowed two parties to reach an agreement about a small piece of land, but there was not enough evidence to go on, said the king, adjourn the case until more be had. Knowing his keen interest, and respecting his advice, the justices would make a note, 'Speak with the lord king about [such and such]' in the margin of the court record. There was the case of a simpleton who confessed to a crime he could not have committed; the king, being consulted, dismissed it. Nor were the king's opinions mere off-the-cuff statements: if the case seemed to warrant it he would go into conference with his advisers, or send out for information about the 'law and custom of the realm'. We can read in the *Curia Regis Rolls* of decisions on technicalities arrived at 'by the king with the advice of his barons', or 'per consilium', and of instructions to justices to allow cases to go forward by such and such a procedure, 'unless reason and the custom of our kingdom stand in the way.'[2]

Respect for John's judicial wisdom was shown also by parties to disputes who asked him to arbitrate, and the many suitors who would come into court and ask for a hearing before the king personally. Whatever else one may say about John, there is no doubt that his royal duty of providing justice was discharged with a zeal and a tirelessness to which the English common law is greatly indebted.[1]

John's handling of his judicial machinery is the clearest evidence of his personal interest in government, and also of that flexibility which he demanded of all branches of his administration. He gathers judicial experts around him, men like Simon Pattishall and Eustace Faucunberg, but he expects them to take on the hack work of the most ordinary pleas waiting in the counties through which he passes. He will despatch them in small groups to hear cases away from the Household, or to attend to general business with no judicial import. Household staff, Exchequer officials, his general henchmen, his sheriffs, as well as barons and bishops (and abbots too) will be pressed into service to man the less exacting but laborious judicial circuits that take pleas in the county courts.[2] In short he expected all his servants to work with the energy and general competence that he displayed himself.

With such a taskmaster there was little chance of the bureaucracy becoming rigid. The danger was all the other way – of complete administrative anarchy. One man is asked to play many parts, separate portions of the Household perform similar functions. It is hard enough to describe; it was even harder to run. The danger was resisted by the careful differentiation of functions even when they were performed by the same man, and to an increasing extent by the keeping of separate records. A Westminster official hearing one kind of plea is a justice *de scaccario*, hearing another kind of plea is a justice *de banco*. Many of the earliest surviving rolls in the Public Record Office were not so much records intended for the archives as memoranda for the information of other members of the Household, and above all for the information of the king himself.

The system worked because the king's hand was firmly upon everything, and because he chose men fit to do his bidding. He picked up able men wherever he could find them, without regard to status or nationality. Many of them earned a reputation for too exclusive a devotion to the royal interests, but this was no doubt a recommendation to their master. He had no 'favourites', pampered flatterers or panderers to his vanity; not even Wendover accuses him of it. His men had to work hard if they were to keep their place, and they had to watch their step. He was generous to the faithful, but exacting and swift to punish laxity. One of the leading justices, John of Potterne, was fined a hundred marks in 1207 for allowing the parties in an appeal to reach an agreement without the king's permission. His chief forester and gaming companion, Hugh Neville, was fined a thousand marks in 1210 for allowing the bishop of Winchester to enclose a park at Taunton without official warrant. The king later let him off payment, but it must have been a sharp warning. The bishop of Winchester was in fact Peter des Roches, one of John's henchmen and close confidants, but that did not excuse misdemeanour. Peter himself was fined a tun of good wine in 1209 'because he did not remind the king to give a belt to the countess of Aumale.'[1]

On the other hand he will make presents to men who have served him well – barrels of wine, it may be, or even a hundred head of deer. When he hears that the son of his henchman William Brewer has fallen into the hands of the French, John helps to pay his ransom. When his valet Petit falls ill and has to stay behind in Somerset, the sheriff is instructed to see that he wants for nothing.[2] John was, it seems, the old-fashioned kind of paternalistic employer who is intolerant of laxity in his workers but ready to set his own shoulder to the wheel, able to talk familiarly with the lowest of them, and remember their birthdays and their babies. John's trouble was that he could not get along with the men who claimed to be his fellow directors.

8. MEETING THE COST

It was John's misfortune to reign in a period of monetary inflation. It shrank his real income at the very time that he badly needed every silver penny he could lay his hands on for the war with Philip. There was more silver available, trade was flourishing, and the standard of living was rising; but the productivity of the land was increasing only slowly, so the prices of agricultural produce went up, and labour was dear. John had to pay two shillings a day to hire a mercenary, for whom Henry II would have paid eightpence. Those who benefited from the situation were those who could call on the free labour services of villeins and put agricultural produce on the market; but hard hit were those who lived on fixed rents or who employed hired labour.[3]

Landholders were able to resist the effects of inflation on their revenues and benefit by the increased prices for agricultural produce by recovering direct control of their estates. Whereas they had formerly let out the bulk of the land they held from the Crown to tenants in return for fixed rents or services, they now went in for farming the land themselves through bailiffs and stewards. The early 13th century saw the landholding classes taking a keen interest in agricultural methods; and the more they realised the profits that could be gained from agriculture the more they resented royal agents selling off the stocks or letting the land go to waste while it was in the Crown's hands in wardship.

The king, of course, was the largest landowner in the realm and had many manors 'in desmesne' in every county.* King Henry II and Hubert Walter, as justiciar in King Richard's time, had shown the way in the better exploitation of desmesne lands, inquiring into lapsed or usurped rights, organising closer supervision and central control, restocking and rack-renting. But the full exploitation of the royal desmesne was defeated by its sheer bulk. Direct cultivation through stewards or custodians accounting for the net profits would have required a machinery for supervision and audit that the Crown could not hope to provide. It was obliged to let most of its manors out to contractors (or 'farmers' as they were known at the time) who arranged in advance to do the job for a lump sum, and pocketed whatever profit they could make in excess of that. The sheriffs were the Crown's principal contractors, and their 'farms' had been fixed early in Henry II's reign. Something was done to bring in higher revenues by withdrawing groups of manors from the sheriff's 'farm' and letting them out to individual farmers at new rates, and also by charging the sheriffs 'increments' over and above the fixed 'farm' for what remained. The charging of increments was unpopular in the country, for it was felt that the sheriffs would thereby be induced to put the screws on other sources of income, such as the profits of jurisdiction, in order to make up their losses. Clause 25 of Magna Carta sought to insist that: 'All counties shall remain at the ancient farms without any increments' – a severe and unfair limitation of the Crown's attempt to take its share of the expanding resources of the country.[1]

John's income from desmesne lands was less than it might have

* Strictly speaking the king was the only *landowner* in the realm; the barons were *landholders* from the Crown. What is referred to here as the king's land (the royal desmesne) are those manors which he retained in his own hands.

been for the reason that much had been granted away in previous reigns. A grant of land was the recognised way of rewarding
the faithful or of buying supporters, and kings were always under
great pressure to alienate their property in this way. Of course
some land fell into them by way of forfeiture for felony, or when a
tenant-in-chief died without an heir (and the land was then said
to 'escheat' to the Crown); but the net result was that John had
to manage on only two-thirds of the land that William the Conqueror had had in desmesne when Domesday Book was compiled.
John tried to arrest the process by granting 'money-fiefs', such as
the 400 marks a year granted to Robert count of Dreux in 1200,
in return for the military service of himself and three knights;
but this, while preserving the Crown's capital resources, put
extra pressure on the king's revenues.[1]

The merchant classes were one section of the community whose
rapidly expanding incomes could be tapped more easily. The
governments of Richard and John encouraged trade by the ready
sale of privileges to towns. It is no accident that many boroughs
hold charters of incorporation dating from this period, nor that
in general the merchants regarded the Angevin rulers with favour.
They could well afford the arbitrary 'tallages' by means of which
the king regularly taxed their profits.[2]

The increased revenue from the desmesne manors and towns
did not by any means meet the king's needs, indeed it probably
only just kept pace with the expansion of the Crown's administration. By careful husbandry, frugality, and the avoidance of
unnecessary war, Henry II was able to keep his treasury well
stocked; but the extravagance of Richard, the gathering tendencies
towards inflation, the hostility of King Philip, and the greater
expense of waging war at the end of the century, posed for John
a severe financial problem. The Norman kings had their armies
largely provided free of charge by their tenants-in-chief, who
jointly owed the services of approximately 6000 knights in return
for grants of land. The feudal army was no longer adequate for
contemporary military operations, however, and the money paid
in scutage and fines by way of commutation of military service
was insufficient to meet the bill for mercenaries. The practice
of taking scutage instead of military service went back almost a
century when John came to the throne, but its antiquity was an
unfortunate drag upon its productivity, for it meant that the

barons were accustomed to paying a mark on the knight's fief, and resented any attempt to push the rate up to meet the higher terms demanded by the mercenaries. King Richard, though he had been very hard pressed for money, had never ventured to ask for more than twenty shillings per knight, but John, in the first year of his reign, fixed the rate at two marks, and this became normal. In 1213–14 he went as high as three marks and was met with flat refusals to pay. Actually three marks was reasonable since he was having to pay three times as much as his father had done to put an army in the field, but it was difficult to make the barons realise the fact – especially since they had little enthusiasm for continental campaigns anyway.

In point of fact the financial burden of scutage did not fall heavily upon the baron himself for he could recover it from his knights, and if he had settled more knights on his land than he owed the king in military service he could actually make a profit. What irked the barons was that whenever the king demanded a scutage for the exemption of knights from service he took a fine for the personal exemption of the tenant-in-chief. Richard had started this practice, assessing the fine roughly on the number of knights the baron owed, and John stepped up the rates. While scutage was taken in 1201 at two marks on the knight's fief, the baron had to pay at the rate of three or four marks for every knight he owed. About £2500 came in from scutage, but over £3000 was picked up in fines. In 1204 the rates for the baron ran at four to seven marks as the king chose, and in 1210 up to ten marks. And besides all the bother of collecting scutage from the knightly tenants, and the burden of paying the heavy fines, the barons had to face the intolerable frequency with which John made demands: he took eleven scutages in sixteen years, in sharp contrast to Henry II's eight in thirty-four years, and Richard's three in ten years.[1] Since military service from the Crown's tenants was obligatory, payment for release from service was inescapable, but the barons bridled discontentedly, and insisted in 1215 that scutage should be levied only with their assent.[2]

If a king were in financial difficulties for some good reason, he could ask his tenants-in-chief for their consent to a general taxation. This was a good way of tapping the hidden wealth of the country, but it could only be taken with the barons' consent and was known as a 'gracious aid'. In 1200 John received an aid to

King John at a stag hunt (from Cotton MS Claudius D. ii, fo. 113, early 14th century). Like most medieval kings of England, John was passionately fond of hunting.

pay the 'relief' of 20,000 marks that had been asked of him by King Philip for his continental inheritance and agreed to at the Treaty of Le Goulet. It went by the technical name of a 'carucage' and was levied at the rate of three shillings on the plough-team, though the king was content to allow individuals or even entire counties to compound for a lump sum.[1]

More profitable, because more in line with economic conditions, were taxes assessed according to people's wealth, reckoned by estimating the value of their movable chattels and their regular revenues. Such a property tax, then a novel device, had been used in Henry II's reign to raise money for the Holy Land, and another was levied in 1193-4 for King Richard's ransom. It was a very unpopular method, partly because juries of neighbours had to be used to assess liability. People could reconcile themselves to it when it was for a pious purpose, or for the king's ransom (to which feudal law obliged them to contribute anyway), but did not like the idea of it becoming a normal method of raising revenue for the Crown. John's government, however, sought to use it to pay for the war with Philip: a seventh of movables was taken in 1203, and a shilling in the mark of property (called for convenience a Thirteenth) in 1207. As 'gracious aids' these property taxes had to be consented to, but this meant the consent of the principal barons, and once that had been obtained every freeman was obliged to pay.[2] To most taxpayers, therefore, a 'gracious aid' was little different from a tyrannous imposition.

Little is known of the Seventh of 1203, but the Thirteenth of 1207 met with a lot of opposition and subterfuge. People tried hiding away their chattels in monasteries, and royal officers carried out raids in search of them. They impounded the building fund of Swineshead abbey as suspect property – not unreasonably since the seneschal of the countess of Aumale had hidden his money there. Richmond castle was seized by the Crown because its constable refused to swear to the value of his chattels and revenue, and was only restored when he paid a fine of two hundred marks and four palfreys. Several men found themselves in prison.[3] The king's own half-brother, Geoffrey archbishop of York, went into exile rather than approve the collection of the tax from his tenants. Many lords compounded with the Crown for the obligations of their tenants, often at an inflated figure, rather than have the royal justices snooping around after defaulters. The bishop of

Durham had to pay £100 for the privilege, but then he had at first tried to deny the king's right to tax the tenants of Church lands.[1]

From the Exchequer's point of view the Thirteenth was enormously successful. Over £60,000 was raised, which was more than double the ordinary revenue for a year, and ten times the amount normally raised from a scutage. So successful was it, indeed, that it formed the model for the later medieval taxation system. But John himself was not able to repeat the method: the necessity of getting the consent of the baronial council forced him into dependence on his barons' goodwill, and it was here that his estrangement from his barons told most powerfully against him. After 1207 no consent was forthcoming, and he was forced to build up his war chest by augmenting the scutages, through economies (such as the sale of surplus wine stocks), the exploitation of windfalls (such as the farming out to contractors of the estates of vacant bishoprics and abbeys, and of baronies in wardship), and by screwing what he could from succession dues and penalties for infringements of the law. In consequence John's government gave the impression of being both burdensome and grasping. In the circumstances the very continuation of the war was a triumph of determination and financial effort; but to many Englishmen the triumph was a tyranny. 'He was a pillager [*depredator*] of his subjects,' says the Barnwell annalist looking back over the reign, and this was one of the chief reasons why 'they forsook him and, ultimately, little mourned his death.'[2]

This unfortunate reputation was probably built up as much by the day-to-day scrounging tactics of the government, which touched the common man most closely, as by the larger attempts at money collecting which hit the purses of the barons and knights. It is very noticeable that when the king is short of money the royal justices come down more heavily on small offenders in the courts. It was easy to get on the wrong side of the authorities, to be adjudged *in misericordiam* – at the king's mercy – and to escape only by paying an 'amercement'. Amercements were not imposed for crimes (upon which death, mutilation, or outlawry were visited) but for misdemeanours, such as neglect of public duties, failing to bring a criminal to justice, or for mistaken or stumbling pleading in a case before the court. 'You were almost bound to come out of the court poorer than you went in,' it has been said, 'whether

you were there as plaintiff or defendant, pledge or juryman.'[1]
This was the unhappy corollary to the provision of good and swift
justice, and men could be forgiven for forgetting to give due credit
to their king when they felt his hands always at their money-
bags. The charges imposed by the justices were not often large,
but they rarely fell below half a mark (6s. 8d.) and this was a
serious burden for many men at a time when a wage labourer
could not expect to make more than thirty shillings a year, and
the goods and chattels of an ordinary peasant were worth little
more than ten shillings.[2] Most men, it seems, could expect to
be amerced at least once a year in the normal course, so it was
intolerable when, as in 1210, special justices came round the courts
in addition to the normal circuit judges, who seemed to have
no object beyond the collection of money for the king's coffers.[3]
Though the barons were not usually amerced themselves, they
were deeply concerned that their peasants and villagers should not
be ruined by hard-hearted royal judges. Hence in Clause 20 of
Magna Carta an attempt was made to mitigate the burden: 'A
freeman shall only be amerced according to the degree of the
offence; and if he has committed a serious offence he shall be
amerced accordingly, but not to the extent that he is unable to
keep up his social position; similarly a merchant shall not lose his
means of trade, nor a villein his crops, if they have fallen into our
mercy; and amercements shall only be assessed by honest men of
the neighbourhood.'[4]

A particularly fruitful source of revenue for the Crown were
penalties for infringements of the Forest Law, which irked everyone, baron and villager alike. Large tracts of land, without regard to who held it, and amounting to about a third of the country
in all, were declared by the Crown to be 'forest' and under the
jurisdiction of forest officials. Therein the 'beasts of the forest'
(the red and fallow deer, the roe, and the wild boar) were protected for the king's hunting. The ordinary life of the countryside
went on there but only under stringent limitations. There was, for
example, a prohibition on the clearance and tillage of virgin land,
so that the protected animals might have cover for breeding, and
there were heavy penalties for anyone who tampered with them
in any way. Woe betide a man who cut a branch off a living tree,
or who was seen with an unslung bow. He could keep a dog only
if it were 'lawed' by having three claws cut from its forepaws.

Some lords had the right to create their own hunting grounds (known as 'chases') on their estates, but they were barred from touching the animals of the forest unless specially privileged – and the privilege never extended beyond the right to take the despised roe. The forest provided fresh meat for the itinerating royal Household, and the Forest Law protected beasts of the chase that would otherwise have been exterminated (the unprotected wolf was nearly extinct by John's day); but it involved restrictions which everyone found irksome. Petty infringements were visited with heavy penalties, and when John was in urgent need of cash he would send round a commission of forest justices. It can be said in his favour that he did not extend the bounds of the forest, as his predecessors had frequently done; but perhaps he had no need to: he made a lot of money out of what there was.[1]

Inevitably John's government appeared to be grasping and money-grubbing; but enterprising and intelligent as it was, it was not content with chivvying half-marks out of petty offenders: it dabbled in new devices for raising money. It thought up the customs duty on foreign cargoes in 1202 and ran it for five years – until a truce with Philip provided for free trade between the two realms.[2] It thought up a tax on wine merchants in 1206.[3] It realised that the age-old practice of farming out the revenues of the shires to the sheriffs for a fixed sum was simple but expensive. The charging of 'increments' over and above the fixed 'farms' did not seem to absorb the extra revenues that the sheriffs were collecting from a country of increasing prosperity, and many were making a large profit. Some of the profit could be tapped by putting up the shires for sale and appointing the highest bidder as sheriff – King Richard did it on a large scale in 1190; but besides the obvious dangers of this practice, the trouble was that no one was quite sure what the shires were now worth. In 1204 John's government thought of a better idea: the experiment was tried of appointing sheriffs to be 'custodians' instead of 'farmers', and having them account for every penny of the revenues. It was tried in about half of the shires, and in several of them joint custodians were appointed as an even better check on honesty. In the first year the net revenues from the shires were increased by a third by this method. It was the sensible solution to the problem, but it was difficult to work: it posed complicated problems of audit for the Exchequer, it defeated the administrative abilities of some of the custodians, and it was difficult to find men to take on such a thankless job. To work properly the system needed a corps of trained 'civil servants' and John had not got them to spare: the men who traditionally came forward to act as sheriffs – the lesser barons – were not interested in acting as custodians. For such reasons as these the experiment soon flagged, and was abandoned altogether in 1207–8. John took its collapse with ill-grace and made the sheriffs who lapsed from custodians into farmers pay fines for having his 'goodwill'. But even if practical difficulties had not wrecked the new system political ones would soon have done so. As the reign went on and the barons became restive and rebellious John needed strong-arm henchmen as sheriffs rather than skilled administrators. Internal defence became more important than extracting the full revenues, and mercenary captains were put into office and allowed to support themselves on whatever profit they could take from the shires.[1]

There could be no harmony in England in the matter of the Crown's finances until the barons, on the one hand, recognised the need for a system of taxation appropriate to the new economic conditions, and the king, on the other hand, limited his extraordinary expenditure to ventures for which he could get approval. As it was, John had to squeeze and wring out the sources that antiquated feudal custom allowed to him, although, as the Thirteenth of 1207 had revealed, the country was prospering and rich. His experiments failed for they were too ambitious, but so were his ventures. That he pursued them unremittingly is testimony to his determination and will-power; but they imparted to his reign a note of financial urgency and strain that mounted to a scream. The extortion of money for an unpopular war by an unpopular king is undoubtedly a factor in his malodorous reputation; but the root cause of it lies in the unpopularity of the war and the unpopularity of the king. The reasons for the former are patent, but the reasons for the latter are not easily laid bare. Monastic writers would like us to believe that it was influenced by King John's persecution of the Church; but did the barons share the prejudices of the tonsured?

5

King versus Pope

'I myself have seen the ungodly in great power: and flourishing like a green bay tree.'   *Psalm xxxvii. 36*

I. THE CLERGY UNDER TWO MASTERS

Many of John's officials and servants were in clerical orders. The archbishop of Canterbury himself was chancellor from 1199 to 1205. Peter des Roches, one of the king's able henchmen, and justiciar towards the end of the reign, was bishop of Winchester. John de Gray, his secretary, was bishop of Norwich. William Wrotham, the organiser of the navy, was archdeacon of Taunton. The treasurer, William of Ely, was archdeacon of Cleveland and a canon of St. Paul's. Most of the officials of the Exchequer and Chancery, and many of the regular justices, were clergymen. The employment of the clergy in the king's business went back to the days when western Europe was ruled by a military aristocracy that left book-learning to the only people who needed it in daily life – those who, at the very least, had to spell out the Bible and intone the liturgy. When great lords needed something written or read they would hire a clergyman to do it. Hence the word 'clerk' acquired in English (and in most north European languages) the double significance of the man in Holy Orders and the man whose job it is to write.

By John's time these barbarous days were becoming only a memory and a higher value was being set on literacy. Kings had come to find it indispensable for themselves, and some, like Henry II of England or Louis VII of France, could take pleasure in reading for its own sake. Indeed, it was a common saying in the middle of the 12th century that 'an unlettered king is a crowned ass.'[1] Literacy spread more slowly among the lay aristocracy who needed it less, but there were literate laymen available for the king's

154

service at the end of the century, like Ranulph Glanville who was Henry II's justiciar, and Geoffrey FitzPeter who was John's until his death in 1213. Nevertheless, clergymen continued to staff the royal administration in large numbers for a variety of reasons. For one thing there were many more clergymen than laymen eager to perform such services for the king or some other great lord. The Church was one of the principal ways of getting on in the world for younger sons or poor men with intelligence, and it provided the means of education in the cathedral schools or the new universities. Many therefore took Holy Orders who had brains but no great religious zeal.

For the lord who needed administrative officials, and for the king especially, who needed them in large numbers, there was a great advantage in employing clergymen for the cost of maintaining them could be reduced by giving them a parish church: the incumbent took the bulk of the revenues and a curate did the work (if the incumbent were conscientious enough to appoint one). If the king had no parishes in his gift available, a canonry or an archdeaconry could often be found, and the most exalted officials could be forced on the electors to a bishopric. Having his officials or former servants in high places in the Church was of further advantage to the king in that it enabled him to exercise some influence in the affairs of the English Church which, after all, had jurisdiction over the two per cent of the population who were in Holy Orders, and was endowed with twenty-five per cent of the land. Most of the bishops and many of the greater abbots were tenants-in-chief of the Crown and owed military service for what were known as their 'temporalities' (that is their landed endowments, in contrast to the 'spiritualities' which were the revenues derived from the performance of ecclesiastical functions), and attended his council as barons. Having clergymen in the royal service was one way of promoting harmony between Church and State; but there was a current of opinion in the 12th century which held that such harmony was bought at too high a price.

It would not be fair to say that the royal clerks were usually indifferent to the spiritual duties of the benefices they held: many, certainly, were secular minded and ambitious, but there were men of personal piety among them, more who were morally upright, and many who used their administrative abilities for the Church's benefit, and who saw to the performance of spiritual duties by deputy if not in person. Nonetheless, such considerations were not closely regarded in their preferment at the king's hands, and a divided allegiance and a double life could not be greatly to the Church's advantage. At the very time, in the early years of the 12th century, when the royal clerks first became exalted enough to be rewarded with bishoprics, their position was being challenged by the first rumblings in England of a revolutionary movement in the Church that was to have a profound influence in the history of western Europe.

In the middle of the 11th century the Apostolic See had been captured from the Roman aristocracy, and rescued from the smothering patronage of the German emperors, by high churchmen bent on bringing the Church, and through it society, closer to the ideal of St Augustine's *City of God*. Many men had had that purpose before and had sought it through monasticism; but these believed that the papacy should use its latent powers for the creation of a new order of righteousness in the world, and that all the clergy, and the secular priests in particular, should be its agents. As a corollary of this purpose it was necessary that the Church's ministers should be disentangled from lay society and worldly cares, and put under close control from Rome. Some of the incidental features of the reforming movement, the outward trappings as it were, came in time to seem obvious and proper: that clergymen should not offer money for benefices, for example, that they should be differentiated from the laity in dress and by being tonsured, that they should be freed from family cares by celibacy, and that they should not hunt. More important, the supreme authority of the Apostolic See, buttressed by a continually developing body of canon law, came to be generally acknowledged, though its exercise was often resented in practice by lay rulers who felt that their own authority was being infringed, and by bishops who felt that their proper jurisdiction was being usurped. Under the steady influence of generations of pontifical statements of principal, of the perseverance of the papal court, of the activity of papal legates and judges delegate, the clergy went a long way towards becoming a separate and privileged caste looking to Rome as the source of authority and guidance – a long way, but not all the way.

The older conception of churchmen working hand in glove with lay lords was never entirely supplanted, reiterated as it was in daily life with the parson paying his respects to the lord of the manor, and the bishops sitting in council with the king.[1] The new ideas transformed but did not overthrow established ways of thought. They were like the arrested dawn of a rainy day. The underlying purpose of the reforming movement failed to gain general understanding or widespread support. It did not even gain the comprehending devotion of a majority of the clergy, who might acknowledge the propriety of papal instructions, but whose vested interests kept their feet moving along the old paths. The implications of the reform movement had to be modified to meet their passive resistance. Ideally the dissociation of the clergy from worldly cares should have meant the surrender of the landed estates which brought them within the framework of feudal society; but to try to meet the impossibility of persuading the clergy to do this by allowing them to retain their estates but at the same time requiring them to disavow the obligations to secular lords that were carried with them, was a prevarication doomed to failure. As often happens with mortal men, the incidental features of a great idea gained the day, but the idea itself got lost on the way.

Nonetheless, the conceptions of the reformers were not lacking in influence. They disturbed and confused old relationships; they made the clergy increasingly conscious of a separateness from lay society; they created the problems of the relations of Church and State. They promoted the authority and jurisdiction of the see of Rome; and they made some men doubt the propriety of the clergy serving lay masters in secular affairs and being rewarded with ecclesiastical preferment.

There was inevitably a tug-of-war between lay rulers and the papacy for control of the clergy. Since neither side could pull the other down, it was eventually called off and relations of mutual accommodation established on a basis of compromise; but in John's lifetime the tug-of-war was still going on, though often shrouded by politeness and goodwill. It was commonly a gentlemanly sort of struggle: popes were usually practical men of affairs who hesitated to fly in the face of the realities of lay power, and kings were respectful and did not readily deny the theological justification of the papal claims. Awkward problems in the relations of Church and State frequently arose in the 12th century and were settled sometimes by compromise, but often by subterfuge on the part of kings and the turning of a blind eye on the part of popes.[1] Points of principle were reiterated more often than they were put into practice. In 1179 Pope Alexander III decreed deposition for clergy who served lay lords and filled secular offices. He thereby established his point but did not press it.[2] The clergy in fact went on serving the king in large numbers. Some were touched in their consciences by such statements of principle, however: Geoffrey Ridel gave up the chancellorship when he was made bishop of Ely; Henry II's bastard son, Geoffrey Plantagenet, resigned the bishopric of Lincoln when his father put him in Ridel's place, and gave up the royal service altogether when he was subsequently made archbishop of York. On the other hand, Hubert Walter, when archbishop of Canterbury, served King Richard as justiciar and was John's chancellor from 1199 until his death in 1205.

Good churchmen would not have denied the pope's authority to condemn the secular activities of the clergy, but nonetheless, some could be found who would defend royal clerks. Peter of Blois, a canon of St Paul's, a scholar, a serious Christian and famous for his letters (which were collected and published), once wrote:

'I do not condemn the life of civil servants, who even if they cannot have leisure for prayer and contemplation, are nevertheless occupied in the public good and often perform works of salvation. All men cannot follow the narrow path – for the way of the Lord is a strait and arduous road, and it is good if those who cannot ascend the mountain can accompany Lot to be saved in the little city of Zoar. . . . I think it is not only laudable but glorious to assist the king, to hold office in the State, not to think of oneself, but to be all for all.'[3]

It was more disturbing that bishops should act as royal judges for this might involve them in death sentences; but Ralph Diceto undertook a defence of them also. It was difficult, he said, for the king to find sufficient men of probity and integrity to take on the necessary task, and in his need he was justified in seeking the help of the clergy. There were advantages for everyone in it, for episcopal judges would not be likely to succumb to bribery, and would do justice in the fear of God.[4] Popes might not like the practice; canon law was against it; but it was acquiesced in. There was always the consolation of hope that clerical servants were infiltrating Christian principles into the business of government. At least a third of the bench of bishops at the close of the 12th century acted as royal judges and did not bother to seek dispensation from the canonical prohibition.[1]

The clergy, in fact, were living under two systems of government, Church and State, *sacerdotium* and *regnum*, papal and royal, express it how one will. The dividing line between the two was indistinct, and the position of the clergy within the realm was always somewhat ambiguous and possibly precarious. Whatever the theory, they were obliged in practice to recognise two masters, and the situation was only tolerable if neither pope nor king harried them too closely. Despite eruptions of principle, both masters were for the most part tacitly agreed that an imperfect peace was preferable to a righteous conflict. To his misfortune, John ran head on into the exceptional situation.

2. A SUCCESSOR FOR ARCHBISHOP WALTER

Principle and practice were clearly at variance in the matter of appointments to bishoprics. According to canon law vacant sees were to be filled by the free vote of the cathedral chapter – subject to confirmation by the papacy, and papal intervention in the case of a disputed election. This procedure had been a strong point with the early reformers, who hoped, rather naïvely, to get the best bishops this way. The procedure was followed at every vacancy in England, but the election was in fact managed by the king whenever he wished to get his own nominee appointed. Henry II at one stage tried to insist on the electors meeting in the royal chapel to hold the election under his eye – a very effective method of getting his own way, but too offensively blatant for any pope's peace of mind.[2] A more acceptable subterfuge was for the king to make his wishes known to the electors when he gave them permission to proceed with the election (a right which was not denied him). This was usually sufficient in a cathedral chapter which contained a large number of canons who were also royal clerks; but ten of the English cathedrals were run by monks, who were too prone to think that a member of their own order would make the best bishop. Here a little more coercion was sometimes required, and Henry's method is well illustrated in a royal writ of 1172:

'Henry king of the English to his faithful monks of the church of Winchester, greeting.

We order you to hold a free election, but nevertheless forbid you to elect anyone except Richard my clerk, the archdeacon of Poitiers.'[1]

John sometimes thought it best to pay a call on the chapter just before an election was held and talk the matter over with the electors.[2]

The Angevin kings were not indifferent to their nominees' fitness for office. None of them gave such cause for scandal as some of the royal servants to whom Henry I gave bishoprics. Bishop Roger of Salisbury, that king's justiciar, lived with baronial splendour, openly kept a mistress, and sired a dynasty of royal servants. Roger's nephew Nigel, the royal treasurer and bishop of Ely, had a son who followed him in office and became bishop of London. One of Henry II's appointments, by contrast, was of Hugh of Avalon, a Carthusian monk of saintly life (he was canonised in 1220) who pulled no punches in his tart criticism of his patron. The king justly boasted of never having taken a bribe to secure a bishopric for anyone.[3] Even Gerald of Wales, who regarded the Angevins and all their works with a jaundiced eye, admitted that Henry II appointed some good bishops.[4] King Richard 'gave the bishopric of Winchester', as a contemporary puts it, to Master Mauger, his physician. Mauger had scruples about accepting it for, as he confessed to the archbishop of Canterbury, he had grave doubts about the legitimacy of his birth. Pope Innocent III, however, had no doubts about Mauger's many fine qualities – 'his education, his honourable character, his virtuous life, and his personal reputation vouched for by some who knew him in the schools' – and indeed of his 'exceptional merits'.[5]

Roger of Howden frequently speaks in his chronicle of the king 'giving' a bishopric to someone. The chapter of course had been through the form of 'free election', but Roger was concerning himself with realities. Thus in 1200 'John de Gray succeeded to the bishopric of Norwich by the gift of King John', and 'In the same year, John King of England, gave Giles son of William de Briouze the bishopric of Hereford.'[6] Gray was the king's secretary and could be trusted with the highest administrative tasks. When Hubert Walter died in July 1205 the king thought to 'give' him the archbishopric of Canterbury.

John was in Buckinghamshire when Hubert died, but went

straight down to Canterbury as soon as he heard the news. Getting Gray through the proper election procedure was not easy, however, because it was not absolutely clear what the proper procedure was in the case of the primacy. The bishops of the province were claiming that they had a right to share in the election with the monks of the cathedral priory, who, of course, hotly disputed it. The king therefore postponed further consideration of the election until the end of November, and both parties to the dispute appealed to the Roman court to have the matter cleared up.[1]

A few weeks later, however, the monks picked up a rumour that the royal agents at Rome were advocating the claims of John de Gray, and they rashly made up their minds to steal a march on the king. They had only recently emerged victorious but exhausted from a long and bitter struggle with two successive archbishops, and they were more than ever determined that one of their own number should fill the vacancy.[2] They secretly held an election and chose their prior, Reginald. They sent him off to Rome with a delegation, but gave him instructions to reveal himself as the chapter's choice only if it were necessary to thwart the king. Reginald, however, fancied himself as archbishop, and as soon as he reached Rome he announced that he had been elected and sought papal confirmation. The royal agents quickly passed the news back to John, who immediately went down to Canterbury and taxed the monks with it. An Angevin in a temper was not to be trifled with, and they hastened to assure him that no election had been made.

John delayed no longer. Early in December he required the monks and the bishops to call off their appeals to Rome in the dispute between themselves, for this had put the whole matter *sub judice* and was holding up a proper election. Then in the king's presence the monks went through the form of election and unanimously chose John de Gray.[3] The bishops were allowed no part in the election but were asked to give their approval to the choice. Papal confirmation was now all that was required for Gray to become primate, and early in 1206 a second delegation of monks arrived at Rome to seek it.

Not unnaturally Pope Innocent III was confused by the babble of claims and counter-claims, assertions and contradiction, of the parties before him. Prior Reginald, of course, denounced the second election as invalid, but the new arrivals repudiated him. John was telling the pope through his agents, probably in good faith, that no previous election had been held; but the second delegation of monks was confusing the issue by insisting that the election of Reginald had been conditional. The bishops' proctor had not got his instructions clear and was still protesting that an appeal on the bishops' claim was pending and had to be decided first. The pope called a halt to the argument, and sent to Canterbury, to the king, and to the bishops, for fresh representatives with power of attorney. Then, taking first things first, he decided against the bishops' claim to share in an election to the primacy. Next he quashed the elections of Prior Reginald and John de Gray on the ground that they had been irregular. Then he called upon the delegates of the cathedral chapter to conduct a fresh election on the spot. Maddeningly they divided equally between Prior Reginald and John de Gray; but Innocent was ready with a solution: he proposed that they consider a new candidate disassociated from their disputes among themselves, and suggested Stephen Langton, cardinal priest of St Chrysogonus. Langton was an Englishman in his late forties, born in Lincolnshire, and until recently a distinguished teacher at the university of Paris. The monks accepted him unanimously.

Innocent had every reason to be delighted with the success of his efforts, for Langton was the ideal type of man to carry out the reform programme that he had very much in mind. There were plenty of conscientious administrators in the hierarchy who could be trusted to apply rules; but the best results could only be obtained if the key positions were held by men with a deep understanding of the purpose of the rules, and the ability to apply them with practical good sense. Langton had given some notable lectures at Paris on the duties of the episcopal office, and his sermons on theological and moral problems were famous. He was also a writer of hymns, and had revised the arrangement of the books in the Bible, and had divided them into the chapters which are still accepted today. Recognising his eminence, Innocent had recently invited him to Rome and made him a cardinal.[1]

The monks were satisfied, the pope was satisfied, propriety and canonical principle was satisfied; the king was furious. Innocent wrote to John telling him of the election of Langton and hoping for his approval. He received a blistering reply. Langton, snorted the king, was quite unacceptable: he had lived among enemies and was not known in England, and, furthermore, it was unheard of that an election to an English see should be made without his licence to elect. Innocent retorted that John's letter was insolent and impudent, and that his arguments were paltry and unjustified. Langton was a loyal subject of the king; it was absurd for John to say that he did not know a man whose reputation stood so high, and anyway, Langton had recently received a letter from the king congratulating him on being made a cardinal and saying that it had been in his mind to invite him to serve in the royal House-hold. As for the matter of the licence to elect, the pope insisted that he had given the king plenty of time and every opportunity, even though it was not usual to wait for a prince's assent to elections conducted at the papal court. John must realise, the pope added, that he had deferred to him more than the law re-quired; but now that the canonical procedures had taken their course it was unthinkable that they should be thwarted. Indeed when a proper election had been made, no pope could impede it without loss of reputation and peril to his conscience.[1]

John relieved his feelings by expelling the monks of Canterbury, and they had to pay for frustrating him by spending many years as refugees in French monasteries.[2] The king could not prevent Langton being consecrated as archbishop but he could prevent him being installed at Canterbury. His father had once said, when the bishop of Chichester told him that only the pope could depose a bishop, 'It is quite true that a bishop cannot be deposed but he can be held out thus' – and pushed out his hands.[3] John could at least use his hands. He refused to allow Langton to enter the country, declared that anyone who called him archbishop should be taken as a public enemy, and seized the estates of the see.[4] The honour of the pope was at stake, the honour of the king was at stake; it was deadlock.

3. WAR BETWEEN CHURCH AND STATE

The matter of elections to bishoprics was close to Innocent's heart. For one thing his reform programme needed sound bishops. For another thing, the principles of a proper election had been laid down at the Lateran Council of 1179 and it fell to him, as an eminent lawyer, to direct how the principles should be worked out in practice. Disputed elections were referred to him for settlement from all over Europe, and jurists crowded his court to hear his decisions and to marvel at the skill with which he marshalled his arguments.

He waited for a year in the hope that John would recognise that the appointment of Langton was canonically proper and for his own 'benefit and salvation' (as the pope put it).[1] But in the summer of 1207 he determined to enforce what was right: he consecrated Langton on 17 June at Viterbo and prepared to use sanctions against the king. In August the bishops of London, Ely, and Worcester (whom he believed he could trust) were instructed to try once more to persuade the king to 'bow to the divine ordinance', and if he still refused to proclaim an interdict on England and Wales.[2]

To proclaim an interdict was to call a general strike of the clergy and stop all the comforts of religion. It was a crude weapon for it made the innocent suffer with the guilty; but from this it derived its effectiveness, for it robbed the offenders of all sympathy, and roused (so it was hoped) the faithful against the faithless. Sentences of interdict had been threatened many times in the 12th century and sometimes actually enforced, but the precise implications of it were still not well regulated in law. Innocent III himself had not been very specific when he laid interdicts on Laon in 1198, on France in 1199, or on Normandy in 1203, and the clergy of those parts had been obliged to ply him with queries. His instructions to the three bishops in August 1207 were couched in rather general terms. They were 'to publish the general sentence of Interdict, permitting no ecclesiastical office save the baptism of infants and the confession of the dying.'[3] There was room for doubt: if infants could be baptised could they not be confirmed? Could the dying be given unction? Was no mitigation to be allowed to pious benefactors? The pope was probably content with a sweeping sentence because he expected it to last only a short time; indeed he perhaps hoped that the threat alone would suffice. King Philip of France had persisted in an adulterous marriage for four years, but submitted to correction within a few months of an interdict being pronounced. But Innocent was mistaken in thinking that John could be brought round with threats, or chastened by the withdrawal of Church services.[4]

In November 1207 the pope wrote an open letter to the barons of England:

'If you pay to King John the loyalty that is due to him, you can be sure that this is pleasing both to God and to us. But because you should so order your loyalty to your earthly king so as never to offend the Heavenly King, you ought to be on your guard to save the king by faithful advice from a policy which he has seemingly adopted in enmity to God – that of persecuting our venerable brother, Stephen archbishop of Canterbury, and through him the church committed to his charge. So, with all your power, save him from rejecting the counsel of good men and from walking in the counsel of the ungodly. . . . Do not fear displeasing him temporarily in the cause of justice – for conduct so upright will not injure you by exciting him to hatred, but will in time work to your benefit by winning his love. For undoubtedly, when he has taken wiser advice and returned to his senses, he will think you very dear friends for the sincerity of your counsel. . . .'[1]

If he hoped that this letter would have any effect, Innocent was being very naïve.

The chronicler of Margam abbey reports that at first 'all the laity, most of the clergy, and many monks were on the king's side.'[2] To people who were ill acquainted with canonical principles in the matter of elections, and ignorant of the full circumstances of the dispute over the see of Canterbury in 1205-6 (and that meant most people in England), it looked as if the pope had simply set aside the election of Gray and appointed his own nominee. It was unheard of that the king should not only fail to have his own man appointed but have someone of whom he disapproved forced upon him. Kings had always got the archbishop they wanted hitherto. It was not as if there were anything wrong with Gray; and the name of Langton meant nothing to most of them. It was only proper that the archbishop of Canterbury, a tenant-in-chief of the Crown, and the king's principal counsellor, should be a man agreeable to him. There was no telling where anyone would be if the pope interfered with tradition in this way. Men wondered what would become of their own ecclesiastical patronage. Canon law had already undermined the old idea that parish churches and abbeys established by pious laymen remained the private property of the founder and his heirs. It still allowed them certain rights in the appointment of parish clergy, but how long would these last if popes were becoming so high and mighty? What hope had the barons of getting canonries and bishoprics for their younger sons if the pope were allowed to thrust in outsiders? Whatever his theoretical powers might be, he should learn to act more circumspectly.

John handled the situation with dexterity. His first reaction had no doubt been one of Angevin rage; but he soon set about creating the impression that it was he, not Langton, who was being persecuted. He staved off the interdict by negotiating: he received Langton's representative, his brother Simon, at Winchester, and sent his own representative, the abbot of Beaulieu, to talk the matter over with the pope. John was merely trying to gain time: he offered concessions and then slithered out of them, he continued to refer to Langton as 'the cardinal', and tried to get an explicit confirmation of his own 'rights' in the matter of episcopal appointments.[1] Within a few months the pope became convinced of the insincerity of the king's offers to come to an agreement, but John was able to give the impression at home that he was trying to be reasonable but was being imposed upon. After the negotiations with Langton's brother he sent letters to be read out in the shire courts, saying:

'You should know that Master Simon Langton came to us at Winchester on Wednesday before the middle of Lent, and asked that we receive his brother Master Stephen Langton as archbishop of Canterbury. And when we spoke to him about preserving our dignity in this matter, he said that he could do nothing for us therein unless we put ourselves completely at his mercy. We tell you this so that you will know the wrong and injury that is done to us.'[2]

By the second week in March 1208 John learned that the pope's patience had come to an end and that the interdict was to be proclaimed at the end of the month. He immediately prepared his counter-attack: special agents were sent into the shires to rally support for his cause, and on the day that the clergy came out on strike (24 March) royal officers moved in to seize their property in the king's name.[3] There was a kind of rough justice in this measure in that the clergy had been endowed with the property to enable them to perform their functions, and it was arguable that they should forfeit it if they withheld their services. At the same time it was a good rejoinder to the pope: if he were penalising the king's subjects, then the king would penalise the pope's. Time would show who could last out longest.

It is a good indication of the pope's authority over the clergy that his instructions were very generally obeyed. The Cistercian monks at first claimed that the Interdict did not apply to them for their privileges exempted them, but they quickly obeyed the pope's order to fall into line. Equally, though, it is eloquent testimony to the efficiency of John's government that he could carry out the wholesale confiscation of clerical property. The sheriffs or specially appointed custodians took charge of it, lay administrators were put into bishoprics and abbeys, and four men were appointed in each parish to assess the clergy's revenues and assign them a maintenance allowance. The pope stopped the clergy ringing their bells, the king locked up their barns.[1]

John, however, could not spare his officers indefinitely for the administration of the Church's estates; nor did he wish to strain the loyalty of the local men who had been called in to help.[2] Within a week or so he let it be known that he was ready, as an act of grace, to allow those clergy who applied to him to recover control of their property – if they were prepared to pay for the privilege. Some favoured clergy, such as the royal clerks, were allowed to recover complete control of their property for a nominal payment; but this was not common. Usually the king allowed the clergy to administer their property but not to dispose freely of their revenues. The abbey of Bury St Edmund's bought itself out of the hands of a royal administrator within three weeks, but on condition that the abbot paid the revenues over to the king, apart from the maintenance allowance which he could deduct. St Edmund's escaped quickly because John was friendly with Abbot Sampson, but many houses soon made similar arrangements. Often the property was transferred from the king's hands to someone who was prepared to act as custodian on behalf of its clerical owners. Barons commonly acted for monasteries with which they had personal connections. The justiciar, Geoffrey FitzPeter, made himself responsible for the whole order of the Knights Templar, and for several monasteries of which he was patron. The prior of the Knights Hospitaller and the master of the Order of Sempringham were allowed to act as administrators for their orders. Bishops, abbots, priors, archdeacons, and parish clergy came to bail out their property, agreeing to be answerable for the revenues to the king. The abbot of St Albans, for example, paid 600 marks for the privilege.[1] The royal records, unfortunately, survive only in fragments for the period of the Interdict, and it is difficult to know how general this conditional recovery of property was; but Adam of Eynsham reports that most rectors redeemed their property on payment of a fine.[2]

It was a clever scheme to impound the clergy's property, make them pay for the privilege of administering it on the king's behalf, and hand over to him a portion of the revenues. They were glad to do it because they could at least prevent their estates being ruined. It is impossible now to know how much John collected from the clergy, but it must have been a small fortune. The sheriff of Northampton, for example, accounted at Michaelmas 1210 for over £1000 in gross receipts from Peterborough in six months. Next year the prior recovered control of the abbey's estates for £600 a year – still a substantial revenue for the Crown, at no cost to the king.[3] The Interdict, in fact, relieved John of financial worries for several years.

With ingenious humour he thought up another scheme for mulcting many of the clergy while they were in his power. The Church authorities had very great difficulty in enforcing celibacy, and it is quite certain that many clergy, particularly parish priests, had gone through a form of marriage, or kept concubines under some such euphemism as 'housekeepers'. Gerald of Wales once remarked that 'the houses and hovels of the parish clergy are full of bossy mistresses, creaking cradles, new-born babes and squawking brats.'[4] Henry I had fined married clergy for disobeying the Church's decrees, but at the same time had sold them licences to do so.[5] John, however, went one better than his grandfather and ordered all the clergy's mistresses, hearthmates (*focariae*), and lady-loves (*amasiae*) to be seized and held for ransom. To the scandal of contemporary moralists many of them hurried to bail their womenfolk out.[6]

4. AN EXCOMMUNICATE KING

The proclamation of the Interdict had failed in its purpose: John was not dismayed, he was merely richer. Writing to the king in January 1209, Innocent threatened sterner measures, and in the summer he instructed Langton to pronounce a sentence of excommunication on John personally whenever he saw fit.[1] The king tried to gain time again by opening negotiations, but his insincerity was patent, and in November he was declared excommunicate.

Excommunication was the ecclesiastical equivalent of outlawry. It put the offender beyond the pale of the Christian community. It should have been a terrible sentence, for the offender's soul was in peril if he died unreconciled to mother Church; but the clergy had unfortunately used it too often for frivolous reasons for it to be seriously regarded by any but the most pious. It imposed disabilities: excommunicates could not plead in the ecclesiastical courts, their oaths were impoverished, and their contracts of dubious validity. These were hardly enough to induce obedience, and the Church in England had in fact been obliged to enlist the king's help in applying sanctions, having offenders sought out and imprisoned by the sheriffs. What Innocent probably hoped for in having John declared excommunicate was an indirect result, for in putting the person of a ruler outside the community of Christians it undermined his relations with his subjects. It was next door to a sentence of deposition: it did not require his subjects to disavow their allegiance, but it protected their consciences if they felt unable to follow a man whom the Church had put asunder.

The only people really disturbed by the sentence on John, however, were some of the English clergy. The bishops of Bath, Lincoln, Rochester, and Salisbury felt unable to keep up relations with the king and retired overseas. They joined the bishops of London, Ely, and Worcester, who had been in exile since proclaiming the Interdict in 1208. A few deans, canons, and archdeacons went too, but there was never a general exodus. The curialist bishops of Winchester and Norwich were quite unmoved, and most of the royal clerks stayed at their posts. Even more striking: two Cistercian abbots remained in attendance upon the king, one of them, the abbot of Bindon, being his almoner.[2] John reacted harshly against those who did go: their estates were seized again and ruthlessly exploited, and in 1212 the clergy appointed to benefices by the absent prelates were expelled and the revenues impounded. The property of the exiles was liable to suffer waste at the king's hands: the woods of the archbishop of Canterbury were sold up, and the bishop of London's castle at Stortford was destroyed.[1]

One of the surprising things about the period of the Interdict is that while chroniclers are prepared to record some of the diplomatic manœuvres, they tell us next to nothing about what effect it had on the life of the English Church. We are left trying to make out the picture on a very incomplete jig-saw puzzle from odd pieces of information. John had no wish, it seems, to disrupt the normal business of ecclesiastical government. As soon as the clergy had bailed out their property they were allowed to bring civil actions in the royal courts. Their own courts continued to function, though no appeals went to Rome (at least after 1210). The dioceses of the absent bishops were run by officials appointed by them, and John did not interfere when, for instance, the bishop of Worcester wrote home with instructions.[2] No doubt ecclesiastical life flagged. It certainly was an unprecedented situation when by the end of 1211 only one bishop remained in England. Besides the bishops who had fled because of the interdict or the excommunication, Archbishop Geoffrey of York had gone into exile in 1207 because of a quarrel with the king over the taxation of his tenants, and Giles de Briouze, bishop of Hereford, had fled in fear because John was having a feud with his family.[3] In addition the bishops of Durham, Lichfield, Chichester, and Exeter had died and the sees remained vacant. Elections were held and the king's friends chosen, but none could be consecrated. John de Gray, bishop of Norwich, was sent to Dublin to be justiciar of Ireland in February 1208; and that left only Peter des Roches, bishop of Winchester.

Even more obscure is the effect of the Interdict on religious life. During the early months there was much earnest debate among those responsible for enforcing it as to what was implied in the ban on 'all ecclesiastical offices save the baptism of infants and the confession of the dying.' Bishops consulted each other, and made inquiries of prominent canon lawyers; the bishop of Salisbury asked the chapter of St Paul's what they thought. In 1209 Innocent allowed monks to celebrate mass once a week behind locked doors, and in 1212 he expressly permitted the dying to receive the *viaticum*, but otherwise he gave no clear guidance.[4] There seem to have been different interpretations in different dioceses: in some babies were baptised at home, in others in church but behind locked doors. People who wished to make offerings could sometimes get access to an altar, and some monasteries surreptitiously admitted pilgrims by a side door. It must be assumed, however, that from the middle of 1208 to the middle of 1214 the laity were denied the sacrament of the altar, could not be married, or be buried in consecrated ground. Graves were dug in woods, or bodies put in roadside ditches. The bishop of Bangor asked to be buried in the market place of his home town of Shrewsbury.[1] Yet there are no signs of popular discontent: it must have been very worrying to pastors, and disturbing to the pope.

Attempts were made to bolster popular piety by non-liturgical means: pilgrimages were encouraged, sermons were preached in churchyards, and crosses were set up in public places on Good Friday. But as the evangelical abbot of Ford lamented in 1210, 'The common people have wanted in continual fasting now for nearly two years, denied all participation in the sacraments, and there is no doubt that they will die on the road and completely cease to remember their fatherland if their hunger goes on increasing.' It had to wait unappeased for four years longer. Moreover, many of the parish clergy, finding little to do, passed their time in taverns or took up secular work. They were a serious problem to their diocesans when the Interdict was over.[2]

It is not surprising that monastic writers should charge John with irreligion. Adam of Eynsham, the biographer of St Hugh of Lincoln, says that John never communicated after he came of age, not even at his coronation.[3] If that were true it is surprising that no other chronicler mentions so remarkable a fact; it is typical, perhaps, of the wild stories that people were prepared to make up about him.[4] As a matter of fact John seems to have been at least conventionally devout: immediately after his coronation he went on a pilgrimage to the shrines of St Thomas Becket, St Alban, and St Edmund, though his presence was urgently needed in Normandy. One of his first acts as king was to give the abbey of Brackley an annuity of five marks to say an obit for his dead brother Richard.[5] He had a special reverence for St Wulfstan and asked to be buried before the saint's shrine in Worcester cathedral.[6] Adam of Eynsham may be right in his story of John on one occasion in church sending a message up to Bishop Hugh to cut the sermon short because he wanted his dinner.[7] His father was restless in church too, chatting with his courtiers or doodling; but both of them had great respect for the saintly Hugh. John visited him in his last illness (though he got a cool reception) and helped to carry the corpse at the funeral.[1] He had indeed no animus against the clergy as such. Abbot Sampson of Bury St Edmunds remained friendly enough to bequeath him his jewels when he died in 1212.[2] In the middle of the Interdict he borrowed some religious books from the abbot of Reading – six volumes of the Bible, Hugh of St Victor on the sacraments, Peter Lombard's textbook on theology, St. Augustine's *City of God*, and the commentaries of Origen – and lent him a copy of Pliny in return.[3] He was alive to religious proprieties: payments for new vestments, books, altar cloths, and crucifixes for the royal chapels figure frequently in the accounts.[4] He was liberal in almsgiving – especially when he had eaten meat on Friday or gone hunting on a holy day. During the Interdict he trebled his customary benefactions to religious houses, as if to advertise his orthodoxy.[5] In 1211 he sent gifts of herrings to nunneries in nearly every shire.[6]

Unfortunately for his reputation John was not a great benefactor to monasteries which kept chronicles. In 1200 he received with sympathy the complaints of twelve Cistercian abbots against the forest officials, and offered not only to redress their grievances but to build them an abbey.[7] Beaulieu rose in accordance with his promise, but the monks there omitted to remind posterity of his munificence. He was very interested in the hand of St James that was the most precious relic of the abbey of Reading, and gave money for a shrine to be made for it.[8] Unfortunately for him the monks there did not keep a chronicle. Nor did the chaplains of Chichester who, for reasons which they have kept to themselves, said masses 'to his blessed memory.'[9]

In the course of the war with the papacy, John never sought to impugn the pope's authority, he merely objected to it being used in a way that infringed the ancient 'rights' of the Crown. He had no real intention of submitting, but he kept up a pretence of being ready to reach a reasonable settlement. In the summer of 1211 a papal legate, Pandulph, was admitted to England and allowed to argue a case before the king's council at Northampton. He offered terms for an end to the Interdict: Langton should be received as archbishop, the exiles should be reinstated, and the confiscated property restored. John rejected them with confidence.[10] Perhaps his pretence to negotiate was a gesture to the barons, but this confident defiance of the pope reveals how far he could trust to their support. Innocent himself tartly commented on the baron's failure to lift a finger to help the Church in her distress.[1]

Not a single comment from a layman on the Interdict is recorded; but though the barons stood by the king in his defiance of the papacy, they cannot have been happy at his demonstration of authority. He had revealed a remarkable power to coerce, and if necessary to break, a large proportion of his subjects at will. The clergy of the realm, great and small, had been at his mercy. Their property had been confiscated, exploited, and sometimes wasted. Their ordered and disciplined life had given way to confusion and uncertainty. Established customs had been overturned at a word. For example, when an abbot died the temporalities of the monastery were taken into the king's hands until a successor were appointed; but long custom distinguished between the abbot's portion of the revenues and the monks' portion, and only the former was enjoyed by the Crown at a vacancy. During the Interdict, however, this custom had been waived, and all the estates had been ruthlessly exploited for the king's benefit. Seventeen monasteries were suffering in this way by 1213.[2] Yet the clergy had seemed to be that class in the country whose rights and privileges were most firmly entrenched by custom and charter. The barons had stood on the sidelines and watched this sort of thing happening; but they could not be indifferent to the spectacle of the fragility of other people's rights in John's fierce hands. Uncertainty had entered into all the barons' relations with him; their rights too were being threatened by arbitrary force, they too passed under the shadow of personal violence. They could not delay for ever in seeking some hope of salvation.

6

King John and his Barons

'Let the things that should be for their wealth be unto
them an occasion of falling.'   *Psalm lxix.* 23

1. ANGEVIN MONARCHY

Although, in the struggle of Crown versus Papacy, John had taken
care to advertise his version of the case, there was little danger
that the barons would espouse the cause of high clericalism. Nevertheless, the fear which must have beset John cruelly in 1208 was
that the Interdict, and more especially his personal excommunication, would give his barons an excuse to disavow their allegiance
and make common cause, one with another, against him. The
spectre of discontent and disloyalty which had seemed just behind
his shoulder in 1204–5, and which had made him so apprehensive
of French invasion, returned to haunt him.

The problem of controlling the barons was not in itself a new
one. The royal government had fifty years' experience behind it
of out-manœuvring the over-mighty subject, taming his ambitions, and curbing his power. The domestic policy of the Angevin rulers had always been to make the monarchy unassailable.
They were not aiming at absolutism – the concept had no meaning
in the middle ages – but they were aiming at maximum security,
and like many rulers before or since who feared for their position
they sought security through dictatorial tyranny and preferred
authoritarianism to appeasement. There was good reason for it:
Henry II became king after nineteen years of civil war between
rival contestants for the throne – his mother Matilda and her
cousin Stephen – and during it the power of the barons had been
greatly enhanced. They had sold their services to one side or the
other, and sometimes to both, in return for concessions and privileges: they had got a grip on royal administration in their neigh-

bourhood, and consolidated their position by building or acquiring castles. Henry set himself to tame and discipline them. As one who knew him personally and approved his work said, 'From the very beginning of his rule he gave his whole mind to crushing by all possible means those who rebelled against peace and were "froward" and sealing up in men's hearts the treasures of peace and good faith.'[1] Some of it was done by indirect means: strengthening and extending the range of the Crown's executive power and discharging it through removable agents instead of dispersing it in the hands of the barons. Some of it was done through the developing machinery of the royal courts: visiting swift and stern justice on any man who had helped himself to another's property in the time of troubles or since. But 'all possible means' included much that was done extra-legally: by forcible expropriation on no other ground than that it was the king's will, and by exploiting the king's discretionary power through loopholes in feudal custom. A powerful barony could be crippled, for example, by demanding an exorbitant succession duty (the 'relief') from an heir, and thereby saddling his revenues with debt for many years or even forcing it into the hands of Jewish moneylenders; or it could be broken up by selling heiresses to the king's friends.

The serious revolt of 1173-4 was the inevitable reaction to royal coercion. The rebellion of the Young King for private grievances against his father was joined by a great number of barons, as Ralph Diceto puts it, 'not because they regarded his as the juster cause, but because the father, with a view to increasing the royal dignity, was trampling upon the necks of the proud and haughty, was overthrowing the suspected castles of the country, or bringing them more under his control; because he ordered and even compelled the persons who were occupying the properties attached to the services of his Household or the Exchequer to be content with their own patrimony.'[2] The suppression of the rebellion enabled the king to complete the work of trimming the power of his over-mighty subjects. He was lenient towards the persons but heavy on the property of the Young King's partisans, and pleadings in the courts a generation later still recall that such and such a man had been disseised of his land 'by decree of King Henry the father because he had been in France with King Henry the Younger.'[3] Physical signs of the clipping of baronial wings were still evident throughout the former

Angevin dominions when the biographer of William Marshal was writing in the 1220s: 'One can still see traces of the war,' he says. 'In Normandy, England, Anjou, Poitou, Maine, and in the duchy of Aquitaine are ruined castles which have not yet nor ever will be restored. So passes the glory of the world.'[1]

This was a turning point in the balance of power between Crown and baronage: the barons were ousted from crucial positions of administrative authority (save in frontier regions where attacks from the Scots, the Welsh, or the Irish, gave them special responsibilities and could be expected to keep them occupied), and castles were withheld from their grasping pride. Expropriation for rebellion was reasonable enough without the formality of judgement and condemnation in the king's court; but the extra-judicial devices for trimming baronial power were maintained in full vigour even when the king had the upper hand – we may even say, especially when the king had the upper hand.

In curbing the disorder of baronial self-help by forcing it under the discipline of the royal courts, the king did not hesitate to use his own self-help which there was no superior court of justice to correct. A Buckinghamshire lord was being merely realistic when he made a grant to a monastery and declared himself ready to guarantee it against all men 'save in the case of royal violence'.[2] Furthermore, the king manipulated his courts to discriminate against his enemies: the courts are not independent, they are creatures of the king's will, he will open and close them as he sees fit, denying a man justice, or making him pay heavily for it as if for a privilege. As John frankly put it, 'It is only reasonable that we should do better by those who are with us than those who are against us.'[3] It could be harder for a rich man to have his right than for a poor man who tendered but half a mark for a writ of *Novel Disseisin* or *Mort d'Ancestor*. The great contradiction of Henry II's reign was that he, the man who made good laws and carried the benefits of royal justice to the most insignificant of freemen, was also, in the phrase of Gerald of Wales, 'a seller and delayer of justice.'[4]

Having the king's goodwill was thus made the *sine qua non* of baronial prosperity, and sometimes even of survival, for the king's ill-will could put a man beyond the protection of the courts. William Turpin put a plea before John soon after he came to the throne, claiming that in the previous reign the earl of Arundel had disseised him of his inheritance simply because it pleased him to do so (*per voluntatem*) and had done it with impunity 'because he knew that King Richard bore ill-will to the said William.'[1] It was lucky for William Turpin that John did not share his brother's malevolence in this particular instance, and he was able to recover his property; but others were not so fortunate. Alexander of Caldbeck in 1206 had a plea about an estate in Cumberland postponed indefinitely 'because it was not pleasing to the king that he should have a jury.'[2]

Cynically and profitably, the Angevin rulers allowed their goodwill, in certain instances at least, to be bought. There is not a Pipe Roll of the period that lacks a crop of offers 'for having the king's benevolence.' 'Adam of Port offers £200 that the king should remit his indignation and receive his homage.' 'Ralph Clare renders account of £60 for having the king's goodwill.' 'Ralph of Betteville renders account of 75 shillings for being freed from the king's ill-will' (*pro habenda pace de malevolentia regis*).[3] These are examples from the reign of Henry II, but they could come as readily from the archives of his sons. Some of the entries are specific: 'for recovering the king's favour in that he took a wife without the king's permission', '. . . in that he failed to render his service'. '. . . in that he allowed prisoners to escape.' But very often the entries are uninformative and we merely know that such a man has crossed the king and had tried to persuade him 'to put aside his anger', 'to abate his ill-will'. The phrases vary, but they all point to the crucial importance in any man's life of a factor of distressing uncertainty – the king's favour, perhaps even his whim.

The other side of the coin is the king's declaration of his 'disfavour', his 'anger', and his 'ill-will', as the sole and indisputable reason for administrative invasion of his subject's property. One could offend the king without breaking the law, and suffer distraint upon one's property or even expropriation. The king's anger could be manifested in this way against any man from an archbishop to a minor servant: Archbishop Becket suffered from Henry II; Archbishop Geoffrey of York from Richard I, while John applies it as a sort of sanction to his administrative orders: 'if our business fail through your default,' he writes to his bailiffs in the ports, 'we shall treat you as we would our enemies.'[4]

It must not be thought that the Angevin rulers acted in this way habitually or that it was wholly irresponsible. Decisive action by decree (*'per preceptum'*, *'per voluntatem'*) was often the best protection of the peace. Furthermore, it was effectively and justifiably used as an adjunct of the royal equity; a man has suffered wrong and cannot obtain justice because, it may be, his opponent is too powerful, the witnesses have been suborned, the jurors bribed, but he can convince the king of the injustice and is restored by the royal *fiat*. At the same time, there was in some respect no more jealous upholder of the customs of the realm than the king. His office, his accepted functions, are justified by custom and tradition. The disorder of strong men's self-help was largely curbed by royal insistence upon due process of law. The demand for due process came initially not from the subject but the ruler. It is the voice of organised authority. But what he firmly denies his vassal he freely practises himself — and he gets away with it while he is too strong to be resisted. When the barons sought from the king in Magna Carta that he could henceforth proceed only upon the judgement of a court and by the law of the land they were turning the tables, obliging him to behave as he insisted they should behave. This may seem only fair and logical: but what is politically just is not always politically expedient. Obstinate political circumstances give the king a Janus face: he feels that he must uphold the law and yet act extra-legally himself when he finds it convenient to do so. This royal schizophrenia is very apparent in the reign of John – a man keenly interested in the proper functioning of his courts of law. He had no desire to dispense with custom. In judicial business it is the *vade mecum*. Let the action proceed, he writes to his justices, 'unless reason and the custom of our kingdom stand in the way'; if an inquest has been taken 'according to the custom of England it should stand, but if otherwise it should be quashed.'[1] But, and here is the rub, a strong monarchy cannot allow itself to be fettered by custom. It must retain room for manoeuvre and be prepared to act quickly and decisively. And so the king will act outside the bounds of his recognised jurisdiction, without seeking a judgement of his court, and enforce obedience to his will by seizing his subjects' chattels and lands without trial.[2] He will even seize their persons. On the death of Henry II, Queen Eleanor, intending that the reign of her favourite son, Richard, should begin on a popular note, released from prison many categories of prisoners, including, her instructions said, 'all those who have been taken and kept by the will of the king or of his justiciar, who were not imprisoned by the judgement of the county or hundred court or on an appeal of felony.'[1]

About 1175, it is said, Roger Asterby, a Lincolnshire knight, conveyed to Henry II a warning about his methods of government. Poor Sir Roger claimed that he was being pestered to do this by St Peter and the Archangel Gabriel and did so only reluctantly. The king was to discharge seven commandments, and if he did so, and went on crusade, he would live for seven years and end his life in happiness; but if he failed to do so he would die miserably within four. Gerald of Wales tells the story and gives the heads of the seven commandments: 'First, the three promises which he had made at his coronation concerning the maintenance of the Church of God. Secondly, concerning the observance of the just laws of the kingdom. Thirdly, that he would condemn no one to death without judgement, even though he were guilty. Fourthly, in the matter of inheritances, that they should be restored and justice done. Fifthly, concerning the rendering of justice freely and without cost. Sixthly, concerning services rendered to his ministers. Seventhly, concerning the Jews: that they should be expelled from his domains with only enough money to pay their fare and support their families, after their securities and title deeds had been taken from them and restored to their owners.'[2] It reads like a summary of the principal provisions of Magna Carta. Henry, Gerald records, was at first contrite and offered to restore to every man his rights, but as people flocked to his court to claim them, he cooled from his previous resolve, and procrastinated from day to day, so that ultimately nothing at all was done.

Inevitably there was persistent grumbling about taxation – the scutages, almost annual under John, the newer taxes on chattels and ploughlands, the levies incidental to feudal tenure that were only occasional but heavy and sometimes crushing, and about the arbitrarily fixed amercements and fines. But in addition – and more telling in producing a general sense of oppression – there can have been few of the hundred and sixty or so tenants-in-chief who had not some personal grievance about royal tyranny, an injury to pride in the destruction of a castle, a sense of injustice in the disposal of a manor, a bitterness about the pillaging of an estate while in wardship, or the indignity of the forced marriage of a widow or an heiress. In this quarter – the Crown's heavy footed and uncontrollable interference in family affairs – was the source of that discontented bickering, that sluggish and unwilling loyalty, that querulous demand by men for their 'rights', that harassed John from his earliest years as king. It is so easy to forget, when studying political and constitutional history, that the first concern of barons was with wives and children, with mothers, cousins, nephews, with manors, castles, and estate boundaries. Because chronicles tell of the politics of the king's council we tend to forget the politics of the bedchamber. A baron's ambition for his heir, his concern for his widow if he died in war, his conversations with his brother-in-law, are no less important, no less a part of the warp and weft of the past, just because we know so little about them. The counterpart of the emergence of the Crown, in the late 12th and 13th centuries, as the dominating influence in public affairs is the establishment of the barons, the military chieftains of earlier days, as a landed aristocracy, learning to exploit the possibilities of estate management. Hence Magna Carta is largely concerned with succession dues and wardship, with widows and fish-weirs, with forest laws and forced marriages. Anyone going to it to learn the barons' thoughts about 'the constitution' or 'the liberty of the individual' will be disappointed to find so little, and that incidental; but such questions, as it happens, were not what the barons thought principally about.

One contemporary was just as disappointed, though for different reasons: chivalry is no more, wailed the biographer of William Marshal, 'Nowadays the great have put chivalry and largesse in bondage, so that the life of errantry and tourneys is deserted for law-suits. But if God wills, King Henry [he meant John's son] will give back joy and laughter to the world.'[1] His hope was vain. His view of the past, his exaltation of the days of his youth as the great age of chivalry, was the narrow view of the knight-errant followers of the Young King, of Philip of Flanders, of Theobald of Blois, and the duke of Burgundy. It was one aspect of medieval life, but a small one – the little world of landless younger sons with idle talents who had found a gentlemanly way of life and aristocratic pursuits in a number of prosperous but transient pleasure-loving courts. The writer's hero, William Marshal, was one of the lucky ones who made the transition from a landless knight-errant to a land-owning magnate, and indeed became the greatest baron in the realm. His biographer could afford the luxury of indulging his nostalgic memories of the gay and ir-responsible days of youth. They were no more. It was the men with families who made politics – and history.

2. JOHN'S WAY WITH HIS BARONS

John, then, had good grounds for being apprehensive when the pope excommunicated him: the fabric of fidelity was riddled with worm-holes of bitterness and remembered grievance; the barons might be expected to rejoice at his difficulties and seek to wrest what advantage they could from them. It was a moment for thought-ful concesssions, for the promotion of confidence between ruler and ruled. John did not take it. It is symptomatic of his tempera-ment that he chose instead to keep his barons in line by fear not affection. He sought to fashion maximum security for the Crown out of the greatest possible insecurity for his subjects. He bore down even harder than his predecessors had done on the point where they were most sensitive – their family interests.

He contrived no new devices for the purpose, but used the old ones more ruthlessly and more generally. His success seemed bound-less – at first. 'No one in the land could resist his will in anything,' says Gervase of Canterbury, 'The king himself seemed alone to be mighty in the land and he neither feared God nor regarded men.'[1]

His reaction to fear of excommunication weakening the bonds of allegiance was to demand hostages from prominent barons. Their sons were made security for their father's good behaviour. It was one of John's favourite devices. He even took them from his mercenary captains. They were not always badly treated: the sons of Richard de Umfraville, for instance, went into the queen's household as pages and took their tutor with them. But if anyone thought the surrender of hostages was nothing more than a nominal security, he had a sharp jolt in July 1212 when John hanged twenty-eight sons of Welsh chieftains because their fathers had broken faith. 'You have given us your son as hostage,' he pointedly reminded the earl of Huntingdon a month later, 'there-fore we require you to yield to us your castle at Fotheringhay.'[2]

Besides thus menacing members of baronial families John kept up a persistent threat to take away their property. He was able to do this very neatly by keeping his barons in a permanent state of financial indebtedness to the Crown. Henry II and Richard I had not hesitated to seize a debtor's chattels and land until he paid up: it was an example of the Crown's arbitrary use of its power, but against persistent defaulters this was reasonable enough. Neither of them, however, went so far as John in deliberately burdening the barons with debt so as to have a ready excuse for expropriating them. It was a clever device for giving the barons an even greater sense of insecurity than periodic displays of arbitrary disseisin would have done.

It was difficult for a baron to avoid getting into the Exchequer's toils; he might commit a misdemeanour – allowing an outlaw to escape from his custody, for example, making a false claim, putting a fish-weir in a river without royal permission – and be at the king's mercy. He might be amerced, but it was generally recognised that a baron's amercements should be assessed by his peers in the king's court, so John would prefer to display his 'anger' and have the baron buy his 'goodwill', often at exorbitant rates. In 1207 Roger de Cressi married an heiress without the king's licence. The lands of both were seized until Roger came to make his peace, and he was then obliged to pledge himself to pay 1200 marks and twelve palfreys for having the king's 'benevolence' and his lands back.[1] This procedure could be used even when there were no sure grounds or clear enough evidence for judicial action; and prowling about the kingdom as was his daily habit, John was adept at smelling out small transgressions and little scandals. Robert de Vaux, one of the principal barons in Cumberland, had to offer the king five first-class palfreys in 1210, 'that he would keep quiet about the wife of Henry Pinel,' and 750 marks for 'goodwill'.[2]

Then again a baron's cupidity or his ambition for his family would lead him to make an offer to the king for some grant or concession – an heiress for his son, perhaps, some fief that had fallen into the king's hands, the guardianship of a minor's estate, the post of warden of a forest, or constable of a castle – and John would draw him on to promise more than he could possibly pay from his revenues or savings. Thomas of Erdington promised 5000 marks for the custody of the FitzAlan barony; William de Briouze was very keen to obtain valuable heiresses for his sons, but he had to pay as much as £1000 each for them. John put the fantastic price of 20,000 marks on his former wife Isabelle, countess of Gloucester, but Geoffrey de Mandeville was prepared to contract for her. William Mowbray was misguided enough to offer the king 2000 marks for justice in his case when William de Stuteville claimed his barony. John accepted the offer, which smacks strongly of a bribe, and then allowed his court to give judgement against Mowbray.[1]

It was, it may be held, a baron's own fault if he became the Crown's debtor of his own free will in this way; but there were frequent occasions when a barony could not help getting into the red at the Exchequer. The king had the whip hand in the matter of succession dues. As the *Dialogus de Scaccario* puts it 'there is no fixed amount which the heir must pay to the king; he must make what terms he can.' Henry I had promised in his coronation charter that 'the heir shall relieve his land by a just and legitimate relief', and it had come to be generally acknowledged that a reasonable relief was £100 for a barony. Very occasionally John would be content with £100, but usually he demanded more. Sometimes he would point to or hint at a possible flaw in the title, but often there seems to have been no excuse. Six hundred marks by way of relief was commonly charged. A man who was out of favour could be asked to pay as much as 7000 marks, as John Lacy was in 1211. William Stuteville and William FitzAlan were each charged the enormous sum of 10,000 marks. Widows were obliged to pay 100–300 marks for having their dower, and if they happened to be heiresses in their own right they might have to promise as much as the 2000 marks that Amabile widow of Hugh Bardolf did.[2]

The relationship of these sums to a baron's ability to pay may be gauged from the fact that the average annual baronial income was something in the region of £200. A small minority could count on about £400 a year, very few on more than £800.[3] The Stuteville inheritance for which Nicholas had to pay 10,000 marks relief in 1205 was worth about £550 a year. This meant of course that the debts were on the king's books for a very long time. It gave him the chance to favour his friends and harass his enemies. He might remit a portion of the debt or even the whole of it. Roger Lacy, the heroic defender of Château Gaillard, was let off a third of the £1000 debt he incurred for having the guardianship of Richard Mountfichet. The relief owed by William Fortibus for the inheritance of his mother, Hawise countess of Aumale, was pardoned altogether, but then she had been the king's mistress.[1] For those who had to pay in full, payment by instalments was arranged. Naturally the king fixed the rates as he wished. They were not usually harsh: grasping though John was he preferred to keep the barons in his power than to have the debts liquidated. Nicholas Stuteville was £9998 in arrears for the several debts he had contracted in John's reign as late as 1230.[2]

To be in debt to the Crown was to give the king a hold over one's property. From the earliest years of the reign he demanded that debtors put their estates in pledge for keeping up their instalments at the Exchequer. In 1201 he went farther and threatened forfeiture of land where the debtor was in default. He could be quite ruthless about it: the whole earldom of Leicester was impounded on this ground in 1207 and held until 1215.[3]

One avenue of escape from threatened foreclosure was to borrow from the Jewish moneylenders; but as often as not one could not escape down it far. For one thing, paying interest to the Jews, heavy enough in itself, was an indirect way of paying a tax to the Crown. The Jews were under royal protection – which meant that they set up in business only on his sufferance – and the king regularly raided their profits by way of arbitrary 'tallages'. Furthermore, the king was every Jew's heir, and when a moneylender died he took over not only his chattels and cash but also his credit notes. So a man who escaped from the Exchequer to the Jews might pay heavy interest for several years and then find that, before he had even reduced the principal, his debt was back in the king's hands.[4]

The king's power to cripple his vassals was all the more disturbing in John because he was capable of using it for no very good reason – a caprice of his twisted suspicions, his dislike of men simply because they were great and powerful. Ranulph earl of Chester had been threatened in 1203–4, and in 1206–7 it was the turn of his Marcher colleagues in south Wales, William Marshal and William de Briouze. Practically anywhere west of the Severn one was in country closely controlled by the earl of Pembroke or by Briouze and his sons and relations. Farther west still, across the Irish Sea, one would again find them the dominating figures. Marshal was lord of Leinster, Briouze was lord of Limerick. The latter's son-in-law, Walter Lacy, was lord of Meath, and Hugh Lacy, his brother, controlled Ulster. Marshal and Briouze were brave men who had served John well and had been handsomely rewarded. Indeed, John was largely responsible for making them the mighty barons that they were. William Marshal was high-minded enough to forgive John the indignities and threats he was made to suffer from 1206 to 1210 and stood by him in the crisis of 1215. William de Briouze could not for he was dead. He died in exile in 1211 after being hounded from his lands and from the country by John's malevolence. His wife and one of his sons died before him, starved to death in King John's prison. The story crops up in every chronicle of the period – which shows how much of a stir it caused at the time.

There seems to be no cause for the king's persecution of these men beyond his own devouring suspicion. It probably had its origin in the arguments and discords of 1205. William Marshal, we know, though he protested his loyalty, provoked John's anger and distrust by his arrangements with King Philip. Briouze may have sided with him, for he too was a Norman baron as well as being a close friend. Certainly both of them were out of favour from then on. Regretting that he had ever made them so powerful, John began harassing tactics. Late in 1206 he encouraged an Irish baron, Meiler FitzHenry, who was also his justiciar in Ireland, to pursue his private ambitions by raiding Leinster and Limerick under the royal protection.[1] In England he lopped off as much as he easily could of their authority by taking back the royal offices that he had bestowed upon them. Marshal lost the posts of sheriff of Gloucester and custodian of Cardigan and the Forest of Dean. Briouze was replaced as bailiff of Glamorgan. In their stead John moved in two of his foreign mercenaries, Gerard d'Athée and Fawkes de Breauté.[2]

So far as the earl of Pembroke was concerned John went no farther than harassing tactics. Marshal preserved his customary correctness and dignity. He spent as much time as possible in Ireland, where he was safer, and met John's demands for the surrender of hostages and castles as pledges of his loyalty with an accommodating promptness. But as for Briouze, John determined in 1208 to break him. We cannot be absolutely certain why. The biographer of Marshal, commenting on the treatment of his patron's friend, says that he does not know what caused it, and if he did he would not tell.[3] Roger of Wendover was not so reticent: the story he knew was that in March 1208 John demanded hostages from Briouze. When the royal messengers arrived 'Matilda the wife of William, with the sauciness of a woman, took the reply out of her husband's mouth and said, "I will not deliver up my sons to your lord, King John, because he basely murdered his nephew Arthur, whom he ought to have kept in honourable custody." William was alarmed at his wife's rash tongue and rebuked her saying, "You have spoken like a stupid woman against our lord the king; for if I have offended him in any way I am ready to make amends without the security of hostages according to the judgement of my fellow barons in his court, if he will fix a time and place for my doing so." When the messengers told the king on their return what they had heard, he was furious and secretly sent knights to seize William and his family, but he, being forewarned by his friends, fled with his wife, his children, and his relatives to Ireland.'[1]

Even if the story were true it could hardly be expected, of course, that John would admit that the reference to Arthur was the cause of his hostility. What he did say, when he issued letters patent about the affair in 1210 as a sort of proclamation, was that William had not kept up the instalments due on the 5000 marks he had promised for Limerick, and had resisted forcibly the very proper efforts of the Exchequer to distrain upon his lands for debt.[2] But Wendover's story, whether or not it is true in all its details, receives support from the way John, in fact, behaved. He was not content with distraint, he wanted forfeiture, and he went about it as if he were going to war. In April 1208 a small army of 500 infantry and 25 mounted sergeants under the command of Gerard d'Athée, now sheriff of Gloucestershire, and Thomas Erdington, sheriff of Shropshire, was moving into the Briouze country; and on 29 April Briouze was ordered to pay 1000 marks within four days to cover the cost of the expedition against him.[3] Furthermore, John pursued Matilda even more relentlessly than he did her husband: when William offered 40,000 marks for recovering the king's goodwill, he refused all terms while Matilda was at liberty.[4]

Briouze was not crushed immediately. In the summer of 1208 he was summoned to appear before John in his court but excused himself on the ground of sickness. Gerard d'Athée, who besides being sheriff of Gloucester had now replaced Briouze's second cousin, Walter Clifford, as sheriff of Hereford, was busily obliging his vassals to disavow their lord. By the autumn William had had enough and fled with his wife and family to Ireland where his friends were strong enough to protect him from the royal justiciar in Dublin. His brother, Giles, bishop of Hereford, went to join those bishops who had already gone into exile because of the interdict.[1]

John let him be in Ireland for a year because he had his hands full in England, but in the spring of 1210 he prepared to cross the Irish Sea with a great army consisting of the feudal levy of England and several companies of Flemish *routiers*. Before he sailed William slipped back to Wales leaving his family in the care of Hugh Lacy in Ulster, and sent messengers to the king seeking terms. John spurned his offers and the Irish expedition went ahead. It was, in fact, part of the king's determined efforts to bring Ireland more firmly under royal control, but he gave out that his purpose was to catch Matilda and to punish the Irish barons who had protected the Briouzes.[2] When he marched on Ulster, Matilda fled with her sons to Scotland, but they were taken by a Scots lord and handed over to John's agents. She offered to ransom herself for 40,000 marks, and William went to meet John on his return to confirm the offer. John later gave out that he agreed to the offer and allowed William to depart to raise the money; but William instead fled to France in despair. Matilda and her eldest son disappeared into prison (at Windsor, probably) and never emerged again. The common report, recorded in half a dozen monastic annals, was that they had been starved to death.[3] William himself died in September 1211, still in exile, at Corbeil in France, and his funeral was conducted by a fellow sufferer from John's tyranny, Archbishop Langton.[4]

John insisted in his proclamation of 1210, which gave his version of the affair up to the point of William's flight to France, that all his actions had been the just and proper response to Briouze's default in payment of his debts and his armed resistance to distraint. But even if the barons accepted John's explanation, they can only have been more alarmed, and felt even more dreadfully insecure, at this terrible illustration of the king's interpretation of his rights. Even the mightiest among them could be crumpled if they lost the king's 'goodwill', and the goodwill of a king, moreover, who was so suspicious and distrustful. His proclamation was witnessed by five earls and seven barons. Six of them were to be among the leaders of the rebels in 1215. Indeed, if one thing above all can be singled out from the many concurrent factors in urging men to united action against the king, it is likely that it was the fate of William de Briouze and his family.[1]

Quite apart from what John actually did there was the objectionable way he went about doing it. He put his deepest trust only in men who were completely dependent upon him, and in practice this meant, very often, the clever and able men he had brought over from the continent: men like Fawkes de Breauté, Savary de Mauléon, Gerard d'Athée, Peter des Roches. The judicious Barnwell annalist was convinced that one of the root causes of the desertion of John by his subjects was the favour he showed to aliens.[2] It is not hard to see why, quite apart from them being outsiders who did not understand English customs, for John entrusted them with his dirtiest work.

Take Gerard d'Athée, who played a prominent part in the destruction of Briouze, as an example. He was a Frenchman from Touraine, and spiteful rumour said that he had been born a serf, and had risen in the world solely by putting his ruthless abilities at the service of a paymaster. In the early days of the reign he had secured Chinon and Loches for John, and had been given the custody of Tours and the seneschalcy of Touraine. When all else in northern France had been lost, he was in 1204 still defending Loches with ferocious bravery until at last he was taken prisoner when the castle fell at Easter 1205. When, in the months that followed, John was moving farther and farther away in spirit from his English barons and felt that there were so few that he could trust, he remembered so clear a demonstration of loyalty, paid the large ransom of 2000 marks which was demanded for Gerard, and brought him to England. He was put in charge of the county and castle of Gloucester when they were taken from William Marshal, of Bristol castle, of the expropriated lands of the bishopric of Bath, and of the county and castle of Hereford. Thus a ruthless adventurer, notorious for his crushing rule in Touraine, became the king's lieutenant in the west country and the approaches to Wales. His establishment there was one of the manifestations of John's distrust of Marshal and Briouze, and when the axe fell on Briouze it was Gerard d'Athée who wielded it. He brought his kinsmen to England with him, and John gave them lands for their maintenance and offices in his service. Gerard died in 1213 before baronial discontent rose to its feet, but he and his kinsmen achieved a perpetual remembrance for they were cited by name in Magna Carta: 'We', the king was made to promise, 'will utterly remove from their offices the relatives of Gerard d'Athée, namely, Engelard de Cigogné, Peter and Guy and Andrew de Chanceaux, Guy de Cigogné, Geoffrey de Martigny and his brethren, Philip Marc and his brothers and his nephew, Geoffrey, together with all their adherents, so that henceforth they shall have no office in England.'[1] Unfortunately we know little more about them than their names, but the hatred of them is obvious enough. John, it is clear, had a corps of strong-arm agents whom he would move into trouble spots to enforce his will at the point of the sword.

Even worse than this there was the way John himself went to work. He prowled the country with a nose alert for scandal or misdemeanour. Yet if Robert de Vaux had to bribe the king to 'keep quiet' about his *affaire* with the wife of Henry Pinel, the king himself gave cause for scandal. He was adulterous, and had five bastards.* They were all old enough to have been the consequences of infidelities to his first wife, but he certainly had mistresses while he was married to Isabelle of Angoulême. There was the unknown one to whom he sent a chaplet of roses from his justiciar's garden in 1212; there was the widow Hawise, countess of Aumale; there was Suzanne and there was Clementia, who were presumably lowborn. He probably had more bastards than his father, who is known to have had three, but can hardly bear comparison with his great-grandfather, Henry I, who had at least twenty-one. The peculiar rub of John's lustfulness, however, seems to have been that it went out after the wives and daughters of his barons. So, at least, barely veiled accusations suggest, but none of them is substantiated, and may have been merely excuses for personal animosity. He is said in his younger days to have lusted after the wife of Eustace de Vesci, but was frustrated by a common woman being secretly substituted.[2] Certainly there was considerable bitterness between the two men, and Eustace was in the forefront of baronial uprisings from 1212 to 1216.

---

* Cf. Painter, *King John*, pp. 232–5. The names of John's known bastards are Joan, who was the daughter of Clementina and married Llewelyn of Wales (*Annales Monastici*, i. 101), Geoffrey (*Curia Regis Rolls*, iii. 321) who helped his father as a commander of troops (*Rot. Pat.*, i. 117), Oliver (Paris, *Chronica Majora*, iii. 41), Richard (Wendover, iv. 29) who served as a captain during the baronial revolt, and Osbert. His mistress Suzanne is referred to as 'domicella, amica domini Regis', *Misae Roll 14 John*, p. 267.

John's humour could be bawdily nasty, as when he held the clergy's concubines to ransom. There is something of the sort too behind a curious but piquant entry on the Oblate Roll for Christmas 1204: 'The wife of Hugh Neville promises the lord king two hundred chickens that she might lie one night with her husband.'[1] Hugh Neville was chief forester and did well for himself as one of John's henchmen, but when the barons rose in revolt in 1216 he joined them.

Then, again, there is the cloak-and-dagger secrecy that John imparted to his administration. He seems to have expected to be cheated and devised elaborate checks on the conveyance of instructions. Castellans who received a writ to hand over their charge to someone else had to report back to the king personally to get confirmation by word of mouth. Secret signs were arranged by which the recipient of an order would know whether the king really sent it. Naturally such secret signs have usually been carried into oblivion, but we know the sort of thing that was going on from the occasions when the king himself had to break the secret because something had gone wrong. The chamberlain had been instructed not to allow anyone to speak to a certain prisoner unless escorted by one of three named members of the royal Household. Unfortunately the king's memory betrayed him: 'and because we do not well recollect who those three were, inform us thereupon that another time we may with more certainty give you our commands.'[2] Robert de Vieuxpont was once instructed not to release a certain prisoner the first time he was instructed to do so[3]: it is clever, too clever by half—that was the trouble with John. His passion for security became almost a mania: Henry of Pomeria and Alan of Dunstanville revealed in court in 1214 that they were members of the Household and as such had been put upon oath that 'if they hear anything hostile to the lord king they were to report it to him.'[4]

There are occasions, too, when John makes his tyrannies seem even worse by unnecessarily underhand or nasty behaviour. When he was forcing the Cistercians to submit to taxation in 1200 he conveyed his instructions privately to his sheriffs 'acting verbally with no written record.' It is Ralph of Coggeshall, himself a Cistercian, who reveals it.[5] In 1214, after he had promised to allow free elections to bishoprics, he wrote to the chapter of York forbidding them to nominate their dean as archbishop, and adding

'if however you do elect him he can never hope to have our peace
or love. This however we wish to be kept secret.'[1] In 1207 the
archbishop of York and the bishop of Durham tried to stop the
collection of the tax of a thirteenth of movable property in the
northern province. Their lands were seized and they came to the
king to plead with him. The archbishop fell at his feet, appealing
to his conscience, whereupon 'the king, in truth, threw himself
at the archbishop's feet and laughing and jeering said, "Look,
my lord archbishop, even as you do so do I".'[2]

As one pursues John through the records one begins not to
need an explicit description of him from a contemporary to know
what he was like, and how he must have appeared to his barons.
He was cultivated in his tastes, fastidious in personal cleanliness,
industrious, clever, and ingenious. At the same time he was hot-
tempered, wilful, and capricious. He was generous to those who
could not harm him, and merciless to anyone who could. Above
and behind all he was secretive and suspicious, over-sensitive to
the merest flicker of opposition, relentless in revenge, cruel and
mocking when he had men in his clutch. Is it any wonder that
men revelled when finally they triumphed over him, and delighted
to tell stories of his wickedness without bothering to establish their
authenticity?

3. MASTER OF THE BRITISH ISLES

John's quest for internal security, driven hard by his anxiety to
get to grips with King Philip again and by his own obsessive
fears, embraced the frontier areas in Wales, Scotland, and Ireland. Here royal authority, at its farthest stretch from the royal
stronghold in the Home Counties and the south, was traditionally
at its most tenuous. The requirements of local defence and the
limitations of the administrative machinery at the disposal of
earlier kings had left in the hands of barons of these parts much of
the local authority that elsewhere was strictly controlled by the
king himself. In some localities, most notably in the Palatinate
of Durham and the Palatinate of Chester, the lord was, in a manner of speaking, a hereditary viceroy, directing on his own authority an administration which, in miniature, mirrored that of the
kingdom at large. He appointed his own sheriffs and justices and
collected revenues into his own exchequer. Other barons of the
border areas enjoyed some but not all of the palatine lords'

privileges: the most extensive being in conquered land in Wales and Ireland. Pembroke, held by William Marshal, was virtually a palatinate, and his authority was only barely less extensive in his Irish lordship of Leinster.

Such barons were by no means insulated from the cares of their colleagues in other parts of the realm, for their estates were not all concentrated within the bounds of these jurisdictional 'liberties'. William Marshal's inherited family manors, for example, were scattered in Wiltshire, Sussex, Berkshire, Worcestershire, and Herefordshire. They were, we may say, ordinary barons with the added advantage of frontier strongholds. It was natural that John should fear the greater liberties, from which his officials were excluded, as likely bases of opposition. He gave them his special attention and did what he could to advertise his authority by personal visitation, by strengthening royal castles there, by intruding trusted men, by revising former concessions in his own favour where he could, and by such demonstrations of power as the destruction of Briouze.[1] No earlier king made himself so felt in the extremities of his realm as did King John.

At the same time, John was concerned that the disaffected should not be able to turn for assistance to the Welsh or Scots, or find refuge in Ireland. His armed expeditions to these parts in 1209–12 were not unrelated adventures or needless dissipations of his military resources; they were integral parts of his design for the security of the realm. They take their place beside the great expenditure on the castles of the eastern and southern coasts, and the establishment of naval flotillas, in John's attempts to guarantee the county's defence before he tried his strength again against Philip.[2]

William the Lion, king of Scots, threatened to give John trouble from the outset of the reign. He had been forced to acknowledge the overlordship of the English Crown when in 1174 he had been captured while trying to profit from the baronial rebellion against Henry II; but King Richard, with typical cavalier disregard for English long-term interests, had thrown this advantage away. With only the thought of raising money for the crusade in mind, he abrogated all the agreements which his father 'by new charters and by reason of the king's capture had extorted', and restored to him the castles of Berwick and Roxburgh for the lump sum of 10,000 marks.[3] Presuming upon this accommodating attitude,

William advanced claims to hold the northern counties (Northumberland, Cumberland, Westmorland, and perhaps part of Lancashire) as a vassal of the English Crown. This was not altogether preposterous: his father had once held the earldom of Northumberland, and his elder brother had been earl both of Northumberland and Cumberland. His younger brother was even now, as a matter of fact, earl of Huntingdon. But William's claim was not seriously entertained.

The king of Scots probably hoped that Richard would be succeeded on the throne by Arthur of Brittany who was his sister's grandson; indeed there is some evidence that he conspired to this end with Chancellor Longchamp.[1] When John succeeded instead, William behaved belligerently, demanding Northumberland and Cumberland, refusing to do homage for his English barony of Tindale, and threatening that if his demands were not met he would do his best to take what he was entitled to. He failed to appear when John summoned him to do homage at York in March 1200, but thought better of it in November and came to John at Lincoln. John postponed discussion of the claim to the northern counties indefinitely, and strained relations between them are witnessed by the seizure of Scottish ships off the coast, and by William's asylum for refugee English bishops, and his demolition of fortifications made by the bishop of Durham on the Tweed.[2]

John was obliged to take the situation in the north very seriously in 1209, for a conspiracy was afoot to start a rebellion there and in Ireland, where the Briouzes were lurking with the Lacys. Philip of France was in touch with the conspirators and seems to have in mind a simultaneous invasion.[3] John determined upon a show of strength before his personal excommunication weakened his position further. In August he appeared at Norham at the head of a large army, demanding that William the Lion give security for his loyalty by surrendering three castles. William did not relish the idea of war and came to make terms. John, thinking he had him on the run, drove home his advantage by adopting a domineering and high-handed attitude, but allowed himself to be pacified by William's complete submission. The Scots king handed over his two daughters as hostages, and promised to pay 15,000 marks within two years for the familiar purpose of having John's 'goodwill'.[4] How he hoped to pay is a mystery for he was already heavily in debt to the Jews; but John had what he wanted: a hold over William and his complete humiliation as an object lesson to anyone who favoured the chances of rebellion.

This demonstration of power in the north was the necessary preliminary to the pursuit of the Briouzes to Ireland, and the proper establishment of the king's authority there. Richard had had no interest in it, indeed so little did he regard it as his concern that he did not deprive John of his title of *Dominus Hiberniae* when his other fiefs were taken away from him in 1194. It is hardly even known who acted as Justiciar in Dublin after John de Courcy was replaced in 1191. For years the country dissolved into a bloody free-for-all in which Irish princes and adventurers from England teamed up indiscriminately against each other. John attempted to do something about it – at a distance – as soon as he came to the throne. One of the survivors of the original conquistadors, Meiler FitzHenry, was put in as Justiciar, the use of the judicial processes by which Henry II had tamed self-help in England was authorised in 1204, and a new coinage was issued in 1207.[1]

The real work of inducing some semblance of order among the lesser barons was, however, carried out by a new generation of lords with English resources behind them: the Lacy brothers in Meath and Ulster, William de Briouze in Limerick, and William Marshal in Leinster. Briouze went over to Limerick as soon as John granted it to him in January 1201, and in getting it under control no doubt used that ruthlessness that had made him the terror of the Welsh March. He had to rejoin John in France in 1202, but his brother-in-law, Walter Lacy, was on hand to watch his interests in Ireland, and in return Briouze looked after Walter's estates which bordered his own in Wales. The Lacys co-operated with the justiciar in subduing the turbulent John de Courcy who was trying to make his own way against the native princes in northern Ireland. In May 1205 John granted Ulster to Hugh Lacy 'as John de Courcy held it on the day when Hugh defeated him.'[2] William Marshal had become lord of Leinster in 1189 in right of his wife, Isabelle, daughter and heiress of Richard 'Strongbow', the most famous of the early adventurers; but he was probably not able to visit it in person until 1207 and then only for a few weeks. He remained there, however, almost continuously from April 1208 until early in 1213, out of favour with John for most of the time, and brought his great province a peace and prosperity unthinkable hitherto.[1]

By comparison with these men, the authority of the Justiciar was feeble, and beyond the Pale hardly visible at all. John realised this forcibly when at the end of 1206 he encouraged Meiler to attack the lands of Briouze and Marshal. When they and their friends in Ireland protested, the king made a great show of insisting that no one should question his Justiciar's right to seize a fief at the king's command.[2] But it was no use the king trying to behave in the arbitrary way he would have done in England when he had not got the force to back up his will. This was only too apparent a few months later: William Marshal shipped over some of his best knights and with the help of Hugh Lacy they overpowered Meiler, devastated his private estates and captured him. News of this did not reach England for several weeks because heavy seas were running, and both the king and Marshal were anxiously on the look-out for messengers. One day at the end of January, as both of them rode out of Guildford together, John asked Marshal if he had heard any word from Ireland, and when he replied that he had not, the king went on to tell him that Meiler's men had worsted William's knights at Kilkenny. William felt sure that John had received no news either and was making up the story to dishearten him and so replied, 'Certainly, Sire, it is a pity about the knights. They were after all your subjects, which makes the affair only more regrettable.'[3]

John's harassing tactics had some effect in that William, bending with the cold wind, consented in March 1208 to accept a new charter for Leinster which extended the reach of royal justice over cases of treasure-trove, rape, ambush, and arson, provided for appeals of default of justice from the lord's court, and gave the king control of the bishopric of Leinster during a vacancy. A month later Walter Lacy accepted similar terms for Meath.[4] But despite this small advance of royal jurisdiction, Meiler was clearly a broken reed, and there were obvious disadvantages in having as justiciar a man who could be discomfited in his private capacity as an Irish baron. So the king replaced him by John de Gray, bishop of Norwich. Gray was one of the best brains of the royal administration, and John had thought him the only possible substitute for Hubert Walter as archbishop of Canterbury. He could ill be spared from the royal service in England, but Dublin was a convenient place to put him in 1208 for no one could afterwards accuse him, a bishop, of having ignored the Interdict: it did not apply in Ireland. Still there was little that Gray could do without an army at his back, beyond investigating the situation with his trained eye. He was not able to hunt down William de Briouze, and could only make verbal protests when William Marshal received him honourably and Walter Lacy gave him asylum.[1]

In the spring of 1210, however, John proposed to give him an army and to lead it in person. The sources for this period of John's reign are, unfortunately, very meagre. We have a Household account roll and can observe his payments to his troops and follow his itinerary in some detail, but the Chancery Rolls for the middle period of the reign have disappeared and John's dealings with his barons are therefore obscure. The triumphant effectiveness of the expedition does not, however, admit of any doubt. It was planned on a major scale and for weeks beforehand stores were being collected from as far apart as Lancashire and Yorkshire, Devon, Somerset, and Sussex. The large force of English knights and Flemish mercenaries who sailed from Pembroke were reinforced on the march through Ireland by the men of the careful William Marshal, and by contingents from the Irish chieftains, whom John seems to have treated with marked favour.[2]

He landed at Crook, near Waterford, and marched through Leinster to Dublin. There, at the end of June, some of the barons of Meath came to intercede for their lord, Walter Lacy, and to offer complete submission, but John would hear no pleas for clemency. He dispossessed Walter and would not restore him until 1215. Hugh Lacy, harbouring Matilda de Briouze in Ulster, presented some show of resistance, and John had to put his army in battle array for the first time when he marched against him in July. The Mourne Mountains gave Hugh a good opportunity for mounting ambushes, but John turned the defences there. He seized Carlingford castle and immediately set about strengthening it, put the main body of his army across Carlingford Lough by means of a bridge of boats, and set them to negotiate the flank of the mountains. He himself, with chosen troops, went by sea to Ardglass and pounced upon the castle of Dundrum which barred the main army's way. As he advanced north again with open country before him, Hugh Lacy decided on flight: with Matilda de Briouze he took ship for Scotland. He left his men to conduct the defence of his main stronghold at Carrickfergus, at the entrance to Belfast Lough, but when John came up to it and made impressive preparations for siege by land and sea, they surrendered. John advanced no farther but sent a contingent to take Antrim castle, and had two galleys built for patrolling Lough Neagh He himself returned to Dublin, and from there at the end of August he sailed to Fishguard.

The Irish lords who had been such mighty nabobs had suddenly seemed small and feeble at the king's coming. It is possible that John prevented the complete conquest of the country by private enterprise, but he had certainly averted the danger from over-mighty subjects, and he was now rich in prisoners, hostages, and confiscated castles. Though we can no longer read the measures he took, it is significant that in time to come men looked on his two months' visit as the foundation of effective royal authority in Ireland. The new stone castle that rose at Dublin, completed in 1215, was the symbol of it.[1]

The situation in Wales was more intractable. English Marcher barons had penetrated deep into south-east Wales and were firmly entrenched on the southern coast. Pembroke, indeed, was already forgetting the Welsh language and becoming 'a little England beyond Wales'. The centre and north of the country, however, were in the hands of quarrelsome Welsh chieftains, sometimes, but never for long, submitting to the rule of one of their number, and owing little more than nominal allegiance to the English Crown. Henry II had struggled in vain in 1165 to mount a full-scale campaign in impossible terrain, and thereafter contented himself with balancing the contending Welsh princes and their English neighbours against each other.[2]

John knew something of Welsh politics from his younger days as earl of Gloucester, and he had to take care that no baron would do as he had done and use his power there as a means of fomenting trouble in England. At the beginning of his reign he built up William Marshal and William de Briouze, who were then in his confidence, in the south, as a balance to Ranulph earl of Chester on the northern border. He tried to play off the Welsh prince Gwenwynwyn, who was strong in the centre, against Llywelyn ap

Iorworth, who dominated Anglesey and the north. When he saw that Llywelyn (who was later to earn the title of Llywelyn the Great) was too wily to be led in this way, he reversed his policy and gave him his illegitimate daughter, Joan, in marriage.

This new policy seemed to pay dividends, for Llywelyn brought a contingent of Welshmen to join the king on his march against Scotland in the autumn of 1209; but in reality the fall of Marshal and Briouze from favour had upset the balance of power in Wales and given Llywelyn scope for his ambitions. Briouze slipped back to Wales on the eve of John's departure for Ireland, and in the king's absence rallied enough supporters to attempt to regain some of his lands there. Llywelyn seems to have given him aid, or at least to have thought the time ripe for creating trouble. The justiciar and the earl of Chester co-operated in leading a force against him, and built three forts on Welsh soil.[1]

This was not enough for John: flushed with his triumph in Ireland, he was in no mood to tolerate an ambitious Welsh chieftain and in May 1211 he gathered an army and Llywelyn's Welsh rivals and marched on the castle of Dyganwy. He was too precipitate: he had not reckoned with the difficulties of fighting in mountainous country. Llywelyn and his men withdrew with their property into the fastnesses of Snowdonia and left John's army nothing to fight but famine: even eggs were hard to come by and the troops resorted to eating horseflesh – a serious matter in the days when the horse was a man's most valuable possession.[2] John retired, but only to prepare himself better. In July he set out again from Oswestry with a larger army and abundant provisions, and marched down the vale of Llangollen and the river Conway to Bangor, building forts as he went. Llywelyn was cowed and sent his wife to plead with her father. John agreed to make peace, but he imposed crushing terms: he took thirty hostages, the region known as the Four Cantreds around St Asaph (thus holding Llywelyn beyond the Conway) and a large indemnity.[3]

Anyone who harboured illusions derived from the fate of Normandy, about John's ability to conduct successful military operations, had them dispelled by 1211. The pursuit to destruction of Briouze had caused ripples of discontent and trouble and had involved him in the extremities of his realm; but he had triumphed. As the Barwell annalist puts it, 'there was now no one in Ireland,

Scotland or Wales, who did not bow to his nod, a situation which, as is well known, none of his predecessors had achieved.'[1] Early in 1212 William the Lion of Scotland, threatened by a Celtic pretender to his throne, sent John his son to pledge their fealty and beseech his aid. With lordly condescension John despatched a force of mercenaries in the spring who quashed the rebellion and hanged the pretender.[2] Well might John think himself ready to renew the war with Philip of France.

4. THE STRUCTURE TOTTERS

John planned his return to France for the summer of 1212. The movement of stores across the country – well on the way to becoming an annual operation – was directed to Portsmouth. Writs went out at Ascensiontide for the summons of knights to Poitou. In anticipation of a prolonged campaign for which all the realm's resources would have to be mustered, an official inquiry was set on foot in every shire to bring up to date the government's knowledge of who was available for military service in respect of land tenure.[3] Three commissions of justices went round the country to search out offenders against the Forest laws. It was a quick way of raising money, and as cash came to hand it was shipped ahead to Poitou.[4] But, as in 1205, the expedition of 1212 was not destined even to board ship.

The first check to it was a Welsh revolt, in which Llywelyn recruited his former rivals in a joint attack on English garrisons. This sudden rising at the end of June, while John was in the north sending help to the king of Scots, was probably quite unexpected. Llywelyn had been entertained by John at Cambridge as recently as Easter. He may, however, have become aware on this visit of how deceptive was John's apparent dominance, and made up his mind, in consequence, to put himself behind the many Welsh chieftains who were bridling at the activities of royal agents in those parts of Wales that were being held for the Crown. The first attack was on the forts that John had built in 1211.[5] At first the king merely thought of a punitive expedition under Brian Delisle, and relief columns for the hard-pressed royal lieutenants there; but by the middle of July he had changed his mind and decided to solve the Welsh problem once for all. The host summoned for Poitou was redirected to muster at Chester on 19 August. The Welsh were to feel the whole weight of the army intended for

Philip of France, and more than that they were to be brought permanently under direct English rule. Castles were to be built as the army advanced. On 10 July instructions were sent out to the sheriffs in thirty shires for the recruitment of 2230 skilled ditchers and carpenters, and 6100 labourers armed with axes. If these plans had gone ahead it seems likely that John, and not his grandson Edward I, would be acclaimed as the conqueror of Wales. Edward, indeed, imitated his grandfather's policy and kept a large labour force at work on castle-building in the wake of his army, though he only recruited half the men for it that John had planned to use.[1]

The preparations came to nothing because a few days before the army was due to start John received alarming news. Rumours were picked up of a conspiracy, in the words of the Barnwell annalist, 'to drive him and his family from the kingdom and choose someone else as king in his place.' Wendover has a more dramatic story of breathless messengers from the king of Scots and from his bastard daughter Joan, Llywelyn's wife, arriving within minutes of each other just as he was sitting down to dinner after hanging the hostages of the Welsh chieftains. They brought similar warnings: if the king went to war in Wales, the barons planned to murder him in the press of battle, or to arrange for him to be captured by the enemy. In some places rumour took on the guise of wish-fulfilment: the king's second son, Prince Richard, had been killed, it was said, the royal treasury at Gloucester plundered, the queen raped.[2]

John acted quickly: the expedition to Wales was called off, his eldest son and heir, Henry (born in 1207), was put in safe-keeping, castles were seized and hostages were demanded. Two barons, Robert FitzWalter and Eustace de Vesci, fled the country.[3] John destroyed two of FitzWalter's castles, Benington in Hertfordshire and Castle Baynard in London, conducted a sharp security check on the personnel of his administration, and went up north, where Vesci was influential, and stamped on the sparks of rebellion.[4]

'The land kept silence', says the Barnwell annalist; but John was no fool to presume twice on his apparent mastery.[5] He seems to have realised that he was driving fierce horses too hard and that they were rearing in their traces. The Barnwell annalist records that in the autumn he stayed the severity of the Forest commissioners, restrained his officials from molesting pilgrims and merchants, and did what he could to make his rule seem less oppressive.[1] It was high time too; an emaciated and probably deranged hermit, Peter of Wakefield, was predicting that John would not reign for more than fourteen years, but would be dead by next Ascension Day, and people were listening to him hopefully. The king laughed at Peter as a madman, but some of his advisers were worried about him stirring up trouble in the disaffected north and had him arrested as a vagrant. Unfortunately this only had the effect of turning him into something of a popular hero – until next Ascension Day came and went, and John was still on his throne.[2]

Wondering upon whom he could rely for advice and help when, as Wendover puts it, 'he had almost as many enemies as barons,' John was grateful to grasp the proffered hand of William Marshal.[3] Though he had been out of favour and maliciously abused for five or six years, William's loyalty to his sovereign was inexhaustible. In these days of 1212, when the skies had suddenly darkened again for the house of Anjou, he persuaded twenty-six of his fellow barons in Ireland to renew their oaths of allegiance and to declare themselves 'ready to live or die with the king, and that till the last they would be faithful and inseparably adhere to him.'[4] William advised John to make peace with the pope and offered his services as negotiator if they were needed. John replied effusively: he was deeply grateful to William for the barons' expressions of loyalty: he much appreciated the earl's offer of his services, but thought that for the moment he would be of more use in Ireland; the justiciar in Dublin had written in warm praise of William's wise counsel and active co-operation, and had insisted that he needed him. As to William's suggestion that he make peace with the pope, he would be pleased if the barons of Ireland would draw up a form of submission which would secure peace without prejudicing the just rights of the Crown. He reported that William's son, who was a hostage at court, was doing well but needed a horse and new clothes. He offered to supply these himself and to put the boy in the care of anyone whom William nominated.[5]

John was clearly ready to cut his losses, and he was quite serious about his willingness to come to terms with the papacy if a reasonable formula could be found. The many adverse rumours that were circulating in the country included a report that Innocent

III had formally deposed him, and had invited Philip of France to take over the kingdom. There was no truth in the story: to the pope John was excommunicate but still king. Nonetheless, Philip was certainly preparing to invade, and it was high time to reduce the number of his opponents and escape from the disabilities of interdict and excommunication. In November a delegation was despatched to Rome.[1]

5. KING PHILIP DISCOMFITED

John authorised his envoys to the pope to accept the terms that had been offered him but rejected the previous summer. As soon as he heard this, Innocent, at the end of February 1213, sent off his legate Pandulph to England to make sure that John was serious, and to absolve him from excommunication if he were truly penitent.[2] Further detailed negotiation would be necessary before the Interdict could be lifted and the English clergy compensated for their losses; but this was tantamount to a truce.

John's representatives had arrived just in time to avert his formal deposition. This was the pope's last resort in a struggle against a ruler who refused to bend to excommunication, but Innocent had hesitated to take it hitherto because he was too much of a statesman to venture a decree he could not enforce. There were new factors in the situation at the close of 1212, however; King Philip was preparing to invade England, and would be delighted to fly the banner of Holy Church. Moreover, the English barons were stirring rebelliously and might be likely now to welcome absolution from their oaths of allegiance. Robert Fitz-Walter, eager to expatiate upon the subject, had joined the exiled bishops in France, posing as a martyr who had forsaken all rather than serve an excommunicate king—a convenient excuse for treason.

Archbishop Langton had visited Rome at Christmas, and had been armed by the pope with letters declaring John deposed and calling on King Philip to take over. He had left for France again before John's delegation arrived, but was overtaken by Pandulph, and the sentence of deposition was never published. On the pope's instructions, Pandulph was to give John until 1 June to ratify his envoys' acceptance of terms; if he failed to do so then Langton was to take over the offensive again. John, however, knew when to submit, and the bulls in Langton's possession became dead letters. In October 1213 the legate Nicholas of Tusculum, who had come to England to arrange the raising of the Interdict, was instructed by Innocent to recover them from the archbishop and have them chopped up into small pieces or burned.[1]

Philip went ahead with his plans to invade England, for his intention was quite independent of papal support. It had been in his mind for many years – in 1205 when he thought he had John on the run, in 1209 when he was in touch with the northern barons who were talking of rebellion. Now his plans were matured and he had been preparing all the winter. He hoped to gain England as an appanage for his son Louis, and at a council at Soissons in April 1213 he went so far as to draft a scheme for the relations between the two countries when Louis should be crowned as king of England.[2]

It is arguable that an invasion of England was one way of preventing John's expedition to Poitou, and Philip may have convinced himself that the disaffection of the English barons was comparable to that in Normandy in 1204; but a seaborne operation of the size necessary for success, and against a hostile coast, was, even on an optimistic assessment of the chances, a hazardous undertaking. Moreover, it was a dissipation of resources and one cannot help wondering why he did not direct them to the seizure of Aquitaine before John could return. One can only conclude that Philip's sense of mission against the house of Anjou had reached the proportion of megalomania, and that he would not be satisfied with anything less than its complete destruction.

Fortunately for John, Philip had trodden on sensitive feet in his arrogant assertion of the claims of his refashioned French monarchy. He quarrelled with Count Renaud of Boulogne in 1211 and expropriated him; whereupon the count set about reviving for John that coalition of princes in the Low Countries which had served Richard so well. Philip went on to make Count Renaud's work easier by allowing his son Louis, in 1213, to seize two towns, St Omer and Aire, in Flanders. Count Ferrand of Flanders was uncertain of his own position: he was a Portuguese prince who had taken over the county as husband of the heiress Joanna, when her father had died as a prisoner of the Bulgarians. His relations with his subjects were not very happy and he had hitherto leaned heavily on the support of his overlord, the king of France. Now he made the restoration of the two towns the price of his participation in the invasion of England. Philip replied by attacking him, and Count Ferrand appealed to John for help.[1]

John meanwhile had been organising the country for defence. The sheriffs were ordered to call out not merely those who owed military service as a condition of tenure, but even landless men who were capable of bearing arms to serve at the king's pay. The justiciar of Ireland came over with a force of 500 knights and a body of mounted sergeants. Philip's expectations of invading a land whose loyalty was dead would have been dimmed had he seen the hosts which converged on the southern and eastern coasts. The problem of feeding them proved to be quite impossible, and after a few days they were whittled down to the most competent, and assembled on Barham Down. John could reduce his army with confidence because his chief reliance was on his navy: 'the king determined to engage his enemies at sea, to drown them before they landed, for he had a more powerful fleet than the French king, and in that he thought his greatest hope of resisting the enemy lay.'[2] He did not even wait for the French armada to put to sea, but tried his ships out in commando raids at Fécamp and Dieppe, and against shipping on the Seine.[3]

It was in this state of preparedness that the messengers of Count Ferrand were received on 25 May. A conference was held that night at Ewell, and on the 28th a fleet of 500 ships put out under the command of William earl of Salisbury, with the counts of Boulogne and Holland aboard, 700 knights, and a large body of mercenaries. On 30 May they made the Flemish coast against awkward off-shore winds, and entered the estuary of the river Zywn. Suddenly, as the harbour of Damme (which was then the port for Bruges) came into view, they were met by an incredible sight: hundreds upon hundreds of French vessels were riding at anchor in the roads, or beached upon the shore. Philip had brought his invasion fleet round while he overran Flanders. The French king's chaplain, who was there at the time, reckons the number of ships at 1700, heavily laden with stores and the personal belongings of the French barons. Reconnaissance revealed that there were only sailors on guard: the troops were away at the siege of Ghent or had gone off for forage or plunder. Salisbury ordered an immediate attack: three hundred French ships were cut adrift and a hundred more were rifled and set on fire.

The next day Count Ferrand himself came up to ratify his

alliance with King John, and the knights disembarked to attack the French at Damme. This was a rash move in the jubilation of the initial success. While they were on the way the main body of the French army with King Philip in command rode into sight, and the English force only just managed to get back to the ships in time to avoid complete annihilation. The English navy had, however, in its first major operation achieved a glowing success. The threat of invasion was completely removed: Philip, unable to get his remaining transports out of the Zwyn, was obliged to burn them lest they fall prey to another sortie. Salisbury triumphantly brought his prizes back across the Channel. 'Never', gloated the biographer of William Marshal, 'had so much treasure come into England since the days of King Arthur.'[1]

7

The Road to Runnymede

'All that they imagine is to do me evil. They hold all together,
and keep themselves close.'   *Psalm lvi.* 5, 6

1. RECONCILIATION WITH ROME

The raising of the Interdict required more from King John than
mere penitence. The envoys that he sent to seek peace with the
pope at the end of 1212 told Innocent on his behalf that he was
ready to ratify any agreement that they might conclude about the
church of Canterbury. But he can hardly have expected to get
away merely with this. As the pope reminded him in reply, 'the
question at issue concerns not merely the church of Canterbury
but the whole English Church which by your impious persecution you are trying to enslave.' Though anxious for peace, of
course, Innocent was not in the least inclined to let John off
lightly. He made it clear that it was only very grudgingly that he
received John's offers to accept the terms of 1211: 'Since it was
your fault that peace was not restored on those terms, and because
you have subsequently attempted worse outrages than before, we
are no longer bound to terms which were for the most part generous, for you have shown yourself unworthy of generosity.' Nevertheless, went on the pope, 'so that we may overcome evil with good
and deprive you of all excuse' the earlier terms would be acceptable 'if before 1 June next, on the oaths of four of your barons,
swearing on your soul in your presence and at your command,
and by your own letters patent, you renew your promise, faithfully and effectively to implement those terms according to the
interpretations and explanations we have thought fit to append for
the removal of every shade of misunderstanding.' The 'interpretations and explanations' amounted, in fact, to an expansion of
the terms to cover all those who had suffered in the war between

Church and State. He was to receive back in peace not only all the clerical exiles, but also Robert FitzWalter and Eustace de Vesci, and was to guarantee the safety of their persons and property. If the king or his agents violated the guarantee he was to lose for ever his right to hold the property of vacant sees, and his rights of patronage. He was to restore all property seized from the clergy and put up £8000 as an initial payment of compensation.[1]

Innocent had cautious doubts about John's good faith, which he opened a week or so later to Langton and some of the English bishops:

'It often happens', he wrote, 'that a ruthless foe, finding himself cornered, treacherously pretends peace and after the peace attempts treachery, in order to outwit by guile those he could not defeat by force. Wishing, therefore, with a careful precaution to guard against such treacheries, by the authority of this letter we grant you this power: if King John should violate the peace that has been restored between him and the English Church, then (unless after due warning he makes proper amends) you will, after consultation with the pope, reduce him and his kingdom, by apostolic authority, to the state of excommunication and interdict that they were in before the restoration of peace.'[2]

He followed this up almost immediately with another letter even sterner:

'Since the perversity of the wicked is sometimes inherited from father to son (as is clearly apparent from the fact that once King Henry persecuted the blessed Thomas archbishop of Canterbury . . . and for a long time now his son John has been unjustly persecuting you . . .) we, therefore, fired by zeal for ecclesiastical liberty, charge you by apostolic letter and strictly command you that, if the king should violate the peace which has been restored between him and the English Church, neither you nor any others should presume to anoint or crown any of his heirs to be king.'[3]

John was trying to break the ice in his relations with the papacy, but it looked as if the atmosphere was to continue very frosty. He had his wits about him, however, and made up his mind that if he were to make a surrender for the sake of dividing his opponents, he might as well make it a big surrender and thaw out the pope completely. What he proposed when he went down to Dover to meet the legate Pandulph at the beginning of May was nothing less than to make England and Ireland feudal fiefs of the Apostolic See. He put his proposal in the form of a charter on 15 May:

'We wish it be known to everyone by this our charter, authenticated with our seal, that we, having offended God and our mother Holy Church in many things, and hence being in great need of the divine mercy, and having nothing but ourselves and our kingdoms that we can worthily offer as due amends to God and the Church, we desire to humble ourselves for Him who humbled Himself for us even unto death; and inspired by the grace of the Holy Spirit – not induced by force or compelled by fear, but of our own free and spontaneous will, and by the common counsel of our barons—we offer and freely yield to God, and His holy apostles Peter and Paul, and to the Holy Roman Church our mother, and to the lord pope Innocent and his catholic successors, the whole kingdom of England and the whole kingdom of Ireland, with all their rights and appurtenances, for the remission of our sins and the sins of our whole family, both living and dead; so that from henceforth we hold them from him and the Roman Church as a vassal. . . . And we have made our homage and sworn allegiance to our lord the pope and his catholic successors, and the Church of Rome, according to the subscription below; and we will make our homage and allegiance for the same in the presence of our lord the pope himself, if we are able to come before him. . . . And as a token of this our perpetual obligation and grant, we will and decree that from our own income and from the special revenues of the aforesaid kingdoms, the Church of Rome shall, for all service and custom that we owe (in addition to the payment of Peter's Pence) receive annually 1000 marks sterling. . . . And if we or any of our successors shall presume to oppose this, let him, whoever he be, forfeit his right in the kingdom. And let this charter of obligation and concession remain for ever valid.'

This charter was witnessed by two of John's episcopal servants, the archbishop of Dublin and the bishop of Norwich, by Geoffrey

FitzPeter, the justiciar, by the earls of Salisbury, Pembroke, Surrey, Winchester, Arundel, and Derby, by the count of Boulogne, and three officials of the Household.[1]

This unexpected move by John worked like a charm. Innocent was absolutely delighted. It was by no means unprecedented for a state to put itself under papal overlordship: Sicily, Poland, Sweden, Denmark, Portugal, and the new kingdom of Aragon were already fiefs of the Apostolic See, but the acquisition, by voluntary surrender, of England and Ireland was a splendid enhancement of papal prestige, and it greatly extended Innocent's opportunities to exercise that influence in secular affairs which he believed St Peter's vicar ought to exercise, but which he was too politic to claim openly. As soon as the news reached him he sent John an effusive letter:

'To Him who is able to bring good out of evil, we render thanks for having mercifully inspired you to make fitting satisfaction for the losses and injuries inflicted upon the Church: for you have not only accepted the form of reparation which had been drawn up after much deliberation, but have also put your person and your realm under apostolic suzerainty. . . . Who but the Divine Spirit that "bloweth where it listeth and one knoweth not whence it comes or whither it goeth" directed and guided you, at once so prudently and so piously, to consult your own interests and provide for the Church? Lo! You now hold your kingdom by a more exalted and surer title than before, for the kingdom is become a royal priesthood and the priesthood a kingdom of priests, as Peter says in his Epistle and Moses in the Law. Come then exalted prince, fulfil the promises given and confirm the concessions offered, so that God Almighty may ever fulfil any righteous desire of yours and confirm any honourable purpose, enabling you so to walk amid temporal blessings as not to fail of winning the eternal.'[2]

Innocent's frosty disbelief in John's good faith thawed out instantly. He even allowed the Interdict to be wound up on lenient terms (at the expense of the English Church). As soon as he was admitted to England, Archbishop Langton set up commissions to assess the clergy's losses, for John had to make recompense before the Interdict could be lifted.[3] The process, however, was necessarily slow, and John had complicated it by bullying monastic houses into giving him quittances for what he had taken from them.[1] After John's submission of the kingdom, however, Innocent sent over a personal representative, Nicholas, cardinal-bishop of Tusculum, 'as an angel of salvation and peace . . . one whom we hold in special affection among our brethren for his piety and integrity – so that in the person of the envoy you may recognise the feelings of the sender.'[2] One can only conclude from the actions of Nicholas that the pope was feeling very complaisant towards his royal client, for the envoy did all he could to end the Interdict on terms advantageous to John. He first of all arranged with the king and the pope to compound the Church's losses at the round sum of 100,000 marks, despite the complaints of the English clergy that this was grossly insufficient, and then allowed this sum to be paid in instalments. The king was to pay 40,000 marks before the Interdict was lifted and 12,000 a year afterwards. Actually John did not even have to pay the full 40,000 marks before the Interdict was officially lifted on 2 July 1214 for Nicholas subsequently allowed him to postpone payment of 13,000 of them.[3]

A generation later there was a feeling that John's submission of the kingdom to the papacy was disgraceful. Matthew Paris calls the charter of May 1213 a 'carta detestabilis', and concludes his account of it with the words 'And so is King John humiliated.'[4] But this feeling was a reaction to the development of papal taxation of the Church to pay for its wars in Italy, for it was mistakenly assumed that John's submission had opened the door to the tax-gatherer. In John's own time there was no such sentiment. King Richard, after all, had made England a fief of the Empire for his own lifetime, as part of the terms for his release; and the emperor himself did homage to the pope for Sicily. The barons evidently thought that it was an astute move on John's part, and two years later the rebels tried hard to persuade Innocent that they had pushed him into it.[5] What they did resent was that for the rest of the reign John was able to count on the unstinted support of the pope against themselves. In fact, after relying on them for support during the Interdict, he simply dropped the defence of lay rights in ecclesiastical appointments, by which he had set so much store, and sold out the barons to buy papal support.[6] It must have been particularly galling for them to find that their past support of the king against the papacy was recalled against them when the pope was John's ally: 'The enemy of the human race who always hates good impulses', wrote Innocent in an open letter of August 1215, 'has stirred up the barons of England with his cunning wiles, so that, with a wicked inconsistency, the men who supported him when he was injuring the Church rebelled against him when he turned from his sin and made amends to the Church.'[1] John, in fact, had taken out an insurance policy (at a premium of 1000 marks a year) that paid off handsomely.

If the barons had been sold out, so too, in a sense, had Langton. Matthew Paris, who regarded the archbishop as a saint and wrote his biography, represented him as regretting and deploring John's submission of the realm to the papacy. In this Paris may have been no more than attributing to Langton his own opinion: he was prone to putting his prejudices into the mouths of his heroes on no better ground than that this was what he felt they ought to have believed.[2] But certainly Langton was chary of the uncontrolled expansion of papal authority. He had no doubt about the pope's supreme authority, but was always careful to speak of Christ as head of the Church, and in all his lectures on the subject hesitated to venture an opinion on the pope's power over temporal princes.[3] He was not the first and he would not be the last medieval churchman to worry about the way the papacy might choose to exercise its admitted authority. Within a few months of his joyful arrival to take up his duties as guide and pastor of the province of Canterbury he was obliged to appeal to Innocent against the legate's appointments to vacant sees and benefices, on the very point for which he had endured years of exile.

The pope had commissioned Nicholas 'to cause suitable persons to be ordained to the bishoprics and abbacies now vacant in England, either by election or canonical appointment, who shall be men not only distinguished by their life and learning, but also loyal to the king, profitable to the kingdom, and capable of giving counsel and help, the king's consent being previously obtained. And while we command the chapters of the vacant churches to accept your recommendation, do you, always having the Lord in view, consult on this matter with prudent and honourable men, who are fully acquainted with the merits of the persons, lest you may be deceived by the guile of anyone; but if any oppose or resist you, do you, by means of the censure of the Church, compel them to obey without appeal.'[4] This in itself was unexceptionable;

nay more, it felicitously united canon law, commonsense, and a readiness to be accommodating. The hub of Langton's objection was that 'canonical appointment'· was in fact used not as an alternative to the customary process of election but as a substitute for it, and that his advice was being ignored. His own appointment had been effected by an exercise of the pope's authority overriding the machinery of election, but that had been a proper use for it because the normal machinery was clogged and misused; now, however, he was being obliged to witness appointments being made by the legate, with the ultimate concurrence of the pope, in undue deference to the royal wishes.[1]

Men who had unblushingly stayed in John's service through the years of Interdict were now by an arbitrary exercise of papal power promoted to the richest prizes. William Cornhill became bishop of Lichfield, Walter Gray was first made bishop of Worcester and then translated to the archbishopric of York. The chapter of Durham presumed from John's submission that it was now free to exercise its ancient and canonical right to elect a new bishop, and chose a man of the highest merit, pious, virtuous, and learned, in Richard Poor, dean of Salisbury. It had presumed wrongly: the election was quashed and the indefatigable justiciar of Ireland, John Gray, bishop of Norwich, was forced upon the electors. The pope was being generous to a king whom he now regarded as sincerely penitent; but in the opinion of Langton and his colleagues he was being generous at the expense of legitimate rights grounded in propriety and justice. It was just such a combination of firmness and generosity as is seen in Innocent's treatment of John that enabled him to establish concordats with secular rulers by which the authority of the Apostolic See was enhanced; but at the same time it was the beginning of the long history of king and pope acting together to resolve difficulties in the relations of Church and State without reference to, and often to the damage of, the native clergy and laity.

The end of the Interdict was, nevertheless, of advantage to the barons in the short term. In the first place it freed them from the awkward situation in which their opposition to John was confused by their support of his stand against papal interference with ancient rights of patronage. In the second place it restored the leaders who had fled in 1212: Robert FitzWalter and Eustace de Vesci, who by an ingenious sleight of hand had successfully posed

The keep of Rochester Castle, Kent. The corner nearest the camera was brought down by John's mining operations in November 1215, and was later rebuilt with a round tower, in contrast with the square towers (dating from *c.* 1130) at the other angles.

Framlingham Castle, Suffolk, built in the early years of John's reign for Roger Bigod, earl of Norfolk, one of the leaders of the baronial rebels in 1215–16. John took Framlingham in March 1216.

as martyrs to their conscientious objections to obeying an ex-communicate king, and had been included in the general settlement.[1] These were the men of commanding personality and ready violence needed to stimulate and marshal the hesitant. In the third place it brought Archbishop Langton, who, as a man of principle, was to prove a surer guide to policy than the greedy passions of men like FitzWalter and Vesci. Though Magna Carta was to be a negotiated settlement, the work of many hands and influences, he more than anyone can be held responsible for it. Indeed he is the only person who deserves to be singled out by name from among its begetters. He was to struggle for it against a king whom he regarded as tyrannous, against a pope whom he regarded as mis-guided, and to save it from shipwreck through baronial folly, in the guiding light of his own clear conscience and his fervent belief in justice.

In politics Langton had hitherto been the schoolman, the theor-ist, apt to turn a nice argument in a lecture or sermon on the nature of kingship or the limitations on obedience to a tyrant; but he had an eminently practical turn of mind, and once in England he showed a quick grasp of political realities and of the need to apply principle to concrete problems. He had an early opportunity. The archbishop's reception by John had been cele-brated in a solemn ceremony at Winchester cathedral on 20 July 1213. The archbishop formally absolved the king from excommu-nication, and John swore upon the gospels that he would love and defend the Church, revive the good laws of his ancestors, especi-ally those of Edward the Confessor, and abolish bad laws, judge all men in accordance with the just judgements of his court, and render his rights to every man.[2] These promises were little more than an embroidery of the coronation oath, yet they pinpointed, at a crucial time, the gulf between Angevin theory and practice. Every time the king acted by decree or at his will he denied just judgement in his court. Roger Asterby had said as much to Henry II. When the earls, at the beginning of the reign and again in May 1201, demanded their 'rights' as a condition of obedience, they were alluding to it. When the Lusignans repudiated the judicial duel and said they would abide only by the judgement of their peers, they were casting into concrete form a developing idea which alone seemed to offer the subject protection against the royal will. It lies at the heart of Magna Carta:

'No freeman shall be arrested, or detained in prison, or deprived of his freehold, or outlawed, or banished, or in any way molested; and we will not go against him, nor send against him, unless by the lawful judgement of his peers and by the law of the land.' (*Clause* 39.)

It needed, perhaps, the hyperbolic interpretations of 17th century lawyers to make this 'the bastion of English liberty', but it was clearly seen in John's reign as the *sine qua non* of particular liberties.

Langton seized upon the principle that is enshrined in this clause in 1213, if indeed he had not grasped its significance earlier, and held his promises at Winchester over the king. The naval victory at Damme inspired John with the notion of taking the army he had gathered for defence immediately to Poitou; but the barons dragged their feet. A variety of excuses was tried. They said at first, with singular lack of consistency, that they could not follow him while he was still excommunicate (for this was in May before Langton arrived to pronounce the formal absolution). Then the knights came in a body to say that they had spent all their ready money while standing on guard against invasion, and could not go unless he paid their expenses. Then, finally, the opposition came out into the open: the northern barons repudiated the summons to Poitou, saying that their conditions of tenure did not bind them to serve there, and that in any case they were exhausted by the recent expeditions within the British Isles.[1] The pattern of 1205 repeated itself: John in a fury put to sea, but was obliged to return when he became sufficiently calm to realise the futility of going alone. Then he gathered his mercenaries and set off for the north to punish the recalcitrants.

It was now late August and Langton was holding a council at St Paul's in London. As soon as he heard of the king's intention he set off in pursuit, caught up with him at Northampton and remonstrated with him, beseeching him not to break his oath at Winchester but to act only on the judgement of his court. The king would not hear of it, and still protesting the archbishop followed him to Nottingham, threatening excommunication on anyone who went on the punitive expedition. At length John gave way and agreed to wait upon judgement; but he still went to the north and marched about there for a fortnight, as if threatening what he might do. The proposed expedition to Poitou was postponed until the spring.[1]

No formal statement either for or against the barons who had refused service issued from John's reluctant consent to wait upon judgement. Perhaps he never bothered to put the matter to the court of their peers, but preferred to let it lie in the air, as it were. Nonetheless, attempts were made at pacification during the autumn and winter as John prepared for his departure in the spring. Nicholas of Tusculum, as part of his commission from the pope, had been instructed to abate 'all conspiracies and factions'. Innocent was under the delusion that baronial restiveness was due entirely to the king's feud with the Church; perhaps FitzWalter and Vesci had encouraged him to think so – he was soon to revise his impression. Still the 'conspiracies and factions' were clearly present in what was now the pope's kingdom, and Nicholas as an 'angel of safety and peace', as Innocent had called him, did what he could with the help of Archbishop Langton.[2]

It is probably to this period of attempted mediation that the document known as the 'Unknown Charter of Liberties' belongs. It acquired this curious title as a result of lying unnoticed in the French royal archives until 1863, and was not generally known in England for another thirty years after that. Whatever else it is, it is certainly not a charter though it purports to be one: it begins in the third person singular, and then switches to the first person singular, whereas a proper charter would have been in the royal plural throughout. It is in fact no more than a draft or a memorandum of proposals, but is nonetheless of considerable interest. It runs like this:

(1) 'King John concedes that he will not take men without judgement, nor accept anything for doing justice, nor perform injustice.

(2) And if my baron or my man should happen to die and his heir is of age, I ought to give him his land at a just relief without taking more.

(3) And if the heir is under age, I ought to put the land in charge of four knights from among the lawful men of the fief, and they with my official ought to render to me the proceeds of the land without sale of anything and without releasing any man and without destruction of park and

beasts; and then when the heir comes of age I will let him have the land quit of payment.

(4) If a woman is heir to land, I ought to give her in marriage on the advice of her relatives, so that she is not disparaged. And if I give her once in marriage I cannot give her a second time, but she can marry as she pleases, though not to my enemy.

(5) If my baron or one of my men should happen to die, I concede that his money be divided as he himself willed; and if he dies intestate through war or illness, his wife or his children, or his parents and close friends, shall divide it for the good of his soul.

(6) And his wife shall not have to leave her house for forty days, and then she shall have her dower decently, and she shall have her marriage.

(7) Furthermore, to my men I concede that they should not serve in the army outside England, save in Normandy or Brittany and this properly; and if anyone owes thence the service of ten knights, it shall be alleviated by the advice of my barons.

(8) And if a scutage should be imposed in the land, one mark of silver will be taken from a knight's fee; and if a greater army shall be needed, more will be taken by the advice of the barons of the realm.

(9) Then I concede that all the forests which my father, and my brother, and I have afforested, shall be disafforested.

(10) Then I concede that knights who have their grove in my ancient Forest, shall have their grove henceforth as to their dwellings and as to clearance; and they shall have their forester; and I only one who protects my beasts.

(11) And if any of my men shall die owing to the Jews, the debt shall not gain interest while the heir is below age.

(12) And I concede that no man shall lose life or limb for Forest offences.'[1]

Stumbling though the phraseology is, it testifies clearly to the matters that touched the barons most. The 'Unknown Charter' bears some striking analogies to the baronial proposals in 1215, and to the final form of Magna Carta, but also some important differences. Most notably, the clause on foreign service (no. 7) does not crop up again. This alone helps to fix the undated document in the winter of 1213–14 when it was obviously a burning issue: by the time of the negotiations preceding Magna Carta service in Poitou had become of merely academic interest.[1]

What we probably see here is the influence of Langton attempting to probe to the roots of baronial discontent, and to secure peace through law and justice. The first clause gives what he takes the king to have already acknowledged; the rest, cast in a different form, represents proposals to which the king's assent was sought. John certainly did not give it at this stage. He might be prepared, from his deep knowledge of and respect for English law, so clearly manifested in his correspondence with his judges, to acknowledge that, properly speaking, the Crown should not go against any man without judgement; but he was not prepared, for he was not yet obliged, to define where justice lay in particular instances. So the 'Unknown Charter' remained merely a dead draft, and no chronicler bothered to mention or record it.

Ralph of Coggeshall says that Nicholas, with the help of Langton and other mediators, managed to reconcile the king and the 'northerners'[2]; but it was only a fragile and uneasy truce, resting solely on the king's overriding anxiety to get to France. The conspiracies went on.

2. DEFEAT AT A DISTANCE

The situation in England then, when the royal galley stood off from the Isle of Wight on 6 February 1214, was uneasy in the extreme. Manifest discontent was neither appeased nor crushed, and only John's anxiety to be in France after so many years of frustrated preparation would have left it so. Many of the earls and barons neither came to the muster themselves nor sent their knights, and it was still an open question whether they would consent to pay fine and scutage in lieu of service. He went committing the realm to the protection of Holy Church and its government to the strong, if not too clean, hands of his ablest henchmen. Peter des Roches, foreign adventurer and bishop of Winchester, was now justiciar in place of Geoffrey FitzPeter, who had died the previous October. He was assisted by William Brewer, who was the sort of man John could confidently entrust with the management of half a dozen shires at once. He was little loved: the men of Devon and Somerset paid 1200 marks to be rid of him in 1210; John acepted the money but doubtless regarded it as a token of Brewer's worth. Another henchman, Richard Marsh, was sent from Poitou to join them in May. They could call at need upon the advice and help of William Marshal, who had sent his knights on the expeditien but would not himself go against his other overlord, King Philip. John had commissioned him to handle the continuing negotiations for the dissolution of the Interdict. There was Stephen Langton too, always ready to be of service in settling the political difficulties of the realm: in June he arranged a truce with the Welsh, neglected but not forgotten since the rising of 1212.[1] This was as good a combination of defenders of the peace as John was likely to get when he set off with, as Coggeshall tells us, 'few earls, but an infinite multitude of low-class soldiers of fortune,' and taking his queen, his son Richard, Eleanor the sister of Arthur of Brittany, and 'an incalculable treasury of gold, silver, and precious stones.'[2]

About the same time, William earl of Salisbury set off for Flanders with a picked company of English troops, a host of Flemish mercenaries, and plenty of money to lay out in subsidies for allies. For years John had been working for the re-creation of a Rhineland confederation in his favour, so secretly indeed that the clerks who paid the expenses of one envoy did not dare to write his name in their accounts.[3] Now, with the help of the count of Boulogne and Philip's arrogance, it was in being, and John's grand design unfolded itself: the king of France was to be crushed on the anvil of Poitou by a hammer from the Low Countries.

John had made a start early in the year because he had much to do. In the counties of Poitou and La Marche, and in the viscounty of Limoges there was hardly anyone upon whom he could rely, and he had to secure his position there before he could risk attacking Philip. La Rochelle was his one secure foothold for its trading connection with England kept it loyal, and from here he probed the surrounding countryside for several weeks. The chroniclers are not at all clear about John's operations from La Rochelle, and the French ones thought to ridicule him for not going out immediately to engage Philip, who was hovering with a considerable army on the Poitevin border. We can trace his itinerary, however, from the dating clause of official documents, and learn from his letters home the necessity and success of his ventures. One or two of the weaker Poitevin barons came in to swear fealty: but one held the castle of Milécu against him, only a few miles from La Rochelle, and had to be reduced by siege.[1] In March John ventured farther afield and took his army down the Charente and through Angoulême to the Limousin, receiving the homage of the barons and appointing officials. From there he scoured Hugh of Lusignan's county of La Marche, and returned through the Limousin again to the Charente. In April he marched into Gascony as far south as La Réole to assure himself of the position there. (*See Map VIII, overleaf.*)

The county of Poitou, however, was still not securely in his grasp, and could not be while the Lusignan family remained hostile. John was prepared to be conciliatory and offered his daughter Joan in marriage to Hugh's heir. Philip, meanwhile, was being excessively cautious and, despite his considerable army, hesitated to come to grips with John. Hearing of the proposed marriage he seems to have put out peace feelers, offering one of his own sons in marriage to Joan. John would not hear of it, and set out early in May to cow the Lusignans by force. He was completely successful and wrote home to tell the government in England about it:

'You should know that when the truce was at an end which we had granted to the counts of La Marche and Eu, and as we did not find them ready to make peace with us, on the Friday before Pentecost we marched with our army upon Mervant, a castle of Geoffrey de Lusignan, and though many believed that it could not be taken by assault, on the day afterwards, that is to say on the eve of Pentecost, we took it by force in one assault lasting from early morning until one o'clock. On the day of Pentecost we laid siege to another of Geoffrey's castles, called Voucant, in which he himself and two of his sons had shut themselves, and when, after a continual battering for three days from our engines, the opportunity for assault was approaching, the count of La Marche came up and induced Geoffrey to put himself at our mercy, together with his two sons, his castle, and everything in it. While we were there we received word that Louis, son of the French king, was besieging Geoffrey's castle af Montcontour; and on hearing it we im-

VIII. The campaigns of 1214

mediately went that way to engage him, so that on Trinity Sunday we were at Parthenay, and there the counts of La Marche and Eu and the aforesaid Geoffrey did homage and fealty to us. And as we had been negotiating with the count of La Marche about giving our daughter in marriage to his son, we granted it to him, although the king of France had sought her for his own son, but deceitfully; for we recalled how our niece had been given to his son Louis, and what the result of that was, and may God grant us more profit of this marriage than we had from that one! Now by the grace of God, we have the opportunity to attack our main enemy, the king of France, beyond Poitou. And we tell you of this that you may rejoice at our success. Given at Parthenay in the sixteenth year of our reign.'[1]

The long list of Poitevin barons who witnessed the contract of marriage between John's daughter and Hugh's son at Parthenay is clear evidence of the success of the preliminary stages of the campaign, and John seems to have decided then to carry his assault into the lost provinces of the Angevin house.[2] Presumably the object of the simultaneous attack on Philip from south-west and north-east was to promote one of two desirable consequences: either Philip would be so distracted by the invasion from the Low Countries that John could overrun his lost provinces, or John's own threat would draw off so much of the available French forces that his allies could march on Paris, and perhaps even on Normandy.

At the beginning of June John first made a feint towards the French army, and then struck north-west across the Loire and seized Ancennis on the border of Brittany and Anjou. It looked as if he were making a move to encircle Angers and come upon it from the rear; but then he suddenly doubled back across the Breton border and attacked the seaport of Nantes, perhaps intending to use it as a base – a more convenient one than La Rochelle now that his operations were in the north. There was a French garrison in the port and it turned out with the citizens to defend the bridge over which John's army would have to cross. John, however, was completely victorious in a sharp encounter and took several important prisoners, including King Philip's cousin, Peter of Dreux, who was count of Brittany in right of his wife Alice, the half-sister of the dead Arthur. Since John had taken the trouble to bring Eleanor of Brittany with him, he may have intended to set up a puppet régime, but nothing is heard of it.

This swift victory prompted the men of Angers to open their gates without a struggle, and in the middle of June John was once more in the ancient capital of his house. The check to the king's complete mastery of Anjou came from William des Roches, appointed by Philip its seneschal, who had built himself a new fortress at Roche-au-Moine, a few miles from Angers. John evidently thought it a crucial stronghold for he spent a fortnight besieging it. Louis seems to have thought so too, and when it seemed in danger of falling made up his hesitant mind to march to its relief. Hearing from his scouts of Louis's approach, John decided that this was the moment for a showdown between the two armies. But then a devastating setback occurred: the Poitevin barons who had been content to join John's siege train refused to fight in a pitched battle. Led by that inveterate turncoat Amery of Thouars, they withdrew for home.

In an impotent fury, unwilling to lose all or even part of the only forces he could rely on – those which he had brought with him – John fell back to La Rochelle.[1] From there on 9 July he wrote a letter to England which, under cover of expressions of confidence, reveals his plight:

'The King to the earls, barons, knights, and all his lieges in England, greeting.

Know that we are safe and well and that everything, by the grace of God, is prosperous and happy with us. We return manifold thanks to those of you who have sent us your knights to serve in the preservation and recovery of our rights, and we earnestly entreat those who have not crossed with us to come to us without delay, being assiduous for our honour, to help in the recovery of our territory (save for those who in the opinion of our reverend fathers the lords Peter bishop of Winchester, our justiciar, and John bishop of Norwich, and of Master Richard Marsh and William Brewer, should stay in England), doing so much in this matter that we are bounden in perpetual thanks to you. Assuredly, if any of you should have understood that we bore him ill-will, he can have it rectified by his coming.'[2]

The enterprise was collapsing for lack of support, and was further jeopardised by lack of co-ordination between its parts:

at the very time when John was languishing in the neighbourhood
of La Rochelle, his initial impetus spent and ready even to forget
old grudges for the sake of reinforcements, the north-eastern forces
were just ranging themselves for the decisive encounter. They had
delayed too long: Philip, gauging perhaps for the first time the
extent of the coalition against him, had been allowed time to call
out the feudal host and the levies of armed citizenry for the
defence of the homeland. The troops under the earl of Salisbury
had been in the field for many weeks in Flanders, scouring the
country for French detachments, but the grand assault waited
upon the arrival of Otto of Brunswick, John's nephew and Holy
Roman Emperor. Otto was as anxious for the destruction of Philip
as was his uncle, for the French supported his rival for the imperial throne; but it was not until the third week in July that he
gathered the Rhineland princes under his banner of the dragon
and the golden eagle at Nivelles, south of Brussels. By this time
Philip was ready to take the offensive and marched into Flanders
as if to cut the Germans and Lorrainers off from the sea and the earl
of Salisbury, who held the money bags. He was too late: the allies
had come up to Valenciennes, and Philip turned back from
Tournai to a place which he judged suitable for battle – an open
plain near the village of Bouvines.

The battle was joined on the morning of a hot summer's day,
27 July. Tactically it was a crude affair, and none of the leaders
sought to prevent it degenerating, as it did, into confused mêlées –
a type of warfare to which the French chivalry was accustomed
by many tournaments. The only man to show any originality
was Count Renaud of Boulogne. From a screen of *routiers* he led
sudden cavalry charges, retiring again behind his protective
phalanx before the French knew what had hit them. On the allied
left the Flemings were put to flight by strong French opposition
and Count Ferrand captured. In the centre the imperial cavalry
broke through the French lines of citizen levies, who had only
come up at the last minute and were hot and tired. Philip himself
was unhorsed and only saved by the courage of his bodyguard.
Thomas of St Valéry swung his cavalry round from the French left
wing to avert disaster in the centre, and it was the turn of the
emperor to be unhorsed. The imperial troops were put to flight,
and Otto himself only just managed to escape to Valenciennes
on the mount of one of his faithful vassals. In just over three

hours the French were almost masters of the field: the imperial eagle lay at Philip's feet. But on the right flank the earl of Salisbury and the count of Boulogne fought on valiantly until the earl was clubbed from his horse, and Count Renaud was captured on one of his sorties. The dust which had risen in clouds to obscure the action settled slowly on a 'medieval Austerlitz', and John's hopes settled with it.[1]

The students of Paris, it is said, danced and sang for seven days, and well they might: the battle of Bouvines meant that the threatened disruption of the French kingdom had been averted, that the Capetians were established securely on their throne, and Otto of Brunswick tumbled from his. John, despondent at La Rochelle, had again been defeated at a distance. The curious feature of his military history is that he, who throughout his reign was never worsted when he led his armies to attack, could never pull off a decisive victory. King Philip, despite his taste of triumph, despite the fact that he had a fresh army ready under Louis, and despite the treacherous submission to him again of Amery of Thouars and other Poitevin barons, did not venture to attack John in Aquitaine. Robert Curzon, an English-born cardinal, commissioned by the pope to persuade the warring kings to fight instead against the Saracens, negotiated a truce to last until Easter 1220.[2] In the middle of October the royal galley put into Dartmouth.

3. THE MUSTER OF REBELLION

One of the most remarkable things about Magna Carta is the obscurity of its antecedents. This obscurity extends from the dating of the charter itself, back over the preceding negotiations and parleys to the muster of rebellion. One of the few things that can be said with certainty is that the hallowed tradition, derived largely from Wendover, is false which pictures a baronage united in arms against the Crown, confronting a cowed and humiliated king at Runnymede on 15 June 1215, and obliging him, with praiseworthy restraint, to set his seal to a statement of constitutional liberties which it had drawn up. It does not make the picture more true merely to darken the colours by saying that the baronial rebels were reactionaries pursuing selfish class interests.

The chroniclers' accounts of events leading up to Magna Carta are scrappy, and often contradictory on points of detail. The documents that might have served to catalogue developments – safe conducts for parleys, draft proposals, preliminary agreements, and the like – have not survived in their entirety; and those that we have got stand so much in isolation that the interpretation of them is often difficult. Papal correspondence does not help much either, for Innocent had to rely on *ex parte* statements, and events often moved too rapidly for him, four or five weeks' distance away, to follow them with any closeness. It is possible to reconstruct something of what happened, but it is rather like restoring a medieval wall-painting of which only a few fragments of coloured plaster remain.

Discontent, it seems, was almost at boiling point when John returned from the continent in October 1214. The strong-arm rule of Peter des Roches as justiciar during the king's absence had emphasised the most unbearable features of Angevin despotism – made even worse by the fact that he was a representative of the foreign dependants upon whom John conspicuously relied.[1] Furthermore, feeling against the king was brought to the point of exasperation by the demand issuing from Poitou in May for the payment of scutage by those who had not joined the expedition. It was met by a widespread though probably unco-ordinated refusal to pay. Very little was extracted from Norfolk and Suffolk, none at all in Essex and Hertfordshire, Lancashire and Yorkshire. The justiciar had ordered distraint upon some of the northern barons, whose truculence seemed most resolute. Eustace de Vesci, for one, was openly defying the royal officers.[2]

It is difficult to say how far King Philip's victory helped to inspire the barons to open defiance. John was certainly not a ruined man at his barons' mercy when he returned; but a defeated John was no doubt less awesome than a victorious John would have been; and it may well have seemed to men already inflamed to the point of conspiracy, that John had been obliged to come to terms with the Church and with the French king and that the next item on the agenda, as it were, was that he should come to terms with them.

The Barnwell annalist has it (though he is not very precise about the details) that in the later months of 1214 a sharp row occurred between John and the defaulting barons. It is easy to believe that he held them responsible for the failure of the expedition. A group of northern barons, however, had an answer, saying (as they had done the previous year) that their conditions of tenure did not bind them to serve outside the kingdom, or to pay scutage in lieu of service. There were no grounds at all for this claim, and John was able to reply that foreign service had been rendered in the days of his father and brother. He had yet to learn that with the barons, as with the Church, 'what has been' was no longer necessarily synonymous with 'what ought to be'. He had given way on Church customs, why should he not also give way on secular customs? Precedent was no infallible guide to justice. Certainly the barons cited or appealed to the custom of the realm with notable frequency, and agreed that it should not be flouted or subverted lightly. But it is easy to emphasise unduly the sanctity of custom in medieval society, and to imagine that it shaped and contained all the thoughts and actions of ordinary men. Appeal to custom was common because custom provided reassuring points of stability in a shifting, changing world: sheet anchors in the rough seas of life. England in the late 12th century was no static society, and men were used to change – even so traditional an institution as the Church was in the van of it. The mutability of all things mortal was a common ingredient of contemporary moralising. Men insist perhaps most firmly on the value of custom when instability and change threaten them most closely; and they are apt to insist most tenaciously of all when in fact they allow the tide of change to carry them along. It gives reassurance that they are moving purposefully, and are not merely adrift on an uncharted sea. In the course of the struggle with John the barons were to loose their hold on part of the past and grab at something new; but they tried all the time to insist that their demands were in harmony with an ancient tradition of just relations between Crown and baronage, which the Angevins, they claimed, had flouted. They talked a lot about the good laws of King Edward the Confessor, but the trouble was that no one was quite sure what these were. They had thought of a better tactic by the end of 1214, and when John met their excuses by reference to the customs of his father's and brother's reigns, they replied by reference to what they believed were the better customs of Henry I's reign. They produced, says the Barnwell annalist, 'a certain charter of liberties granted to the English by Henry I' which they sought to have observed by demanding its confirmation by the king. He put the matter off until the new year; and when the barons came again to renew their demands at London at Epiphany he procrastinated further, and said he would give them a definite answer at Easter.[1]

This charter of Henry I has nothing to say about military service or scutage; but it had a lot to say of interest to the barons about reliefs and wardship and marriage and debts to the Crown and the restoration of the 'law of King Edward'. They were side-stepping the issue of service and going straight to the deeper causes of discontent. The charter had been granted by Henry I in 1100 when he was trying to rally support for his seizure of the throne. The promises in it were couched in rather vague terms, and Henry I had in fact never kept them; but they provided a useful precedent for the establishment of good custom by royal charter. Moreover, the charter referred to the bad customs of the king's predecessor which he sought to amend. John's barons had reached the point of demanding that he do the same.[2]

Wendover has a similar story, indeed he makes much of Henry I's coronation charter and gives it in full in his chronicle. He does not, however, leave its initial appearance in the argument in the hands of the northern barons, as the Barnwell annalist does. Wendover never talks of a group of rebels but gives the impression that the baronage was united to a man against John and his 'most evil counsellors'. He has it that shortly after the king's return in the autumn of 1214 'the earls and barons of England' met at Bury St Edmunds as if on a pious pilgrimage, but conferred secretly about Henry I's charter. 'And so they all gathered in St. Edmund's church and starting with the most eminent they all swore on the high altar that if the king refused to grant them the said liberties, they would go to war against him, and withdraw their allegiance, until he should confirm by a charter under his own seal everything they should require.'[3] Even shorn of its exaggeration and detail this story supports the impression which is to be derived from the safer Barnwell annalist – the rebellious barons were on a new tack: in place of the conspiracy to murder John and set up a new king, which had been their one policy in 1212, they were now waving a charter. No more is heard of Henry I's charter afterwards, but this was the crucial development and its influence can be seen in Magna Carta.

Wendover has a dramatic tale, too, about the origin of this development. 'The story goes', he writes, that when Archbishop

Langton had in August 1213 held a service in St Paul's before a great concourse of ecclesiastics and barons 'the archbishop called some of the lords aside and began to speak privately with them as follows, "You have heard", he said, "how I made the king swear, when I absolved him at Winchester, that he would abolish bad laws and recall good ones, such as those of King Edward, and have them observed by everyone in the kingdom; well, a charter of King Henry I has now been found by which you can, if you will, recover your long-lost liberties and your former condition." And placing a document before them he had it read aloud for all to hear. . . . And when it had been read and understood by the barons, they rejoiced with exceeding great joy, and all swore in the archbishop's presence that when the time was ripe they would fight for these liberties even unto death. The archbishop also promised them his loyal support as far as in him lay, and this agreement having been made betwen them the conference broke up.'[1]

It is easy to understand why Wendover has had such a lasting influence: this is the sort of thing that Sellar and Yeatman call the 'Memorable History of England' – a secret meeting in the sacristry, the dramatic production of a newly found charter that would solve all the barons' problems, the oath to act together when the time was ripe. Much of the story has, unfortunately, to be discounted: Henry's charter was already well enough known in legal circles. But there is nothing inherently improbable in the belief (and Wendover admits that his story is no more than a rumour) that Langton first pointed out its significance to the barons in its formal abrogation of the bad, and establishment of good customs, and its value as indicating a sound line of policy; indeed, that he should have done so is in line with all that is known of his attitude.

It seems clear, then, that by the beginning of 1215 baronial dissidents were loudly demanding a royal charter of liberties; but who were they? Apart from Wendover with his insistence upon a well-nigh united baronage, the rest of the chroniclers were almost unanimous in talking of them as 'the Northerners', and indeed the phrase strays into the royal records as a general description of the rebels.[2] It is not surprising that the north should be the home of revolt against John: for one thing, it had in Eustace de Vesci, lord of Alnwick, one of his most bitter foes; and on more general grounds, it was likely to react sharply against John's rule because it was less inured to Angevin government by long sufferance than regions farther south. John had carried direct rule, and indeed personal visitation, into the northern counties as his predecessors had never done. Here the barons who had felt but little the whips of the father kicked out most vigorously against the scorpions of the son.

Nonetheless, the description is misleading if it is taken to imply that the rebellion was exclusively a northern movement. Undoubtedly it had a numerous northern element and a strong northern flavour; it may indeed be described as a northern movement in inception, which contingents from other parts later joined; but these other contingents were very prominent. The northern element contained few great barons – it was mainly composed of second rankers. The prestige, the weight, the leadership, came from the eastern counties and the London region. The man who took command of the movement was John's old enemy Robert Fitz-Walter, lord of Dunmow and hereditary holder of Barnard's Castle in the city of London: 'one of the foremost barons of England and one of the most powerful', admits a hostile contemporary.[1] He brought with him a family group, Geoffrey de Mandeville earl of Essex, Henry Bohun earl of Hereford, Robert de Vere earl of Oxford, and Geoffrey de Say, together with his neighbours of the great houses of Clare and Bigod. There was a west country movement too, and a rising in Devonshire which the earl of Salisbury went to suppress with a troop of mercenaries in the spring and found too strong for him.[2] Following the northern initiative, it seems, barons rose in revolt wherever the king's power was not overwhelmingly strong on the ground. He held the midlands and the central southern counties firmly with his mercenaries and castles; outside this area rebels could be looked for.

Their numbers should not be exaggerated. The militants who came out into the open in the spring of 1215 numbered few more than forty holders of baronies, supported, of course, by their sons, their lesser vassals, and their knights. Some of them, perhaps many, felt the sharp edge of personal grievance. Nicholas Stuteville had in mind, perhaps, the debt of 10,000 marks at the Exchequer, with which John had saddled him as relief from his inheritance. William Mowbray had been simmering with fury for a long time over the trick John had played upon him in making him promise

2000 marks for justice in the law-suit about his barony, when he allowed the case to go against him, but still demanded the money – and this after he had spent four years as a hostage in Germany for the payment of King Richard's ransom.[1] Giles de Briouze, bishop of Hereford, was thinking no doubt of the fate of his brother and sister-in-law. But the most impenetrable mystery of all is what spurred on the chief agitators and promoters of rebellion, Robert FitzWalter and Eustace de Vesci. They put out stories of John's lecherous designs upon their women folk – an easy enough charge to make, but the stories they told were so confused and unsubstantiated as to be beyond unravelling, let alone belief.[2] They seem indeed to be unintelligent fabrications to cover lack of rational excuse; and it is hard to believe that FitzWalter and Vesci were anything more than baronial rough-necks. They had been out simply for John's blood in the conspiracy of 1212, with no thought of a charter, and in thrusting themselves to the fore in 1215 seem to have changed their intentions very little.

FitzWalter was altogether disreputable and mischievous, rescued from ignominy only by his great fiefs, and owing his leadership largely to his dominating aggressiveness. He was quick to take offence and draw his sword. One chronicler tells how his son-in-law, Geoffrey de Mandeville, once slew a servant of William Brewer in a sordid squabble over lodgings when the royal court was putting up for the night at Marlborough. John threatened to hang him for murder, and FitzWalter broke out with 'You will not hang my son-in-law! By God's body you will not! You will see two hundred laced helms in your land before you hang him!' And when the king put the case up for trial, FitzWalter appeared at court with five hundred armed knights.[3] He was not a whit more commendable than John's strong-arm mercenaries, like Fawkes de Breauté, Gerard d'Athée, and Engelard de Cigogné, against whom he was setting himself up as baronial champion. Indeed, he was rather less commendable for he had not even their virtue of staunch loyalty. Gerard had stoutly defended Loches against the French king when all else seemed lost; FitzWalter and Saer de Quenci (another of the confederate barons) had cravenly opened the gates of the vital stronghold of Vaudreuil in Normandy, and had been despised for it even by the French. William Marshal one day asked King Philip why he bothered to have truck with such traitors, and Philip replied that such men were like torches, to be used and then thrown in the cesspool.[1] The rebellious barons might make such a man their leader, but they could not make him a shining champion of English liberty.

The men who formed the king's party in the months of crisis were perhaps slightly less numerous than the rebels, but they were more weighty in power, influence, and sagacity. The most notable of them were William Marshal and Ranulph de Blundeville, earl of Chester. These men, the most powerful in the land, had also suffered from John's malevolence, but had survived it with courage and forbearance. When the time came to line up for or against the king, their oaths of allegiance counted for more than remembered grievance. Pembroke carried with him his Irish colleagues, standing by their promise of 1212 to live or die with the king. Chester carried with him his friend William Ferrers, earl of Derby. Three other earls, those of Salisbury, Warwick, and Devon, were prepared to draw swords for the Crown, and two more, Arundel and Earl Warren of Surrey, could be counted on in the crisis of 1215, though they wavered later.

The rest of the barons of England, a hundred or more, would rather have held their hand. When pressed for a decision their families tended to split: heirs and younger hotheads joined the rebels, 'intending to make a name for themselves in arms', says the Barnwell annalist, while their fathers, the fief holders, were mindful of their oaths and stood by their lord.[2] The Marshal family was a case in point: the earl was the king's man, his eldest son fought for the rebels.

Paradoxical as it may seem, it was this large body of neutralist, hesitant opinion, wavering between the banners of revolt against tyranny and instinctive if reluctant fidelity to the Crown, that was really responsible for the birth of Magna Carta. It ensured that the demand for confirmation of Henry I's charter was turned into something concrete, and prevented the period of manœuvre from degenerating into a straight fight for dominance between the king and the militant rebels.

In coming out into the open at the beginning of 1215 the militants were taking a big risk. The king was not defenceless: he had well-fortified castles and many of them; he had mercenary captains and seasoned troops. It was quite possible that he would repeat his performance of 1212 and smother the fires of rebellion with a blanket of armed might. A demand for a charter was the militant's surest shield: bloodthirsty treason sheltered behind justifiable requests. While they kept these in the foreground they could be certain of having the sympathies of all the barons – even of those who would stand to arms with the king. John could fight two score rebels, but he could not fight the whole baronage: it was like Normandy over again – few might be actively against him, but he could not number his possible enemies. The hesitant barons might follow their oath and come to his standard, but he could not plumb the depths of their reluctance, or be certain that they would not desert when he tried to strike hard. His only course was to strip the rebels of their advantage by conceding many of the demands. He had to restrain his temper, negotiate, be accommodating and reasonable.

The militants probably hoped that he would lose his temper and with it all loyalty. They certainly went about to provoke him: when he showed signs of willingness to negotiate they stepped up their demands; when he offered concrete proposals, they cried 'not enough' and flew to arms. In doing so they were in danger of losing sympathy themselves: Roger Wendover, even, shows signs of turning against them when they risked civil war – 'promoters of pestilence' he calls them.[1] It was at this point that the rest of the baronage was put to the test, hotheaded sons made their way to the rebel army, but their fathers lined up with their lord. The day was saved, and the charter too, by a middle party of barons and bishops, headed by Stephen Langton, who kept negotiations open, brought everyone together at Runnymede, and arranged the final terms. This at least was the firm belief of two contemporaries, a monk of Canterbury and the abbot of Coggeshall.[2] We can get no closer.

4. THE CHARTER OF LIBERTIES

John handled the situation with a sensitivity to its delicate balance and a resourceful ingenuity which, whatever one thinks of him as a man, can only enhance his reputation as a ruler of consummate ability. His first move in response to the rebels' initiative in demanding a charter was to play for time – he would give them his answer at Northampton on the Sunday after Easter. This respite he used to reinforce his position. Envoys were packed off to the realm's new overlord at Rome (the rebels were quickly off the mark, too, and sent their men in pursuit). Mercenaries were summoned from Poitou, but, to avoid prejudicing the king's position with the hesitant barons, many of them were diverted to Ireland under the command of Savary de Mauléon. John was evidently aware of the futility of strong-arm methods in the present situation; but it was convenient to have his forces close at hand if a showdown were forced upon him. Then on 4 March he took vows as a crusader. This was a brilliant move to give himself a protective screen – almost as good as the rebels' use of a charter. It put his person and his property under the protection of the Church, and gave him a crusader's respite of three years in meeting his secular obligations.[1]

Archbishop Langton seems to have resented John's attempts to wriggle off the hook, and refused to act as a negotiator while mercenaries were being mustered. The king was conciliatory, and informed some of the Poitevins who had arrived in England that their services were no longer required and they could go home.[2] It was fortunate for him that he kept up this accommodating front, because his envoys to the pope did not return home until the end of April, and the king had to retreat from his promise to give an answer on the 26th and play for more time by keeping the discussions going through Langton and William Marshal.

The pope's letters, when they arrived, were to the king's advantage. They urged the barons to abandon conspiracies and any thought of force, and to make such requests as they had respectfully. They upbraided Langton for favouring the king's opponents, and ordered him to forbid conspiracies under pain of excommunication. They also proposed 'three-fold peace terms' (*triplex forma pacis*). What these were is not known, though they are later referred to as 'thoroughly honourable and reasonable and worthy of acceptance by God-fearing men', and as involving a provision for safe-conducts for the barons 'so that if they could not arrive at agreement, the dispute might be decided in his court by their peers according to the laws and customs of the kingdom.'[3] A *détente* of this kind was not in the rebels' interest: they had to plug away with their demands to provoke the king to attempt to crush them and so rally the neutrals to their support, if they were to get their way.

Gathered at Brackley, near Northampton, they issued demands. Again we are in the dark: we do not know what these demands were; but they must have been stiff because the king took the risk of rejecting them outright. The rebels therefore sought to push matters to a head: on 3 May they formally renounced their hom-age and fealty, and, in contemporary parlance, 'defied' the king. FitzWalter was appointed commander, and took the grandi-loquent title of 'Marshal of the army of God'. Perhaps he was trying to repeat his earlier performance of posing as a champion of Christian conscience; but this time it did not work – the king had bought himself the pope as ally. The rebels put up a brave show and marched to Northampton where they attacked the castle, held for the king by one of Gerard d'Athée's relatives, Geoffrey de Martigny.

John did not attempt to take the field against them. Instead he moved quickly to corner the moderates. On 9 and 10 May he issued letters offering to put all grievances to papal arbitration, and renouncing, as a basic concession, the use of arbitrary ad-ministrative action without prior judgement. 'Know', he wrote, 'that we have granted to our barons who are against us that we shall not take them or their men, nor disseise them, nor go upon them by force or by arms, except by the law of our realm or by the judgement of their peers in our court.'[1] This, a reflection of the first clause of the 'Unknown Charter', was to come up in very similar words, as the thirty-ninth clause of Magna Carta. It tackled the basic problem of the whole trouble between Crown and baronage, and was one of the few clauses of real constitutional significance in the Charter. As examples of what he took this concession to imply, John at the same time offered to have the reliefs imposed on two of the rebel leaders, the earl of Essex and the bishop of Hereford, for the Mandeville and Briouze inheritances, reviewed by their peers in court.[2] This was tantamount to an admission that there were wrongs to be righted, and a surrender of the Crown's uncontrolled coercion of the barons. The king was being very reasonable: he was conceding the vital point now, and put-ting up specific grievances to arbitration. He was still hedging, of course, on the question of a charter: he was prepared to settle outstanding grievances, but not to bind himself in general terms for the future. As a reasonable offer it must have appealed strongly to those reluctant to rebel, and John went on to buttress reluctance by granting out the lands of some of those who had renounced their allegiance to his supporters. This in itself had immediate effect. Simon Pattishall's manor of Wasden was granted to Robert Courtenay on 15 May, but within a week the abbot of Woburn came to plead for Simon, and secured a safe-conduct for him to come to make his peace. Henry Braybrooke had two manors seized, but was granted a safe-conduct to come to speak with the king.[1]

It looked as if John had stayed the tide of rebellion, and, without striking a blow, was bringing some of the rebels back. 'The Army of God', meanwhile, was not doing very well. For a fortnight it sat fruitlessly before Northampton castle, unable to take it because it was stoutly defended, and because the rebels had no siege engines. They moved off instead to take possession of the far less important castle at Bedford, which was held by a sympathiser. They had made a poor show so far, and John, having established his reasonableness, felt that he would no longer alienate the rest of the barons if he moved against them. Savary de Mauléon's mercenaries were brought over to Winchester; the earl of Salisbury and the Flemish mercenaries were directed to move into London.

John was closing in for the kill; but then the rebels brought off a coup. They beat the earl of Salisbury to London, were let in by friends there, and took possession with very little resistance. This was early on 17 May, a Sunday morning. The prestige of holding what was already becoming the capital city restored the rebels' fortunes – at least it put them back into the fight, though their position was still far weaker than they could have hoped. How weak is revealed by Wendover: 'They sent letters throughout England', he says, 'to those earls, barons, and knights, who appeared to be still faithful to the king (though they only pretended to be so) exhorting them with threats, as they were mindful of their property and possessions, to abandon a king who was perjured and hostile to the barons, and to form a united front with them in a fight for liberties and peace; and that if they declined to do so they would be treated as public enemies, war made upon them, their castles brought down, their homes and buildings burned, their warrens, parks, and orchards destroyed.'[2] So much for a united baronage in arms against King John – despite Wendover's attempt to gloss the evidence: the rebels were letting out a desperate cry. The effect, if we may believe the Barnwell annalist, was that heirs rode off to London while their fathers kept peace with the king: in this way both sides were placated. It was a stalemate: the rebels stayed in the city, the king held his troops back. Here was the opportunity for the moderates, and under the energetic leadership of Langton they took it. Mediators and negotiators rode to and fro between the rebels at London and the king in the neighbourhood of Windsor, trying to hammer out a formula for peace.

On 10 June the king himself came down from Windsor to the water meadows by the Thames near Staines to meet leaders of the opposition, and there he committed himself to a draft schedule. This survives in a document known as 'The Articles of the Barons'. Some of the clauses dealing with vital points had been worked out in some detail, but others were left merely as headings or notes ('That measures of corn, wine, breadths of cloth and other matters be amended; also of weights', says the twelfth clause).[1] Although it was therefore a rather rough and ready document, the product of urgency, the king allowed his Great Seal to be affixed to it as an indication that he had committed himself. When this had been carried back to the rebels and discussed by them, they came in a body to meet the king at Runnymede on the 15th to join in a formal ceremony of acceptance. Magna Carta itself concludes with the words 'Given in the meadow that is called Runnymede between Windsor and Staines, 15 June'; but this was simply a nominal date, recalling the moment at which general agreement had been reached. In fact it took several days after the 15th for the precise wording in proper legal terms to be worked out, with the co-operation of the Chancery clerks. The handing over of copies for general distribution only followed a ceremony at which the rebels formally renewed their oaths of allegiance to the king, and this took place on 19 June. After all, a charter records a solemn grant by the Crown and this could hardly be made to rebels at war with the king.[2]

Magna Carta* is an unrewarding document for the general reader. It bristles with the technicalities of feudal law, and when these are cleared away most of its provisions seem very mundane. There is in it no high-sounding statement of principle and no clearly defined political theory. It is, in fact, a Charter of Liberties not a Charter of Liberty, concerned to secure practical re-

* See Appendix B, p. 265–77.

forms which would protect the upper classes against an over-mighty ruler in current matters of grievance, not to enunciate abstract 'rights of man'.[1]

In the forefront of the Charter were provisions designed to block up the loopholes in feudal custom through which the Angevins had shot down their vassals. Vexed questions in the law about reliefs, wardship, marriage, the position of the widows of tenants-in-chief, and the payment of debts to the Crown were cleared up by defining the king's rights and establishing protection for the vassal. Here the technical language in which the provisions were expressed was of particular importance in eliminating ambiguity. Scutage, it was declared, should be taken 'only by the common counsel of our kingdom'. This was to be interpreted, not as it often had been in the past as the approval of the king's chosen advisers, but as the consent of a body consisting of all the tenants-in-chief, the greater of whom were to be summoned individually, and the lesser collectively through the sheriff. The prerogative of the Crown to commandeer wagons and supplies was curtailed, and evil customs of the forest were to be rooted out after a commission of inquiry had reported.* The advantages to litigants in the new developments in legal procedure, which had brought much business to the royal courts, was tacitly recognised in not being attacked; but the barons objected to the ways in which the king manipulated the system for his own advantage. He was not in future to deny a man justice, to take money from anyone for helping him to get a favourable verdict, or for delaying a suit, to try to make a profit out of the sale of writs which started actions, or to sell writs indiscriminately which would bring into the royal courts cases with which the feudal courts of the barons were perfectly competent to deal.[2] The principle (which John had already recognised) that executive action against an offender should not deprive a man of his liberty, rights at law, or property 'except by the lawful judgements of his peers or by the law of the land', was reiterated.[3] An attempt was made to curb the high-handedness of the king's foreign helpers by insisting that no one should be put

---

* In 1217 the clauses concerning the forest were withdrawn, expanded, and put into a separate charter. The documents together were referred to as 'the charters of liberties', but from the middle of the 13th century it became common to distinguish them as 'the big charter' and 'the little charter' (or charter of the forest)—hence the designation 'Magna Carta'.

in a position of authority (such as sheriff or justice) who did not know the law of the land and mean to observe it. John promised to restore immediately all lands, castles, liberties, or rights which he had taken from anyone without proper judgement, and to have claims against similar acts by his father or brother investigated and put right when he returned from crusade.

Though the Charter was primarily concerned with matters which touched the barons most closely, other interests were not entirely neglected. The rebels would have been helpless without the support of their own knights, of course, and in common prudence, if nothing more, they had allowed in their draft proposals that any rights and liberties which were established should be recognised by them in their dealings with their own men. A clause to this effect was incorporated in the Charter, and with it clauses protecting the interests of the rebels' friends in London, and their allies, Llewelyn of Wales and the king of Scotland. The barons, too, realised the growing importance of the merchant classes and sought protection for the privileges of towns, freedom of movement for merchants, and a national standard of weights and measures. Everybody benefited from the clause mitigating the burden of amercements, but this is the only one that specifically mentions the unfree peasants. A paragraph guaranteeing the liberties of the English Church was put at the head of the Charter, though it had found no place in the 'Articles of the Barons' – an interesting side-light on the rebels' attitude to Langton and the struggle with the pope. As the Articles were being worked over another valuable change was made: the words 'any baron' were changed, where appropriate, to 'any free man' (*liber homo*), which may have seemed a small point of phraseology at the time, but which was of great importance in giving the Charter a wider application in the future.

The great majority of the provisions were a commentary not upon John's reign alone, but upon half a century of vigorous Angevin government. Only in one or two of the later clauses were features of the political situation peculiarly characteristic of his reign attacked. He was obliged 'to restore all hostages and charters which were delivered to us by Englishmen as security for the peace or for faithful service,' to remove from office the kinsmen of Gerard d'Athée, and to dismiss 'all alien knights, crossbowmen, serjeants, and mercenaries, who have come with horses and arms to the injury of the kingdom.' Even here he had not created precedents; indeed, John designed no new instruments of oppression, but he had applied the final and paralysing turns of the screw.

The most startling and revolutionary change proposed in Magna Carta was contained in clause 61 – called in the Articles 'the form of security for the preservation of the peace and liberties between king and kingdom.' Nothing, hitherto, had obliged a king to keep his sworn promises save his own fear of God and the possibility of rebellion, and the barons evidently felt that the Charter would be little more than a catalogue of empty promises unless provision were made for sanctions. They therefore proposed the establishment of a standing committee of twenty-five barons who would act as guardians of the law and receive complaints against the actions of the king or his officials. The Twenty-five were in the first instance to be chosen by the barons and were subsequently to keep up their strength by co-option. If a complaint which they thought justified were not remedied within forty days they were to compel the king by calling out 'the community of the whole land' to seize his castles, lands, and possessions, and by injuring him in any way they could, sparing only the persons of himself and his family. Everyone was to take an oath to obey the instructions of the Twenty-five – or of a majority of them, if all could not agree. It was common practice for a person to be obliged to keep his contractual obligations by the threat of distraint upon his property, and the clause was drawn up in the familiar form of a covenant for distress.[1] Nonetheless, the familiar form of the machinery could not disguise its novelty when applied to the relations between a king and his subjects. The clause did not authorise civil war, but it was hardly likely that this would be avoided in practice, especially since the extremist barons insisted on electing the Twenty-five exclusively from among themselves.[2] Moreover, the 'form of security' was full of novel and alien implications about the nature of kingship. It imposed a new oath on everyone superior to the hitherto supreme oath of allegiance to the king, and people might well ask if the Twenty-five had not been set above him. Indeed, the king was virtually reduced to the role of executive officer of the law under the supervision of a baronial committee. Everyone agreed that a ruler who paid no heed to law and custom and listened only to the dictates of his arbitrary will was a tyrant and not a true king, but the device for restraining tyranny forced upon John in 1215 was crude in its methods and disturbing in its implications. The search for an alternative was to be the *motif* of political struggles for the next two centuries.

Magna Carta, as it emerged from the crisis of 1215, was the work of many hands and influences, and the formal phraseology of the Chancery clerks who drafted it gives a spurious unity to a medley of provisions, some just and reasonable, some salutary and convenient, some unfair and impracticable, and some vindictive. Stephen Langton himself, when he had a hand in running the country during the minority of John's son, was prepared to see some of the clauses dropped altogether and others drastically amended.[1] He could be content to do so because for him, and for posterity, the chief value of the Charter did not lie in its specific provisions. Many who knew little and cared less about the contents of the Charter have, in nearly all ages, invoked its name, and with good cause, for it meant more than it said. For one thing it was a code of law (the longest ever issued since the Conquest) established by royal charter at the prompting of the king's subjects. As such it opened the way to periodic revisions of custom and law, and implied that government should not be conducted to the damage of the governed. Moreover, merely by existing it was a standing condemnation of the rule of arbitrary will.[2] Even in the emasculated form in which it eventually got on to the statute book, an appeal to Magna Carta was a shorthand way of proclaiming the rule of law. Its actual provisions exercised little influence on the development of the constitution until misinterpreted by 17th century lawyers to mean trial by jury and no taxation without the consent of representatives; yet their interpretations were not wholly absurd, for they accurately reflected the spirit, if not the purpose, of the 13th century original. It should be remembered, however, that the charter which the 17th century politicians studied with such zeal was not the one issued by John in 1215, but a truncated and modified version promulgated by his son, Henry III, in 1225.[3] Historically John's Charter is of great interest, but legally it is little more than a curiosity, for it lived for no longer than ten weeks. Within a couple of months, in fact, it had been dropped to the ground by the extremists of both sides, and was then knocked on the head by the pope.

8

The Road to Newark

'They gat not the land in possession through their own sword: neither was it their own arm that helped them.' *Psalm xliv.* 3

I. A HOLLOW PEACE

John, it seems, had recognised in the summer of 1215 that he had gone too far: that he had treated the barons with intolerable harshness, and trampled too recklessly on their property rights. They had justifiable grievances about particular royal acts, and he was ready to give them satisfaction. In this he was very likely more pragmatic than penitent, but nonetheless he seems to have been genuinely prepared to set matters right. A spate of writs went out from Chancery on and after 19 June dealing with the grievances of individuals. Saer de Quenci was given possession of Mountsorrel castle that he claimed had been unjustly detained by the king from his share of the Leicester inheritance. Richard FitzAlan got back Richmond castle which for generations had been in his family's keeping. Robert FitzWalter was allowed the custody of Hertford castle. The town of Buckingham was given into the the keeping of Richard earl of Clare to hold for his grandson, John de Briouze, who was a minor in wardship. The earl of Huntingdon got back Fotheringhay castle that had been taken from him in 1212 by royal officers bearing writs from the king that threatened his hostage. Richard Montfichet was allowed the office of forester in Essex, which his father and grandfather had held in days gone by. Royal officers in Durham were instructed to allow Eustace de Vesci his ancient hunting rights. There are many similar concessions.[1] Though crippled by gout, the king struggled to a council meeting at Oxford in July, where some of the more debatable claims and the replacement of unpopular officials were to be discussed.[2]

On the other hand, while prepared as a matter of commonsense tactics to remedy the grievances of individuals, he was not ready to see the Crown's initiative, its freedom to act in its own best interests, fettered permanently by a charter which converted loose and malleable custom into the rigid bonds of law, and one, moreover, which saddled him with a commission of baronial policemen who were also to be the judges of what constituted an injustice. On the morrow of granting the charter he sent off a tendentious account of what had happened to the pope, seeking its annulment. This was double-dealing of the most contemptible, though yet secret, kind – for at the same time he was instructing his sheriffs to carry out the provisions of the Charter, and to see that everyone took the required oath to the Twenty-five.[1]

The charge of double-dealing cannot, however, be levelled at him alone. On the baronial side there were diehard extremists who were bitterly disappointed that John should escape destruction by coming to terms with their less blood-thirsty colleagues. If we can believe the Barnwell annalist, there were rebels who slipped away from Runnymede, so that they could continue hostile acts with the excuse that the peace did not bind them because they had not been present when it had been made.[2] Others, less extreme but truculently suspicious, were unwilling to accept the consequences of peace and break up their military formations. They organised tournaments as an excuse for remaining in arms, but would not venture far from London to which they obstinately clung as a fortified base. A tournament arranged for 6 July at Stamford was transferred to Hounslow so as to be nearer the city, in case anyone tried to take possession during their absence. FitzWalter, still calling himself 'Marshal of the army of God', wrote to tell William d'Albini of this and remarked, 'You well know how useful it is for us to hold the city of London, which is our refuge, and how damaging it would be to us to lose it.'[3] In council with the king a week later at Oxford they publicly insulted him by refusing to stand at his entrance.[4] When he suggested at this council meeting that it was about time they recognised that peace had been made and gave up guarding London, they countered by saying that not everyone had yet taken the oath to the Twenty-five, and that all their demands for castles and privileges had not yet been satisfied. The moderates had to intervene to arrange a compromise: the archbishop of Canterbury should hold the Tower of London, and the baronial leaders could retain the rest of the city in the king's name until the Feast of the Assumption (15 August), and could continue to hold it if their claims had not been satisfied by then and the oath taken by everyone.[1]

Archbishop Langton himself, and a number of his suffragans, evidently felt that the baronial extremists had failed to keep their part of the bargain at Runnymede, for they let it be known by letters patent that the rebels had not fulfilled their promise to give security for their fidelity in the future. They had failed to set their seals to a document which ran, 'Know that we are bound by oaths and homage to our lord John, king of England, to protect faithfully his life, limbs, and worldly honour, against all mortal men, and to guard and defend his rights, the rights of his heirs, and his realm.' At the same time, says the Barnwell annalist, they were fortifying their castles, including the ones they had just recovered from the king.[2]

In August there was every sign of a swift movement towards a renewal of hostilities. Some of the barons were encouraging physical assaults on royal officials. The king had his recruiting officers out for mercenaries in Aquitaine and Flanders. He even wrote to the count of Brittany, offering to grant him the honour of Richmond, which previous counts had held, if he would come 'with well armed knights in all haste to serve us.'[3] An actual outbreak of war was only delayed because the king had disbanded his mercenaries as a condition of coming to terms, and did not expect to get them together again before Michaelmas, and because the rebels were hampered in collecting enough men by the needs of the harvest. Archbishop Langton tried to take advantage of the lull to get the moderates to mediate again; but unfortunately his authority was at this point undermined by the arrival of a powerful papal letter.

This letter was, as a matter of fact, completely out of date: it referred to the situation at the end of May when John had complained of conspiracies against him and the archbishop's sympathy with his enemies. It is remarkable that Innocent had any time at all to spare for English affairs: he was in the midst of his great ecumenical council at the Lateran which was seeking to set the whole world to rights. A baronial revolt in his feudal kingdom of England was hampering his grand design for a crusade

243

to the Holy Land; he had imbibed the king's version of what was happening and minced no words. Addressing the bishop of Winchester, the abbot of Reading, and the legate Pandulph, he said:

'We are driven to express amazement and irritation that when the king of England has, to a greater degree than might have been expected, made amends to God and the Church and especially to Stephen archbishop of Canterbury and his fellow bishops, some of them, showing less respect than was either proper or seemly for the Crusade, for our instructions, and for the oath of fealty that they had taken, have shown him neither help nor favour against the disturbers of the realm, which is now acknowledged to belong to the see of Rome by right of feudal wardship; they thus appear to be accomplices, if not sharers, in a wicked conspiracy. See how these bishops defend the patrimony of the Roman Church! See how they protect crusaders! They are worse than Saracens for they are trying to unseat a king who, it was especially hoped, would succour the Holy Land. . . . Even if the king were remiss or lukewarm about the Crusade, we would not allow such great wickedness to go unchecked, for by God's grace we know how to punish, and we can punish such shameless presumption. Lest their insolence should have the effect of endangering the realm of England and of ruining other realms, and above all of wrecking the Crusade, we excommunicate all such disturbers of the king and king-dom, together with their accomplices and supporters, and we lay their lands under interdict, most strictly requiring the arch-bishop and bishops to have these sentences solemnly published throughout England every Sunday and every feast day, with the tolling of bells and candles extinguished, until, having made amends to the king for the losses and wrongs inflicted on him, they humbly return to his service. If any bishop should avoid obeying our order, let him know that he is suspended from episcopal office. . . .'[1]

This letter must have come as a nasty shock to the bishops who had been working tirelessly as mediators throughout the perilous spring. What made it worse, indeed intolerable, was that the addressees of the letters and the pope's commissioners for its execution were firm supporters of the king who endeavoured to

Dover Castle, Kent, successfully defended for John by the justiciar, Hubert de Burgh, against the attacks of Louis of France.

King John, close side view of the effigy surmounting his tomb in Worcester Cathedral.

press the pope's commands despite the fact that they were given in ignorance of the settlement at Runnymede and for an entirely different situation. Langton insisted that they were out of date and refused to promulgate the sentences of excommunication and interdict. The commissioners, however, were able to point to the last paragraph of the pope's letter which said:

'That our mandate may not be impeded by anyone's evasion, we entrust you with the execution of the above instructions, and charge you to proceed as you see fit, disregarding all appeals. If you cannot all discharge the business, let two of you do so.'

On 5 September they issued a reasoned case for applying the instructions to the still truculent barons, condemned all conspiracies and excommunicated the barons and their supporters, including the citizens of London. Since Langton refused to co-operate with them they suspended him from office.[1]

Disconsolate and helpless, Langton set off at the end of September for Rome to plead with Innocent. In the bitterness of the moment, outmanœuvred by the king whom ironically the pope had sent him to England to tame, he thought of resigning his see and becoming a Carthusian monk.[2] As he journeyed a further papal letter crossed his path on its way to England, which killed off the infant for whom he had been a tireless midwife. Innocent had now heard of Magna Carta. Despite all his pleas for reasonableness, he wrote, despite the king's offer to put the grievances of the barons to papal arbitration, despite the protection he should have received from the bishops as a crusader, the king

'was forced to accept an agreement which is not only shameful and base but also illegal and unjust. . . . We refuse to pass over such shameless presumption, for thereby the Apostolic See would be dishonoured, the king's right injured, the English nation shamed, and the whole plan for the Crusade seriously endangered; and since this danger would be imminent if concessions thus extorted from a great prince who had taken the Cross, were not cancelled by our authority, even though he himself should prefer them to be upheld, on behalf of Almighty God, Father, Son and Holy Ghost, and by the authority of Saints Peter and Paul His apostles . . . we utterly reject and

condemn this settlement, and under threat of excommunication we order that the king should not dare to observe it
and the barons and their associates should not insist on it being
observed. The charter, with all undertakings and guarantees,
whether confirming it or resulting from it, we declare to be null
and void of all validity for ever.'[1]

When this crushing letter reached its destination, England was
already in the throes of civil war.

2. CIVIL WAR

John expected his hired *routiers* to arrive from the continent in
time for a muster at Dover at Michaelmas: he was down on the
Kent coast in September waiting for them. There were delays,
however, due to autumn gales: Hugh de Boves, an experienced
organiser of commercial armies, was drowned when his transports
bearing Flemish mercenaries were overwhelmed by heavy seas.
Many corpses were washed up on the coast of Suffolk.[2]

The rebels decided to take advantage of the delay by a bold
march on Rochester to bar the king's advance on London. The
royal castle there was in the keeping of the archbishop of Canterbury, and held for him by Reginald of Cornhill. Reginald had
done well for himself over many years as an agent of the royal
administration, but he readily opened the gates at the approach of
the 'Army of God'. This was particularly infuriating to John:
Rochester was second only to Dover in strength and importance
among the castles of Kent, and he had been politely requesting
that it be handed over to a castellan of his own choosing for some
time.[3] He moved immediately to assault it, though he had with
him as yet only a small force gleaned from castles, and his mercenary bodyguard. 'In truth, sire,' remarked one of his Flemings,
'you hold your enemies of little account if you go to fight them with
so small a force.' 'I know them well enough,' answered John,
'they are not to be made much of or feared. We could safely fight
them with fewer men than we have.'[4] His confidence was not
misplaced: after vainly trying to prevent the king's men de-
stroying the bridge over the Medway, Robert FitzWalter retired
to London, leaving a garrison in the castle.

The rebels had already opened negotiations at the French
court for the support of an invading army, and they expected

Rochester to hold out until it arrived – certainly they made no serious effort to relieve it. They had reckoned, however, without French caution and without John's determination. Though ill-provisioned, the castle was well manned by ninety-five knights and forty-five men-at-arms under William d'Albini, lord of Belvoir, one of the ablest of the rebel commanders. But John, when roused, was irresistible. He had all the smiths in Canterbury working day and night on siege equipment. 'Living memory does not recall a siege so fiercely pressed or so staunchly resisted', says the Barnwell annalist. John remained there for seven weeks personally conducting the operations. The keep resisted all attempts at battery, and the king resorted instead to mining. A tunnel was dug, shored by timbers, filled with combustibles, and fired with the fat of forty bacon pigs.[1] As the timbers were burned away and collapsed, one of the corner towers of the keep came crashing down. On 30 November the garrison surrendered. One crossbowman was hanged who had been in John's Household since his youth; the rest were held for ransom. After the siege of Rochester 'there were few who would put their trust in castles.'[2]

Wendover has nothing but scorn for the rebels in London who had failed to come out against John. He portrays them 'playing at damnable dice, selecting for themselves the best wine for drinking, and practising who knows what else besides.'[3] It is similar to his comment on John's apparent inactivity in Normandy, and similarly somewhat unfair. The rebels were trying to set up an administration in those parts of the country controlled by their adherents, the eastern counties and the north. They even summoned Yorkshire landholders to a council meeting at London to debate 'the affairs of the kingdom'. They were trying to apply the sixty-first clause of Magna Carta and ordered distraint upon the king's property.[4] They were handicapped, however, by their lack of effective force. There were something like a hundred and fifty castles held against them for the king, and they still had, it seems, no siege train. They had missed the opportunity of attacking the king when he came up to Rochester, and since then he had been steadily reinforced by swarms of mercenaries from the continent. They badly lacked a properly equipped field army and thought that they could find one only through external allies. Llewylyn's Welshmen were on their side, but would not stray far from their hills, and were being contained by the men of the earls of Chester and Pembroke. Alexander II of Scotland, forgetting that he owed his throne to John, was eager to take advantage of a disordered England; but no one would expect him to field a very formidable army. Their hopes in consequence were pinned on French help; Philip, after all, was well known to have had an invasion of England very much in mind.

While John was preoccupied with the siege of Rochester, the rebels sent off a delegation to the French court begging for help and offering the crown to Philip's son Louis. Louis was quite eager, but his father was lukewarm: he wished to know if the rebels were determined or merely desperate, and he demanded security.[1] He was, in fact, not very disposed to break his truce with John, and even less disposed to have papal fulminations flying about his head. Innocent III had clearly been touched to the quick by the baronial revolt: it imperilled his dearest desire, a great crusade. Philip had had enough of papal interdict as a result of his adulterous marriage, and did not relish more. Louis, however, promised to send what help he could in a private capacity. He deferred coming over himself but sent a contingent of his knights at the end of November. They landed in the Orwell estuary and made their way to the rebel headquarters in London, but were not much help to the cause. They remained there all winter, remarks one of John's Flemish mercenaries scornfully, having to make do with unaccustomed beer because the wine had run out.[2]

John did not treat their advent very seriously. On 20 December he held a council at St Albans and decided to divide his army: a detachment under the earl of Salisbury, Fawkes de Breauté, and Savary de Mauléon, was left to keep the rebels pent up in London while he set about recovering control of the counties dominated by the rebels' adherents. This is a typical example of his reluctance to commit himself to decisive military action: the rebellion would have collapsed had London been recaptured. The rebel headquarters there were the nettle that he should have grasped and uprooted without flinching. He was ready enough to conduct a punitive expedition in the north, but the risks there were slight. It is possible to defend his actual course of action: a siege of London would have been very difficult and prolonged. A pressing problem for him, very likely, was that of paying his mercenaries. His Household was struggling to keep the machinery of administration going, but the revenue-collecting system of the country had been badly disrupted for many months, and John was probably living largely on the stored wealth of his castle treasuries. It could be argued that the surest means of keeping his mercenaries content was a plundering expedition at the rebels' expense. If, at the same time, he could bring all the rest of the country outside the London area under his control, the financial administration could be restored and his coffers replenished. Furthermore, the loss of their estates and castles might convince the rebel leaders of the futility of continuing the struggle. These are powerful arguments; but one cannot help feeling that a Richard or a Philip would have gone straight for the hardest task and sought a decisive victory. John had to pay dearly for taking the course of least resistance and seeking his ends by indirect means.

In December 1215, then, he set off (*see Map IX*) on that most fearful of medieval military operations – the harrying expedition. Christmas day was spent at Nottingham, 'not in the usual fashion but as one on the warpath.'[1] As he marched to the farthest reaches of his kingdom detachments of *routiers* scoured the countryside after his enemies. There was a rough kind of discipline about it: one man who took a cow in a churchyard had his hand cut off in punishment, but the pillaging of rebels and their lands was freely licensed.[2] The chroniclers speak with horror of the fearful passage of this terrible army. From the king's point of view the expedition was eminently successful. Alexander of Scotland had advanced as far south as Newcastle, but he scuttled back at John's approach. Swearing that he would 'run the sandy little fox-cub to his earth', John pursued him to Berwick, seized the town, butchered its inhabitants, and mounted punitive raids into the Scottish lowlands.[3] As he marched north the gates of towns and castles had been opened to him in fear. His finances were strengthened by the fines he took for recovery of his good will: Laxton, for example, offered a hundred pounds, York a thousand. The barons of the north came to seek 'the mercy of the merciless one, or fled before his face.' Rebel leaders like Eustace de Vesci and Robert de Ros were cowed into making overtures for peace.[4]

At the end of January he turned south again, returning by a different route, and took his flock of predators through Suffolk and Essex, to try to persuade the eastern leaders to a similar submission. Colchester surrendered after the shortest of sieges; Castle

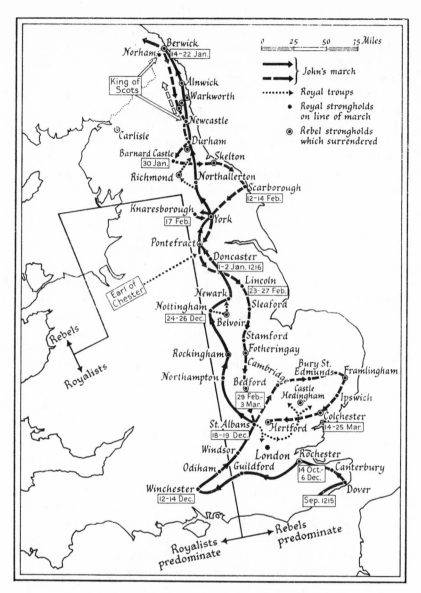

IX. John's march through rebel territory (September
1215 to March 1216).

Hedingham was given up after three days, and its lord, the earl of Oxford, came to seek the king's peace. In three months he had knocked the heart out of resistance everywhere save in London; but there the rebels still defied him, and the time for a decisive victory over them had passed. Louis had ferried more troops into the city in January and February and was proposing to come over himself at Easter.

The pros and cons of intervention were discussed by the French barons at Melun in April 1216. The French king and his son had in fact by this time made up their minds to invade England; it remained to justify the venture to the French barons, and especially to the papal legate Gualo, who had been sent by Innocent to succour his English vassal with all possible ecclesiastical help. A barrage of fictions and half-truths was put up by Philip and Louis. John could not have submitted his realm to the papacy, they alleged: it was not his to give for he was not rightfully king since he had been condemned for treason in King Richard's court. If he had properly become king, he nonetheless stood condemned in the French court of the murder of Arthur, and had been rejected by his barons. Louis had a claim to the throne through his wife, Blanche, granddaughter of Henry II, and the English barons had chosen him to be their new lord. Louis then enacted a little scene in which he insisted that his father might be his liege lord in France, but could not forbid him prosecuting his wife's rights in England, for it was outside his jurisdiction. He himself, he claimed, was not bound to the truce with John since he had not been a party to it. All he required was his father's blessing to lead the men of his own fiefs and whoever else would follow him on a private enterprise. He got it. Gualo, fulminating excommunication on anyone who joined Louis, left for England.[1]

John spent the end of April and the beginning of May preparing to repel invasion. The sheriffs were ordered to proclaim a general safe-conduct for anyone who came to make his peace within a month of Easter; anyone who failed to do so would be disinherited for ever.[2] He gathered his forces in Kent and went there himself to await developments. His prime reliance, however, was again upon his navy. All ships were ordered to gather at the mouth of the Thames or in the Dover roads in preparation for an attack upon Louis' vessels before they could put out from Calais. Throughout the night of 18 May, however, a gale howled, and in the morning his ships lay broken upon the shore or scattered at sea.[1] On the 21st watchmen on the coast of Thanet detected sail on the horizon, and next day John himself watched the hostile fleet pass in safety across the mouth of Pegwell Bay. The trumpets were sounded, the troops were fallen in; but the order to charge was never given, for at the last minute John hauled off for Winchester. Once more he had baulked the decisive encounter.

Again there were good arguments for it, and William Marshal himself was urging the king to retire, perhaps in fear for his safety. The mercenaries were unreliable, it was argued: their pay was in arrears, and since many of them were Louis' subjects they might change sides. Possibly it was hoped that foreign invasion would rally the realm to the king's side; but this did not happen, rather the reverse. The arrival of Louis revealed how attenuated any residual loyalty to John had become. The realm was thrown into chaos. Rebels who had lately made their peace hastened to Louis' camp. Men who had hesitated to break with the king for fear of the consequences plucked up courage now. Alexander of Scotland led his army across the border again. Most serious of all, Louis' rapid conquest of the southern counties led to some surprising defections – the earl of Arundel, the earl of Surrey, William of Aumale earl of York, and, most shattering of all, the king's half-brother, William of Salisbury, who lately had been one of his chief commanders. They were joined by some royal servants, such as Hugh Neville, and Warin FitzGerold, one of the chamberlains of the Exchequer.[2] It seems that such men, hitherto loyal, reckoned that John's cause was hopeless and were merely taking thought for their own future; but they were mistaken, he was not beaten yet.

Up and down the country castles were held for him by determined men who owed everything to John. Engelard de Cigogné hurled defiance at rebel besiegers from the walls of Windsor. Hugh Balliol held out at Barnard Castle against the Scots, and Philip Oldcoates in Durham. Hubert de Burgh, now justiciar, sat tight in Dover against all that Louis could do against him from July to October. Odd sparks of loyalty fired local resistance movements: the citizens of the Cinque Ports had been obliged to take an oath to Louis, but their vessels harried French shipping; William of Kensham, operating under the name of 'Willikin of the Weald', organised a band of loyalists that preyed on Frenchmen in Sussex and Kent.[1] The west midlands were held securely for the king (after a little cleaning up of defectors) by the vassals of the two elder statesmen, William Marshal and Ranulph of Chester. They had served his father, and despite the insults they had suffered, would not desert the son. Thither John retired with Savary de Mauléon and the Poitevin mercenaries.

By the end of the summer the confused situation was clarifying itself. Two-thirds of the barons had gone over to Louis, but there the rot stopped. He could not take Dover though he personally directed operations against it. Relations were becoming strained between the rebels and the French barons who had come not as allies but in hope of rich fiefs. The more English barons who went over, the less the French liked the situation. Moreover, the rebels had lost some of their firebrand leaders. Eustace de Vesci was killed helping the king of Scots in the fruitless siege of Barnard Castle. Geoffrey de Mandeville had been accidentally killed in a joust with a Frenchman.[2] The earl of Salisbury and the earl of York returned to their allegiance; William Marshal's son came in to make peace with his father's party. 'Day by day the adherents of the Frenchmen dwindled', says the annalist of Dunstable.[3]

Emboldened by this unlooked-for swing of fortune, John went over to the offensive in mid-September. From the security of the Cotswolds he marched with Savary de Mauléon's men down the valley of the Thames, skirted Windsor in a successful attempt to draw off its besiegers, and then headed for the eastern counties. His aim, presumably, was to cut the country in two, drive back the king of Scots who had advanced as far as Cambridge, and bring relief to hard-pressed Lincoln, where the hereditary castellan, Dame Nicola da la Hay, held out valiantly against the rebel earl of the county. John was at Lincoln at the end of the month, and from there went to Lynn. Townsmen, on the whole, were in favour of Angevin kings; they readily sold privileges, and none more so than John, and strong rule was good for trade. The citizens of Lynn welcomed him and feasted him well; but there, it seems, he contracted dysentery as a result of over-indulgence in their hospitality when fatigued by long days of hard riding. Lynn was the principal port handling the important victualling trade of East Anglia, and one of the five most prosperous seaports of England. John's main purpose in visiting it seems to have been to arrange for supplies to be sent to his northern strongholds.[4]

On 11 October he went from Lynn to Wisbech, and on the following day made his way through the difficult country of the numerous rivers which empty into the Wash to the abbey of Swineshead in Lincolnshire. Some time in the course of that journey occurred the famous but in fact somewhat obscure accident to his baggage train popularly known as 'the loss of King John's treasure in the Wash'. The impression of a major disaster derives from a melodramatic but far from precise account by Roger of Wendover. He tells of an 'unforeseen accident in the river Wellstream', in which 'the ground opened up in the midst of the waves, and bottomless whirlpools sucked in everything'. The king lost, he would have us believe, in addition to numerous foot-soldiers, 'all his wagons, carts, and packhorses, with the treasures, precious vessels and all the other things of which he was especially fond'. A major loss of baggage could indeed have been serious, for John had gathered in, and was presumably carrying with him, all his jewels, ornamental plate and regalia from its former safe-deposit in monastic houses. It should be noted, however, that Ralph of Coggeshall, a more sober and reliable chronicler than Roger of Wendover, writes of it more in terms of a mishap than a disaster, which befell not the whole baggage train but merely the vanguard. Attempting to ford the Wellstream, packhorses became trapped in quicksand 'because they had hastily and incautiously set out before the tide had receded'. Some members of the king's household were sucked into the quicksand, but the loss of baggage was confined to household effects, the equipment of the chapel and its holy relics. Whichever of the two accounts comes nearer the truth must remain in doubt, and not even the location of the accident can be fixed with certainty.*

The illness that John had contracted at Lynn worsened, and he could barely sit his horse. He rested at Sleaford on 14–15 October and then struggled on to the bishop of Lincoln's castle at Newark; but he could go no farther, and the abbot of Croxton, who had a reputation for medical skill, was fetched to tend him. In the early hours of 18 October a furious wind howled round the rooftops of the town. Messengers struggled through the storm with letters

---

* The possible but widely varying interpretations of the scanty evidence are discussed in Appendix C.

from a number of rebels who wished to make their peace, but the king could not read them for his life was ebbing away. The abbot of Croxton heard his confession and performed the last rites.[3]

Before he died John dictated a brief but dignified will:

'Being overtaken by a grievous sickness, and so incapable of making a detailed disposition of my goods, I commit the ordering and execution of my will to the fidelity and discretion of my faithful men whose names are written below, without whose counsel, were they at hand, I would not, even in health, ordain anything; and I ratify and confirm whatever they shall faithfully ordain and determine concerning my goods, in making satisfaction to God and Holy Church for the wrongs I have done them, sending help to the Holy Land, rendering assistance to my sons for the recovery and defence of their inheritance, rewarding those who have served us faithfully, and distributing alms to the poor and to religious houses for the salvation of my soul. And I pray that whosoever gives them counsel and aid in their endeavours may receive the grace and favour of God; and may he who violates the settlement they make incur the curse and wrath of God Almighty, of the Blessed Mary, and of all the saints.

First, then, I desire that my body be buried in the church of the Blessed Virgin and St Wulfstan at Worcester. Next, I appoint as ordainers and executors of my will the following persons: the lord Gualo legate of the Apostolic See, Peter lord bishop of Winchester, Richard lord bishop of Chichester, Silvester lord bishop of Worcester, Brother Amery of Ste Maurie, William Marshal earl of Pembroke, Ranulph earl of Chester, William earl Ferrers, William Brewer, Walter Lacy, John of Monmouth, Savary de Mauléon, and Fawkes de Breauté.'[1]

His intestines were taken away by the abbot of Croxton, but his body was borne in a funereal convoy of armed mercenaries right across the country to Worcester cathedral and there laid, as he had requested, before the altar of St Wulfstan (though the monks of the abbey he had founded at Beaulieu begged for it).[2]

When the news of the king's death reached the royalists in the west country, his eldest son, Henry, nine years old and 'a pretty little knight', was brought up from Devizes to Gloucester, and there in the abbey church on 28 October, under the directions of the papal legate Gualo, he was crowned by the bishop of Winchester with a circlet provided by his mother. The loyalist barons, it is said, were deeply moved by the ceremony; and meeting next day in the great hall of the castle to decide how best to protect the interests of their new young king, they prevailed upon William Marshal (who was now in his seventies) to act as regent. The situation in England was precarious but Ireland at least was still loyal and, declared Marshal, leaning with his back against the wall as he addressed the assembled company, he would carry the young king from land to land on his shoulders if need be, 'one leg here, the other there', rather than give in.

But serious as the situation was, it was not quite so grim as Marshal imagined. John's death itself helped the cause of his house, for many who had opted for Louis in his stead bore no animosity against his infant son. Anyone who believed that in persisting in rebellion he was upholding the cause of justice and the rule of law was contradicted on 11 November, when at a solemn meeting of the royalist magnates at Bristol, the Charter of Liberties was reissued in the young king's name. Some of the more disturbing or hampering of the clauses of the charter of 1215 were omitted, modified, or held over for further consideration, but its essential spirit was preserved. It is the supreme irony of Magna Carta that, after being demanded by rebels and killed by the pope, it should have been brought back to life as a royalist manifesto.

Many barons hesitated to declare for Henry during the winter months of restricted military activity until they could see whether Louis and his Frenchmen would prevail; but when spring came and a strong party of diehard rebels and French knights was routed by William Marshal and Fawkes de Breauté at Lincoln, they flocked to take the oath of allegiance to the young king. Louis expected strong reinforcements from the continent, but on their way across the Channel in August they were caught by the royal fleet off Sandwich and drowned, captured, or dispersed, so he had no option but to seek terms. On 12 September 1217 peace was restored to England.[1]

3. EPILOGUE

So passed King John, vigorous upholder of the Crown's authority.

He figures as a tyrant and oppressor of his subjects' liberty, yet to the end he was protesting his respect for English law. A letter he wrote after the siege of Rochester to Hubert de Burgh, then his justiciar, reveals most clearly the paradox of his character:

'Dear Hubert,

If you have any power by English law to deprive the archbishop of Canterbury of his temporalities by a judgement of our court, although you cannot deliver judgement against him in his absence, do not fail to do so. For he is a notorious and barefaced traitor to us, since he did not render up our castle of Rochester to us in our so great need. And also because, though frequently requested and repeatedly summoned, he has not done us the service he was bound to do for his temporalities. And although there is no one to give judgement against, since he is not present, keep the temporalities in our hand all the same, if it is in any way possible by process of law; a thing which will rejoice the hearts of our friends at court.

Inquire with care, moreover, from your prisoners and others whether they acted on the archbishop's advice. And have a diligent inquiry made to see if you can find the letters that he sent to barons and others at the time of the rebellion against us; and send them, together with what the prisoners have told you, as speedily as you can to the Lord Pope and to us. . . .

With best wishes.'[1]

'A great prince certainly,' says the Barnwell annalist, 'though scarely a happy one, and like Marius experiencing the ups and downs of fortune.'[2]

The monster of personal depravity portrayed by Wendover and Paris must be dismissed for ever. The gossip which Wendover retailed so credulously was a by-product of the loathing the barons felt for the way in which John strove to maintain the dominant position of his predecessors in conditions of ever-increasing difficulty, and of their own fearful uncertainty for their families and lands in the face of his arbitrary oppressions. But if the barons were woefully uncertain of retaining their status, so too was the king. His most reprehensible acts of wilful violence were attempts to still his nagging fear of traitors and rebels. It was uncertainty and not 'superhuman wickedness' (to quote Miss Norgate)[3] that darkened the years of John's reign. He could be mean and

257

nasty, and there was an ignoble small-mindedness about his suspicion; but he was not a devil incarnate, and the Barnwell annalist gets nearer the mark than Wendover and Paris; but even he misses it.

Throughout his reign John's overriding objective was to rule his inheritance in peace: to be able to ride, like his father, from the Cheviots to the Pyrenees, wearing his crown in undisputed majesty receiving the homage of his vassals, doing justice. 'Greatest of earthly princes', Richard FitzNigel had called Henry II.[1] His father's position appeared to John not so much a challenge as a birthright. His ambition was not wanton, but he committed wanton acts in trying to achieve it. He possessed the high administrative ability of a great ruler, but he had the opportunity to use it only incidentally in the intervals of pursuing what he took to be his primary task. From the moment he began to rule, rivals and traitors conspired to cheat him of his inheritance. His reaction was a display of ruthless determination: anyone who impeded him ruling as his father had done was his enemy, be he baron, king of France, or pope; but as he wrestled with one, more foes sprang upon his back. Though he flinched sometimes in moments of danger, he never gave up. It could have been an epic struggle, but the story is marred by flaws in the character of the protagonist.

One of his greatest enemies was his own impatience. The rivalry of Arthur of Brittany and the implacable hostility of King Philip could have been met successfully by John only with the willing support of his vassals. His real strength lay in them, not, as he seems to have supposed, in the coffers of his treasury. It was, indeed, a supremely difficult task for John to win the support of his barons, for with his lands he inherited a legacy of long-standing resentment and flagging loyalty; but the basic case against him is that he did not even try. The interests of king and barons were not fundamentally incompatible, as the future was to show, and the tensions could have been resolved with patience and tact. What John had to contend with at home were grievances that had gone too long without remedy, and which went deeper than the superficial appearance of resentment and chagrin, for they touched basic conceptions of justice and the rule of law. John could recognise this – and did eventually, for he was sensitive to the requirements of law and justice – but he responded only at the sword point of rebellion. The warning cries had sounded from the earliest moments of his reign, but he ignored them. He could not claim that the imperious demands of war gave him no opportunity to set his house in order, for he won a respite by his campaign in 1199 and by the Treaty of Le Goulet, but threw it away by his reckless provocation of the Lusignans. Victory made him foolhardy and power corrupted his judgement. He made political difficulties for himself by turning upon the great barons whose support ensured the stability of his throne – men like William des Roches, William de Briouze, and William Marshal – and by his prolonged refusal to come to terms with the papacy, and his ill-conceived hatred for Stephen Langton. The time for reconciliation with the barons was in 1204–5 when their reluctance to support him was manifest, or at the very latest in 1212 when his throne rocked on the swelling tide of disaffection. It was his own fault that the baronial cause fell into the hands of violent men like Robert FitzWalter. John's one answer to opposition was to crush it out of existence, instead of trying to build up the sure defences of goodwill. His failure to recognise that the justifiable grievances of his barons were the basic problem and took precedence over the challenge posed by King Philip debars him from the title of 'great prince' that the Barnwell annalist bestows on him, and to which his undoubted practical abilities might otherwise have urged a claim.

Perhaps, though, even greater patience would not have smoothed John's path as king. It is impossible, the evidence being what it is, to pronounce finally upon his character as a man, but it seems clear that he was inadequate for the tasks confronting him as king. Even in his achievements there was always something missing. He subdued nations to his will, but brought only the peace of fear; he was an ingenious administrator, but expedients came before policy; he was a notable judge, but chicanery went along with justice; he was an able ruler, but he did not know when he was squeezing too hard; he was a clever strategist, but his military operations lacked that vital ingredient of success – boldness. He had the mental abilities of a great king, but the inclinations of a petty tyrant.

Appendices

The Trials of John at the French Court in 1202 and 1203

(See above, Chapter 3, pp. 74–5)

THE TRIAL OF 1202

Ralph Coggeshall, alone of the chroniclers, gives an explicit account of the French court proceeding to judgement on John in 1202.[1] Because his testimony was unsupported Miss Norgate dismissed it, maintaining that there had been no formal trial, but that Philip fabricated reports of a suppositious trial a few years later to justify his forcible expropriation of John.[2] Petit-Dutaillis contested this opinion. Coggeshall he holds was a selective chronicler who confined himself, by and large, to events of which he had special knowledge. The other chroniclers, though they do not explicitly support him, do not in any way contradict him. Moreover Pope Innocent III, writing on 31 October 1203 was confident that a trial had taken place, and his words imply that a judgement had been given.[3]

THE FIEFS WHICH JOHN WAS DECLARED TO HAVE FORFEITED IN 1202

Coggeshall wrote that 'the assembled court of the king of France adjudged the king of England to be deprived of all his lands which he and his forefathers had hitherto held of the king of France.' But the French chronicler, Rigord, is clear that he was cited only in respect of the counties of Poitou and Anjou and the duchy of Aquitaine.[4] If Normandy was omitted in April 1202 this would be a reason for holding another session of the court in 1203 to get the legal position clear. Some historians, however, refuse to believe that any trial was held in 1203.

[1] Coggeshall, pp. 135–6.

[2] K. Norgate, 'The Alleged Condemnation of King John by the Court of France in 1202,' *Transactions of the Royal Historical Society*, new series, xiv. (1900), 56–68; *John Lackland*, p. 84.

[3] Ch. Petit-Dutaillis, *Studies Supplementary to Stubbs*, i. 107–15; Innocent III, Letters, Bk. VI, no. 167; Migne, *Patrologia Latina*, ccxv. 183–4.

[4] Rigord, i. 151–2.

THE ALLEGED TRIAL OF 1203

A second trial was not mentioned in any chronicle or surviving document until 1216. Philip's son Louis then recalled it in attempting to justify his claim to the throne of England. The claim was very dubious and the arguments in support of it tendentious, so belief in the trial of 1203 is not encouraged by its mention in this connection. Moreover, Louis asserted that John had then been declared to have forfeited all his lands because of the murder of Arthur. Since no one knew that Arthur was dead in 1203 the assertion is absurd. In consequence many historians have dismissed the whole thing as a fable.[1] Nonetheless it is possible that the palpable nonsense of Louis' description in 1216 of the trial of 1203 has inclined scholars to dismiss the fact of a second trial without full justification. While Innocent could write in 1203 feeling that he knew what had happened at the trial of 1202, in March 1205 he said that Philip claimed Normandy by judgement of his court, but professed himself ignorant of the circumstances and the law involved.[2] This was in reply to a request from the bishops of Normandy as to how they should conduct themselves towards Philip who had taken over the duchy by force. The implication is that Normandy had not been included in the trial of 1202 but that Philip, so he claimed, had rectified the omission at a second trial. Further support for a belief in a trial in 1203 has been advanced by B. C. Keeney. I have tentatively assumed in the narrative that the trial took place, but the question is still very open. The question is of some importance in the development of the feudal prerogatives of the French Crown and the jurisdiction of its court, but it is not crucial in the history of John's reign. He lost his French fiefs in the fortunes of war.

[1] Ch. Bemont, 'De condamnation de Jean sans-terre par la cour des Pairs de France en 1202,' *Revue Historique*, xxxiii. (1886), 33–72, 290–311. Ch. Petit-Dutaillis, *Le Desheritement de Jean sans-terre et le meurtre d'Arthur de Bretagne* (Paris 1925). The attempt of P. Guilhiermoz to rehabilitate the second trial, *Bibliotheque de l'Ecole des Chartes*, lx. (1899), 45–85, was severely handled by critics.

[2] Innocent III, Letters, Bk. viii, no. 7, Migne, *Patrologia Latina*, ccxv. 564.

Magna Carta

Translated by HARRY ROTHWELL, M.A., PH.D.
Professor of History, University of Southampton

There is no 'original 'of the Charter of Liberties of 1215. *Four copies sent out from the royal chancery shortly after the meeting at Runnymede on* 19 *Jun-survive: two are in the British Museum, one at Lincoln Cathedral, and one at Salisbury Cathedral. Each consists of a single sheet of parchment measuring approximately* 15 × 20 *inches. The punctuation, division into paragraphs, and numeration of them in the translation which follows are in accordance with the practice of modern editors.*

There has been no full-scale commentary on the Charter since W. S. McKecknie, Magna Carta. *The* 2nd *edition of this (Glasgow,* 1914) *was much revised from the first. Its interpretations of John's government and the baronial purpose need much further revision in the light of modern knowledge, but its elucidae tions of the technicalities of the Charter can be read with much profit.*

THE CHARTER OF LIBERTIES OF 1215

John, by the grace of God, king of England, lord of Ireland, duke of Normandy and Aquitaine, and count of Anjou, to the archbishops, bishops, abbots, earls, barons, justiciars, foresters, sheriffs, stewards, servants, and to all his bailiffs and faithful subjects, greeting. Know that we, out of reverence for God and for the salvation of our soul and those of all our ancestors and heirs, for the honour of God and the advancement of holy Church, and for the reform of our realm, on the advice of our venerable fathers, Stephen, archbishop of Canterbury, primate of all England and cardinal of the holy Roman Church, Henry archbishop of Dublin, William of London, Peter of Winchester, Jocelyn of Bath and Glastonbury, Hugh of Lincoln, Walter of Worcester, William of Coventry and Benedict of Rochester, bishop, of Master Pandulf, subdeacon and member of the household of the lord pope, of brother Aymeric, master of the Knights of the Temple in England, and of the noble men William Marshal earl of Pembroke, William earl of Salisbury, William earl Warenne, William earl of Arundel, Alan of Galloway constable of Scotland, Warin son of Gerold, Peter son of Herbert, Hubert de Burgh seneschal of Poitou,

Hugh de Neville, Matthew son of Herbert, Thomas Basset, Alan Basset, Philip d'Aubigny, Robert of Ropsley, John Marshal, John son of Hugh, and others, our faithful subjects:

[1] In the first place have granted to God, and by this our present charter confirmed for us and our heirs for ever, that the English church shall be free, and shall have its rights undiminished and its liberties unimpaired; and it is our will that it be thus observed; which is evident from the fact that, before the quarrel between us and our barons began, we, willingly and spontaneously granted and by our charter confirmed the freedom of elections which is reckoned most important and very essential to the English church, and obtained confirmation of it from the lord pope Innocent III; the which we will observe and we wish our heirs to observe it in good faith for ever.[1] We have also granted to all freemen of our kingdom, for ourselves and our heirs for ever, all the liberties written below, to be had and held by them and their heirs of us and our heirs.

[2] If any of our earls or barons or others holding of us in chief by knight service[2] dies, and at his death his heir be of age and owe relief[3] he shall have his inheritance on payment of the old relief, namely the heir or heirs of an earl £100 for a whole earl's barony,[4] the heir or heirs of a baron £100 for a whole barony; the heir or heirs of a knight 100s., at most, for a whole knight's fee[5]; and he who owes less let him give less according to the ancient custom of fiefs.

[3] If, however, the heir of any such be under age and a ward, he

---

[1] This confirmation, in general terms, of the liberties of the Church in England has no place in the Articles of the Barons, and was presumably included at the request of Archbishop Langton and his suffragans. The charter referred to in the text was one issued on 21 November 1214 and re-issued on 15 January 1215 setting out the procedure for elections to episcopal sees and abbacies in a form acceptable to the pope. (For the text of it see Stubbs' *Select Charters* pp. 283-4; translation in Stephenson & Marcham, *Sources of English Constitutional History*, pp. 114-15.)

[2] *In chief by knight service*: i.e., directly from the king by the service of rendering a stipulated number of knights for service in the feudal army or for castleguard. The *others holding of us in chief* included all the bishops (except the bishop of Rochester who held of the archbishop of Canterbury), and the abbots of the greater abbeys founded before 1070.

[3] The *relief* was a succession duty taken from anyone entering upon an inheritance held by military tenure. If the heir were under age his person and his lands were held in wardship by his overlord until he came of age, and in such cases relief was not normally exacted.

[4] *Barony*: a conventional term for a large estate held of the king by knight service.

[5] *Knight's fee* (or fief): an estate charged with the service of providing one fully equipped knight (or his monetary equivalent). Its size depended upon the accident of grant and might be anything between 5 and 20 curacates. The curacate was not itself a uniform land measure, though for fiscal purposes it was often reckoned at 100 or 120 acres. The knight's fee was the basic unit in reckoning taxes based upon liability for military service, but individual holdings of a fraction of a knight's fee were common.

shall have his inheritance when he comes of age without paying relief and without making a fine.[1]

[4] The guardian of the land of such an heir who is under age shall take from the land of the heir no more than reasonable sums, reasonable customary dues and reasonable services, and that without destruction and waste of men[2] or goods; and if we commit the wardship of the land of any such to a sheriff, or to any other who is answerable to us for its revenues, and he destroys or wastes what he has wardship of, we will take compensation from him and the land shall be committed to two lawful[3] and discreet men of that fief, who shall be responsible for the revenues to us or to him to whom we shall assign them; and if we give or sell to anyone the wardship of any such land and he causes destruction or waste therein, he shall lose that wardship, and it shall be transferred to two lawful and discreet men of that fief, who shall similarly be responsible to us as is aforesaid.

[5] Moreover, so long as he has the wardship of the land, the guardian shall keep in repair the houses, parks, preserves, ponds, mills and other things pertaining to the land out of the revenues from it; and he shall restore to the heir when he comes of age his land fully [*totam*] stocked with ploughs and the means of husbandry [*waynagüs*] according to what the season of husbandry requires, and what the revenues of the land can reasonably bear.

[6] Heirs shall be married without disparagement,[4] yet so that before the marriage is contracted those nearest in blood to the heir shall have notice.

[7] A widow shall have her marriage portion[5] and inheritance forthwith and without difficulty after the death of her husband; nor shall she pay anything to have her dower or her marriage portion or the inheritance which she and her husband held on the day of her husband's death; and she may remain in her husband's house for forty days after his death, within which time her dower shall be assigned to her.

[8] No widow shall be forced to marry so long as she wishes to live without a husband, provided that she gives security not to marry

[1] *Fine:* the word was not confined at this period to a monetary penalty for an offence, but was used of any offering acceptable to the king for having something from him, be it his peace or the grant of a privilege.

[2] *Waste of men:* an estate could be wasted by selling freedom to villeins and so depriving the heir of labour services that his ancestors had enjoyed.

[3] *Lawful men:* men of free status (in contrast to villeins) who have not been outlawed.

[4] *Without disparagement:* i.e., not to social inferiors. Kings were prone to sell heiresses to the highest bidder without regard to social considerations.

[5] *Marriage portion:* an endowment in property bestowed on the wife at the time of marriage by her own family, as distinct from the *dower* – the property which the husband assigned to her at the same time, as a provision for her widowhood.

without our consent if she holds of us, or without the consent of the lord of whom she holds, if she holds of another.

[9] Neither we nor our bailiffs will seize for any debt any land or rent, so long as the chattels of the debtor are sufficient to repay the debt; nor will those who have gone surety for the debtor be distrained so long as the principal debtor is himself able to pay the debt; and if the principal debtor fails to pay the debt, having nothing wherewith to pay it, then shall the sureties answer for the debt; and they shall, if they wish, have the lands and rents of the debtor until they are reimbursed for the debt which they have paid for him, unless the principal debtor can show that he has discharged his obligation in the matter to the said sureties.

[10] If anyone who has borrowed from the Jews any sum, great or small, dies before it is repaid, the debt shall not bear interest while the heir is under age, whosoever tenant he may be; and if the debt falls into our hands, we will not take anything except the principal mentioned in the bond.[1]

[11] And if anyone dies indebted to the Jews, his wife shall have her dower and pay nothing of that debt; and if the dead man leaves children who are under age, they shall be provided with necessaries befitting the holding of the deceased; and the debt shall be paid out of the residue, reserving, however, service due to lords of the land; debts owing to others than Jews shall be dealt with in like manner.

[12] No scutage or aid[2] shall be imposed in our kingdom unless by common counsel of our kingdom, except for ransoming our person, for making our eldest son a knight, and for once marrying our eldest daughter; and for these only a reasonable aid shall be levied. Be it done in like manner concerning aids from the city of London.

[13] And the city of London shall have all its ancient liberties and free customs as well by land as by water. Furthermore, we will and grant that all other cities, boroughs, towns and ports shall have all their liberties and free customs.

[14] And to obtain the common counsel of the kingdom about the assessing of an aid (except in the three cases aforesaid) or of a scutage, we will cause to be summoned the archbishops, bishops, abbots, earls

---

[1] Since usury was prohibited to Christians by the Church, the Jews were the principal moneylenders. They were under the protection of the Crown, but the king was every Jew's heir. See above, p. 184.

[2] *Scutage:* literally 'shield-money' – a payment made to the Crown in lieu of military service. In origin the payment of scutage was probably a privilege granted to those for whom the rendering of knight service was an inconvenience; but it was later demanded by the Crown from those liable for knight service as a means of raising money. *Aid:* a general word for a money payment to an overlord to help him in difficult financial circumstances.

and greater barons, individually by our letters – and, in addition, we will cause to be summoned generally through our sheriffs and bailiffs all those holding of us in chief – for a fixed date, namely, after the expiry of at least forty days, and to a fixed place; and in all letters of such summons we will specify the reason for the summons. And when the summons has thus been made, the business shall proceed on the day appointed, according to the counsel of those present, although not all have come who were summoned.

[15] We will not in future grant anyone the right to take an aid from his own freemen, except for ransoming his person, for making his eldest son a knight and for once marrying his eldest daughter; and for these only a reasonable aid shall be levied.

[16] No one shall be compelled to do greater service for a knight's fee or for any other free holding than is due from it.

[17] Common pleas shall not follow our court, but shall be held in some fixed place.[1]

[18] Inquests of *novel disseisin*, of *mort d'ancestor*, and of *darrein present-ment*,[2] shall not be held elsewhere than in the court of the county to which they relate [*in suis comitatibus*] and in this manner – we, or, if we should be out of the realm, our chief justiciar, will send two justices through each county four times a year, who, with four knights of each county chosen by the county, shall hold the said inquests [*assisas*] in the county court, on the day and in the place of meeting of the county court.

[19] And if [all] the said inquests [*assisas*] cannot be held on the day of the county court, there shall stay behind as many of the knights and freeholders who were present at the county court on that day as are necessary for the sufficient making of judgements, according to the amount of the business.

[20] A freeman shall not be amerced[3] for a slight offence except in

---

[1] *Common pleas:* suits between subject and subject about real property. It was a serious inconvenience for suitors who wished to bring civil suits before a royal justice to have to chase the peripatetic royal household, and this clause sanctions the practice of establishing commissions of justices to hear such pleas. These justices came to be known as the Bench and their place of meeting was the palace of Westminster.

[2] *Inquests (recognitiones* – inquiries) involved a legal procedure (the use of a jury of neighbours) that could be authorised only by a royal writ. The necessary writ was sued out of chancery by the plaintiff who claimed that another had recently forcibly dis-possessed him of his property (*novel disseisin*), was depriving him of his inheritance (*mort d'ancestor*), or was seeking to present to him an ecclesiastical benefice to which the plaintiff had presented at the last vacancy (*darrein presentment*). These writs (sometimes referred to as the possessory writs or 'assizes') instructed the sheriff to empanel a local jury (a 'jury of recognition') who from their local knowledge answered certain specific questions which he put to them. The sheriff then acted according to the tenor of their replies. See above, p. 142.

[3] *Amerced:* fined in a court of law. For discussion of this clause see above, pp. 150–1.

accordance with the degree of the offence, and for a grave offence he shall be amerced in accordance with its gravity, yet saving his way of living [*contenementum*]; and a merchant in the same way, saving his stock-in-trade [*mercandisa*]; and a villein shall be amerced in the same way, saving his means of livelihood [*waynagium*] – if they have fallen into our mercy: and none of the aforesaid amercements shall be imposed except by the oath of upright men of the neighbourhood.

[21] Earls and barons shall not be amerced except by their peers, and only in accordance with the degree of the offence.

[22] No clerk shall be amerced in respect of his lay holding except after the manner of the others aforesaid and not in accordance with the amount of his ecclesiastical benefice.

[23] No community or individual [*nec villa nec homo*] shall be compelled to make bridges at river banks, except those who from of old are legally bound to do so.

[24] No sheriff, constable, coroners, or other of our bailiffs, shall try [*teneant*] pleas of our Crown.[1]

[25] All counties, hundreds, wapentakes and trithings shall be at the old rents without any additional payment, except our demesne manors.[2]

[26] If any one holding a lay fief of us dies and our sheriff or bailiff shows our letters patent of summons for a debt that the deceased owed us, it shall be lawful for our sheriff or bailiff to attach and inventory chattels of the deceased found upon the lay fief to the value of that debt under the supervision of law-worthy men, provided that none of the chattels shall be removed until the debt which is manifest [*clarum*] has been paid to us in full; and the residue shall be left to the executors for carrying out the will of the deceased. And if nothing is owing to us from him, all the chattels shall go to the deceased, saving to his wife and children their reasonable shares.

[27] If any freeman dies without leaving a will, his chattels shall be distributed by his nearest kinsfolk and friends under the supervision of the church, saving to every one of the debts which the deceased owed him.

[28] No constable or other bailiff of ours shall take anyone's corn or other chattels unless he pays spot cash for them or can delay payment by arrangement with the seller.

---

[1] *Pleas of the Crown:* the more serious criminal charges reserved for judgment in the royal courts.

[2] The *hundred* was an administrative subdivision of the county. In the counties of Derby, Nottingham, Lincoln, Leicester, and parts of Yorkshire, the hundred was known by the name of *wapentake*, a word of Danish origin. The *trithings* were the modern Ridings of Yorkshire. *Desmense manors* were those directly exploited by the lord through bailiffs, as distinct from manors which were leased to others.

[29] No constable shall compel any knight to give money instead of castle-guard if he is willing to do the guard himself or through another good man, if for some good reason he cannot do it himself; and if we lead or send him on military service, he shall be exempt from guard in proportion to the time that because of us he has been on service.

[30] No sheriff or bailiff of ours, or anyone else [*aliquis alius*], shall take the horses or carts of any freeman for transport work save with the agreement of that freeman.

[31] Neither we nor our bailiffs will take other people's timber for castles or other works of ours except with the agreement of him whose timber it is.

[32] We will not hold for more than a year and a day the lands of those convicted of felony, and then the lands shall be handed over to the lords of the fiefs.

[33] Henceforth all fishtraps shall be cleared completely from the Thames and the Medway and throughout all England, except along the sea coast.

[34] The writ called *Praecipe* shall not in future be issued to anyone in respect of any holding whereby a freeman may lose his court.[1]

[35] Let there be one measure for wine throughout our kingdom, and one measure for ale, and one measure for corn, namely 'the London quarter'; and one width for cloths whether dyed, russet or halberget, namely two ells within the selvedges. Let it be the same with weights as with measures.

[36] Nothing shall be given or taken in future for the writ of inquiry concerning life or limbs, but it shall be granted free of charge and not withheld.[2]

[37] If anyone holds of us by fee-farm, by socage, or by burgage,[3] and holds land of another by knight service, we will not, by reason of that fee-farm, socage, or burgage, have the wardship of his heir or of his land that is of the fief of the other; nor will we have wardship of the fee-farm, socage, or burgage, unless such fee-farm owes knight service. We will not have the wardship of anyone's heir or land which he holds

---

[1] The writ *praecipe* instructed the sheriff to command the defendant to restore property of which the plaintiff claimed he was being wrongfully deprived or to appear in court before royal justices to show good cause for not doing so. This was a speedy means of getting an action about title started in the royal courts, and the writ was very popular. For the purpose of the clause see note 2 to p. 237.

[2] The writ referred to here is the writ *de odio et atia*. A person who had been challenged to a judicial duel by having a case brought against him by another purely 'out of spite and hatred' could apply for this writ and have a jury of neighbours decide whether the charge were reasonable or not. If they decided that it had been brought out of spite the case was quashed.

[3] These are three free, though non-military, tenures, usually involving a money rent. Burgage tenure was confined to tenements within towns.

of another by knight service by reason of any petty serjeanty which he holds of us by the service of rendering to us knives or arrows or the like.[1]

[38] No bailiff shall in future put anyone to trial upon his own un-supported testimony, without reliable witnesses brought for this pur-pose.

[39] No freeman shall be arrested or imprisoned or disseised or outlawed or exiled or in any way destroyed, neither will we set forth against him or send against him, except by the lawful judgement of his peers and [vel] by the law of the land.[2]

[40] To no one will we sell, to no one will we refuse or delay right or justice.

[41] All merchants shall have safe and secure exit from, and entry into England, and dwelling and travel in England as well by land as by water, for buying and selling by the ancient and right customs, free of all evil tolls, except in time of war and if they are of the land that is at war with us. And if such are found in our lands at the beginning of a war, they shall be taken and kept in custody [attachientur], without injury to their persons or goods, until we, or our chief justiciar, know how merchants of our land are treated who were found in the land at war with us when war broke out [tunc], and if ours are safe there, the others shall be safe in our land.

[42] Without prejudicing the allegiance due to us, it shall be lawful in future for any one to leave our kingdom and return safely and se-curely by land and water, save, in the public interest, for a short period in time of war – except for those imprisoned or outlawed in accordance with the law of the kingdom and natives of a land that is at war with us and merchants (who shall be treated as aforesaid).

[43] If anyone who holds of some escheat[3] such as the honor of Wallingford, Nottingham, Boulogne, Lancaster, or of other escheats which are in our hands and are baronies dies, his heir shall give no other relief and do no other service to us than he would have done to the baron, if that barony had been in the baron's hands; and we will hold it in the same manner in which the baron held it.

[1] Serjeanty tenures were a very miscellaneous class. Their characteristic feature was that they involved the rendering of some special service. These services ranged up-ward from petty services such as the annual render of a pair of spurs, a cloak, a falcon, an arrow head, or the service rendered on Christmas day by the tenant of the manor of Kingston Russell of counting the king's chessmen and putting them back in their box when he had finished his game, to the grand services rendered, for example, at the coronation. Many serjeanties were already an anachronism by the 13th century and were being commuted into money payments.

[2] For discussion of this clause see above, pp. 213–14, and note 3 to p. 237.

[3] Escheat: an estate which has reverted to the overlord, e.g., for lack of an heir, or on forfeiture for felony.

[44] Men who live outside the forest[1] need not henceforth come before our justices of the forest upon a general summons, unless they are impleaded or are sureties for any person or persons who are attached for forest offences.

[45] We will not make justices, constables, sheriffs or bailiffs save of such as know the law of the kingdom and mean to observe it well.

[46] All barons who have founded abbeys, in respect of which they have charters of the kings of England or of which they have had long tenure, shall have custody of them in a vacancy, as they ought to have.

[47] All forests that have been made forest in our time shall be immediately disafforested; and so be it done with river-banks that have been made preserves[2] by us in our time.

[48] All evil customs connected with forests and warrens, foresters and warreners, sheriffs and their officials, river-banks and their wardens shall immediately be inquired into in each county by twelve sworn knights of the same county who are to be chosen by good men of the same county, and within forty days of the completion of the inquiry shall be utterly abolished so as never to be restored, provided that we, or our justiciar if we are not in England, have previous intimation thereof.

[49] We will immediately return all hostages and charters given to us by Englishmen, as security for peace or faithful service.

[50] We will entirely remove from their bailiwicks the relations of Gerard d'Athée so that in future they shall have no bailiwick in England, namely Engelard de Cigogné, Peter and Guy and Andrew de Chanceaux, Guy de Cigogné, Geoffrey de Martigny and his brothers, Philip Marc and his brothers and his nephew Geoffrey, and all their following.[3]

[51] As soon as peace is restored, we will remove from the kingdom all foreign knights, cross-bowmen, serjeants, and mercenaries, who have come with horses and arms to the detriment of the kingdom.

[52] If any one has been dispossessed or removed by us without the legal judgement of his peers from his lands, castles, franchises or his right, we will immediately restore them to him; and if a dispute arises over this, then let it be decided by the judgement of the twenty-five barons who are mentioned below in the clause [61] for securing the peace: for all the things, however, from which any one has been dispossessed or removed without the lawful judgement of his peers by King Henry, our father, or by King Richard, our brother, which we have in our hand or are held by others, to whom we are bound to

---

[1] For the *forest* see above, pp. 151–2.
[2] *Preserves:* literally 'put "in defence".'
[3] For Gerard d'Athée and his kin see above, pp. 188–9.

warrant them, we will have the usual period of respite of crusaders, excepting those things about which a plea was started or an inquest made by our command before we took the cross[1]; when however we return from our pilgrimage, or if by any chance we do not go on it we will at once do full justice therein.

[53] We will have the same respite, and in the same manner, in the doing of justice in the matter of the deafforestation or retention of the forests which Henry our father or Richard our brother afforested [*cf. clause* 47], and in the matter of the wardship of lands which are of the fief of another, wardships of which sort we have hitherto had by reason of a fief which anyone held of us by knight service [*cf. clause* 37], and in the matter of abbeys founded on the fief of another, not on a fief of our own, in which the lord of the fief claims he has a right [*cf. clause* 46]; and when we have returned, or if we do not set out on our pilgrimage, we will at once do full justice to all who complain of these things.

[54] No one shall be arrested or imprisoned upon the appeal of a woman, for the death of anyone except her husband.[2]

[55] All fines made with us unjustly and against the law of the land, and all amercements imposed unjustly and against the law of the land, shall be entirely remitted, or else let them be settled by the judgement of the twenty-five barons who are mentioned below in the clause [61] for securing the peace, or by the judgement of the majority of the same, along with the aforesaid Stephen, archbishop of Canterbury, if he can be present, and such others as he may wish to associate with himself for this purpose, and if he cannot be present the business shall nevertheless proceed without him, provided that if any one or more of the aforesaid twenty-five barons are in a like suit, they shall be removed from the judgement of the case in question, and others chosen, sworn and put in their place by the rest of the same twenty-five for this case only.

[56] If we have dispossessed or removed Welshmen[3] from lands or liberties or other things without the legal judgement of their peers in England or in Wales, they shall be immediately restored to them; and if a dispute arises over this, then let it be decided in the March by the judgement of their peers – for holdings in England according to the law of England, for holdings in Wales according to the law of

---

[1] For John 'taking the cross' see above, p. 233.

[2] An *appeal* (in the legal sense here used) was a formal accusation of felony or treason made by an individual. The appellant had to be prepared to support the charge 'with his body' (i.e., in a judicial duel). A female appellant, however, was allowed to appoint a proxy to fight for her, and before the limitations imposed by this clause the possibilities of abuse were great.

[3] The rebel barons were allied with the Welsh under Llywelyn.

Wales, and for holdings in the March according to the law of the March. Welshmen shall do the same to us and ours.

[57] For all the things, however, from which any Welshman has been dispossessed or removed without the lawful judgement of his peers by King Henry, our father, or Richard, our brother, which we have in our hand or which are held by others, to whom we are bound to warrant them, we will have the usual period of respite of crusaders, excepting those things about which a plea was started or an inquest made by our command before we took the cross; when however we return, or if by chance we do not set out on our pilgrimage, we will at once do full justice in accordance with the laws of the Welsh and the foresaid regions.

[58] We will give up at once the son of Llywelyn and all the hostages from Wales and the charters that were handed over to us as security for peace.

[59] We will act towards Alexander, King of the Scots, concerning the return of his sisters and hostages and concerning his franchises and his right in the same manner in which we act towards our other barons of England, unless it ought to be otherwise according to the charters which we have from William his father, formerly King of the Scots, and this shall be according to the judgement of his peers in our court.

[60] Moreover, all these aforesaid customs and liberties which we have granted shall be observed in our kingdom as far as it pertains to us towards our men, all of our kingdom, clerks as well as laymen, shall observe as far as it pertains to them towards their men.

[61] Since,[1] moreover, for God and the amendment of our kingdom and for the better allaying of the discord that has arisen between us and our barons we have granted all these things aforesaid, wishing them to enjoy the use of them unimpaired and unshaken for ever, we give and grant them the under-written security, namely, that the barons shall choose any twenty-five barons of the kingdom they wish, who must with all their might observe, hold and cause to be observed, the peace and liberties which we have granted and confirmed to them by this present charter of ours, so that if we, or our justiciar, or our bailiffs or any one of our servants offend in any way against any one or transgress any of the articles of the peace or the security and the offence be notified to four of the aforesaid twenty-five barons, those four barons shall come to us, or to our justiciar if we are out of the kingdom, and, laying the transgression before us, shall petition us to have that transgression corrected without delay. And if we do not correct the transgression, or if we are out of the kingdom, if our justiciar does not correct

---

[1] For discussion of this clause see above, pp. 239-40.

it, within forty days, reckoning from the time it was brought to our notice or to that of our justiciar if we were out of the kingdom, the aforesaid four barons shall refer that case to the rest of the twenty-five barons and those twenty-five barons together with the community of the whole land shall distrain and distress us in every way they can, namely, by seizing castles, lands, possessions, and in such other ways as they can, saving our person and the persons of our queen and our children, until, in their opinion, amends have been made; and when amends have been made, they shall obey us as they did before. And let anyone in the country who wishes to do so take an oath to obey the orders of the said twenty-five barons for the execution of all the aforesaid matters, and with them to distress us as much as he can, and we publicly and freely give anyone leave to take the oath who wishes to take it and we will never prohibit anyone from taking it. Indeed, all those in the land who are unwilling of themselves and of their own accord to take an oath to the twenty-five barons to help them to distrain and distress us, we will make them take the oath as aforesaid at our command. And if any of the twenty-five barons dies or leaves the country or is in any other way prevented from carrying out the things aforesaid, the remainder of the aforesaid twenty-five barons shall choose as they think fit another one in his place, and he shall take the oath like the rest. In all matters the execution of which is committed to these twenty-five barons, if it should happen that these twenty-five are present yet disagree among themselves about anything, or if some of those summoned will not or cannot be present, that shall be held as fixed and established which the majority of those present ordained or commanded, exactly as if all the twenty-five had consented to it; and the said twenty-five shall swear that they will faithfully observe all the things aforesaid and will do all they can to get them observed. And we will procure nothing from anyone, either personally or through any one else, whereby any of these concessions and liberties might be revoked or diminished; and if any such thing be procured let it be void and null, and we will never use it either personally or through another.[1] And we have fully remitted and pardoned to everyone all the ill-will, anger and rancour that have arisen between us and our men, clergy and laity, from the time of the quarrel. Furthermore, we have fully remitted to all, clergy and laity, and as far as pertains to us have completely forgiven all trespasses occasioned by the same quarrel between Easter in the sixteenth year of our reign and the restoration of peace. And, besides, we have caused to be made for them letters testimonial patent of the lord Stephen archbishop of Canterbury, of the lord Henry archbishop of Dublin and of the aforementioned bishops

---

[1] Some editors begin a new clause (no. 62) at this point.

and of Master Pandulf about this security and the aforementioned concessions.[1] Wherefore we wish and firmly enjoin that the English church shall be free, and that the men in our kingdom shall have and hold all the aforesaid liberties, rights and concessions well and peacefully, freely and quietly, fully and completely for themselves and their heirs from us and our heirs, in all matters and in all places for ever, as is aforesaid. An oath, moreover, has been taken, as well on our part as on the part of the barons, that all these things aforesaid shall be observed in good faith and without evil disposition. Witness the abovementioned and many others. Given by our hand in the meadow which is called Runnymede between Windsor and Staines on the fifteenth day of June, in the seventeenth year of our reign.

[1] Some editors begin a new clause (no. 63) at this point.

The Accident to King John's
Baggage Train in October 1216

THE accounts given by the chroniclers, in order of composition, are as follows:

RALPH, ABBOT OF COGGESHALL, *Chronicon Anglicanum*, pp. 183–4

Moreover the greatest distress troubled him, because on that journey [from Lynn] he had lost his chapel with his relics, and some of his packhorses with divers household effects at the Wellstream, and many members of his household were submerged in the waters of the sea, and sucked into the quicksand there, because they had set out incautiously and hastily before the tide had receded (*quia incaute et precipitanter se ingesserant aestu maris nondum recedente*).

ROGER OF WENDOVER, *Flores Historiarum*, ii. 195–6

Then, heading for the north, he lost, by an unexpected accident, all the wagons, carts, and packhorses, with the treasures, precious vessels, and all the other things which he cherished with special care; for the ground was opened in the midst of the waves, and bottomless whirlpools engulfed everything, together with men and horses, so that not a single foot-soldier got away to bear tidings of the disaster to the king. The king, however, barely escaping with his army, spent the following night at the abbey called Swineshead.

MATTHEW PARIS, *Historia Anglorum*, ii. 190

Paris, writing a generation after the event, offers an embroidered version of Wendover's story:

King John, heading for the north, . . . attempted to cross, without a guide, the place where sea and river water mingle, known as Wellstream, and narrowly escaping himself, he lost there irretrievably the carts and packhorses bearing his booty and loot, and all his treasure and household effects. For the ground opened in the midst of the waves, and the sand which is called quick sucked in everything – horses and men, weapons, tents, victuals, and all the things which the king valued too highly in the world – apart from his life.

The inconsistencies of these accounts make it hard to gauge the magnitude of the accident or to describe precisely what happened; and none gives sufficient information to make it possible even to place it exactly. Two further difficulties beset any attempt to reconstruct

x. The accident at the Wellstream.

what happened. The first of these is the transformation of the coastline in this region of the Wash as the result of drainage, the alteration of watercourses, and the silting up of estuaries. Where John's baggage was submerged is now almost certainly dry land.[1] The second difficulty arises from the king's itinerary as revealed by the dating clauses of letters patent and close. These show him to have remained at Lynn until 11 October (though he may, of course, have left early on the morning of that day), to have been at Wisbech on 12 October, and to have reached Swineshead on the same day. The obvious interpretation of the chroniclers' accounts is that trouble befell John's baggage train as it attempted to shorten the journey from Lynn to Swineshead by crossing the sands of the Wellstream estuary at low tide; but if so, why should the king have been at Wisbech, which the short cut should have bypassed?

W. St John Hope sought to resolve these difficulties in a brilliantly

[1] For the fenland in the middle ages see G. Fowler, *A Guide to Wicken Fen* (National Trust, 1947), H. C. Darby, *The Medieval Fenland* (Cambridge, 1940), and the articles cited in the other footnotes in this appendix.

argued paper read to the Society of Antiquaries in 1906.[1] He suggested that on leaving Lynn on 11 October the king and the army went via Wisbech, but that the cumbersome and slow-moving baggage train was instructed to take a more direct route across the sands of the Wellstream estuary and meet up with him on the Lincolnshire side next day. By offering a reasoned guess at the size of the baggage train and its rate of progress, by calculating the time of low water on the day in question, by a close study of local topography, and by consulting descriptions of the passage of the former estuary recorded by local historians, St John Hope felt able to offer a plausible account of what happened. There was at one time (his account runs) a recognized route across the estuary, four and a half miles long, from Cross Keys to Long Sutton, though it was advisable to have a guide prodding the route with a long pole for the sands were treacherous. On 12 October 1216 it would have been nearly spring tide and at low water, about noon, the sea would be far out. But October is generally a bad month on the fens for the mist hangs low for some time after sunrise, and the wagons, therefore, probably started late upon the sands, and with little margin of safe time to cross fanned out to get over hurriedly. Trouble arose at the attempt to ford the channel of the Wellstream.

Here would begin the great danger that a guide might have averted, the quicksands which are still the terror of the Wash. If once the leading horses and vehicles got involved the fate of the train was sealed. The vanguard would quickly become a struggling and shouting mass of men trying to extricate themselves and their charges, or to turn back, while the rest of the train would block the retreat and the rearguard continue to press on until halted by the confusion ahead. Meanwhile carts and wagons, horses and men, would settle deeper and deeper into the quicksands, and any possible margin of time in which to effect a safe crossing would quickly pass. The turning of the tide would mean, too, the conversion into quicksands of much of the dry bed already traversed, and in them the rest of the helpless team would also become involved and so eventually perish.

This vivid reconstruction has for long been the accepted account (and has led to several expensive attempts to find the treasure in the neighbourhood of Long Sutton); but it was challenged by Mr Gordon Fowler in 1952.[2] Fowler casts doubts upon the validity of several of the premises of St John Hope's argument, and questioned his reliance upon Paris and Wendover. Fowler could find no evidence of quicksand in the ancient estuary and was convinced that in the early thirteenth

[1] W. St John Hope, 'The Loss of King John's Baggage Train in the Wellstream in October 1216', *Archaeologia*, lx (1906), 93–110.

[2] G. Fowler, 'King John's Treasure', *Proceedings of the Cambridge Antiquarian Society*, xlvi (1953), 4–20.

century the estuary was not passable at any state of the tide north of Wisbech. He contended, then, that both the king and the baggage train were obliged to pass through Wisbech on their way to Swineshead. This meant that they were obliged to ford the Wellstream on the road between Walsoken and Wisbech, and it was there, Fowler concluded, that the accident took place. The banks of the estuary were at this point only a quarter of a mile apart, and the river bed was a mere forty yards wide. Normally this crossing presented no difficulties and John's misadventure must be attributed to an infrequent but well attested phenomenon known locally as a 'stolen tide' – a sudden tidal surge some two hours before expected low water, creating an eagre or bore that instantly raises the level of the water in a tidal river by several feet. Exceptional tide surges occur from time to time in the North Sea between the Humber and the Thames, and shortly after Fowler wrote his paper there occurred the devastating one of the night of 31 January 1953.

Fowler's interpretation had the advantage over St John Hope's that it invoked fewer debatable suppositions; but it had the serious weakness of being incompatible with the most sober and trustworthy of the chronicle accounts – that of the abbot of Coggeshall. Ralph of Coggeshall speaks clearly of quicksand and of an incautious attempt to cross before the tide had receded, not of an unforeseeable accident caused by an incoming tide when fording a river. Moreover, a tidal surge of the kind that would create a dangerous bore on the Wellstream would no doubt have left its mark elsewhere on the east coast that day, but Coggeshall, an assiduous recorder of natural phenomena, knew nothing of it.

More recently Professor J. C. Holt has offered yet another closely argued interpretation.[1] Since Fowler wrote, evidence has come to light of the existence of wet quicksand at medieval levels on the site of the former estuary and near the possible line of a natural causeway across it several miles north of Wisbech. Moreover, it is unlikely that Fowler was right in supposing that Wisbech lay on the normal route across the fens in the thirteenth century. Holt is therefore inclined to revert to the theory that it was in an attempt to cross the broad estuary that John's baggage train encountered misadventure, though he would place the route south of that selected by St John Hope, and suggests that it ran between Walpole and Tydd Gote. He points out, as both St John Hope and Fowler had omitted to do, that such a route was not merely shorter than the road through Wisbech, it also avoided the treacherous marshes north-west of Wisbech, and the difficult

[1] J. C. Holt, 'King John's Disaster in the Wash', *Nottingham Medieval Studies*, v (1961), 75–86.

crossing of the western branch of the river Nene. On the other hand, he rejects, like Fowler, St John Hope's assumption that King John and the baggage train parted company on leaving Lynn, and reinforces this view with the contention that any such division would have been dangerous and inconvenient:

in an area like the Fenland which was predominantly rebel in sympathy and where travel by road was difficult, there would be powerful reasons for keeping an undivided column. The army could not be separated from its supplies; government could not be separated from its impedimenta; the king, especially, was unlikely to let such of his regalia, money and precious movables as he had with him, far from his sight. In 1216 only some great urgency could have created the kind of separation which St John Hope imagines.

This, of course, leaves Holt with the problem of explaining King John's presence in Wisbech on 12 October, but this very problem suggests to him an interpretation of what happened. Following Coggeshall, he accepts that the baggage train met with an accident caused by an over-confident and hasty attempt to cross the Wellstream before low tide. The attempt to cross was then abandoned and instead the army made its way to Wisbech. This detour was made necessary by the loss of packhorses in the accident: 'baggage could be salvaged where packhorses would drown, and, if the king was suddenly faced with a surplus of baggage over packhorses, sea transport was the obvious alternative.' The Patent Rolls show that at Wisbech the king engaged eight shipmen and their vessels to transport his 'goods and merchandise' to Grimsby.[1] Having solved his immediate problem the king made his way, with a reduced baggage train, to Swineshead.

This is an ingenious solution to the problem of reconciling all the known facts and filling in the blanks in the contemporary reports; but there are weaknesses in it. The assumption that packhorses drowned but most of their loads of baggage were saved is large and not very convincing. If the packhorses were being sucked into the sands, as the chroniclers relate, the first action of rescuers would naturally be to cut free their loads, but in these circumstances the lightened packhorses would stand as much – or as little – chance as men who attempted to struggle to firmer ground with the baggage. That the net result was a 'surplus of baggage over packhorses' does not sound very probable. If, nevertheless, we accept Holt's contention that there was such a surplus – creating a problem so serious that it could be solved not by commandeering pack animals locally but only by seeking sea transport – why go on to Wisbech? The sensible course in this predicament would have been to return to Lynn. The journey to Lynn was little longer and the

[1] *Rot. Pat.*, p. 199.

chance of finding ships at that thriving port very much greater than at the small township of Wisbech. Indeed John had already arranged at Lynn the transport of victuals to Nottingham and 'merchandise' of his own to Lincoln, and the obvious course would have been to have added his surplus baggage to it.[1]

If we discount the argument for a serious surplus of baggage, how are we to explain the arrangements made with the eight shipmen at Wisbech on 12 October to transport the king's *res et mercandise* to Grimsby? We may in passing wonder why he should purpose sending surplus baggage to Grimsby; but these letters patent of 12 October are easily explicable if we suppose that their purpose was similar to that of the letters patent drawn up at Lynn on 10 October. They are indeed very similar in form. It should be noted about the Wisbech letters that they give no indication that the vessels concerned are lying at Wisbech – no point of departure is mentioned. Furthermore, the safe conducts that they decree for the shipmen and the goods loaded in their vessels are post-dated by two days: 'These letters,' they say, 'are to be valid from Friday next (14 October) . . . and for eight days thereafter.'[2] This would seem to indicate that the ships were lying somewhere else – possibly at Lynn. We may indeed go further than this and reconstruct the situation as follows. There were sufficient ships lying at Lynn to transport all the winter supplies John had acquired for his north-eastern strongholds, but some of the shipmen, he was told, had gone down to Wisbech on business. Anxious to be on his way, John decided to pursue them to Wisbech: his business was important and urgent, and his personal presence would expedite it wonderfully; but the baggage train would be an encumbrance on such a mission (and pose problems in the marshlands on the further side of Wisbech), so he instructed it to take the convenient route across the estuary and to rendezvous with him on the morrow. This, of course, is to revert to St John Hope's hypothesis of a divided column, but is this so improbable? Holt's objections to a separation carry some

[1] *Rot. Pat.*, p. 199, *Rot. Claus*, i. 291.

[2] The entry may be translated:

'The king to all etc. You should know that the goods and merchandise which are in the ship which Ralph FitzWalter brings are ours: we have ordered them to be conducted to Grimsby. And therefore we command you neither to do nor to allow to be done any harm or hindrance to the said Ralph or to the goods or merchandise on board his ship. These letters are to be valid from Friday next after the feast of St Denis in the 18th year of the king's reign and for eight days following, and in witness of this we have caused etc. Witness myself at Wisbech on 12 October in the 18th year of the reign.

Godfrey le Pohier, Osbert Fitzwalter, Benedict de Beautre, Thomas de Beautre, William the German, Reginald But, and John FitzAlan have letters similar in all respects. Witness the king at Wisbech in the 18th year of the reign.'

weight, but they are not conclusive. John had on previous occasions divided his forces while in rebel territory. Would it have been so very dangerous on this occasion for John with some of his *familia* and a strong escort to leave for one day and a few miles the baggage train protected by the rest of the army? There was no rebel army in the vicinity, and an ambush in open fen country was hardly likely.

The accident, then, may be reconstructed as follows. The king, leaving Lynn on 11 October, probably reached Wisbech before dusk and concluded his business there early on the morrow. Meanwhile the rest of the army, having ferried the baggage over the river Nar near Lynn, made its way to the banks of the Wellstream estuary where it bivouacked for the night. Unfortunately, the time of low water was not until noon on 12 October, and the baggage train, with a long journey ahead of it, and anxious not to keep an impatient king waiting, started too early upon the sands. Some, at least, of the heavily laden packhorses found themselves being sucked into the sands and men who went to help them got into difficulties too. If we accept Cogge-shall's report of limited losses instead of the total disaster described by Wendover and Paris, we may assume that since the tide was still receding conditions steadily improved and those who were not involved in the initial mishap successfully made their way to the further side.

Wendover relates that the king himself 'barely escaped with his army'. He may here be embroidering his tale in ignorance of the king's absence; though it would be possible to explain his words by supposing that the king had reached Tydd Gote, attempted to organize rescue operations, but had to abandon them hurriedly as the tide turned and the sands became treacherous again. If we suppose this, however, it becomes difficult to believe that John would have had time to reach Swineshead the same day, where the Patent Rolls show him to have been. It would be better to suppose that Swineshead was the intended rendezvous, that John reached it in time, but that the delayed baggage train perhaps failed to arrive that day. Wendover tells us one moment that no one survived to tell him of the disaster, the next moment that the king himself barely escaped – clearly his account is so confused that it is profitless to try to wring a meaning from it.

What was lost? Between May 1215 and March 1216 John gathered in a great quantity of his jewels, ornamental plate, and regalia from safe-deposit in monastic houses. This property is minutely inventoried in the Patent Rolls and includes dozens of gold and silver goblets, flagons, basins, candelabra, phylacteries, pendants, and jewel-encrusted belts, the coronation regalia, and the regalia his grandmother had worn as Empress of Germany – the great crown, purple robes, the gold wand with a dove, the sword of Tristram. Wendover tells us that in the accident at the Wellstream John lost 'the treasures, precious vessels, and all the other things which he cherished with special care'; and if we consult the inventory of the regalia gathered together for the coronation of Henry III in 1220 we find that very little of it tallies with what John is known to have possessed four years earlier. The imperial regalia of Empress Matilda are never heard of again.[1]

We should, however, hesitate before jumping to the conclusion which these facts suggest. For one thing, we cannot be sure that Wendover is correct in the description he gives of what the quicksand claimed: the abbot of Coggeshall, a more trustworthy informant, tells only of the loss of 'his chapel with his relics and some packhorses with divers household effects (supellectilis)'. If we accept the Coggeshall account we must find some other explanation for the disappearance of John's treasures; but this is not difficult. John almost certainly collected in his valuables from safe-deposit so as to be able to sell or pawn them to raise ready money to pay his mercenaries if civil war created a financial emergency, and it is very likely that he disposed of some of them, at least, in this way before setting off on campaign in September 1216.[2] This explanation cannot, however, be held to cover the regalia, for it is unlikely that either selling them or putting them in pledge would make them disappear without trace. It is possible then that they were indeed swallowed up by the sands of the Wellstream estuary. But anyone who hopes to find them there should note the further possibility that John was robbed of them on his deathbed: a priest who went to Newark to say a mass for the dead king's soul subsequently told the abbot of Coggeshall that he had seen men leaving the city laden with loot.[3]

---

[1] For full details of these inventories see A. V. Jenkinson,' The Jewels Lost in the Wash', *History*, viii (1923–4), 163–6.

[2] Cf. Holt, op. cit., p. 85.   [3] Coggeshall, p. 184.

Notes

NOTES

Full details will be found in the Bibliography of works cited by short title in the Notes. In the case of a number of frequently occurring works more drastic abbreviations have been used as follows:

Annals of Dunstable   *Annales Monastici*, ed. H. R. Luard (Rolls Series, 1864–6), iii. 3–408.

Annals of Margam   *Ibid.*, i. 3–40.

Annals of Waverley   *Ibid.*, ii. 127–411.

Barnwell   Annals of Barnwell priory in *Memoriale Walteri de Coventria*, ed. W. Stubbs (Rolls Series, 1872–3), ii. 196–279.

Biog. Marshal   *Histoire de Guillaume le Maréchal*, ed. P. Mayer (Paris, 1891–1901).

Coggeshall   *Radulphi de Coggeshall Chronicon Anglicanum*, ed. J. Stevenson (Rolls Series, 1875).

Devizes   Chronicle of Richard of Devizes in *Chronicles of the Reigns of Stephen, Henry II, & Richard I*, ed. R. Howlett (Rolls Series, 1884–90), iii. 379–454.

Diceto   *Radulphi Diceto Opera Historica*, ed. W. Stubbs (Rolls Series, 1876).

E.H.R.   *English Historical Review*.

Foedera   *Rymer's Foedera* (Record Commission, 1816–69).

Gerald of Wales   *Giraldi Cambrensis Opera*, ed. J. S. Brewer, J. F. Dimock, & G. F. Warner (Rolls Series, 1861–91).

Gervase   *The Historical Works of Gervase of Canterbury*, ed. W. Stubbs (Rolls Series, 1879–80).

Gesta Henrici   *Gesta Regis Henrici Secundi Benedicti Abbatis*, ed. W. Stubbs (Rolls Series, 1867).

Gesta Ricardi   *Ibid.*, ii. 72–252.

Howden   *Chronica Magistri Rogeri de Houdene*, ed. W. Stubbs (Rolls Series, 1868–71).

Life of St Hugh   *Magna Vita S. Hugonis Episcopi Lincolniensis*, ed. J. F. Dimock (Rolls Series, 1864).

Misae Roll 14 John   Printed in *Documents Illustrative of English History in the 13th & 14th Centuries*, ed. H. Cole (Record Commission, 1844).

Newburgh	'The Historia Regum Anglicarum of William of Newburgh' in *Chronicles of the Reigns of Stephen, etc.* (as above), i. & ii.
Pipe Roll (followed by regnal year of king)	*The Great Rolls of the Pipe,* published by the Pipe Roll Society.
Rigord	*Oeuvres de Rigord et de Guillaume le Breton,* ed. H. F. Delaborde (Paris, 1882–5).
Rot. Chart.	*Rotuli Chartarum,* ed. T. D. Hardy (Record Commission, 1837)
Rot. Claus.	*Rotuli Litterarum Clausarum, 1204–27,* ed T. D. Hardy (Record Commission, 1833).
Rot. de Lib.	*Rotuli de Liberate ac de Misis et Praestitis regnante Johanne,* ed. T. D. Hardy (Record Commission, 1844).
Rot. de Oblat.	*Rotuli de Oblatis et Finibus,* ed. T. D. Hardy (Record Commission, 1835).
Rot. Pat.	*Rotuli Litterarum Patentium,* ed. T. D. Hardy (Record Commission, 1835).
T.R.H.S.	*Transactions of the Royal Historical Society.*
William the Breton	*Oeuvres de Rigord et de Guillaume le Breton,* ed. H. F. Delaborde (Paris, 1882–5).
Wendover	*Chronica Rogeri de Wendover liber qui dicitur Flores Historiarum,* ed. H. G. Hewlett (Rolls Series, 1886–9).

page 1, 1. Herbert of Bosham, *Liber Melorum*, in Migne, *Patrologia Latina*, cxx. 1322.

    1, 2. Gerald of Wales, viii. 214; Walter Map, *De Nugis Curialium* (ed. M. R. James), pp. 237, 249; Peter of Blois, letter 14 in Migne, *Patrologia Latina*, ccvii. 48, and letter 66, *ibid.*, 195–210; *The Chronicles of Ralph Niger* (ed. R. Anstruther), p. 169.

page 2, 1. Newburgh, p. 500; cf. Diceto, ii. 162.

    2, 2. Gervase, ii. 100.

    2, 3. Letter of Archbishop Becket in *Materials for the History of Thomas Becket*, ed. J. C. Robertson (Rolls Series, 1875–85), vi. 71–2.

    2, 4. Biog. Marshal, iii. 156.

    2, 5. Devizes, p. 408.

    2, 6. Gerald of Wales, viii. 309.

page 3, 1. *Ibid.*, viii. 301–2.

page 5, 1. Map, *De Nugis Curialium*, pp. 238, 241–2.

    5, 2. Life of St Hugh, pp. 92–3.

    5, 3. Gerald of Wales, iv. 47, 51, viii. 128.

    5, 4. John of Salisbury in J. A. Giles, *Patres Ecclesiae Anglicanae*, ii. 202. Cf. Letter of Becket, *Materials for the History of Thomas Becket*, vi. 245, vii. 248; Gerald of Wales, viii. 160.

    5, 5. Printed in Gerald of Wales, vol. viii.

page 6, 1. *Curia Regis Rolls*, iv. 270.

    6, 2. Newburgh, p. 283.

    6, 3. *Itinerarium Peregrinorum* (in *Chronicles & Memorials of the Reign of Richard I*, ed. W. Stubbs, vol. i), pp. 224–5, 344–5. The author was probably Richard, canon of Holy Trinity, Aldgate.

    6, 4. Howden, iii. 93–4.

    6, 5. Gerald of Wales, viii. 247.

page 7, 1. Coggeshall, pp. 97–8; cf. Gerald of Wales, viii. 326. Gervase had no love for him, cf. Stubbs, preface to *Historical Works of Gervase of Canterbury*, p. xlviii.

page 8, 1. Household accounts for John's reign have been published by H. Cole, *Documents Illustrative of English History*, and by T. D. Hardy, *Rotuli de Liberate ac de Misis et Praestitis regnante Johanne.* An Itinerary of John, compiled from the dating clauses of documents issued by his Chancery, has been published by T. D. Hardy as part of the introduction to *Rotuli Litterarum Patentium.*

8, 2. Gervase, i. 87. For a review of the man and his work see the preface by Stubbs to each of the two volumes.

page 9, 1. See preface by J. Stevenson to *Radulphi de Coggeshall Chronicon Anglicanum.*

page 10, 1. Cf. Stubbs, preface to *Memoriale Fratris Walteri de Coventria,* vol. i, pp. x, lxxxvi–viii.

10, 2. Barnwell, pp. 199, 232, 203.

10, 3. J. R. Green, *Short History of the English People* (Everyman edition), i. 114. This book has been a best seller since its first appearance in 1875, and has been translated into French, German, Russian, Japanese, and (in part) Chinese. Historians like Sir Charles Firth and Sir John Marriott have testified that it 'marked an epoch in their lives.' It was carried to the loneliest outposts of the Empire, found a place on the shelves of missionaries and merchant seamen, and dropped with an officer of the 1st Airborne Division at Arnhem in 1944. See W. G. Addison, *J. R. Green* (London, 1946), chapter 4.

page 11, 1. Wendover, i. 315, 316–17; ii. 46, 52–3, 55, 63.

11, 2. *Ibid.,* ii. 16–35.

11, 3. Wendover introduces no hint of doubt or qualification into his fabulous tales, and seems to have been remarkably gullible, even by the standards of his own day. Contrast William of Newburgh (p. 82) telling the tale that was current at the end of the 12th century about two green children from an underground city, who emerged one day from an old wolf-pit, drawn by the sound of the bells of Bury St Edmund's: 'Though it is asserted by many, I have been in doubt about it for a long time, for I thought it ridiculous to credit an event supported on no rational foundation, or at least of a very mysterious character. Yet at length I was so overwhelmed by the weight of so many and such competent witnesses that I have been compelled to believe and wonder over a matter which I was unable to comprehend or to unravel by any powers of intellect.'

page 12, 1. Wendover, ii. 47–8.

12, 2. *Rot. Claus.,* i. III. It was John's policy at the time to persuade the English clergy to ignore the Interdict and maintain normal relations with the Crown.

12, 3. Wendover, ii, 52–3.

page 13, 1. The other accounts are investigated by S. Painter, *The Reign of King John,* pp. 270–2.

13, 2. This passage is not in the Rolls Series edition for it was erroneously supposed that Wendover only wrote the portion from

1154. It will be found in Wendover, *Chronica sive Flores Historiarum* ed. H. O. Coxe (English Historical Society, 1841–4), i. 1–2.

page 14, 1. Matthew Paris, *Chronica Majora*, ed. H. R. Luard (Rolls Series, 1872–4), ii. 559, applied to the death of Geoffrey Fitz-Peter in 1213; *Historia Anglorum* (in *Matthiae Parisiensis Historia Minor*, ed. F. Madden (Rolls Series, 1866–9)), ii. 104, applied instead to the death of Archbishop Walter in 1205. The speech of the archbishop at the coronation of John, *Chronica Majora*, ii. 454, is probably an example of Paris's powers of invention. He over-reaches himself when he says that in 1215 John counterfeited the seals of all the bishops and used them on letters sent to every nation to tell them that the English were apostate and detestable to all the world, *ibid.*, ii. 588. It seems that Paris himself came to feel that he had turned a lurid portrait into an impossible caricature, and in his second version, the *Historia Anglorum*, he tones the picture down considerably, and even says something to John's credit – equally unreliable. See V. H. Galbraith, *Roger Wendover & Matthew Paris*, and R. Vaughan, *Matthew Paris*.

page 15, 1. *Chronica Majora*, ii. 560–3; cf. Kate Norgate, *John Lackland*, p. 182, n. 2, for criticisms of the anecdote.

page 16, 1. Stubbs, preface to *Memoriale Fratris Walteri de Coventria*, vol. ii, p. xi. Stubbs was the doyen of English medieval historians in the 19th century, and his judgements had, and still have, much influence.

16, 2. *Short History*, ii. 114, quoting Paris, *Chronica Majora*, ii. 669.

CHAPTER 2. GAINING A KINGDOM

page 17, 1. Devizes, p. 402.

page 18, 1. There have been several biographies of Eleanor of Aquitaine, but none that survives critical examination. For some aspects of her life see F. M. Chambers, 'Some Legends Concerning Eleanor of Aquitaine', *Speculum*, xvi. (1941), 459–68; A. Duggan, *Devil's Brood*; A. Richard, *Histoire des comtes de Poitou*; W. Stubbs, preface to *Memoriale Fratris Walteri de Coventria*, ii. pp. xxviii–xxxi.

page 20, 1. For the feudal structure of 12th cent. France see R. Fawtier, *The Capetian Kings of France;* and for Henry's fiefs, J. Boussard, *Le Gouvernment d'Henri II Plantagenet*.

page 21, 1. A lively account of the lives of Henry and Eleanor (largely from the writings of Gerald of Wales) is given in A. Duggan, *Devil's Brood*. For the early history of Anjou and of Henry, see Kate Norgate, *England under the Angevin Kings*.

page 23, 1. Boussard, *Le Gouvernment d'Henri II Plantagenet*.

23, 2. Peter of Blois, letter 66, in Migne, *Patrologia Latina*, ccvii. 197–8; cf. Gerald of Wales, viii. 214–15, *Chronicles of Ralph Niger*, p. 169.

page 24, 1. Peter of Blois, letter 14, *Patrologia Latina*, ccvii. 48–9.

24, 2. *Ibid.*, letter 66, *Patrologia Latina*, ccvii. 198. Cf. Stubbs, 'Learning & Literature at the Court of Henry II', *Lectures on Medieval & Modern History*.

page 25, 1. Biog. Marshal, iii. 37–8.

25, 2. *Ibid.*, iii. 87–90.

25, 3. *Gesta Henrici*, i. 42–3; Howden, ii. 47; Coggeshall, p. 146. They had been reading too much of Geoffrey of Monmouth's very popular but fabulous *History of the Britons*; cf. V. H. Galbraith, *Historical Research in Medieval England*.

page 26, 1. *Chronica Monasterii de Melsa*, ed. E. A. Bond (Rolls Series, 1866–8), i. 256; Gerald of Wales, viii. 232; cf. *Gesta Henrici*, ii. 160. The story of his seduction of Alice does not appear in French chronicles. The name of one of his mistresses is known from an entry in the exchequer accounts: 'for clothes for the queen and Bellebelle *ad opus regis*. £55 17*s*,' *Pipe Roll 30 Henry II*, p. 134.

26, 2. Gerald of Wales, viii. 165–6; Chambers, 'Some Legends concerning Eleanor of Aquitaine,' pp. 463–5; Howden, iii. 167–8

26, 3. Richard, *Les comtes de Poitou*, ii. 375; *Gesta Henrici*, i. 7, 305, 308.

page 27, 1. Printed by J. Stevenson in *Radulphi de Coggeshall Chronicon Anglicanum*, pp. 324–5. For Fulk FitzWarin see Painter, *King John*, pp. 48–54.

27, 2. Cf. Stubbs, preface to *Gesta Henrici*, ii. xviii–xix.

27, 3. *Pipe Roll 8 Henry II*, p. 43.

page 28, 1. Cf. Poole, *Domesday Book to Magna Carta*, pp. 324–5.

28, 2. Newburgh, p. 146. For its use by French chroniclers see Norgate, *John Lackland*, p. 2, n. 2.

page 29, 1. Newburgh, p. 170. For the negotiations with Maurienne and the sequel see *Gesta Henrici*, i. 35–42.

29, 2. Diceto, i. 355; Gervase, i. 242; *Gesta Henrici*, i. 42.

29, 3. *Gesta Henrici*, i, 43 ff.

page 30, 1. *Ibid.*, i. 77–9; *Foedera*, i. i. 30; Robert of Torigni in *Chronicles of Reigns of Stephen*, etc., iv. 268.

30, 2. Gerald of Wales, viii. 245–6; Devizes, p. 401.

page 31, 1. For the Young Henry see Gerald of Wales, viii. 173–5; Thomas Agnellus in *Radulphi de Coggeshall Chronicon Anglicanum*, ed. Stevenson (Rolls Series), pp. 265–73; and for a critical view, Map, *De Nugis Curialium*, pp. 139–40.

31, 2. *Gesta Henrici*, i. 308.

31, 3. See Poole, *Domesday Book to Magna Carta*, p. 486, n. 1.

page 32, 1. The author of the *Gesta Henrici*, probably Roger of Howden, see D. M. Stenton in *E.H.R.*, lxviii. (1953), 574–82.

32, 2. Gerald of Wales, viii. 177–9. Gerald unfortunately indulges at this point in such tortured rhetoric that it is difficult to get a clear statement out of him.

32, 3. *Gesta Henrici*, i. 335–6; Diceto, ii. 32–3; Gerald of Wales, viii. 202–3.

page 33, 1. Diceto, ii. 33–4; cf. Gerald of Wales, viii. 208–9; Gervase, i. 32; Newburgh, p. 247.

33, 2. Cf. Newburgh, p. 166, who quotes liberally from Bede about Ireland.

page 34, 1. For the foregoing and the rest of this section see Orpen, *Ireland under the Normans*.

page 35, 1. *Gesta Henrici*, i. 162–5.

35, 2. *Ibid.*, i. 336.

35, 3. Gerald of Wales, v. 380–1. The crown, sent by Urban III, was never used. The hitch led to the historical accident of no separate kingdom of Ireland being formed in the middle ages. When John, still *Dominus Hiberniae*, became also king of England, he merely linked the two titles together, and this practice was followed until Tudor times. For the use of the title *Dominus*, see Poole, *Domesday Book to Magna Carta*, p. 3, and n. 1.

35, 4. Gerald's *Topographia Hibernica* is printed in *Giraldi Cambrensis Opera*, ed. Dimock, v. 3–204.

page 36, 1. Gerald of Wales, v. 388–92; cf. *Gesta Henrici*, i. 339.

36, 2. Gerald of Wales, v. 395–7.

page 37, 1. *Gesta Henrici*, i. 350.

page 38, 1. *Ibid.*, ii. 60–1, 66.

38, 2. *Ibid.*, 67–71; Howden, ii. 366–7.

38, 3. Devizes, p. 384.

38, 4. *Gesta Ricardi*, ii. 90.

38, 5. Devizes, p. 388.

page 39, 1. See below, p. 66.

page 40, 1. For the arrangements and affairs during Richard's absence see Stubbs' masterly introduction to *Chronica Rogeri de Houedene*, iii.

40, 2. *Gesta Henrici*, ii. 206; Devizes, p. 382.

40, 3. Newburgh, pp. 337–8; Devizes, p. 406.

40, 4. Devizes, p. 406.

page 41, 1. See *Gesta Henrici*, i. 305, 308.

41, 2. Gerald of Wales, iv. 411, 424. For Longchamp's support of

Arthur's claims see Newburgh, pp. 335–6. The sentiments of the clerks are expressed in *Pipe Roll 2 Richard I*, p. 116: he owes £20 for the scutage of Wales; but there are many of his men serving in the army 'therefore with angels and archangels he is quit.' They drew caricatures of his brother Osbert in the first letter of his name, see *Pipe Roll 9 Richard I*, p. xxvi. For chroniclers' abuse of him see *Gesta Ricardi*, ii. 216; Howden, iii. 142; Gerald of Wales, iv. 418–20.

41, 3. Newburgh, p. 333.

page 42, 1. Cf. Stubbs, *op. cit.*, pp. liii–liv.

42, 2. The confused chronology of events, which seems to have led Stubbs astray, is disentangled by Landon, *Itinerary of Richard I*, p. 192.

page 43, 1. Devizes, p. 415: 'summus rector totius regni.'

43, 2. *Ibid.*, pp. 430–2; *Gesta Ricardi*, pp. 236–7.

page 44, 1. Devizes, pp. 433–5; *Gesta Ricardi*, p. 239.

page 45, 1. Howden, iii. 198.

45, 2. *Ibid.*, iii. 205, 207–8, 216–17.

45, 3. *Ibid.*, iii. 229.

page 46, 1. *Ibid.*, iii. 237–8, 241–2; cf. Annals of Margam, p. 24.

46, 2. Biog. Marshal, iii. 136–7; cf. Diceto, ii. 114, Howden, iii. 252.

page 47, 1. Howden, iii. 286.

47, 2. *Ibid.*, iv. 5, 16; Newburgh, p. 493.

47, 3. Howden, iv. 60.

47, 4. *Ibid.*, iv. 81.

page 48, 1. Coggeshall, pp. 94–6; Howden, iv. 82–3.

48, 2. Life of St Hugh, p. 287.

page 49, 1. Glanville, *De Legibus et Consuetudinibus Angliae*, ed. Woodbine, pp. 101–4.

49, 2. *Le Trés Ancien Coutumier de Normandie*, ed. Tardif, pp. 12–13.

49. 3. Biog. Marshal, iii. 159–60.

49, 4. Howden, iv. 86–7; Life of St Hugh, pp. 287 ff.

page 50, 1. *Ibid.*, p. 296.

50, 2. Biog. Marshal, iii. 160-1; Coggeshall, p. 98; Howden, iv. 88–9.

50, 3. Coggeshall, p. 99; Howden, iv. 88–90.

CHAPTER 3. LOSING A DUCHY

page 51, 1. She had done homage to king Philip, Rigord, i. 146, and then later installed John as co-ruler, *Rot. Chart.*, i. 30.

page 53, 1. Howden, iv. 95.

53, 2. Cf. Powicke, *The Loss of Normandy*, p. 198 & n. 2.

53, 3. Howden, iv. 93; *Rot. Chart.*, i. 30, 31. Gerald of Wales (i. 118) remarks that fighting between Philip and Baldwin 'qui regi Angliae Johanni tunc adhaes erat' made travelling difficult between Flanders and France.

page 54, 1. Howden, iv. 96; Biog. Marshal, iii. 168–9; *Rot. Chart.*, i. 30.

54, 2. Gervase, ii. 92.

page 55, 1. The treaty is printed in A. F. Teulet, *Layettes du trésor des chartes*, i. 217, no. 578. The versions in the chronicles are faulty.

55, 2. It is of some interest, however, that Henry II, defeated by the alliance of Richard and Philip in 1189, agreed to pay the sum of 20,000 marks as part of the terms of peace. He had previously renounced his homage to the French king and was now obliged to renew it (Diceto, ii. 63; *Gesta Henrici*, ii 70). It is not clear if the payment and the renewal of homage were linked, but Philip may have wished to give that impression. That the sum demanded in 1200 was the same may thus be more than coincidence. Henry died before paying; Richard agreed to discharge his father's debt (*Gesta Ricardi*, p. 74), but it is doubtful if Philip ever got the money.

page 56, 1. Cf. treaty between Henry I and Count Robert of Flanders, F. Lot, *Fidèles ou Vassaux?* (Paris 1904), pp. 23–5.

56, 2. Gervase, ii. 92–3.

page 57, 1. Cf. the comments of R. C. Smail, *Crusading Warfare* (Cambridge 1956), pp. 60–2, 204 ff.

page 58, 1. Powicke, *Loss*, pp. 288–90, 303–5, 346.

58, 2. Cf. Powicke, *Loss*, pp. 294–9.

58, 3. Relief was allowed at the Norman exchequer for mills wasted by Count John, *Magni Rotuli Scaccarii Normaniae*, ed. T. Stapleton (London 1840), ii, 292.

page 59, 1. Howden, iv. 40; Life of St Hugh, p. 248; *The Chronicle of Jocelin of Brakelond*, ed. H. E. Butler (London 1949), pp. 85–6; *Pipe Roll 9 Richard I*, xix–xxii.

59, 2. A judicial duel fought between the parties to an action in the courts (or between champions in a civil action) was a recognised method of proving an accusation or its rebuttal. The practice was introduced to England by the Normans.

page 60, 1. Newburgh, pp. 484–5.

60, 2. They lived like gypsies, dragging their miserable families around with them; cf. Powicke, *Loss*, p. 337 & n. 4.

60, 3. Cf. J. O. Prestwich, 'War & Finance in the Anglo-Norman State,' *T.R.H.S.*, 5th ser., iv. (1954), 19–43.

page 61, 1. *Dialogus de Scaccario*, p. 1.

61, 2. Newburgh, p. 406.

61, 3. Some were still struggling to pay off their contributions in 1203, *Rotuli Normanniae*, ed. T. D. Hardy (Record Comm. 1835), p. 79.

page 62, 1. See A. L. Poole, 'Richard I's Alliances with the German Princes in 1194', *Studies presented to Powicke*, pp. 90–9.

62, 2. Howden, iv. 62–3, on the articles of the eyre of 1198: 'By these and other exactions, whether just or unjust, the whole of England from sea to sea was reduced to poverty.'

62, 3. Howden, iv. 46 ff., 66.

62, 4. *Pipe Roll 9 Richard I*, p. xxix.

62, 5. J. H. Round, 'Richard's Change of Seal (1198)', *Feudal England*, pp. 539–51.

62, 6. 'Saviez qu'à Chinon, Non a argent ni denier,' A. J. V. Le Roux de Lincy, *Receuil de chants historiques français* (Paris 1841–2), 1. 65–7. The treasury of Anjou was kept at Chinon.

page 63, 1. Howden, iii. 254–5; Diceto, ii. 115, 144.

63, 2. Life of St Hugh, p. 282.

63, 3. Rigord, i. 141.

63, 4. Howden, iv. 68, 80.

page 64, 1. Howden, iv. 119: 'non est inventus qui ei resisterit.'

64, 2. Richard, *Comtes de Poitou*, ii. 353; *Rot. Chart.*, i. 30.

64, 3. Cf. *Calendar of Documents preserved in France*, ed. J. H. Round (London, 1899), i. 471.

page, 66, 1. Isabelle was granddaughter of Robert, earl of Gloucester, natural son of Henry I and half-brother to John's grandmother, Matilda. See H. G. Richardson, 'The Marriage & Coronation of Isabelle of Angoulême,' *E.H.R.*, lxi. (1946), 289 ff.

66, 2. *Gesta Ricardi*, p. 236.

66, 3. Diceto, ii. 166–7, gives a trial before the bishops of Lisieux, Bayeux, and Avranches in 1199; Howden, iv. 119, a trial before the archbishop of Bordeaux and the bishops of Saintes and Poitiers in 1200. Richardson's attempt (*op. cit.*, pp. 291–5) to antedate John's divorce to at least two years before his accession is barely tenable. He bases his argument on Howden's citation of Bishop William of Poitiers who had died in 1197; but it is more likely that in this instance Howden has the name wrong rather than the date. (Cf. Biog. Marshal, iii. 161.) John had neither standing in nor connection with Aquitaine before his accession, and there is no good reason why the case should have been put before the bishops of the duchy.

page 67, 1. *Rot. Chart.*, 1. 57, 58, 97; Diceto, ii. 170.

67, 2. *Chroniques de Saint-Martial de Limoges*, ed. H. Duplès Agier

(Paris 1874), p. 67, n. 3: *Memorials of St Edmund's Abbey*, ed. T. Arnold (Rolls Series 1890–6), ii. 8.

67, 3. F. A. Cazel & S. Painter, 'The Marriage of Isabelle of Angoulême,' *E.H.R.*, lxii. (1948), 85–6.

67, 4. Cf. J. Boussard, *Le Gouvernment d'Henri II*, pp. 119 ff.; Powicke, *Loss*, p. 44 & n. 1.

page 68, 1. Diceto, ii. 54.

68, 2. The title had been bought by Henry II in 1177 from the last count, who wished to go on crusade, Boussard, *op. cit.*, p. 133.

68, 3. See S. Painter, 'The Lords of Lusignan in the 11th & 12th cents.', *Speculum*, xxxii. (1957).

68, 4. *Ibid.*, p. 43; *Rot. Chart.* i. 58.

page 69, 1. Painter, *William Marshal*, p. 27.

69, 2. Biog. Marshal, iii. 162–3; Howden, iv. 19; Coggeshall, p. 103.

69, 3. Cf. Richardson, 'The Marriage & Coronation of Isabelle of Angoulême,' pp. 307–11. It was a particularly solemn affair, making Isabelle vice-regent.

page 70, 1. Historians have frequently remarked that John was the first king since the Conquest who knew England really well, but have implied that this was a consequence of his loss of Normandy. His confinement to England after 1204 of course increased his knowledge, but his itinerary in 1200–1 shows that personal inclination preceded political accident.

70, 2. Howden, i. 209, iv. 141.

70, 3. Life of St. Hugh, p. 371.

page 71, 1. Howden, iv. 114.

71, 2. *Ibid.*, iv. 97.

page 72, 1. *Rot. Chart.*, i. 102–3.

72, 2. *Ibid.*, i. 102; cf. Howden, iv. 160–1; William the Breton, i. 207.

72, 3. Innocent III, Letters, Bk. VI, no. 167; Migne, *Patrologia Latina*.

72, 4. Howden, iv. 163.

page 73, 1. *Ibid.*, iv., 161, 164; Gervase, ii. 93; Rigord, i. 150.

73, 2. *Rot. Pat.*, i. 5.

73, 3. Howden, iv. 164, 172. The alliance was concluded at Angoulême on 4 February 1202, *Rot. Pat.*, i. 3, 5; Powicke, *Loss*, p. 215.

page 74, 1. Howden, iv. 176: 'dicentes quod nemini responderent nisi pari suo.'

74, 2. William the Breton, ii. 155–8.

74, 3. Gervase, ii. 93; Diceto, ii. 173.

74, 4. Rigord, i. 151–3; William the Breton, i. 207; Gervase, ii. 93.

74, 5. *Historiae Francorum Scriptores*, ed A. Du Chesne (Paris 1636–49), iv. 411. He was summoned, it seems, for marrying Eleanor, without the consent of his overlord, Louis VII. 'Qui citatus ad curiam, venire noluit ad jus faciendum, vel capiendum in regis praesentia palatii judicium omnino respuit et contempsit.'

page 75, 1. Cf. Keeney, *Judgment by Peers*, p. 129, n. 94.

75, 2. *Rot. Pat.*, i. 14, cf. *ibid.*, i. 10.

75, 3. Rigord, i. 152–3; William the Breton, ii. 155.

75, 4. Biog. Marshal, iii. 163; *Hist. des ducs de Normandie*, pp. 104–5.

page 76, 1. Cf. Robert of Auxerre in *Historiens de France*, xviii. 263: 'juvenis quidem remissioris animi, amansque quietis.'

page 77, 1. Cf. Petit-Dutaillis & Guinard, *L'Essor des Etats d'Occident*, p. 138.

77, 2. *Rot. Pat.*, i. 10–12.

page 79, 1. These seem to be the highlights of the battle: the chroniclers tell rather different stories; see *Hist. des ducs de Normandie*, pp. 94–5; Coggeshall, pp. 137–8.

79, 2. Coggeshall, pp. 137–8.

79, 3. Biog. Marshal, iii. 165–6.

page 80, 1. E.g., the keepers of Geoffrey de Lusignan were instructed to admit a visitor only if he were accompanied by one of three named members of the royal household, *Rot. Pat.*, i. 17.

80, 2. Guy of Limoges was the only other possible leader, but he too was in John's hands by the beginning of September, Rigord, i. 152; cf. *Rot. Pat.*, i. 18.

80, 3. *Hist. des ducs de Normandie*, p. 94.

page 81, 1. Coggeshall, p. 138; Biog. Marshal, ii. 170. The attempt to placate the Poitevins was not altogether misguided or fruitless. Savary de Mauléon, who was taken at Mirebeau and imprisoned at Corfe castle, was released on giving hostages, and remained faithful to John throughout all the later troubles; cf. Coggeshall, p. 146.

81, 2. Annals of Margam, p. 26.

81, 3. Powicke, *Loss*, pp. 453–81, 'King John & Arthur of Brittany', *E.H.R.*, xxiv. (1909), 659–74.

81, 4. Paris, *Historia Anglorum*, iii. 221.

81, 5. Coggeshall, pp. 139–41.

81, 6. Powicke, *Loss*, 455.

page 82, 1. Newburgh, pp. 235, 463–4; for the stirrings of nationalism see V. H. Galbraith, *T.R.H.S.*, 4th ser., xxiii. (1941), 113–28; Cheney, *From Becket to Langton*, pp. 100–3.

82, 2. Barnwell, p. 196.

82, 3. Wendover, ii. 48–9.

page 83, 1. Annals of Margam, p. 27; Powicke, *Loss*, pp. 466ff.

83. 2. Coggeshall, p. 145. He suspected something in October 1203; in granting castles to Guy of Thouars a clause was written into the charter 'saving the rights of Arthur if he still lives', Delisle, *Cat. des Actes de Philippe Auguste*, no. 783. But this may have been merely intended to reinforce the suspicions of the Bretons, following the false report of Arthur's death which, according to Coggeshall, was put out by Hubert de Burgh.

83, 3. Coggeshall, p. 145.

83, 4. *Rot. Claus.*, i. 144, 150, 157, 168; *Pipe Roll 6 John*, pp. 92, 213, 219.

page 84, 1. Paris, *Chronica Majora*, ii. 659.

84, 2. For the military history of 1203 see Powicke, *Loss*, pp. 232ff; Norgate, *John Lackland*, pp. 89ff.

page 86, 1. Biog. Marshal, iii. 171–2.

86, 2. Coggeshall, pp. 143–4; *Rot. Pat.*, i. 31. Its custodians were Robert FitzWalter and Saer de Quinci. It is noticeable that John did not help to pay their ransoms as he did the other constables who were captured by the French.

86, 3. Norgate, *Richard the Lion Heart*, pp. 311–13.

page 87, 1. William the Breton, ii. 181–92.

page 88, 1. Wendover, i, 316–17. Wendover gives a similar explanation (*Ibid.*, ii. 8) of John's apparent inactivity in 1204 when Philip was seizing Normandy and much of Poitou: 'When this was told the king of the English he was enjoying all the pleasures of life with his queen, in whose company he believed that he possessed everything that he wanted.'

88, 2. *L'Essor des Etats d'Occident*, p. 137.

88, 3. Biog. Marshal, iii, 171; Gervase, ii. 95; Barnwell, p. 197; cf. *Selected Letters of Innocent III*, ed. Cheney & Semple, p. 40.

88, 4. Coggeshall, p. 144.

page 89, 1. The key fortress of Gisors had then been lost through the treachery of its castellan, Howden, iii. 206; cf. Powicke, *Loss*, pp. 144, 146–7.

89, 2. *Ibid.*, p. 126.

page 90, 1. Gerald of Wales viii. 257; cf. Powicke, *Loss*, pp. 435ff.

90, 2. Biog. Marshal, iii. 58.

90, 3. For Robert of Auxerre's comment, see above, p. 76, n.1; Howden, iii. 198; Newburgh, p. 391.

90, 4. Gervase, ii. 92: "Sed processu temporis mollities illa in tantem crudelitatem versa est, ut nulli praedecessorum suorum coaequari valeret, ut in sequentibus patebit."

page 91, 1. *Foedera*, i. i. 84–5.

    91, 2. *Rot. Pat.*, i. 20, November 1203.

    91, 3. See Powicke, *Loss*, p. 339.

    91, 4. Biog. Marshal, iii. 171; cf. *Rot Pat.*, i. 35, 7 November 1203.

    91, 5. *Pipe Roll 6 John*, p. 150.

page 92, 1. See Powicke, *Loss*, pp. 237, 347–8, 354.

    92, 2. *Ibid.*, pp. 329–30, and 'The Angevin Administration of Normandy,' *E.H.R.*, xxii. (1907), 42, n. 118.

    92, 3. Biog. Marshal, iii. 175.

    92, 4. *Ibid.*, iii. 93–4.

page 93, 1. *Ibid.*, iii. 175.

page 94, 1. *Ibid.*, iii. 174.

    94, 2. Wendover, iii. 318, 320.

page 95, 1 See D. M. Stenton, introduction to *Pipe Roll 6 John*; *Rot de Lib.*, 84–5.

    95, 2. *Rot. de Lib.*, 82–3.

    95, 3. For a detailed description of the siege, compiled from French chronicles, see Norgate, *England under the Angevin Kings*, ii. 411–23.

page 96, 1. Gervase, ii. 95; Coggeshall, p. 147; *Rot Pat.*, i. 39; *Rot. de Lib.* pp. 85, 87, 96.

    96, 2. Gervase, ii. 95–6; Coggeshall, pp. 144–5; Biog. Marshal, iii. 176.

    96, 3. Annals of Waverley, p. 256; Coggeshall, p. 144.

    96, 4. On the imperial character of Rouen see C. H. Haskins, *Norman Institutions* (Cambridge, Mass., 1925), p. 144, n. 72.

page 99, 1. *Rot de Lib.*, pp. 102–3.

    99, 2. Wendover, ii. 8.

CHAPTER 4. KING OF ENGLAND

page 100, 1. Wendover, ii. 8–9.

    100, 2. The Patent Rolls are not mentioned here because they are rather sketchy for the years 1204–5.

page 101, 1. See D. M. Stenton, introduction to *Pipe Roll 6 John*, pp. xi–xxxiii; *Pipe Roll 6 John*, p. 147; and for the currency reform, S. Smith, introduction to *Pipe Roll 7 John*, pp. xxvii–xxxii.

page 102, 1. Coggeshall, p. 152; William the Breton, i. 223. Thouars was made seneschal in Thornham's stead.

    102, 2. Coggeshall, p. 103.

page 103, 1. Cf. Powicke, *Loss of Normandy*, p. 445.

    103, 2. *Curia Regis, Rolls 7–8 John*, pp. 101–2.

page 104, 1. See Powicke, *Loss*, pp. 411–26.

    104, 2. Biog. Marshal, iii. 176–8. William met Philip in the later stages of the Normandy campaign and ratified the arrangement by charter, Deslisle, *Actes de Philippe Auguste*, no. 818, p. 186.

page 105, 1. That this was his attitude may be deduced from his conviction that John had no chance in Normandy, and from his negotiations with Philip, see above p. 92, and below p. 113 ff.

    105, 2. Coggeshall, p. 151; cf. *Pipe Roll 7 John*, p. xix, n. 4.

page 106, 1. Painter, *King John*, p. 10.

page 107, 1. Painter, *William Marshal*.

page 108, 1. Painter, *King John*, pp. 41–5; Powicke, *Loss*, pp. 187 n., 468–70, 489; Powicke, *Christian Life in the Middle Ages*, p. 148.

    108, 2. E.g., *Rot. de Lib.*, pp. 139–40; Painter, *King John*, p. 40.

    108, 3. *Selected Letters of Innocent III*, p. 40.

page 109, 1. Painter, *King John*, pp. 25–9.

    109, 2. Howden, iv. 88.

page 110, 1. *Ibid.*, 161.

    110, 2. Gervase, ii. 97–8.

    110, 3. Assize of Arms, 1161, Stubbs, *Select Charters*, pp. 183–4; *English Historical Documents*, ii. 416–17.

page 111, 1. Gervase, ii. 96–7.

    111, 2. Deslisle, *Actes de Philippe Auguste*, no. 910, p. 209; Coggeshall, pp. 148–9; Powicke, *Loss*, pp. 390–1; Norgate, *John Lackland*, p. 108; *Rot. Pat.*, i. 50.

page 112, 1. *Rot. Pat.*, i. 55.

    112, 2. Gervase, ii. 98; Coggeshall, p. 152; Biog. Marshal, iii. 180; cf. *Pipe Roll 7 John*, pp. xviii–xx, xxxiv.

page 113, 1. *Rot. Claus.*, i. 25–42 *passim*; *Pipe Roll 7 John*, pp. xiii–xxv; Coggeshall, pp. 152–3 (he says that 14,000 seamen were in the king's service); Gervase, ii. 98.

    113, 2. Painter, *King John*, p. 138.

    113, 3. Biog. Marshal, iii. 178–9. The biographer maintains that John commissioned William to treat for peace, but deliberately kept it secret from the chancellor, Hubert Walter. This sounds pointless and improbable, especially since the vice-chancellor accompanied William to the French court. John may have been ready enough for a truce, but the initiative in raising the question of a treaty is more likely to have come from William himself.

page 115, 1. *Ibid.*, iii. 180–2.

    115, 2. Coggeshall, pp. 152–3.

    115, 3. *Ibid.*, p. 153; Gervase, ii. 98; Wendover, ii. 10.

page 116, 1. Coggeshall, pp. 154–5; cf. *Pipe Roll 8 John*, pp. xiii–xiv.

    116, 2. *Rot. Pat.*, i. 61; *Rot Claus.*, i. 55.

page 117. 1. *Pipe Roll 8 John*, p. xiii. Wendover says that on the abandonment of the expedition of 1205 'the king took an immense sum
of money from the earls, barons, knights, and prelates, accusing
them of refusing to accompany him overseas to recover his lost
inheritance.' No trace of such an 'immense sum' can be found
on the Pipe Roll, so it seems that Wendover is, once again, in
error.

117, 2. *Rot. Pat.*, i. 62.

117, 3. *Rot. Claus.*, i. 70. Freebooters and pirates were welcomed
if they brought ships to the king's service, cf. *Rot. Pat.*, i. 65:
loan and safe conduct to Eustace the Monk, a notorious Channel
pirate. For the preparations see *Pipe Roll 8 John*, pp. xv–xix.

117, 4. Wendover, ii. 13–14; *Annales Monastici*, v. 394; cf. Barnwell, p. 198. Montauban fell on 1 August.

page 119, 1. Annals of St Aubin under the year 1206, in *Receuil d'-
annales angevines et vendomoises*, ed. L. Halphen (Paris, 1903); cf.
Rigord, i. 164; William the Breton, i. 223–4.

119, 2. Foedera, i. i. 95. The Lusignan brothers, Hugh and
Ralph, represented Philip on the truce commission, Savary de
Mauléon and William de Chantemerle acted for John. Philip had
determined to absorb Normandy into the desmesne of the French
Crown and it was an extensive operation. Some of the Normans
were regretting the passing of the Angevin connection: the
men of Dieppe went so far as to send ships to join John's expedition
to Poitou, Powicke, *Loss*, pp. 387–8.

page 121, 1. Cf. *Pipe Roll 30 Henry II*, p. 87.

121, 2. For the early history of the Cinque Ports as a confederation see Miss K. M. E. Murray, *The Constitutional History of the
Cinque Ports* (Manchester 1935).

121, 3. William the Breton, ii. 183; Brooks, *The English Naval
Forces 1199–1272*, p. 136.

121, 4. *Victoria County History, Hampshire*, iii. 172 ff.; *Curia Regis
Rolls*, vi. 305. In 1197–8 money was spent on improving the houses
and hall of the king at Portsmouth.

page 122, 1. *Rotuli Scaccarii Normaniae*, p. 218.

122, 2. The existing order is of June 1204, but the levy was
in operation two years before, *Rot. Pat.*, i. 42, cf. 146. For control
of shipping and merchants see reference in *Pipe Roll 7 John*, pp.
xxxii–iii: e.g., Bartholomew of Ypres paid £2 for permission to
take a load of tin and other merchandise to whatever destination
he pleased; the men of Dunwich offer 100,000 herrings that they
may 'safely and securely go with their ships.'

122, 3. *Rot. Pat.*, i. 15.

122, 4. *Ibid.*, i. 52. The dispositions of the ships was noted down on the back of the Close Roll for 7 John, *Rot. Claus.*, i. 33.

page 123, 1. *Pipe Roll 7 John*, p. 10; *Rot. Claus.*, i. 55.

123, 2. *Pipe Roll 14 John*, p. xix; *Rot. Claus.*, i. 117.

page 124, 1. *Rot. Claus.*, i. 62–3.

page 125, 1. See F. W. Brooks, 'William Wrotham & the Office of Keeper of the King's Ports & Galleys,' *E.H.R.*, xl. (1925), 570–9; W. R. Powell, 'The Administration of the Navy & the Stannaries,' *E.H.R.*, lxxi. (1956), 177–88; Patricia M. Barnes, introduction to *Pipe Roll 14 John*, pp. xvii–xx; *Curia Regis Rolls*, vi. 124.

125, 2. Brooks, *English Naval Forces*, pp. 141, 175; Beryl E. R. Formoy, 'A Maritime Indenture of 1212,' *E.H.R.*, xli. (1926), 556–9; *Rot. Claus.*, i. 117, 118, 120.

125, 3. Biog. Marshal, iii. 202; see below, pp. 204–5.

page 126, 1. Cf. V. H. Galbraith, *Studies in the Public Records*, chapter 3. A biography of John is not a suitable place for a detailed analysis of the machinery of Angevin government. See S. B. Chrimes, *An Introduction to the Administrative History of Medieval England.* I am here concerned to distinguish the chief features of the machinery John had at his disposal, as a preliminary to seeing what he did with it.

page 127, 1. For translations of long passages from Glanville's treatise see *English Historical Documents*, ii. 462–79.

page 128, 1. *Dialogus de Scaccario*, ed. C. Johnson; H. Jenkinson, 'Financial Records of the Reign of King John,' in *Magna Carta Commemoration essays*, ed. Malden; H. G. Richardson, 'William of Ely, the King's Treasurer (?1195–1215)', *T.R.H.S.*, 4th ser., xv. (1932), 45–90.

page 129, 1. Howden, iv. 90–1.

page 131, 1. *Curia Regis Rolls*, i. 462; cf. C. Flower, *Introduction to the Curia Regis Rolls* (Selden Society, vol. xlv).

131, 2. *Curia Regis Rolls*, v. 327; cf. H. G. Richardson, introduction to *Memoranda Roll 1 John*, pp. xi–xv.

page 133, 1. Newburgh, p. 399.

133, 2. *Chronicon Monasterii de Abingdon*, ed. J. Stevenson, (Rolls Series 1858), ii. 230; cf. J. E. A. Jolliffe, *Angevin Kingship*, pp. 61 ff.

133, 3. Jolliffe, *loc. cit.;* Stubbs, preface to *Gesta Henrici*, ii. lxvi–viii; cf. Form of proceeding on a judicial visitation, 1194, Stubbs, *Select Charters*, p. 251; articles of general eyre of 1208–9 in *Munimenta Gildhallie Londoniensis*, ed. H. T. Riley (Rolls Series, 1859, 1862).

133. 4. Gervase, ii. 95.

133. 5. *Pleas before the King & his Justices*, ed. D. M. Stenton, nos. 3112–3230.

133, 6. 'Regnavit autem satis laboriose,' Coggeshall, p. 184.

page 134, 1. See n. 1 to p. 14 above. Wendover has a different and more temperate story, though equally fantastic: Hubert died, he says (ii. 10), 'to the great delight of the king, by whom he was suspected of being too familiar with the king of the French.' Miss Norgate, *John Lackland*, p. 113, repeats him in good faith. Elsewhere (p.105) she makes the staggering statement that 'Of all John's ministers, the one whom he most disliked and mistrusted was the one whose constitutional position made him absolutely irremovable from the royal counsels—the archbishop of Canterbury, Hubert Walter.'

134, 2. *Curia Regis Rolls*, iii. 124. In a case in which William Marshal claimed the manor of Sturminster, the king consulted those in attendance on him, but they professed themselves too inexperienced to deal with such a weighty matter, and asked for postponement until the arrival of the archbishop of Canterbury and other wise men.

page 135, 1. *Foedera*, i. i. 75–6; *Curia Regis Rolls*, i. 331.

135, 2. Duplicate copies of some outgoing writs had been made before, and were known as *contra brevia*, some of which survive. The systematic enrolment of all outgoing letters of importance was 'a change which was in effect a revolution' (V. H. Galbraith, *An Introduction to the Use of the Public Records* (Oxford 1934), p. 20). Patent Rolls begin in the 3rd year of John's reign. The Close Rolls survive from the 6th, but grew, somewhat earlier than this, out of the Liberate Rolls which begin in the 2nd year (Galbraith, *Studies in the Public Records*, pp. 71–5); and for a contrary view that enrolments began earlier, Richardson, introduction to *Memoranda Roll 1 John*, p. xxi.) Charters and Letters Patent were similar in appearance—an open document, having the seal hanging from the bottom on ribbons, though the latter were much less solemn in wording than the former, and did not carry long lists of witnesses. The difference in form and phraseology reflects the different use made of them (though there was no rigid consistency): charters were used for grants in perpetuity, letters patent usually for grants of a more temporary nature. Thus land would be granted to a monastery, a fair to a borough, or an earldom created by charter; a sheriff would be appointed or a castellan commissioned by letters patent. Letters Close took the form of small pieces of parchment, folded, and sealed where the folds overlapped, so that they could only be opened and read by breaking the seal. They were much quicker and cheaper to produce than letters patent or charters, and were used to convey instructions privately to individuals. Writs of Liberate were similar in form, so that it is not surprising that they and letters close were put on the same roll to start with, but since writs of liberate dealt with financial matters which had to be brought to the attention of the Exchequer, it was really much more convenient to enrol them separately.

135, 3. Galbraith, *Studies in the Public Records*, p. 80.

135, 4. *Dialogus de Scacarrio*, pp. 41–2.

page 136, 1. This does not exhaust the list of John's residences. Other places frequently visited where there was no royal castle, were Ashley (Hants), Bradenstoke (Wilts.), Crambourne, Dorchester (Dorset), Farnham (Surrey), Havering (Essex), Lambeth (Surrey), Laxton (Notts.), Melksham (Wilts.), Pontefract (Yorks.). See also *Pipe Roll 9 John*, p. xiv.

page 137, 1. Cf. D. M. Stenton, *English Society in the Middle Ages*, chapter 1; Jolliffe, *Angevin Kingship*, chapter 9.

137, 2. W. H. St John Hope in *Archaeologia*, lx (1906), p. 104; Cole, *Documents Illustrative of English History*, p. vi: carters bringing wine from Southampton held up for three days at the river Trent, unable to cross.

137, 3. Cole, *op. cit.*, pp. ix–x.

137, 4. Itinerary in introduction to *Rot. Pat.*; *Misae Roll 14 John*, p. 234.

page 138, 1. J. E. A. Jolliffe, 'The Chamber & the Castle Treasuries under John', *Studies presented to Powicke*, pp. 117–42.

page 139, 1. See *Pipe Roll 6 John*, pp. xxxiv, xxxvi; for an example of ' a generous gift to a knight see *ibid.*, p. 213.

139, 2. *Rot. de Lib.*, p. 151.

139. 3. *Pipe Roll 7 John*, p. 112; *Rot. Claus.*, i. 8, 10. For gifts to second wife, *Pipe Roll 4 John*, p. 280, *Pipe Roll 5 John*, pp. 139, 154–5, *Pipe Roll 6 John*, p. 213 (a robe costing the considerable sum of £23 11s. 1d.), *Pipe Roll 7 John*, pp. 12, 121.

139, 4. For sugar and spices see *Pipe Roll 8 John*, p. xxvi, and *Pipe Roll 13 John*, p. xxii. For the Staffordshire potteries see *Pipe Roll 7 John*, p. 160. For the preparations at Windsor for Christmas 1211, *Pipe Roll 13 John*, pp. 109 and xxii.

page 140, 1. *Misae Roll 14 John*, 4 March 1212: 100 marks paid to Henry de St Helena to purchase precious stones to put in the gold crown he was making for the king. The executors of the bishop of Durham tender 2000 marks and all his jewels in payment of debt, *Pipe Roll 10 John*, p. 59. William son of Gerold owes a ruby worth 20 or 30 marks, *Pipe Roll 9 John*, p. 72. The monks of Bury

St Edmund's bring in Abbot Sampson's jewels, *Curia Regis Rolls*, vi. 189. The jewels that John intended as a gift for St Edmund's are referred to *Rot. Pat.*, p. 13. Innocent III's letter accompanying his present of jewels is printed in *Foedera*, i. i. 93. For jewels, etc., deposited in monasteries see *Rot. Chart.*, i. 134, *Rot. Pat.*, i. 145–50. For the transport of the jewels he liked to have with him see *Pipe Roll 2 John*, p. 150, *Pipe Roll 13 John*, p. 109.

140, 2. *Rot. de Lib.*, p. 23; *Pipe Roll 4 John*, p. 276.

140, 3. *Pipe Roll 5 John*, p. 139: 43*s.* 10*d.* paid to John of Kempsey for chests and carts to carry the king's books (libros Regis) oversea; *Rot. Claus.*, i. 108; *ibid.*, i. 29: 'Romancium Historia Anliae'.

140, 4. E.g. *Misae Roll 14 John*, pp. 239, 249, 252–4.

140, 5. *Hist. des ducs de Normandie*, p. 109.

page 141, 1. For the acquisition of hawks, *Pipe Roll 3 John*, p. xviii, *Pipe Roll 6 John*, pp. xlv, 99, *Pipe Roll 7 John*, p. 9. For John feasting paupers to ease his conscience over hunting see, e.g., *Misae Roll 14 John*, pp. 250, 253, *Rot de Lib.*, p. 124.

141, 2. See Jolliffe, *Angevin Government*, chapter 7.

141, 3. Assize of Northampton (1176), clause 7.

141, 4. On the general subject of John's concern with justice and the operations of his courts see Lady Stenton, 'King John & the Courts of Justice', *Proceedings of the British Academy*, xliv (1958), 103–28; Fowler, *Introduction to the Curia Regis Rolls;* A. L. Poole, review of *Pleas before the King & his justices 1198–1202*, ed. D. M. Stenton, in *E.H.R.*, lxx. (1955) 278–81.

page 142, 1. For the procedures in the royal courts at the end of the 12th century, see the *De Legibus et Consuetudinibus Angliae* attributed to Ranulph Glanville. Extracts in translation are printed in *English Historical Documents*, ii. 462–79.

page 143, 1. *Rot. Claus.*, i. 270.

143, 2. *Curia Regis Rolls*, i. 382, vi. 203–4, 351, 382; for decisions 'per consilium' see, e.g., *ibid.*, i. 142, 162, 392; cf. D. M. Stenton, 'King John & the Courts of Justice', pp. 104–5.

page 144, 1. D. M. Stenton, introduction to *Pipe Roll 6 John*, p. xxxiii: 'Whatever may be the final judgement of history upon King John, if history can ever venture on a final judgement, his interest in legal development, his untiring activity in hearing pleas, and his readiness to admit litigants not only to his court but to his presence must be remembered in his favour. It was very largely the attitude of the king himself which made the first fifteen years of the 13th century so fertile a period in the growth of English law.'

144, 2. Judges on the northern circuit in 1202 seem to have worked through from June to the beginning of December without the normal month's holiday at harvest time. The circuits seem to have been arranged so that men could serve near their estates and during a lull in judicial business could slip away to attend to their own affairs; see Poole in *E.H.R.* lxx. (1955), p. 279.

page 145, 1. Stenton, 'King John & the Courts of Justice,' p. 113; *Pipe Roll 12 John*, p. 203; *Pipe Roll 11 John*, p. 172.

145, 2. The hundred deer went to Bishop Jocelin of Bath, former Chancery clerk, justice, and Exchequer official, J. Armitage Robinson, *Somerset Historical Essays*, p. 149; *Pipe Roll 6 John*, p. 192; *Rot. Claus.*, i. 48.

145, 3. Cf. J. H. Ramsay, *Dawn of the Constitution*, p. 301; for increasing trade see *Pipe Roll 4 John*, pp. xxi–ii; *Pipe Roll 7 John*, pp. xxxii–iii.

page 146, 1. Cf. *Pipe Roll 7 John*, p. xxvi; R. S. Hoyt, *The Royal Desmesne in English Constitutional History*.

page 147, 1. For pensions granted in return for service see, e.g., *Rot de Lib.*, pp. 4, 13.

147, 2. For towns and trade see Poole, *Domesday Book to Magna Carta*, chapter 3; J. Tait, *The Medieval English Borough* (Manchester 1936); *Pipe Roll 1 John*, pp. xviii–xix, *Pipe Roll 2 John*, pp. xvii–xviii. For the development of tallage see Hoyt, *The Royal Desmesne*, pp. 107 ff.

page 148, 1. S. K. Mitchell, *Studies in Taxation under John & Henry III*; Painter, *King John*, pp. 127–8.

148, 2. Magna Carta, clause 12: 'Scutage or aid shall be levied in our kingdom only with the common counsel of our kingdom . . .'

page 149, 1. Mitchell, *Studies in Taxation*, pp. 32–4.

149, 2. In the writs requiring payment the Thirteenth of 1207 was said to have been authorised by 'the common counsel and assent of our council at Oxford for the defence of our realm and the recovery of our rights', *Rot. Pat.*, i. 72.

149, 3. For money hidden in Swineshead abbey, *Rot. Claus*, i. 85, *Rot. de Oblat.*, p. 393; *Pipe Roll 9 John*, p. 29; for the constable of Richmond castle, *Rot. Pat.*, i. 72–3, *Rot. Oblat.*, p. 373; for imprisonments, *Rot. Pat.*, i. 73, *Rot. de Oblat.*, p. 430, *Pipe Roll 9 John*, p. 45.

page 150, 1. Painter, *King John*, pp. 134–5; Mitchell, *Studies in Taxation*, pp. 84–92.

150, 2. Barnwell, p. 232; for the sale of surplus wine stocks see *Pipe Roll 4 John*, pp. xvi–xvii.

page 151, 1. Poole, *Obligations of Society in the 12th & 13th cents.*, p. 89.

151, 2. *Ibid.*, pp. 78–9.

151, 3. Pollock & Maitland, *History of English Law*, ii. 513, 519.

151, 4. See Poole, *Obligations of Society*, pp. 89–90. I have translated the clause freely to convey the sense behind the technicalities.

page 152, 1. Cf. *Pipe Roll 14 John*, p. xxiv; M. L. Beazley, 'The extent of the English Forest in the 13th century,' *T.R.H.S.*, 4th ser., iv. (1921), 146–8. For the customs of the forest see Poole, *Domesday Book to Magna Carta*, pp. 28–34; G. J. Turner, introduction to *Select Pleas of the Forest* (Selden Society, 1899); D. M. Stenton, *English Society in the Early Middle Ages*, pp. 97–119.

152, 2. Painter, *King John*, pp. 136–9.

152, 3. It did it by close inquiry into infringements of the regulations on the sale of wines, and by heavy penalties for offences. They were so numerous as to require a special section of the accounts for several counties, headed *Amerciamenta vinitariorum*, and few merchants seem to have escaped. See *Pipe Roll 8 John*, pp. xxv–xvi.

page 153, 1. Painter, *King John*, pp. 115–23.

CHAPTER 5. KING VERSUS POPE

page 154, 1. Cf. V. H. Galbraith, 'The Literacy of the Medieval English Kings', *Proceedings of the British Academy*, xxi. (1925), 201–30.

page 157, 1. Cf. Diceto, i. 335: 'Ecclesiastical dignity rather advances than abolishes royal dignity, and royal dignity is wont to preserve rather than to destroy ecclesiastical liberty; for the two, the ecclesiastical dignity and the royal, meet as it were in a mutual embrace, since kings cannot obtain salvation without the Church, and the Church cannot obtain peace without the protection of the kings.'

page 158, 1. See C. R. Cheney, *From Becket to Langton*, esp. chapter 4.

158, 2. Canon 12 of the Third Lateran Council (1179); cf. Cheney, *op. cit.*, pp. 21–2.

158, 3. Peter of Blois, Letter 150, Migne, *Patrologia Latina*, ccvii. 440–1; cf. R. W. Southern, *The Making of the Middle Ages* (London 1953), pp. 210–14.

158, 4. Diceto, i. 435.

page 159, 1. Cheney, *From Becket to Langton*, p. 24.

159, 2. Constitutions of Clarendon (1164), clause 12, printed in Stubbs, *Select Charters*, p. 166, translated in *English Historical Documents*, ii. 721.

page 160, 1. L. Deslise & E. Berger, *Receuil des Actes de Henri II* (Paris 1909–27), i. 587.

160, 2. Knowles, in *E.H.R.*, liii. (1938), 216.

160, 3. *Gesta Henrici*, i. 346.

160, 4. Gerald of Wales, iv. 345.

160, 5. Howden, iv. 78; *Selected Letters of Pope Innocent III*, ed. C. R. Cheney & W. H. Semple, pp. 16–22.

160, 6. Howden, iv. 125.

page 161, 1. For the manœuvres in the election see M. D. Knowles, 'The Canterbury Election of 1204–5,' *E.H.R.*, liii. (1938), 211–20.

161, 2. See M. D. Knowles, *The Monastic Order in England* (Cambridge, 1949), pp. 319–22, 325–7.

161, 3. Allegations that John had used violence to persuade the monks to elect Gray were naturally made (Gervase, ii. 99), but the pope exonerated him; cf. C. R. Cheney, 'A Neglected Record of the Canterbury Election of 1205–6', *Bulletin of the Institute of Historical Research*, xxi (1918), 234, n. 1.

page 162, 1. For Langton's early career, see Powicke, *Stephen Langton*; Beryl Smalley, *The Study of the Bible in the Middle Ages* (Oxford 1941), chapter 5.

page 163, 1. *Selected Letters*, pp. 86–90.

163, 2. Cf. Knowles, *The Monastic Order in England*, p. 365.

163, 3. Cheney, *From Becket to Langton*, p. 94.

163, 4. Barnwell, p. 199. The writ for the seizure of the estates was issued on 11 July 1207, *Rot. Pat.*, i. 74.

page 164, 1. *Selected Letters*, p. 93.

164, 2. *Ibid.*, pp. 91–6.

164, 3. *Ibid.*, p. 94.

164, 4. For the law and practice of medieval interdicts see E. B. Krehbiel, *The Interdict, its History & Operation* (Washington, 1909).

page 165, 1. *Selected Letters*, pp. 97–9

165, 2. Annals of Margam, p. 28.

page 166, 1. Cf. Coggeshall, p. 163: 'Rex Anglorum misit Roman, et se satisfacturum per omnia Deo et Sanctae Ecclesiae ac domino papae spopondit; sed minime tenuit.' For the negotiations see Painter, *King John*, pp. 173–4.

166, 2. *Rot. Pat.*, i. 80.

166, 3. The Interdict was proclaimed in churches on Sunday 23 March to come into effect the following day. See C. R. Cheney, 'King John & the Papal Interdict', *Bulletin of John Rylands Library*, xxxi. (1945), 295.

page 167, 1. The evidence for the preceding section and for what follows has been gathered together by C. R. Cheney, *op. cit.*, pp. 300 ff., and 'King John's Reaction to the Interdict on England', *T.R.H.S.*, 4th ser., xxxi. (1949), 129–50.

page 167, 2. Peter of Blois reported having seen 'bands of four rustics wickedly standing guard over the clergy's barns'; quoted in Cheney, 'King John's Reaction', p. 131.

page 168, 1. *Gesta Abbatum S. Albani*, ed. H. T. Riley (Rolls Series 1867–9), i. 241–3.

168, 2. Life of St Hugh, pp. 303–4.

168, 3. *Pipe Roll 12 John*, pp. 215–16; *Pipe Roll 13 John*, p. 65.

168, 4. Gerald of Wales, iv. 313. The sons of priests are a not uncommon phenomenon in the records. The father, grandfather, and great-grandfather of Ailred, the saintly abbot of Rievaulx, had been parish priests of Hexham. Innocent III in 1203 remonstrated with the bishop of Norwich about the numbers of clergy in his diocese who had gone through a form of marriage. See J. R. H. Moorman, *Church Life in England in the 13th century* (Cambridge 1946), pp. 63–7.

168, 5. Poole, *Domesday Book to Magna Carta*, p. 183.

168, 6. Annals of Waverley, p. 261: cf. Cheney, 'King John & the Papal Interdict,' p. 306. Abbot John Ford, preaching in 1210, attacked those priests who thought this measure the worst feature of the Interdict and spent their money on ransom.

page 169, 1. *Selected Letters*, pp. 117–20, 123.

169, 2. Cf. Cheney, 'King John & the Papal Interdict,' pp. 310–11.

page 170, 1. Cf. Cheney, 'King John's Reaction', pp. 147–8, and 'King John & the Papal Interdict', pp. 304–5.

170, 2. *Ibid.*, pp. 308–11.

170, 3. See above, p. 149 and below, pp. 185 ff., 191.

170, 4. Gervase, ii. cviii–cx; Barnwell, p. 199. Coggeshall, p. 65.

page 171, 1. Annals of Waverley, p. 273; cf. Cheney, 'King John & the Papal Interdict', pp. 279–300.

171, 2. *Ibid.*, p. 314.

171, 3. Life of St. Hugh, p. 293.

171, 4. As a matter of fact a similar accusation was levelled against Richard I (Coggeshall, p. 96), probably with as little justification; cf. Norgate, *England under the Angevin Kings*, ii. 386, n. 1.

171, 5. *Pipe Roll 1 John*, p. 4.

171, 6. Cf. Powicke, *Stephen Langton*, pp. 86–8.

171, 7. Life of St Hugh, p. 292.

page 172, 1. *Ibid.*, pp. 335, 371.

172, 2. *Curia Regis Rolls*, vi. 189.

172, 3. *Rot. Claus.*, i. 108.

172, 4. Cf. *Pipe Roll 3 John*, p. xix; *Pipe Roll 4 John*, p. 12; *Pipe Roll 6 John*, pp. 94, 131; *Pipe Roll 7 John*, p. 133; *Rot. Claus.*, i. 39.

172, 5. For John's penances, see above, p. 141; for his almsgiving during the Interdict, see Poole, *Domesday Book to Magna Carta*, pp. 477-8.

172, 6. See *Pipe Roll 13 John*, p. xxxvii.

172, 7. Howden, iv. 144-5.

172, 8. *Pipe Roll 2 John*, p. xviii.

172, 9. *Chichester Chartulary* (Sussex Record Society, xlvi, 1946), no. 410.

172, 10. Rumours and apochryphal stories, but little more, got into the chronicles about the conference, see Powicke, *Stephen Langton*, pp. 86-7, & 87, n. 1; Painter, *King John*, pp. 186-7. For the terms see Innocent's commission to Pandulph, *Selected Letters*, pp. 125-7.

page 173, 1. *Selected Letters*, p. 213.

173, 2. Cheney, 'King John's Reaction', pp. 142-5.

CHAPTER 6. KING JOHN AND HIS BARONS

page 175, 1. *Dialogus de Scaccario*, p. 75.

175, 2. Diceto, i. 371.

175, 3. *Curia Regis Rolls*, i. 415.

page 176, 1. Biog. Marshal, iii. 33.

176, 2. *Early Buckinghamshire Charters*, ed. Fowler & Jenkins (Bucks. Archaeological Soc., Records Branch, 1939), p. 3: 'praeter regiam violentiam.'

176, 3. *Rot. Claus.*, i. 87.

176, 4. Gerald of Wales, viii. 160; cf. the hostility of Ralph Niger to all Henry's legal reforms, *Chronicles of Ralph Niger*, p. 168.

page 177, 1. *Curia Regis Rolls*, i. 285.

177, 2. *Ibid.*, iv. 99.

177, 3. *Pipe Roll 34 Henry II*, pp. 173, 86; *Pipe Roll 21 Henry II*, p. 114.

177, 4. *Rot. Pat.*, i. 85; cf. Jolliffe, *Angevin Kingship*, esp. chapters 3 & 4.

page 178, 1. Stenton, 'King John & the Courts of Justice', pp. 104-5.

178, 2. This schizophrenia is readily apparent in the *Curia Regis Rolls*. John will lay down that cases should proceed according to custom despite any instructions he has issued to the contrary (iii. 27-8, 57); but at other times he will insist that a royal command takes precedence over custom (iii. 215). The royal justices sometimes made a note on their rolls when custom had been flouted: 'on the order of the lord king, not by consideration of the court or according to the custom of the realm' (ii. 189). See J. C. Holt, 'The Barons & the Great Charter', *E.H.R.*, lxx. (1955), 5 ff.

page 179, 1. *Magna Carta Commemoration Essays*, p. 114; cf. Howden, iii. 3.

179, 2. Gerald of Wales, viii. 183–6.

page 180, 1. Biog. Marshal, iii. 38; cf. Painter, *William Marshal.*

page 181, 1. Gervase, ii. 100.

181, 2. *Rot. Claus.*, i. 162, 122; Wendover, ii. 61; Barnwell, p. 207; *Rot. Pat.*, p. 94.

page 182, 1. *Rot. Claus.*, i. 84.

182, 2. *Pipe Roll 12 John*, p. 139: 'Robertus de Vallibus debet quinque optimos palfridos ut R. taceret de uxore Henrici Pinel.'

page 183, 1. *Rot. de Oblat.*, p. 531; *Pipe Roll 5 John*, p. 197; *Rot. de Oblat.*, pp. 520, 102.

183, 2. *Dialogus de Scaccario*, p. 96. Reliefs of 600 marks, e.g., *Pipe Roll 8 John*, p. 104, *Pipe Roll 9 John*, pp. 77, 157. Lacy's relief, *Rot. de Oblat.*, p. 495; Stuteville's, *Rot. Claus.*, i. 45; FitzAlan's, *Pipe Roll 16 John*. Widows paying for dower, e.g., *Pipe Roll 3 John*, p. 18, *Pipe Roll 4 John*, p. 126, *Pipe Roll 5 John*, pp. 22, 104, *Pipe Roll 7 John*, p. 34.

183, 3. Cf. Painter, *The English Feudal Barony*, chapter 7.

page 184, 1. *Pipe Roll 6 John*, p. 30; *Rot. Chart.*, i. 201.

184, 2. Painter, *Feudal Barony*, p. 187.

184, 3. Howden, iv. 152, cf. Jolliffe, *Angevin Kingship*, pp. 79–84.

184, 4. Cf. Painter, *Feudal Barony*, pp. 185–6; for extortion practised on the Jews by John see Norgate, *John Lackland*, p. 137.

page 185, 1. When Marshal and Briouze protested to the king he ordered Meiler to restore any men and booty that he had captured, but instructed him to hold on to the city of Limerick if he had taken it, *Rot. Claus.*, i. 77.

185, 2. *Rot. Pat.*, i. 68, 78; Painter, *William Marshal*, pp. 144–69.

185, 3. Biog. Marshal, iii. 195.

page 186, 1. Wendover, ii. 48–9. For Matilda Briouze see Powicke, *Christian Life in the Middle Ages*, p. 151.

186, 2. *Foedera*, i. i. 107–8.

186, 3. *Rot. Pat.*, i. 81; *Rot. Claus.*, i. 112–13.

186, 4. See Painter, *King John*, p. 247.

page 187, 1. *Curia Regis Rolls*, v. 152; *Rot. Pat.*, i. 86; *Annales Monastici*, iv. 396; Annals of Margam, p. 29; *Hist. des ducs de Normandie*, p. 112.

187, 2. See Painter, *William Marshal*, pp. 163–4.

187, 3. Coggeshall, p. 164; Wendover, ii. 57; Barnwell, p. 202. *Annales Monastici*, i. 30, 59, ii. 81, 265, iv. 399.

187, 4. Annals of Margam, p. 31.

page 188, 1. Norgate, *John Lackland*, pp. 287–8; Painter, *King John*, pp. 238–50.

188, 2. Barnwell, p. 232.

page 189, 1. See F. W. Maitland, *Pleas of the Crown for the County of Gloucester . . . in* 1221 (London 1884), pp. xiii ff.

189, 2. Newburgh, p. 521.

page 190, 1. *Rot. de Oblat.*, p. 275; cf. Painter, *King John*, pp. 231–2.

190, 2. *Rot. Pat.*, i. 17. Cf. *ibid.*, i. 116: 'The King to . . . John of Bassingbourne, greeting. Know that we have restored to . . . Ralph, count of Eu, the honor of Tickhill with the castle and all its appurtenances as the right of Alice his wife; and because we believe that you would be unwilling to deliver up the castle to him on the sole authority of our letters, we send you our beloved and faithful Master Richard March, archdeacon of Northumberland, whom you may and ought to credit as ourselves. . . .'

190, 3. *Rot. Pat.*, i. 66.

190, 4. *Curia Regis Rolls*, viii. 170.

190, 5. Coggeshall, p. 102.

page 191, 1. *Rot. Chart*, i. 207: 'si quis autem ipsum elegerit nunquam poterit sperare se pacem aut amorem nobiscum habiturum. Hoc autem secretum esse volumus.'

191, 2. Gervase, ii. lix: 'Rex vicissim procidit ad pedes ejus et ridendo ac irridendo dixit, "Ecce, domine archiepiscope, eece tantum feci tibi quantum tu mihi". Et sic dimisit eum non consolationem sed irrisionem solam reportantem.'

page 192, 1. As examples of John placing trusted men in border areas we may note the appointment of Fawkes de Breauté as bailiff of Glamorgan, and Gerard de Athée as sheriff of Gloucester and sheriff of Hereford (*Rot. Pat.* i. 68, 78). Both were mercenary captains. Some time before he died in 1213 Gerard was replaced as sheriff of Gloucester by his kinsman Engelard de Cigogné. When the bishop of Durham died in 1208 his castles and men were put under the command of another mercenary captain, Philip of Oldcoates (cf. Painter, *King John*, p. 252, n. 92). Owing to the Interdict the see of Durham was not filled until 1213. Roger Lacy, constable of Chester and defender of Château Gaillard, was in December 1204 appointed sheriff of Cumberland and Yorkshire (*Rot. Pat.*, i. 48). Robert de Vieuxpont, one of John's most trusted and indefatigable henchmen, was in March 1205 granted the barony of Westmorland (*Rot. Pat.*, i. 51).

Considerable sums of money were spent on royal castles at Scarborough, Knaresborough, and Lancaster, and some too at Newcastle upon Tyne, and Tickhill. See R. Allen Brown, 'Royal

Castle Building in England, 1154–1216', *E.H.R.*, lxx (1955), 353–98. Some of the building work followed a visit from John, e.g., on 15 February 1206, the day after leaving Knaresborough, he wrote to the constable: 'We require you to go ahead with the repairs to the house and castle of Knaresborough as we have arranged and as we discussed with you' (*Rot. Claus.*, i. 65).

192, 2. The castles of Scarborough, Corfe, and Dover received special attention at this time, and in addition John built a new castle at Odiham in Hampshire at a cost of over £1150. See R. Allen Brown, *op. cit.*

192, 3. *Foedera*, i. i. 50.

page 193, 1. Newburgh, pp. 335–6.

193, 2. Howden, iv. 91, 107, 140–2; Poole, *Domesday Book to Magna Carta*, p. 282.

193, 3. Painter, *King John*, pp. 253–6.

193, 4. Gervase, ii. 102–3; *Foedera*, i. i. 103.

page 194, 1. See Orpen, *Ireland under the Normans*, vol. ii.

194, 2. *Rot. Pat.*, i. 54.

page 195, 1. Orpen, *op. cit.*, chapter xx; Painter, *William Marshal*, pp. 149–69.

195, 2. *Rot. Pat.*, i. 72.

195, 3. Biog. Marshal, iii. 191–2.

195, 4. *Rot. Chart.*, i. 176, 178; cf. Painter, *William Marshal*, pp. 159–60.

page 196, 1. Briouze was driven by storms to land at Wicklow where Marshal was staying, and was entertained for three weeks. The justiciar protested that he was harbouring a traitor, but the earl replied that he was doing no more than giving shelter to his lord, as feudal law required. It is not known just how Briouze could have been Marshal's lord, but the complexities of feudal tenure were such that it is quite possible that the latter held a fief of Briouze in Wales somewhere. He escorted the fugitive to the borders of Meath, where Walter Lacy was waiting to receive his father-in-law. Biog. Marshal, ii. 196–7.

196, 2. *Pipe Roll 12 John*, xxxii. For the expedition see Orpen, *op. cit.*, ii. 242–77.

page 197, 1. Wendover (ii. 56) says that 'he caused to be set up there English laws and customs, establishing sheriffs and other officers who should judge the people of the realm according to English laws.' He is certainly mistaken: sheriffs had been appointed in the time of Henry II (and for one 1205 see *Rot. Claus.*, i. 218); but it shows how men of Wendover's day looked on John's work there.

It is confirmed by references in Henry III's charters, see Orpen, *op. cit.*, ii. 273.

197, 2. For Wales in this period see J. E. Lloyd, *A History of Wales*, i., chapters 16–17.

page 198, 1. Cf. Lloyd, *op. cit.*, i. 631–2; Annals of Dunstable, p. 32.

198, 2. Lloyd, *op. cit.*, i. 634–5.

198, 3. *Ibid.*, i. 635–6; *Annales Monastici*, i. 60.

page 199, 1. Barnwell, p. 203.

199, 2. *Ibid.*, p. 206.

199, 3. It is a great pity that the returns for this inquest, a remarkably searching one, have not survived entire. Had they been written up at the Exchequer we should have had a record comparable to Domesday Book. The surviving returns are printed in the *Book of Fees*, pp. 52–228, and throw much light on early 13th-century feudal society. Cf. Painter, *King John*, pp. 208–11.

199, 4. *Pipe Roll 14 John*, pp. xxiii–iv; *Rot. Claus.*, i. 117.

199, 5. Lloyd, *op. cit.*, i. 637; *Annales Monastici*, ii. 81; *Memorials of St Edmund's Abbey*, ed. T. Arnold (Rolls Series 1890–6), ii. 24.

page 200, 1. Cf. J. G. Edwards, 'Edward I's Castle Building in Wales', *Proceedings of the British Academy*, xxxii. 57–8; *Pipe Roll 14 John*, pp. xv–vi; *Rot. Claus.*, i. 131.

200, 2. Barnwell, p. 207; Wendover, ii. 61. For the rumours see *Memorials of St Edmund's Abbey*, ii. 23; Annals of Dunstable, pp. 33–4, Coggeshall, p. 165.

200, 3. *Rot. Claus.*, i. 121: Stephen of Thornham was to allow no one to see Henry who did not carry special letters of authorisation. Barnwell, p. 207; Annals of Dunstable, pp. 33–4; Wendover ii. 62; Annals of Waverley, p. 268; Coggeshall, p. 165.

200, 4. For the details of John's measures see Painter, *King John*, pp. 267–72. Three Exchequer officials fell under suspicion: William Cornhill was imprisoned but bought the king's good will; William of Necton fled to France; Geoffrey of Norwich was imprisoned and died there. Wendover embroidered the fate of the last named into the tale of the crushing of 'Geoffrey, archdeacon of Norwich' under a cope of lead, and ascribed it to 1209 as an example of John's treatment of the clergy during the Interdict; see above, pp. 12–13.

200, 5. Barnwell, p. 207: 'et siluit terra.'

page 201, 1. *Ibid.*

201, 2. Barnwell, p. 208 ('Homo iste simplex et rusticanus, sed vitam agens in pane et aqua, quasi futura praedicens habebatur in populo.'); Wendover, ii. 62–3; *Hist. des ducs de Normandie*, pp. 122–3; Annals of Dunstable, p. 34 (where he is called Peter of Pontefract).

page 201, 3. Wendover, ii. 63.

   201, 4. *Cal. of Documents relating to Ireland*, ed. H. S. Sweetman, i, no. 448.

   201, 5. *Rot. Claus.*, i. 132.

page 202, 1. For the rumours of papal deposition, which some chroniclers recorded as fact, and many modern historians have believed, see C. R. Cheney, 'The Alleged Deposition of King John', *Studies presented to Powicke*, pp. 100–16.

   202, 2. Cheney, 'Alleged Deposition', p. 110.

page 203, 1. *Selected Letters*, p. 164. Prof. Cheney ('Alleged Deposition') does not believe that Innocent ever went so far as to depose John and call upon Philip to invade. He assumes that the bulls that Nicholas was instructed to destroy had been issued specifically as an insurance against John's possible failure to ratify the agreement before 1 June. I fully accept his argument that he never treated John as deposed, and that Philip had no ground for complaining that the pope had given him authority to invade and then withdrawn it. Prof. Painter, on the other hand (*King John*, pp. 190–2), sides with the confused chronicle accounts that assume both these developments. The fact that the bulls were still in Langton's possession shows that they had never been delivered to their addressees; but I am prepared to believed that Innocent had gone farther along the road to deposition than Prof. Cheney seems to allow, and had put the bulls decreeing it in Langton's possession when he visited Rome around Christmas 1212. Though never published, their contents would be known to Langton and the exiled bishops, and later talk in ecclesiastical circles would account for the very general, though mistaken, belief among the chroniclers that the king had actually been deposed. After John's timely intervention, the pope would naturally not allude to what was an unrealised intention, though he kept the bulls in reserve until he was sure of John's good faith.

   203, 2. *Foedera*, i. i. 104, dated wrongly; Deslisle, *Cat. des Actes de Philippe Auguste*, no. 1437.

page 204, 1. See Poole, *Domesday Book to Magna Carta*, pp. 453–5.

   204, 2. Wendover, ii. 66–8.

   204, 3. Poole, *op. cit.*, p. 459 & n. 2.

page 205, 1. Biog. Marshal, iii. 202; William the Breton, i. 251; Barnwell, p. 211; Wendover, ii. 78–80; A. Cartellieri, *Philip IV August* (Leipzig, 1899–1921), iv. 363 ff.

CHAPTER 7. THE ROAD TO RUNNYMEDE

page 207 1. *Selected Letters*, pp. 130–6.

   207, 2. *Ibid.*, p. 141.

   207, 3. *Ibid.*, p. 142.

page 209, 1. *Ibid.*, pp. 178–80; *Rot. Chart.*, i. 195; *Foedera*, i. i. 115.

   209, 2. *Selected Letters*, pp. 149–51, 6 July 1213. The confirmation asked for was discharged by John on 3 October 1213 when he repeated his oath of homage in the presence of Nicholas of Tusculum (sent by the pope as a personal representative) and sealed with a golden seal, see *ibid.*, pp. 177–83.

   209, 3. *Foedera*, i. i. 114; *Rot. Claus.*, i. 164.

page 210, 1. He had first done this in the summer of 1212. The Chancery prepared documents in the following form: 'Know thty when our lord John . . . was ready to restore to us all the monea that he had received from our house from his first coronation until the feast of the Nativity of the Blessed Virgin Mary in the 14th year of his reign (8 September 1212) we in good spirit and entirely of our free will gave him that money.' *Rot. Chart.*, i. 191–2. Innocent, while still distrustful of John, instructed Langton to ignore such documents (*Selected Letters*, pp. 137–8). John later had his Chancery draft a different form: 'We wish it to be known that our lord John . . . has fully satisfied us and our church in respect of all that was received by him or any of his men from the goods of our house from the beginning of the Interdict to [such and such a day]', *Rot. Pat.*, i. 140–1; *Annals of Waverley*, p. 268; Coggeshall, p. 165.

   210, 2. *Selected Letters*, p. 150, 6 July 1213.

   210, 3. Cf. Cheney, 'King John's Reaction to the Interdict on England,' p. 129; Wendover, ii. 94, 100–3; *Selected Letters*, pp. 171–2; *Rot. Chart.*, i. 208–9.

   210, 4. Paris, *Historia Anglorum*, ii. 146–8.

   210, 5. *Foedera*, i. i. 120.

   210, 6. The surrender of royal control over episcopal appointments in the acceptance of Langton without qualification was made explicit in a charter of 21 November 1214, *Foedera*, i. i. 126, *Selected Letters*, pp. 199–201. In it John declared that:

'Whatever custom has so far been observed in the English Church during our own and our predecessor's reigns and whatever jurisdiction we have so far claimed in the election of whatever grade of prelate, this we have now conceded . . . voluntarily and of our own free will, and with the general consent of our barons; and we have decreed and by this our charter confirmed that for the future in all and each of the churches and monasteries, cathedral or conventual, through our whole realm of England there should be for ever free elections . . . saving only the securing to us and our heirs the custody of the vacant churches and monasteries that belong to us. We also promise that we will not hinder, nor permit or instigate our agents to hinder the electors . . . from freely appointing a pastor over them whenever they so wish after the prelacy has become vacant, provided that permission to elect be first sought of us and our heirs, a permission which we will not refuse or postpone. And if (which God forbid) we should refuse or postpone, the electors will nevertheless proceed to make a canonical election. Similarly after an election let our assent be sought, which similarly we will not refuse unless we have offered and lawfully proved, some reasonable cause to justify our refusal. . . .'

Although the king's grant is said to be 'with the general consent of our barons', John was in fact conciliating the barons at the moment of moving against the rebellious barons. In practice, kings were usually able to get their own way in the matter of elections, even after this charter, often by arrangement with the papacy. The 12th century struggles over 'free elections' ended in king and pope jointly gaining control at the expense of the interests of the ordinary electors.

page 211, 1. *Selected Letters*, p. 213.

211, 2. Paris, *Historia Anglorum*, ii. 146–8; cf. Powicke, *Stephen Langton*, pp. 104, 130, 134.

211, 3. *Ibid.*, p. 98.

211, 4. *Selected Letters*, pp. 166–7.

page 212, 1. Coggeshall, p. 170; Barnwell, pp. 213–14; Wendover, ii. 97–8.

page 213, 1. *Selected Letters*, p. 133. John did not let their cunning pass without a gesture of protest: on the same day that he issued a safe conduct, he ordered the destruction of Vesci's castle at Alnwick, *Rot. Pat.*, i. 99.

213, 2. Wendover, ii. 81.

page 214, 1. *Ibid.*, ii. 80, 82; Coggeshall, p. 167.

page 215, 1. Wendover, ii. 82–3; Coggeshall, p. 167; *Rot. Pat.*, i. 103.

215, 2. Coggeshall, p. 167. The commission to Nicholas is as follows: '. . . By the authority of this letter we command that, as soon as the Interdict on England is relaxed, you will by our authority declare to be null and void all conspiracies and factions which were formed because of the quarrel between the kingdom and the priesthood, since, with the disappearance of the cause, the effect ought to disappear also.' *Selected Letters*, p. 165.

page 216, 1. Published by Teulet in *Layettes du Trésor des Chartes*, i. 423, and by J. H. Round, 'An Unknown Charter of Liberties', *E.H.R.* (1893), viii. 288 ff. The original is not divided into paragraphs. The divisions used here for convenience are those in McKechnie's edition, *Magna Carta*, pp. 485–6.

page 217, 1. See Painter, *King John*, pp. 311–15, for comparisons with the baronial proposals in 1215. There is much dispute among historians about the date of the 'Unknown Charter', see McKechnie, *Magna Carta*, pp. 172–5, for a summary of the arguments. I am in agreement here with Painter, *op. cit.*, p. 314.

217, 2. Coggeshall, p. 167. *Annals of Dunstable*, p. 40: 'On 1 November at Wallingford the Northerners were reconciled to the king by the legate, and admitted to the kiss of peace.'

page 218, 1. *Pipe Roll 12 John*, p. 175 (for the offer of Devon and Somerset to be rid of Brewer); *Rot. Pat.*, i. 139; *Foedera*, i. i. 118; Lloyd, *History of Wales*, i. 641.

218, 2. Coggeshall, p. 168.

218, 3. *Misae Roll 14 John*, p. 157: 'quia non ausi sumus scire nomen ejus, ideo non ponitur in hoc scripto.'

page 219, 1. *Rot. Pat.*, i. 111.

page 221, 1. Wendover, ii. 99–100. Treaty with Lusigans, *Rot. Chart.*, i. 197.

221, 2. See *Foedera*, i. i. 125 for the large numbers of Poitevin barons attending John.

page 222, 1. William the Breton, i. 263–4; Coggeshall, pp. 169–70; Wendover, ii. 104–5.

222, 2. *Rot. Pat.*, i. 118.

page 224, 1. F. Lot, *L'Art Militaire et Les Armees du Moyen Age*, i. 223–5; C. Oman, *The Art of War in the Middle Ages*, pp. 457–9.

224, 2. *Foedera*, i. i. 124–5.

page 225, 1. Annals of Waverley, p. 281: 'potestate sua non bene utens, iram baronum converti fecerat contra regem.'

225, 2. *Rot Claus.*, i. 166, 213; *Foedera*, i. i. 126; Mitchell, *Studies in Taxation*, pp. 112–13 & n. 84.

page 227, 1. Barnwell, pp. 217–18.

227, 2. In the document in which the 'Unknown Charter' survives, it immediately follows a copy of Henry I's Coronation Charter. Some historians have argued that it dates from this point. For the text of Henry I's charter, Stubbs, *Select Charters*, pp. 117–20; translation in *English Historical Documents*, i. 400–2.

227, 3. Wendover, ii. 111–12.

page 228, 1. *Ibid.*, ii. 83–7.

228, 2. Roger Cressi, a baron from Norfolk, is said to be 'unus ex Norensibus qui habent pacem usque ad clausum Pasche', *Curia Regis Rolls*, vii. 315. See Poole, *Domesday Book to Magna Carta*, p. 409 & n. 1.

page 229, 1. *Hist. des ducs de Normandie* quoted in Norgate, *John Lackland*, p. 290.

229, 2. *Hist. des ducs de Normandie*, pp. 147–9. There is no contemporary analysis of the adherents of rebellion. Such evidence as there is is collected by Painter, *King John*, pp. 286 ff. J. H. Round, 'King John & Robert FitzWalter', *E.H.R.*, xix. (1904), 707–11, and Powicke, *Stephen Langton*, pp. 207–13, discuss the subject and emphasise the non-northern elements. It is difficult, however, to go against the testimony of so many chronicles, and particularly those for the eastern counties – Coggeshall, Barnwell, Dunstable – and discredit the description of the rebels as the 'Northerners' altogether. No doubt it soon became an inadequate label, but the impression on contemporaries of its being a northern movement is clearly very strong.

page 230, 1. Cf. Painter, *King John*, pp. 29–30.

230, 2. See Norgate, *John Lackland*, pp. 289–93.

230, 3. *Hist. des ducs de Normandie*, pp. 116–18. FitzWalter seems to have had a grudge against Brewer, who held some of the Lacy fiefs that he seems to have thought belonged to him, see Painter, *King John*, pp. 75–6.

page 231, 1. *Biog. Marshal*, iii. 172–3. Marshal and Quenci, it seems, could not abide each other, see Painter, *King John*, p. 295 & n. 3.

231, 2. Barnwell, p. 220.

page 232, 1. Wendover, ii. 114: 'pestes incentores.'

232, 2. Gervase, ii. 109; Coggeshall, p. 172.

page 233, 1. This interpretation of the several moves by the king and the barons is largely my own, but I have followed the skilful reconstruction of the preliminary events by Prof. Cheney, 'The Eve of Magna Carta', *Bulletin of John Rylands Library*, xxxviii. (1955–6), 311–41. For the events of June 1215, leading up to the promulgation of the charter, I have been convinced by the arguments of J. C. Holt, 'The Making of Magna Carta', *E.H.R.*, lxxii. (1957), 401–22, which suggests a rather different reconstruction from Prof. Cheney's.

233, 2. *Rot. Pat.*, i. 130.

233, 3. *Magna Carta Commemoration Essays*, p. 44; *Selected Letters*, p. 214.

page 234, 1. *Rot. Chart.*, i. 209.

   234, 2. *Rot. Pat.*, i. 141.

page 235, 1. Cheney, 'Eve of Magna Carta', p. 231; Painter, *King John*, p. 307.

   235, 2. Wendover, ii. 117.

page 236, 1. The Articles of the Barons are printed in Stubbs, *Select Charters*, pp. 284–91, and McKechnie, *Magna Carta*, pp. 487–93.

   236, 2. There has been much argument among scholars as to the nature of the formal negotiations at Runnymede, and the actual date of the surviving documents. I follow Holt, 'The Making of Magna Carta.'

page 237, 1. To the early 13th century, 'rights' meant property and 'liberties' meant something more akin to privileges than to freedoms.

   237, 2. Clause 34 reads: 'The writ which is called *praecipe* shall not for the future be issued to anyone, regarding any tenement by which a freeman may lose his court.' An older generation of scholars, reacting against excessive adulation of Magna Carta, fastened on this clause (exaggerating its importance in the process) as typical of the barons' short-sighted pursuit of self interest, and as an attack upon legal progress. Thus Maitland describes it as 'a victory for feudalism consecrated by the Great Charter', and McKechnie as 'one of the most reactionary clauses in the Charter.' This, however, is a far-fetched and misplaced interpretation. The writ *praecipe* did indeed peremptorily draw a case into the royal court without reference to other competent jurisdictions, but Miss N. D. Hurnard ('Magna Carta, Clause 34', *Studies presented to Powicke*, pp. 157–79) has shown that the barons could always claim a case when it came up for a hearing. By this clause they were seeking to save themselves the inconvenience of claiming by asking that the Chancery exercise more discrimination in issuing the writ. What is really remarkable is that they did not seek to go further.

   237, 3. The phrase 'per legem terrae' means, roughly, 'by any recognised procedure at law'. There were many different courts and several procedures. The barons did not wish to insist upon any particular procedure; they were merely seeking to provide some safeguard against arbitrary administrative action without the sentence of a proper court at all. Trial by peers ('per iujicium parium') would apply where the law were uncertain or the court not competent to deal with a case. Cf. F. M. Powicke in *Magna Carta Commemoration Essays*, pp. 96 ff. See also Keeney, *Judgment by Peers*, chapter 3.

page 239, 1. Cf. T. F. T. Plucknett, *The Legislation of Edward I* (Oxford 1949), pp. 75–6.

239, 2. The names are given by Paris, *Chronica Majora*, ii. 604–5.

page 240, 1. Magna Carta as subsequently amended will be found in Stubbs', *Select Charters*, pp. 336–9, 340–8, 349–50, and McKechnie *Magna Carta*, pp. 497–512. Stephenson & Marcham, *Sources of English Constitutional History*, pp. 115–26, prints in italic the portions of the Charter of 1215 which were omitted or changed in reissues.

240, 2. The emergence of the principle of the rule of law in the late 12th century is examined in an interesting article by J. C. Holt, 'The Barons & the Great Charter', *E.H.R.*, lxx. (1955), 1–24. It is particularly valuable for showing how the assumptions and ideas of ordinary men can be recovered from the records of lawsuits, etc., in the royal archives.

240, 3. John's Charter was only dimly known in the 17th century. Selden printed a copy drawn from Paris's chronicle in 1610, but it was Henry III's Charter of 1225 that Coke used in his famous commentary, though he says in a footnote that there was a charter in John's reign also called Magna Carta. See H. Butterfield, *The Englishman & his History* (Cambridge 1945), pp. 26 ff.

CHAPTER 8. THE ROAD TO NEWARK

page 241, 1. *Rot. Pat.*, i. 143–5; *Rot. Claus.*, i. 215–16. For further examples see Painter, *King John*, pp. 330–3.

241, 2. *Hist. des Ducs de Normandie*, p. 151; Painter, *King John*, pp. 337–8.

page 242, 1. *Rot. Pat.*, i. 140, reinforced by further letters a week later, *ibid.*, i. 145. Mr. H. G. Richardson has made a brilliant reconstruction of how the Charter was put into effect, 'The Morrow of the Great Charter', *Bulletin of John Rylands Library*, xxviii (1944), 422–43, xxix. (1945), 184–200. I am unable, however, to see the baronial leaders in as favourable a light as he does.

242, 2. Barnwell, p. 222.

242, 3. Wendover, ii. 137.

242, 4. *Hist. des Ducs de Normandie*, p. 151.

page 243, 1. *Foedera*, i. i. 133.

243, 2. Barnwell, p. 222. The letters (*Rot. Pat.*, i. i. 181) were issued over the names of the archbishops of Canterbury and Dublin, the bishops of London, Winchester, Bath, Lincoln, Worcester, Coventry, Chichester, and the papal legate.

243, 3. Barnwell, p. 222; *Rot. Pat.*, i. 152, 153.

page 244, 1. *Selected Letters*, pp. 207–9. I have pruned the quotation of formalities and repetitions which were part of the contemporary idiom, but which impede the modern reader.

page 245, 1. Cf. Powicke, 'The Bull *Miramur plurimum* and a Letter to Archbishop Stephen Langton, 5 September 1215', *E.H.R.*, xliv. (1929), 87–93; Richardson, 'The Morrow of the Great Charter', p. 193, and the comments of Painter, *King John*, pp. 344–7.

245, 2. See Powicke, *Stephen Langton*, pp. 132–4, for a fascinating letter that the old and still testy Gerald of Wales sent Langton urging him to give up neither Canterbury nor hope.

page 246, 1. *Selected Letters*, pp. 212–16, dated 24 August.

246, 2. Barnwell, p. 224; Wendover, ii. 147–8.

246, 3. *Rot. Pat.*, i. 181.

246, 4. *Hist. des Ducs de Normandie*, pp. 158–9.

page 247, 1. *Rot. Claus.*, i. 231; Barnwell, p. 227; *Rot. Claus.*, i. 238: letters to the justiciar, 25 November, 'We order you to send us with all haste forty bacon pigs of the fattest and those less good for eating to use for bringing fire under the tower.'

247, 2. Barnwell, p. 227; *Hist. des Ducs de Normandie*, p. 163. Wendover (ii. 150) has a story that John would have hanged all the inmates, but was restrained by Savary de Mauléon who protested that this would be a bad example to his enemies.

247, 3. Wendover, ii. 149.

247, 4. Richardson, 'Morrow of the Great Charter.'

page 248, 1. Barnwell, p. 226; Coggeshall, p. 177; *Hist. des Ducs de Normandie*, p. 160; Wendover, ii. 173.

248, 2. *Hist. des Ducs de Normandie*, pp. 160–1; cf. Coggeshall, p. 176.

page 249, 1. Barnwell, p. 228.

249, 2. *Rolls of the Justices in Eyre for Yorkshire, 1218–19* (Selden Society, 1937), no. 851.

249, 3. *Hist. des Ducs de Normandie*, pp. 163–4.

249, 4. Poole, *Domesday Book to Magna Carta*, p. 481; Coggeshall, pp. 178–9; *Rot. Pat.*, i. 162, 168, 169.

page 251, 1. See Wendover, ii. 177 ff., for a colourful account. Louis expounded his case in a letter to the abbot of St Augustine's, Canterbury, *Foedera*, i. i. 140.

251, 2. *Rot. Claus.*, i. 270.

page 252, 1. *Hist. des Ducs de Normandie*, pp. 167–8; Coggeshall, p. 181.

252, 2. *Hist. des Ducs de Normandie*, pp. 174–7; Coggeshall, p. 182; Barnwell, p. 232; *Rot Pat.*, i. 190.

page 253, 1. *Foedera*, i. i. 142; *Rot. Pat.*, i. 196; G. R. Stephens, 'A Note on William of Cassignham,' *Speculum*, xvi. (1941), 216–23.

253, 2. Wendover, ii. 176, 193–4; Coggeshall, p. 179.

253, 3. *Hist. des Ducs de Normandie*, p. 179; Annals of Dunstable, p. 49.

253, 4. *Rot. Pat.*, p. 199. *Rot. Claus.*, i. 291.

page 254, 1. Coggeshall, p. 184; Barnwell, p. 231; Wendover, ii. 195–7; Annals of Dunstable, p. 48.

page 255, 1. *Foedera*, i. i. 144.

255, 2. Barnwell, p. 232; *Foedera*, i. i. 192. The monks of Worcester fasted annually for his soul, *Early Compotus Rolls of the Priory of Worcester*, ed. J. M. Wilson & Cosmo Gordon (Worcs. Historical Soc., 1908), p. 60.

page 256, 1. See F. M. Powicke, *King Henry III & the Lord Edward* (Oxford, 1947), i. 1–19; *The Thirteenth Century* (Oxford, 1953), pp. 1–14.

page 257, 1. Public Record Office, Ancient Correspondence, i. 6, transcribed in Galbraith, *Studies in the Public Records*, pp. 161–2, and translated pp. 136–7.

257, 2. Barnwell, p. 232.

257, 3. Kate Norgate, *John Lackland*, p. 286.

page 258, 1. *Dialogus de Scaccario*, p. 2.

Bibliography

BIBLIOGRAPHY

The following list of authorities is not intended to be an exhaustive survey of works bearing upon John's reign. Articles and books on special points referred to in the notes are generally not included. The arrangement is as follows:

I *The Sources*

    (*a*) Chronicles, biographies, and memoirs.
    (*b*) Records and other documents.
    (*c*) Works bearing upon the sources.

II *Modern Works*

    (*a*) General.
    (*b*) Upon particular aspects.

I

The Sources

(a) CHRONICLES, BIOGRAPHIES, AND MEMOIRS

Annales Monastici, ed. H. R. LUARD, 5 vols. (Rolls Series, 1864–9). [Containing the annals of Margam, Tewkesbury, Winchester, Waverley, Dunstable, and Worcester.]

Chronica Magistri Rogeri de Houedene, ed. W. STUBBS, 4 vols. (Rolls Series, 1868–71).

Chronica Rogeri de Wendover liber qui dicitur Flores Historiarum, ed. H. G. HEWLETT, 3 vols. (Rolls series, 1886–9).

Chronica sive Flores Historiarum, ed. H. O. COXE, 5 vols. (English Historical Society, 1841–4).

Chronicles of the reigns of Stephen, Henry II, & Richard I, ed. R. HOWLETT, 4 vols. (Rolls Series, 1884–90). [Containing the chronicles of Richard of Devizes, Robert of Torigni, and William of Newburgh.]

The Chronicles of Ralph of Niger, ed. R. ANSTRUTHER (Caxton Society, London, 1851).

Chroniques de Saint-Martial de Limoges, ed. H. DUPLÈS AGIER (Société de l'Histoire de France, Paris, 1874).

De Nugis Curialium, ed. M. R. JAMES (Oxford, 1914).

Gesta Regis Henrici Secundi Benedicti Abbatis, ed. W. STUBBS, 2 vols. (Rolls Series, 1867).

Giraldi Cambrensis Opera, ed. J. S. BEWER, J. F. DIMOCK, & G. F. WARNER, 8 vols. (Rolls Series, 1861–91).

Histoire de Guillaume le Maréschal, ed. P. MEYER, 3 vols. (Société de l'Histoire de France, Paris, 1891–1901).

Histoire des Ducs de Normandie et des Rois d'Angleterre, ed. F. MICHEL (Société de l'Histoire de France, Paris, 1840).

The Historical Works of Gervase of Canterbury, ed. W. STUBBS, 2 vols. (Rolls Series, 1879–90).

Magna Vita S. Hugonis, Episcopi Lincolniensis, ed. J. F. DIMOCK (Rolls Series, 1864).

Memoriale Fratris Walteri de Coventria, ed. W. STUBBS, 2 vols. (Rolls Series, 1872–3). [Containing the annals of Barnwell.]

Oeuvres de Rigord et de Guillaume le Breton, ed. H. F. DELABORDE, 2 vols. (Société de l'Histoire de France, Paris, 1882–5).

Radulphi de Coggeshall Chronicon Anglicanum, ed. J. STEVENSON (Rolls Series, 1875). [Containing also *The Legend of Fulco Fitz-Warin* and *Magistri Thomae Agnelli, Sermo de Morte et Sepultura Henrici Regis Junioris*.]

Radulphi de Diceto Opera Historica, ed W. STUBBS, 2 vols. (Rolls Series, 1876).

Recueil d'annales angevines et vendômoises, ed. L. HALPHEN (Paris, 1903).

(b) RECORDS AND OTHER DOCUMENTS

Catalogue des Actes de Philippe Auguste, ed. L. DESLISLE (Paris, 1856).

Curia Regis Rolls, vols. i.-vii., ed. C. T. FLOWER (London, 1923–35).

Dialogus de Scaccario, ed. C. JOHNSON (London, 1950).

Documents illustrative of English History in the 13th & 14th centuries, ed. H. COLE (Record Commission, 1844).

English Historical Documents, vol. ii. (1042–1189), ed. D. C. DOUGLAS & G. W. GREENAWAY (London, 1953).

English Historical Documents, vol. iii. (1189–1327), ed. H. ROTHWELL (London, 1961).

The Great Rolls of the Pipe, 1–14 John, ed. with introductions by D. M. STENTON, S. SMITH, H. M. KIRKUS, C. F. SLADE, P. M. BARNES (Pipe Roll Society, London, 1933–55).

Layettes du Trésor des Chartes, ed. A. F. TEULET (Paris, 1863–1909).

Magna Carta, ed. W. S. MCKECHNIE, 2nd edition (Glasgow, 1915).

Magni Rotuli Scaccarii Normanniae sub Regibus Angliae, ed. T. STAPLETON (London, 1840).

Patrologiae cursus completus, series Latina, ed. J. P. MIGNE (Paris, 1844–64).

Pleas before the King or his Justices, 1198–1202, 2 vols., ed. D. M. STENTON (Selden Society, 1952–3).

Rotuli Chartarum, ed. T. D. HARDY (Record Commission, 1837).

Rotuli de Liberate ac de Misis et Praestitis regnante Johanne, ed. T. D. HARDY (Record Commission, 1844).

Rotuli de Oblatis et Finibus temp. Regis Johannis, ed. T. D. HARDY (Record Commission, 1835).

Rotuli Litterarum Clausarum, 1204–27, vol. i., ed. T. D. HARDY (Record Commission, 1833).

Rotuli Litterarum Patentium, vol. i., ed. T. D. HARDY (Record Commission, 1835).

Rotuli Normanniae, ed. T. D. HARDY (Record Commission, 1835).

Select Charters, ed. W. STUBBS, 9th edition (Oxford, 1921).

Selected Letters of Pope Innocent III concerning England (1198–1216), ed. C. R. CHENEY & W. H. SEMPLE (London, 1953).

(c) WORKS BEARING UPON THE SOURCES

[The chronicles in the Rolls Series editions cited in section (a) above are prefaced by valuable introductions.]

BARLOW, F., 'Roger of Howden', *English Historical Review,* lxv. (1950), 352–60.

FLOWER, C. T., *Introduction to the Curia Regis Rolls, 1199–1230* (Selden Society, 1944).

GALBRAITH, V. H., *Historical Research in Medieval England* (London, 1951).

GALBRAITH, V. H., *Roger Wendover and Matthew Paris* (Glasgow, 1944).

GALBRAITH, V. H., *An Introduction to the Use of the Public Records* (Oxford, 1934).

RICHARDSON, H. G., introduction to *The Memoranda Roll for the Michaelmas Term of I John, 1199–1200* (Pipe Roll Society, 1943).

SALTER, H. E., 'William of Newburgh', *English Historical Review*, xxii. (1907), 510–14.

STENTON, D. M., 'Roger of Howden & Benedict', *English Historical Review*, lxviii. (1943), 574–82.

VAUGHAN, R., *Matthew Paris* (Cambridge, 1958).

II

Modern Works

(a) GENERAL

DUGGAN, A., *Devil's Brood: The Angevin Family* (London, 1957).

LLOYD, J. E. *A History of Wales*, 2 vols., 3rd edition (London, 1939).

NORGATE, K., *England under the Angevin Kings*, 2 vols. (London, 1887).

NORGATE, K., *John Lackland* (London, 1902).

ORPEN, G. H., *Ireland under the Normans*, vol. ii. (1169–1216) (Oxford, 1911).

PAINTER, S., *The Reign of King John* (Baltimore, 1949).

PETIT-DUTAILLIS, CH., & GUINARD, P., *L'Essor des États d'Occident*, new edition (Paris, 1944).

POOLE, A. L., *From Domesday Book to Magna Carta (1087–1216)* (Oxford, 1951).

POWICKE, F. M., 'Richard I & John', *Cambridge Medieval History*, iv. 205–51.

STENTON, D. M., *English Society in the Early Middle Ages.* (London, 1951).

(b) UPON PARTICULAR ASPECTS

BOUSSARD, J., *Le Comté d'Anjou, 1151–1204* (Paris, 1938).

BOUSSARD, J., *Le Government d'Henri II Plantagenet* (Paris, 1956).

BROOKS, F. W., *The English Naval Forces, 1199–1272* (London, 1933).

BROOKS, F. W., 'William de Wrotham & the Office of Keeper of the King's Ports & Galleys', *English Historical Review*, xl. (1925), 570–9.

BROWN, R. A., *English Medieval Castles* (London, 1954).

BROWN, R. A., 'Royal Castle-Building in England, 1154–1216', *English Historical Review*, lxx. (1955), 353–98.

CARTELLIERI, A., *Philip II August*, 4 vols. (Leipzig, 1899–1921).

CAZEL, F. A., & PAINTER, S., 'The Marriage of Isabelle of Angoulême, *English Historical Review*, lxii. (1948), 83–9; lxvii. (1952), 233–5.

CHAMBERS, F. M., 'Some Legends concerning Eleanor of Aquitaine', *Speculum*, xvi. (1941), 459–68.

CHENEY, C. R., 'The Alleged Deposition of King John', *Studies . . . Presented to F. M. Powicke* (Oxford, 1948), pp. 100–16.

CHENEY, C. R., 'King John & the Papal Interdict', *Bulletin of John Rylands' Library*, xxxi. (1948), 295–317.

CHENEY, C. R., 'King John's Reaction to the Interdict in England', *Transactions of the Royal Historical Society*, 4th series, xxxi. (1949), 129–50.

CHENEY, C. R., *From Becket to Langton* (Manchester, 1956).

CHENEY, C. R., 'The Eve of Magna Carta', *Bulletin of John Ryland's Library*, xxxviii. (1955–6), 311–41.

CHRIMES, S. B., *An Introduction to the Administrative History of Medieval England* (Oxford, 1952).

GALBRAITH, V. H., *Studies in the Public Records* (London, 1948).

HOLT, J. C., 'The Barons & the Great Charter', *English Historical Review*, lxx. (1955), 1–24.

HOLT, J. C., 'The Making of Magna Carta', *English Historical Review*, lxxii. (1957), 401–22.

HOPE, W. ST JOHN, 'The Loss of King John's Baggage Train in the Wellstream in October 1216', *Archaeologia*, lx (1906), 93–110.

HOYT, R. S., *The Royal Desmesne in English Constitutional History*, 1066–1272 (New York, 1950).

HURNARD, N. D., 'Magna Carta, Clause 34', *Studies . . . Presented to F. M. Powicke* (Oxford, 1948), pp. 157–79.

JENKINSON, A. V., 'The Jewels Lost in the Wash', *History*, new series, viii. (1923), 161–8.

JOLLIFFE, J. E. A., 'The Chamber & the Castle Treasuries under King John', *Studies . . . Presented to F. M. Powicke* (Oxford, 1948), pp. 117–42.

JOLLIFFE, J. E. A., *Angevin Kingship* (London, 1955).

KEENEY, B. C., *Judgment by Peers* (Cambridge, Mass., 1949).

KNOWLES, M. D., 'The Canterbury Election of 1205–6', *English Historical Review*, liii. (1938), 211–20.

KNOWLES, M. D., *The Monastic Order in England, 943–1216* (Cambridge, 1949).

KREHBIEL, E. B., *The Interdict, its History & Operation* (Washington, 1909).

LANDON, L., *The Itinerary of Richard I, with studies on certain matters of interest connected with his reign* (Pipe Roll Society, 1935).

LOT, F., *L'Art Militaire et les Armées au Moyen Age*, 2 vols. (Paris, 1946).

Magna Carta Commemoration Essays, ed. H. E. MALDEN (London, 1917).

MITCHELL, S. K., *Studies in Taxation under John & Henry III* (New Haven, 1914).

MOORMAN, J. R. H., *Church Life in England in the 13th century* (Cambridge, 1946).

MORRIS, W. A., *The Medieval English Sheriff* (Manchester, 1927).

NORGATE, 'The alleged Condemnation of King John by the Court of France in 1202', *Transactions of the Royal Historical Society*, 2nd series, xiv. (1900), 53–67.

NORGATE, K., *Richard the Lion Heart* (London, 1924).

OMAN, C., *A History of the Art of War in the Middle Ages* (London, 1898).

PAINTER, S., *William Marshal* (Baltimore, 1933).

PAINTER, S., *Studies in the History of the English Feudal Barony* (Baltimore, 1943).

PETIT-DUTAILLIS, CH., *Le Deshéritement de Jean Sans Terre et le meutre d'Arthur de Bretagne* (Paris, 1925).

PETIT-DUTAILLIS, CH., *Studies & Notes Supplementary to Stubbs' Constitutional History*, vol. i. (Manchester, 1911).

POOLE, A. L., *Obligations of Society in the 12th & 13th centuries* (Oxford, 1946).

POWELL, W. R., 'The Administration of the Navy & the Stannaries, 1189–1216', *English Historical Review*, lxxi. (1956), 177–88.

POWICKE, F. M., 'The Angevin Administration of Normandy', *English Historical Review*, xxi. (1906), 625–49; xxii. (1907), 15–42.

POWICKE, F. M., *The Loss of Normandy* (Manchester, 1913).

POWICKE, F. M., *Stephen Langton* (Oxford, 1928).

POWICKE, F. M., 'The bull "Miramur plurimum" and a letter to Archbishop Stephen Langton, 5 September 1215', *English Historical Review*, xliv (1929).

POWICKE, F. M., *The Christian Life in the Middle Ages, and other essays* (Oxford, 1935).

RICHARD, A., *Histoire des comtes de Poitou* (Paris 1903).

RICHARDSON, H. G., 'William of Ely, the King's Treasurer (?1195–1215)', *Transactions of the Royal Historical Society*, 4th series, xv. (1932), 45–90.

RICHARDSON, H. G., 'The Morrow of the Great Charter', *Bulletin of John Rylands' Library*, xxviii. (1944), 422–43; xxix. (1944), 184–200.

RICHARDSON, H. G., 'The Marriage & Coronation of Isabelle of Angoulême', *English Historical Review*, lxi. (1946), 289–314.

RICHARDSON, H. G., 'King John & Isabelle of Angoulême', *English Historical Review*, lxv. (1950), 360–71.

ROUND, J. H., *The Commune of London, & other studies* (London, 1899).

ROUND, J. H., 'King John & Robert FitzWalter', *English Historical Review*, xix (1904), 707–11.

STUBBS, W., *Seventeen Lectures on Medieval & Modern History* (Oxford, 1887).

Studies in Medieval History Presented to F. M. Powicke, ed. R. W. HUNT, W. A. PANTIN, R. W. SOUTHERN (Oxford, 1948).

STENTON, D. M., 'King John & the Courts of Justice', *Proceedings of the British Academy*, xliv (1958), 103–28.

TOUT, T. F., *Chapters in the Administrative History of Medieval England*, vol. i. (Manchester, 1920).

TOY, S., *A History of Fortifications from 3000 B.C. to A.D. 1700* (London, 1955).

The following works have been published since this book was written:

APPLEBY, J. T., *John, King of England* (London, 1960).

ASHLEY, M., *The Life and Times of King John* (London, 1972).

CHENEY, C. R., *Hubert Walter* (London, 1967).

CHENEY, C. R., *Pope Innocent III and England* (Stuttgart, 1976).

CROSLAN, J., *William the Marshal* (London, 1962).

English Historical Documents, vol. iii, *1189–1327*, ed. H. Rothwell (London, 1975).

The Great Roll of the Pipe, 17 John, ed. with an introduction by Patricia M. Barnes (Pipe Roll Society, London, 1962).

HOLLISTER, C. W., 'King John and the Historians', *Journal of British Studies*, i (1962), 1–19.

HOLT, J. C., *King John* (Historical Association Pamphlet, G.53, London, 1963).

HOLT, J. C., *Magna Carta* (Cambridge, 1965).

HOLT, J. C., *The Northerners; a study in the reign of King John* (Oxford, 1961).

JONES, J. A. P., *King John and Magna Carta* (Seminar Studies in History, London, 1971).

LE PATOUREL, J., 'The Plantagenet Dominions', *History*, 1 (1965), 289–308.

The Letters of Pope Innocent III concerning England and Wales, ed. C. R. and M. G. Cheney (Oxford, 1967).

MILLER, E., 'The background of Magna Carta', *Past and Present*, no. 23 (1962).

RICHARDSON, H. G., and SAYLES, G. O., *The Governance of Medieval England from the Conquest to Magna Carta* (Edinburgh, 1963).

WARREN, W. L., *Henry II* (London, 1973).

WARREN, W. L., 'John in Ireland in 1185', in *Essays Presented to Michael Roberts*, ed. J. A. Bossy and P. J. Jupp (Belfast, 1976).

WEST, F., *The Justiciarship in England, 1066–1232* (Cambridge, 1966).

Index

Index

Medieval surnames which are clearly derived from the name of a place have been spelt according to the modern spelling of the place-name. The 'de' in such names has generally been omitted or translated as 'of' in names of English origin, but retained in names of French origin

INDEX

Geoffrey, *illeg. son of Henry II, see* Plantagenet, Geoffrey.

Geoffrey, *illeg. son of John (see endpapers)*, 112.

Geoffrey, *son of Henry II, duke of Brittany (see endpapers)*, 17, 28, 29, 30; character of, 31–2; 33; death of, 37.

Gerald of Wales, *see* Wales, Gerald of.

Gervase of Canterbury, *see* Canterbury, Gervase of.

Glanville (Glanvill), Ranulph, *justiciar under Henry II*, tutor to John, 26, 41; views on succession, attributed to, 48–9; conversation with Gerald of Wales on state of Normandy, 89; & the *De Legibus Angliae*, 127; 155.

Gloucester, Isabelle of, *daughter of earl of Gloucester, wife to John (see endpapers)*, 30; marriage to John, 60; divorce of, 66; gifts to by John, 139; 182.

Goodwill (*benevolentia*), the king's, 176–7; fines for, 177; 187.

Gournai, Hugh of, 62–3.

Gray (Grey), John de, *bishop of Norwich (1200–14)*, 154, 160; royal nominee for primacy, 160–2, 165; justiciar of Ireland, 170, 195–6; 201, 204, 212, 222.

Gray (Grey), Walter de, 212.

Green, J. R., *historian*, on John, 10; his *Short History*, 284.

Gualo, *papal legate*, 251, 255.

Hawking, John's interest in, 139–40.

Henry I, *king of England (1100–35)*, 1, 21, 23, 48, 183; coronation charter of, produced in 1214, 226–7, 228.

Henry II, *king of England (1154–89) (see endpapers)*, character of, 1, 2; attitude of chroniclers to, 4–6; marriage, 20–1; becomes king of England, 21; methods of government, 21 ff.; his court, 23–5; estrangement from wife, 25–6; adultery of, 26, 286; plans for succession, 27 ff.; rebellion of Young King against, 29; declines offer of crown

of Jerusalem, 32–3; refuses to let John go to Holy Land, 33; & Ireland, 33 ff.; defeated by Richard and Philip II, 38; death of, 38; feudal position of vis-à-vis king of France, 54–6; strategic policy of, 57; & William Marshal, 106; 110, 111,132; & royal desmesne, 146; 154; & appointments to bishoprics, 159–60, 163; taming of barons by, 174 ff.; & revolt of 1173–4, 175; manipulates law courts, 176; fines by, for 'goodwill', 177; failure to conquer Wales, 197.

Henry, *son of King Henry II (see endpapers)*, 17; character of, 25, 31; 26, 27, 29, 30; death of, 30–1; 90, 107, 175.

Henry III, *son of John, king of England (1216–72) (see endpapers)*, 200, 240; succession of, 256.

Henry VI, *Holy Roman Emperor (1190–4)*, 44, 45.

Hereford, Henry de Bohun, earl of, 229.

Histoire de Guillaume le Maréschal, author of, *see* Marshal, William, anonymous biographer of.

Hostages, demanded by John from barons, 181, 200; Welsh, execution of, by John, 200.

Household, the royal, 127, 129–30; description of, 135–9, 140, 144–5; members of, on oath to report rumours to John, 190.

Howden, Roger of, *chronicler*, on Richard I, 6; on Geoffrey, 32; death of, 100; on royal appointments to bishoprics, 160.

Hugh, St, of Avalon, *bishop of Lincoln (1186–1200)*, & Henry II, 5, 70; 49, 63; character, death of, 70; 160.

Hunting, John &, 95, 140–1.

Huntingdon, David, earl of, 181, 193, 241.

Innocent III, *pope (1198–1216)*, attitude of to death of Arthur, 84; &

343

tured at Mirebeau, 79, 80; released, 80; 102; comes to terms with John, 219–21.
Lusignan, Ralph of, *count of Eu*, 68, 72, 73, 79.
Lynn, 253.

McMurrough, Dermot, *king of Leinster*, 34.
Magna Carta (translated & annotated, 265–77), 110; sheriff's 'farm' in, 146; amercements in, 151; & due process of law, 178; & Asterby's warning to Henry II, 179; nature of, 180; relatives of Gerard d'Athée in, 189; judgement by peers in, 213–14, 234; & the 'Unknown Charter', 216–17; obscurity of antecedents of, 224–5; inception of, 231–2; drawn up, 236; analysed, 236–40; origin of name, 237 n.; 'forma securitatis' in, 239–40, 247.
Maine, county of, 20, 21, 23, 27; accepts Arthur of Brittany, 49, 51; 53, 54, 64, 103.
Mandeville, Geoffrey de, *earl of Essex*, 182, 229, 230, 234 253.
Map, Walter, on Henry II, 5.
Marc, Geoffrey, 188–9.
Marc, Philip, 137, 188–9.
Margam, anonymous annals of abbey of, on fate of Arthur, 82–3, 107; on reaction to Interdict, 165.
Marsh, Richard, 218, 222, 307.
Marsh, William, 125.
Marshal, William, anonymous biographer of, value for John's reign, 7; on the Young King, 25; on the succession to Richard, 49; on state of Normandy under John, 88, 90; on use of mercenaries in government of Normandy, 91; on John's flight from Normandy, 92–3; on origins of John's hostility to William Marshal, 114–15; on surviving traces of rebellion of 1173–4, 176; laments decline of chivalry, 180; on naval victory at Damme, 205.

Marshal, William, *earl of Pembroke, lord of Leinster*, discusses succession, 49; supports John, 50; attitude of to Lusignans, 69; 79, 81; & attempt to relieve Château Gaillard, 87; advises John to abandon Normandy, 92; mission to Philip II in 1204, 96; affect of loss of Normandy on, 103; his arrangement with Philip about his Norman estates, 104–5, 113–14; early career & character of, 106–7; his attitude to John, 107; at odds with John, 113–14; dissuades John from leaving England in 1205, 115; 180; John's persecution of, 184–5; authority of in Pembroke & Leinster, 192; work in Ireland, 194–5; concedes greater royal control of Leinster, 195; shelters William de Briouze, 196, 308; co-operates with John's expedition to Ireland in 1210, 196; 198; persuades Irish barons to offer support to John in 1212, 201; assists in government of England during John's absence, 218; conversation with Philip II about FitzWalter, 230–1; supports king in 1214–15, 231 ff.; acts as mediator in 1215, 233; supports king in civil war, 248, 253; urges John to abandon resistance to French landing, 252; executor of John's will, 255; leads royalists in support of Henry III, 255.
Martell, Alan, 103.
Martigny (Martinni), Geoffrey de, 188–9, 234.
Matilda, *mother of Henry II*, 1, 20–1, 33.
Matilda, *dau. of Henry II* (*see endpapers*), 17. 24.
Mauger, *physician to Richard I*, 160, *see also* Worcester, bishop of.
Mauléon, Savary (Savaric) de, 79, 117, 188; leads Poitevin mercenaries to England in 1214–16, 233, 235, 248, 253; executor of John's will, 255; 292, 296.